The Blue Guides

D1099430

Please write to us with your suggestions and corrections for the next edition of this guide. Writers of the best letters will be awarded a free Blue Guide of their choice.

If you would like to receive further information about Blue Guides, please write to us at Freepost, A & C Black (Publishers) Ltd, Cambridgeshire, PE19 3EZ, or e-mail us at travel@acblack.co.uk

Morocco

Jane Holliday

BLUE GUIDE

A&C Black • London
WW Norton • New York

Third edition May 1998

Published by A & C Black (Publishers) Limited
35 Bedford Row, London WC1R 4JH

Maps and plans © A & C Black, drawn by Welton Cartographics, and Penny Mills
Illustrations © by Colin Ross
'Blue Guides' is a registered trademark

A CIP catalogue record of this book is available from the British Library.

ISBN 0-7136-4677-2

Published in the United States of America by
WW Norton and Company, Inc.
500 Fifth Avenue, New York, NY 10110

Published simultaneously in Canada by
Penguin Books Canada Limited
10 Alcorn Avenue, Toronto, Ontario M4V 3BE

ISBN 0-393-31802-X USA

The author and publishers have done their best to ensure the accuracy of all the information in *Blue Guide Morocco*: however, they can accept no responsibility for any loss, injury or inconvenience sustained by any traveller as a result of information or advice contained in this guide.

Jane Holliday is a graduate in English Literature (University of London) and a *diplomée* in *Civilisation Française* (Sorbonne, Paris). When married to a senior diplomat, she lived and worked in Sweden, Bolivia and, latterly, Morocco, where she spent over four years becoming familiar not only with the major cities but also with the most remote corners of the country. Still a regular visitor to Morocco, she now lives in Oxfordshire, works as a charity consultant and writes travel guides.

The **cover photograph** is of the ruins of a kasbah, Dades Gorge, Getty Images. The **title page illustration** is the view from a window of Glaoui kasbah, Telouet.

Printed and bound in Great Britain by Butler and Tanner Limited, Frome and London

Contents

The Guide

Maps and Plans

Preface

Morocco, only 14km from Europe and bounded by both the Atlantic and the Mediterranean, is the ideal gateway to both the African continent and the Arab world. It is easily accessible from both Europe and North America and, with the liberalisation of air transport and plans afoot to build a tunnel under the Strait of Gibraltar, is likely to become even more so. This richly diverse country has something to suit all tastes—rugged mountains, the emptiness and great beauty of the Sahara, 3800km of coastline with uncluttered sandy beaches, cedar forests, and an inexhaustible supply of atmospheric old towns and kasbahs.

The main attraction for the discerning visitor is, without doubt, the quartet of 'Imperial Cities'—Fes, Marrakesh, Meknes and Rabat—so called because each at some time has been capital of the empire of the Moroccan rulers that stretched northwards into much of Spain and southwards beyond Timbuktu (now in Mali). Each of these cities has its own unique and irresistible atmosphere and nowhere more so than Fes, the oldest of all, founded in 808 and now preserved as a national treasure with the aid of UNESCO. Marrakesh, equally rich in historic monuments, with a near perfect climate and easy access to the High Atlas, has become one of the world's most desirable tourist destinations. Meknes is Morocco's very own Versailles, while Rabat gives living proof that modern and traditional architecture can exist harmoniously side by side.

The imperial cities, above all others, bear witness to over a thousand years of unbroken royal succession and strong Islamic tradition. Unlike its neighbours, Algeria and Tunisia, Morocco was never invaded by the Turks, and successive ruling dynasties, whether Berber or Arab, have always sprung up from within the country itself. Even the 44 years of French and Spanish occupation earlier this century left the culture largely unchanged (whilst hugely benefiting the infrastructure and educational system). So it is that Morocco retains to this day a remarkably homogeneous cultural heritage, and a wealth of Islamic architecture which reflects the extraordinary energy of its sultans and frequently a touch of extra refinement reimported from Moorish Spain (*el Andalus*).

All of Morocco is fascinating and most of it is accessible via a good rail and bus network and excellent roads, of which an additional 10,000km are promised for the near future to end the economic disparity between the highly developed north and west of the country and the more remote areas to the south and east. There is also a well-distributed hotel infrastructure, with a comprehensive classification system and clear pricing, described on page 18. Moreover, in the last few years measures have been taken to check harassment of tourists in souks and at major sites and there has been a noticeable improvement on this score in places such as Marrakesh and Fes.

It is the purpose of *Blue Guide Morocco* to help readers feel at home in the great medinas of the historic cities and also to encourage them to look beyond the obvious places—to enjoy the supreme majesty of the Atlas, the hot colours of the Sahara, the huge enveloping silence of the forests and the excitement of the country souks. The text is based on the personal experience and observations of the author who lived in Morocco for over four years, has visited and re-visited all the great cities and travelled extensively in the rural areas. She has been helped and encouraged by a wide variety of people, ranging from the poorest desert nomads to the wisest academicians in the land—all happy to satisfy her curiosity and proud to talk of the country's origins, its problems and its promise.

Acknowledgements. The author would like to express her gratitude to all her friends in Morocco who have so willingly given of their time and experience to make the writing and revision of this book possible. Special thanks are due to officials of the Moroccan National Tourist Office in Rabat, and to Delegates in Ouarzazate, Tinerhir and Laayoune; and in particular to Ali El Kasmi, Director of OMNT in London and his Press & Media Officer, Jamal el Jaidi, for their kindness in arranging complex itineraries and responding to endless queries; also to Sarah and Peter Holliday, Selby Martin, Elise Bayley, Tim Brierly and many others whose help and constructive criticism have been invaluable.

Note. Readers will find that spellings of Moroccan words can vary considerably between different maps and guide books, and even within the same book (for example, Tangiers, Tangier or Tanger). There are several different systems for transliterating Arabic into Western languages, and the influence of the country's French and Spanish heritage also affects spellings. This applies particularly to the names of places and people. In *Blue Guide Morocco*, conventional spellings are used for the name of the Prophet Muhammad and for certain words that have entered the English language, such as kasbah and mihrab. Elsewhere, we have tried to make consistent spellings from a multitude of sources, while retaining those still commonly used in Morocco itself (for example, Avenue Mohammed V).

Practical information

Tourist information and the ONMT

The Moroccan National Tourist Board (abbreviated to ONMT in Morocco and in the rest of this guide) has offices all over the world which will provide information on all aspects of tourism in Morocco, including lists of hotels and a huge array of leaflets about the principal towns, sites and activities. It will not, however, book accommodation; this is best done through tour operators (see next section) or directly through the hotels themselves. The Ministry of Tourism in Rabat is responsible for Morocco's tourist policy and also controls hotel rates.

UK. 205 Regent St, London WIR 7DE. ☎ (0171) 437 0073 fax (0171) 734 8172.
USA. 20 East 46th St, Suite 1201, New York, NY 10017. ☎ (212) 557 2520 fax (212) 949 8148.
Canada. 2001 Rue Université, Suite 1460, Montreal, Québec, P.O. Canada H3A 2A6. ☎ (514) 842 8111 fax (514) 842 5316.
Australia. 11 West St North, Sydney NSW 2060. ☎: (02) 922 4999 fax (02) 923 1053.

Every major town in Morocco has a tourist information office (*office de tourism*) and/or a *syndicat d'initiative*. Both fulfil the same function, providing information and leaflets on request. Staff are invariably extremely helpful and speak two or three languages. Addresses are given as part of the practical information in each section of *Blue Guide Morocco*.

Tour operators

Abercrombie & Kent, Sloane Square House, Holbein Pl., London SW1W 8NS. ☎ (0171) 730 9600 fax (0171) 730 9376. General and 11-day escorted tours from Spain to Morocco by 4WD vehicle.
Acacia Expeditions Ltd, 27d Stable Way, Latimer Road, London W10 6QX. ☎ (0181) 960 5747 fax (0181) 960 1414. Transafrican expeditions; 'Moroccan Experience'; 'High Atlas Trek'; 15-day tours.
Aeroscope, Scope House, Hospital Road, Moreton-in-Marsh, Gloucestershire GL56 0BQ. ☎ (01608) 650 103 fax (01608) 651 295. 'Fly-drive and Stay in'; general.
Africa Explored Ltd, Rose Cottage, Summerleaze Magor, Newport NP6 3DE. ☎ (01633) 880 224 fax (01633) 882 128. Adventure tours and expeditions.
African Safari Trails, 113–19 High St, Hampton Hill, Middlesex TW12 1PS. ☎ (0181) 941 7400 fax (0181) 9415 168. 'Imperial Cities'; 'Mountains and Valleys Tour'; 'Kasbah Trail'.
Alecos Tours, 3a Camden Road, London NW1 9LG. ☎ (0171) 267 2092 fax (0171) 284 2891.
Andante Travels Ltd, Grange Cottage, Winterbourne Dauntsey, Salisbury, Wiltshire SP4 6ER. ☎ (01980) 610 555 fax (01980) 610 002. Cultural tours; 'Grand Tour of Ancient Morocco'.
Artscape Painting Tuition, 7 Clifton Parade, Southend-on-Sea, Essex SS1 1DP. ☎: and fax (01702) 435 990. Painting holidays.

Atlas Travel Agency, 59 Praed St, London W2 1NS. ☎ (0171) 262 1172 fax (0171) 262 0097. 'Morocco à la Carte': tailor-made itineraries all over Morocco. Fly-drive, escorted tours, conferences and incentives.

Best of Morocco, Seend Park, Seend, Wiltshire SN12 6NZ. ☎ (01380) 828 533 fax (01380) 828 630. General; also luxury villas, tailor-made holidays, horse- and camel-trekking, walking holidays, Sahara Landrover safari, golfing, skiing, and film production.

British Airways Holidays, Astral Towers, Betts Way, London Road, Crawley, West Sussex RH10 2XA. ☎ (01293) 723 100 fax (01293) 722 702. Marrakesh.

Bruma Overland Expeditions, 3 Wynford Pl., Grosvenor Road, Belvedere, Kent DA17 5LZ. ☎ (01322) 442484 fax (01322) 434 333. Casablanca to Casablanca; 15-day camping tours.

Cadogan Travel, 9–10 Portland St, Southampton, Hampshire SO14 7EB. ☎ (01703) 332661 fax (01703) 228 601. General; also tailor-made holidays, golfing.

CLM (Morocco Made to Measure), 4a William St, London SW1X 9HL. ☎ (0171) 235 0123 fax (0171) 235 3851. General; also garden tours, butterfly tours, birdwatching, golfing, tennis, trekking on foot, horseriding, conferences, bridge holidays in Tangier, and 'Thalassotherapy'.

Club Medierannée, 106–110 Brompton Road, Knightsbridge, London SW3 1JJ. ☎ (0171) 581 1161 fax (0171) 581 4769. All-inclusive holidays in Agadir, El Jadida, Marrakesh, Ouarzazate, Smir. Conference groups in Marrakesh and Agadir.

Condor Travel (UK) Ltd, 234 Earls Court Road, London SW5 9AA. ☎ (0171) 373 0495 fax (0171) 835 1052. General; also conference groups and holidays.

Cosmos Coach Tours, 17 Homesdale Road, Bromley, Kent BR2 9LX. ☎ (0181) 464 3444 fax (0181) 466 6640. Marrakesh; 'Moroccan Adventure'; 8-day coach tour starting in Spain.

CV Travels, 43 Cadogan St, London SW3 2PR. ☎ (0171) 581 0851 fax (0171) 584 5229. General; also tailor-made itineraries and touring holidays.

Destinations by OCA, 3 Sycamore Dene, Chesham, Buckinghamshire HP5 3JT. ☎ (01494) 792 184 fax (01494) 773 576. Tailor-made group travel to the Imperial Cities etc. Also Rif, Atlas and 'Deep South'/Ouarzazate.

Discover Adventure, 1 Wick Farm Cottage, Wick Lane, Salisbury, Wiltshire SP5 3NH. ☎ and fax (01725) 512 161. Cycling tours in Anti Atlas and Jbel Sirwa; High Atlas and Jbel Sarhro; High Atlas and Berber villages.

Dragoman, Camp Green Kenton, Debenham, Suffolk IP14 6LA. ☎ (01728) 861 133 fax (01728) 861 127. Western Transafrican combinations: Sahara and West Africa (9 weeks); Western Transafrica (20 weeks).

Dust Trails, Unit 11, Deveril Road Trading Estate, Sutton Veny, nr Warminster, Wiltshire. ☎ (01985) 841 184. Motorcycle tours (16 and 23 days).

Elegant Resorts Ltd, The Old Palace, Little St John St, Chester CH1 1RB. ☎ (01244) 877 777 fax (01244) 897 770. Marrakesh and Taroudannt.

Encounter Overland, 267 Old Brompton Road, London SW5 9JA. ☎ (0171) 370 6951 fax (0171) 244 9737. Transafrican expeditions, including Morocco (17, 23 or 27 weeks).

Exodus Travels, 9 Weir Road, London SW12 0LT. ☎ (0181) 675 5550 fax (0181) 673 0779. Escorted adventure tours, 8 or 15 days; also biking adventures and overland expeditions.

Explore Worldwide Ltd, 1 Frederick St, Aldershot, Hampshire GU11 1LQ. ☎ (01252) 319 448 fax (01252) 343 170. Treks, rambles and cultural adventures; Imperial Cities and desert; 'High Atlas Trek'; Jbel Sarhro.

First Choice Holidays and Flights Ltd, First Choice House, London Road, Crawley, West Sussex RH10 2GX. ☎ (01293) 560 777 fax (01293) 588 680. Marrakesh.

Forte Travel Services, Crawley, West Sussex RH10 1JA. ☎ (01293) 614 040 fax (01293) 512 232. Casablanca (3–7 nights at *Hôtel Royal Mansour*).

Goldenjoy Holidays, 36 Mill Lane, London NW6 1NR. ☎ (0171) 794 9767 fax (0171) 794 9850. Agadir, Marrakesh; 'Great South Tour' (8 days).

Golf International, International House, Priestley Way, London NW2 7AW. ☎ (0181) 208 4555 fax (0181) 208 3894. Golfing holidays; Rabat and Marrakesh.

Guerba Expeditions, Wessex House, 40 Station Road, Westbury, Wiltshire BA13 3JN. ☎ (01373) 826 611 fax (01373) 858 351. Expeditions: 'Morocco Desert and Mountain'; 'High Atlas Trail'; 'South Morocco Trek'; 'Trans-Sahara Adventure'.

Hayes & Jarvis, Hayes House, 152 King St, London W6 0QU. ☎ (0181) 748 5050 fax (0181) 741 0299. 'Great South and Kasbahs'; 'Grand Tour of Morocco'. Tailor-made holidays, trekking, golfing, special interest, 4WD tours.

Headwater Holidays, 146 London Road, Northwich, Cheshire CW9 5HH. ☎ (01606) 486 99 fax (01606) 48761. Around the Sahara and the High Atlas (11 days).

Inspirations, Victoria House, Victoria Road, Horley, Surrey RH6 7AD. ☎ (01293) 822 244 fax (01293) 821 732. General; also camel treks, horseriding, painting holidays, golfing, birdwatching, Imperial Cities, 4WD tours.

International Chapters, 102 St John's Wood Terrace, London NW8 6PL. ☎ (0171) 722 9560 fax (0171) 722 9140. High-standard villas in Marrakesh.

Marrakesh Express, 81 St George's Road, Glasgow G3 6JA. ☎ (0141) 332 1991 fax (0141) 332 1881. General; also golf, skiing, desert excursions, TV and film co-production.

Martin Randall Travel, 10 Barley Mow Passage, Chiswick, London W4 4PH. ☎ (0181) 742 3355 fax (0181) 742 1066. Cultural tour with lecturer; 'The Moroccan Gold Route'; 'From Tangier to Marrakesh' (11 days).

Moroccan Travel Bureau, 304 Old Brompton Road, London SW5 9JF. ☎ (0171) 373 4411 fax (0171) 244 8174. Flights and/or accommodation. Also tailor-made holidays, birdwatching, fly-drive, walking and trekking. Mountains and desert areas.

Nomadic Thoughts, 23 Hopefield Ave, London NW6 6LJ. ☎ (0181) 960 1001 fax (0181) 960 1006. Honeymoons; holidays for individuals, small groups and incentives.

Nouvelles Frontieres, 2/3 Woodstock St, London W1R 9HE. ☎ (0171) 629 7772 fax (0171) 491 0684. Agadir, Marrakesh, Ouarzazate, Tangier.

Oasis, Box 43, Welwyn Garden, Hertfordshire AL8 6PQ. ☎ (01707) 373 988 fax (01707) 333 276. Adventure tours to Marrakesh for 20–35 age group.

Panworld Holidays, 8 Great Chapel St, London W1V 3AG. ☎ (0171) 734 2562 fax (0171) 287 0554. Agadir, Marrakesh, Tangier.

Peregrine Holidays (Equitour), 40/41 South Parade, Oxford OX2 7JP. ☎ (01865) 511 642 (01865) 512 583. Horseriding, 'Royal Cities Ride', Berber villages.

Prestige Holidays, 14 Market Pl., Ringwood, Hampshire. ☎ (01425) 480 400 fax (01425) 470 139. Agadir, Marrakesh, two-centre holidays. Car hire.

Prospect Music & Art Tours Ltd, 454–58 Chiswick High Road, London W4 5TT. ☎ (0181) 995 2151 fax (0181) 742 1969. Cultural tours. Marrakesh and the Southern Oasis Route.

Ramblers Holidays, Box 43, Welwyn Garden, Hertfordshire AL8 6PQ. ☎ (01707) 331 133 fax (01707) 333 276. Walking, trekking, sightseeing. Marrakesh and southern Morocco.

Sherpa Expeditions, 131a Heston Road, Hounslow, Middlesex TW5 0RD. ☎ (0181) 577 2717 fax (0181) 572 9788. Walking in the High Atlas, Jbel Sarhro, Jbel Toukbal, M'Goun Massif. Siroua expedition.

Solos Holidays Ltd, 54–58 High St, Edgware, Middlesex HA8 7ED. ☎ (0181) 951 2800 fax (0181) 951 1051. Holidays for singles. Imperial Cities.

Steppes East Ltd, Castle Eaton, Cricklade, Wiltshire SN6 6JU. ☎: (01285) 810 267 fax (01285) 810 693. Tailor-made itineraries throughout Morocco. Trekking with small groups. Natural history escorted tours.

Tarik Travel, 9 Windy Hall, Fishguard, Pembrokeshire SA65 9DP. ☎ (01348) 874 361 fax (01348) 874 380. Casablanca, Marrakesh, Tangier, Agadir. Personalised itineraries. Business travel.

Travelscene Ltd, 11–15 St Ann's Road, Harrow, Middlesex HA1 1AS. ☎ (0181) 427 4445 fax (0181) 861 4154. Marrakesh short breaks.

Travelsphere Holidays, Compass House, Rockingham Road, Market Harborough, Leicestershire LE16 7QD. ☎ (01858) 410 456 fax (01858) 466 477. Marrakesh, Agadir.

Worldwide Journeys & Expeditions, 8 Comeragh Road, London W14 9HP. ☎ (0171) 381 8638 fax (0171) 3810 836. Trekking and safari holidays; High Atlas mountains and Sahara.

Getting to Morocco

By air

Morocco has twelve international airports, Agadir, Al Hoceima, Casablanca, Dakhla, Fes, Laayoune, Marrakesh, Ouarzazate, Oujda, Rabat-Salé, Tangier, and Tetouan. The national airline, **Royal Air Maroc**, has direct flights from **London** Heathrow to Casablanca, Tangier, Agadir and Marrakesh on a daily basis. There are direct flights to Ouarzazate twice weekly, and frequent connections between the Moroccan airports. For further information, contact Royal Air Maroc, 205 Regent St, London WIR 7DE. ☎ (0171) 439 4361 fax (0171) 287 0127.

GB Airways operate scheduled services from Heathrow and Gatwick to Casablanca, Tangier, Agadir, and Marrakesh. For further information contact British Airways, ☎ (0345) 222 111 or (01293) 664 275.

Charter flights are also widely available from various regional UK airports, particularly to Tangier and Agadir. These are often much cheaper but usually limit you to a two-week stay. Consult your local travel agent or look in the classified ads in Sunday newspapers.

While most North American travellers fly to Morocco via Europe rather than t, Royal Air Maroc runs direct flights from **New York** to Casablanca, er, Agadir and Marrakesh almost daily. For further information, contact

Royal Air Maroc, 666 Fifth Ave at 53rd St, New York, NY 10103.☎ (212) 974 3850 fax (212) 974 0612.

Royal Air Maroc also runs direct flights from **Montreal** to Casablanca, Tangier, Agadir and Marrakesh almost daily. For further information, contact Royal Air Maroc, 1001 de Maisonneuve Ouest, Montreal PQ, Canada H3A 3C8. ☎ (514) 285 1937 fax (514) 285 1878.

By train

There are two ways to travel from the UK to Morocco by train. The first involves taking **Eurostar** from London to Paris, then a train to Madrid and either Algeciras or Malaga, thence the ferry to Tangier. This takes two days. The adult return fare as far as Algeciras or Malaga is (at time of writing) £306.20, with the additional cost of the ferry across the Strait of Gibraltar (see below). There is a discount of £20 for people under 26. The second route also takes the train (not Eurostar) and ferry to Algeciras or Malaga. This takes three days and costs £219 return with a discount of £22 for people under 26. Again, the cost of the ferry is additional.

An **Inter-Rail pass**—valid for one month—can be bought for £279 by travellers under 26. This covers all train travel in Europe and Morocco (except certain express trains and Eurostar), and leaves only the ferries to pay. The pass should be available at any major rail station in the UK and at youth/student travel agencies such as STA. BIGE tickets also offer discounted train travel for those under 26, and are marketed as Eurotrain by Campus Travel, 52 Grosvenor Gardens, London SW1W 0AG, ☎ (0171) 730 8518.

For all **information** regarding rail travel from the UK, contact the The Rail Shop, 179 Piccadilly, London W1V 9DB, ☎ (01891) 515 477 fax (0171) 633 9900. Or call the International Rail Information Line,☎ (0171) 834 2345.

By coach

Eurolines run coaches from London to Tangier—by way of Dover and Paris—and thence onwards to Rabat, Casablanca, Marrakesh, Agadir and Tiznit, or Meknes, Fes, Taza, Oujda and Nador. Coaches for both routes depart from the Eurolines Desk at Victoria Coach Station: the first leaves at 22.00 on Tuesday and arrives in Tiznit at 15.00 on Friday; the second leaves at 22.00 on Monday and Wednesday and arrives in Nador at 11.00 on Thursday or Saturday. The peak season (July–August inclusive) return fare to Tangier, Rabat or Casablanca is £190; the off-peak fare is £170. Return fares to all the other destinations are £200 (peak) and £180 (off-peak). Note that a departure tax of 30 francs is charged in Paris. There are no discounts. The services run all year except during Ramadan.

For further details on Eurolines services, contact National Express Coaches, ☎ (0990) 808 080.

By car and ferry

Whether travelling through France or Spain, a number of ferry services are available from the following ports:

Sète in France to Tangier takes 38h. There are 3–6 crossings per month, depending on the season. Bookings through COMANAV, 7 Blvd de la Resistance, Casablanca, ☎ (02) 302 006 or SNCM, 4 Quai d'Alger, Sète, ☎ 747 055.

Algeciras in Spain to Tangier takes 2h 30min. There are 3–6 crossings daily. Bookings through Southern Ferries, 179 Piccadilly, London W1V 0BA, ☎ (0171) 491 4968, or COMARIT, 7 Rue Mexique, Casablanca, ☎ (02) 931 220, or from any travel agent in Algeciras. Algeciras to Ceuta (car ferry) takes 1h 30min. There are 6–12 crossings daily. Algeciras to Ceuta (hydrofoil, passengers only) takes 1h. There are 4–8 crossings daily. Booking as above.

Malaga in Spain to Melilla takes 8h 30min. There is one crossing per day. Bookings through Transmediterannea, 4 Calle Juan Diaz, Malaga, ☎ 224 393, or Southern Ferries as above.

Gibraltar to Tangier takes 3h. There are 2 crossings weekly. Bookings through Tour Africa, ICC, Casemates Square, Gibraltar, or Southern Ferries, as above.

Another option is to take the ferry from Plymouth to Santander in northern Spain and thence onwards by car. There is no direct ferry service from the UK. It is worth noting that customs and other formalities in both Melilla and Ceuta, as Spanish enclaves within Morocco, can be very time-consuming. Casablanca and Tangier are usually much quicker in this respect and are generally more convenient ports of entry if you wish to visit other parts of Morocco.

Travelling around Morocco

By car

The international highway code is observed, with road signs written in French and Arabic (except in some remote rural areas where they appear only in Arabic). **Speed limits** are 120kph on motorways, 100kph on other roads, and 40–60kph in built-up areas. The rule of priority for the car coming from the right is ruthlessly enforced. The wearing of seat belts is compulsory.

An **International Driving Licence** is necessary to drive in Morocco (in the UK this is obtainable from any AA or RAC office). The minimum age for driving in Morocco is 21. Third party **insurance** is compulsory and the international green card is valid. If you do not have it on arrival, you can buy an *Assurance Frontière* at your port of entry.

At time of writing, both super and unleaded **petrol** (*essence*) costs 7.84dh a litre, which makes it a little cheaper than in the UK. Unleaded petrol (*sans plomb*) can be difficult to find, however: most large cities will carry it at main entry and exit points; small towns and villages have often never heard of it. Diesel (*gasoil*) is also widely available and costs around 5dh a litre.

If your vehicle has a **breakdown**, most Moroccan garage mechanics can perform miracles, though these may only last long enough to get you home. They are particularly at home with French cars. If you drive a hire car, you will be given contact numbers to phone in case of breakdown.

The more expensive hotels carry their own **parking** areas: otherwise, wherever you park, whether in the city centre or the middle of nowhere, it will be necessary to pay a *gardien* who will appear as if by magic. He may be an official wearing a badge, or an enterprising child simply wanting to earn a dirham or two. Whichever, you cannot avoid engaging him. It is wise always to carry a few loose dirhams specifically for this purpose: 5dh for an hour or so, 10dh for a day, or overnight, and less for small children who will be even more delighted with pens (*stylos*) or sweets (*bonbons*). If there is a group of children, be careful only to engage one of them, and ask his or her name.

The big international **car hire** companies such as Hertz, Avis and Europcar are well represented in all the main Moroccan cities, and on the whole provide excellent service, enabling one to collect the vehicle at one place and leave it at another, which is a great advantage. It is advisable to arrange car hire at home before leaving. The smallest car (group A) is usually a Renault 4 or Fiat Uno, a group B car is usually a Peugeot 205 or Ford Fiesta, and so on. Fiat Unos are now assembled in Morocco and garage mechanics can repair them more readily than other makes should they break down. Insurance usually covers unlimited liability, theft and fire damage and coverage for collision damage, but obviously all this must be carefully checked before signing an agreement. Minimum driver's age is 21. There are also a number of Moroccan car rental firms, often with very competitive rates. It is also possible to hire a local driver through a car-hire company; costs for this are usually somewhat lower than they would be in Europe or North America.

Morocco has the best **road network** in North Africa. This has recently been improved with the completion of the motorways between Rabat and Casablanca (toll 15dh) and between Larache and Kenitra, with an extension to Rabat underway. A motorway between Rabat and Fes is about to be constructed with funding from the World Bank, France, Italy and the Gulf States. Trunk roads are exceptionally good and uncluttered; secondary or B- roads are narrower, often only one car wide due to erosion of both edges, but sometimes almost completely empty. C-roads, to be found in rural areas, may well be unsurfaced tracks or **pistes**, which fall into three categories: those which are passable all the year round in any type of car; those which are open to non-4WD cars in the dry summer season only; and those which are passable only by 4WD vehicles at any time of year. Information as to the state of *pistes*, of fords after rain, and other hazards, is always available from local authorities.

Make sure your spare wheel is in place and usable, and that you have supplies of spare fuel and water on board. It is hard to imagine the degree of remoteness of some of the mountain and desert *pistes*. Moreover, if setting off on a desert journey, go with another vehicle, or at least take a local guide; it is so very easy to get lost, or stuck in sand.

In general, driving in Morocco can be sheer pleasure for anyone coming from congested European roads. However, roads in and around big cities such as Casablanca are to be avoided if possible, especially during rush hours, when they become seriously congested and badly polluted by lorries and buses which are not yet legally bound to clean up their engines. Intercity trunk roads hide other **problems**: as nearly all fields and forests are unfenced, there is a danger of untended cattle or donkeys or camels straying onto the roads. You are also likely to come across heavily laden horse-drawn carts creeping slowly along in the middle of the road. Moroccan country people seem blissfully unaware of danger and their children will dash out without so much as a glance. Some ancient vans and cars may not have any lights at all.

By train
The railway system, with its 1893km of track, is concentrated in the north of the country (see map on page 16). Some major cities are not served by rail, but the **ONCF** (*Office National de Chemin de Fer*) provides bus connections to them (see below). Contact the ONCF in Morocco on ☎ (07) 774 747 fax: (07) 774

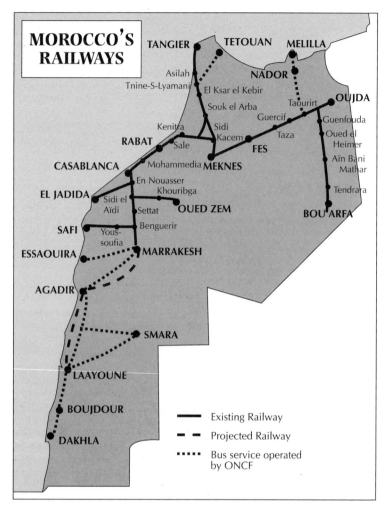

MOROCCO'S RAILWAYS

TANGIER
TETOUAN
MELILLA
Asilah
NADOR
Tnine-S-Lyamani
El Ksar el Kebir
OUJDA
Souk el Arba
Taourirt
Guercif
Guenfouda
Kenitra
Sidi
Taza
Oued el
RABAT
Kacem
Heimer
Sale
FES
Aïn Bani
CASABLANCA
Mohammedia
MEKNES
Mathar
En Nouasser
EL JADIDA
Khouribga
Tendrara
Sidi el
Aïdi
Settat
OUED ZEM
SAFI
Benguerir
BOU ARFA
Youss-
soufia
ESSAOUIRA
MARRAKESH
AGADIR
SMARA
LAAYOUNE
BOUJDOUR
DAKHLA

— Existing Railway

– – Projected Railway

····· Bus service operated by ONCF

480. Otherwise, information can be had from ONMT offices both in Morocco and abroad (see list above).

Trains have first-, second- and economy-class carriages. If you are travelling in the hot season it is certainly worth paying the small supplement for first class in order to benefit from the **air-conditioning**. Most trains have restaurants or buffet cars and, for long journeys, night sleepers or **couchette** facilities are usually available. Trains are modern, clean and comparatively cheap.

There is an excellent **inter-city service** between Rabat and Casablanca which takes 1h and runs throughout the day. It takes approximately 6h to get from Casablanca to Fes, and 7h from Casablanca to Tangier (both via Rabat). Casablanca to Marrakesh takes 4h.

By bus

The main national coach company, CTM-Lignes Nationales, operates services to most towns of any size. Most of their coaches are air-conditioned and comfortable. Fares are cheap by European standards. For information contact CTM, 23 Rue Léon l'Africain, Casablanca. ☎: (02) 448 127 fax: (02) 317 406.

ONCF, the railway, runs express coach services to a number of towns which are not connected to the rail network. Private companies such as SATAS supplement these networks, mainly in the south. Beware of very small companies which only have one or two buses and whose timetables are notoriously unreliable.

In general, bus services are punctual and are cheaper than trains, with offices and stations in all the major cities. Buses travel fast on inter-city routes; on minor routes, however, they may well stop at every little town for anything between five and 30 minutes, and always at a café. In the more remote areas the arrival of the coach is a great event for local people and they are liable to produce singers, dancers, acrobats, as well as anything from whole sheep to sticky cakes for sale. Life is never dull and time can be of supreme unimportance. This is a wonderful way to get to know the rural areas.

By air

For those who are really short of time, **Royal Air Maroc** operates regular services between Tangier, Casablanca, Marrakesh, Ouarzazate, Agadir, Al Hoceima, Oujda, Fes, Meknes, Rabat, Laayoune and Dakhla. This is a comparatively expensive way to travel but, given the vast size of the country, can make a lot of sense and save a great deal of time.

By taxi

Taxis are easy to find, particularly at railway and coach stations. They are also very cheap, compared with European taxis, and drivers do not expect to be tipped.

Petits taxis have a distinctive bright colour for each town: red in Casablanca, blue in Rabat, and so on. They cruise around or wait in ranks, and are metered. They are usually plentiful and hotel porters seem to have no trouble whatsoever in finding them when needed. They will usually only take up to three people and will not go outside city boundaries. Within the city they are the ideal way to sightsee without hassle. Rates usually rise after 20.00, although this may vary from city to city. You should enquire about this, and negotiate a fare, in advance, should the meter not work.

Grands taxis do not cruise around but wait in ranks, usually by bus and train stations. They are big cars, usually old Mercedes, and cover longer distances, between cities or from airport to city. In country districts they act like mini-buses and have specific collection points, usually insisting on six passengers before they will move at all. It is essential to negotiate a price before starting a journey; otherwise unsuspecting tourists can be seen as fair game. It is a good idea to take advice from hotel porters or airport information desks as to rates, particularly those from airports to town centres, which are usually standard.

Accommodation and food

Hotels

There are more than 550 **classified hotels**, offering 100,000 beds, in Morocco. The Ministry of Tourism classifies these hotels from one to five stars and prices are as follows:

5* single room 650–1450dh	double room 800–1650dh
4* single room 317–950dh	double room 396–1138dh
3* single room 110–382dh	double room 143–475dh
2* single room 131–194dh	double room 146–226dh
1* single room 68–138dh	double room 89–160dh

The ONMT produces a full list of classified hotels detailing their respective facilities, number of rooms, and so on. A few luxury-class hotels, such as the *Mamounia* in Marrakesh, the *Palais Jamai* in Fes and the *Gazelle d'Or* in Taroudannt, operate independently and their prices do not fall within the above scale. Information can be obtained from them direct, or through a tour operator such as *Best of Morocco*. In general, classified hotels are located in the new sections of towns, or around tourist sites in the medinas. Facilities according to star rating are as follows:

5* Bath and shower, telephone, heating, air-conditioning, television; restaurant, bar, nightclub, conference room, hairdresser, boutique; tennis, swimming pool; garage/parking

4* Bath and shower, telephone, heating, air-conditioning, television; restaurant, bar, boutique; swimming pool; garage/parking

3* Bath and shower, telephone, heating, air-conditioning (in a few cases only), television (not all hotels); restaurant, bar; swimming pool (not all hotels); garage/parking

2* Shower, heating; restaurant (in a few cases only); garage/parking (very few)

1* Shower

A selected list of hotels appears after the description of each major town in *Blue Guide Morocco*, and gives star classifications, number of rooms, addresses and telephone numbers. All of these have been visited either by the author or by reliable people known to the author. Judgements as to quality are, of course, subjective, and no responsibility can be taken for changes in management or falling standards of any hotel listed.

There are also 1000 **unclassified hotels** and pensions with 25,000 beds. They are usually to be found in the medinas of big cities, and in small towns. They are often very cheap, though even their prices can fluctuate with the season. Standards vary greatly, particularly with regard to washing facilities and size of rooms. It is important to ask to see the room, or make careful enquiries over the telephone, before making a booking.

Youth hostels

The Royal Federation of Moroccan Youth Hostels is affiliated to the International Federation of Youth Hostels. There are hostels in Asni, Azrou, Casablanca, Chaouen, Fes, Laayoune, Oujda, Marrakesh, Meknes, Rabat and Tangier. Prices vary from 15 to 30dh per person per night. Hostels are reserved for 13–30 year-olds. Some twenty **rest centres** do not have an age limit. A full list of youth hostels and rest centres is available from the ONMT, at the addresses given above, or from

Royal Moroccan Federation of Youth Hostels, Parc de la Ligue Arabe, BP 15988, Casablanca. ☎ (02) 220 551 fax (02) 226 777 or

Cultural Tourism Service for Young People & Rest Centres: 6 Rue Soumaya, Rabat Agdal. ☎ (07) 672 772 fax (07) 670 388.

Campsites

There are 87 camping and caravanning sites in Morocco, providing 41,000 places. They are usually in well-chosen locations, close to beaches or in woods. All those listed offer showers/WC, laundry facilities, groceries and may also have snack bars or restaurants and swimming pools. Rates are, on average, 15dh per person per night, plus 15dh for the car and caravan. Campsites are listed in each section of *Blue Guide Morocco*.

A full list of campsites can be obtained from the ONMT, at the addresses given above.

Refuges

There are many refuges for hikers and trekkers in forest and mountain areas, as well as overnight stopovers in the homes of local people, known as *gîtes d'étape*. Rates depend on the category and the season, but broadly range between 15 and 50dh per person per night. A full list is available from the ONMT, at the addresses given above, or from Club Alpin Français, BP 6178 Casablanca 01. ☎ (02) 270 090 fax (02) 297 292.

Restaurants

It is possible to eat very well for a reasonable price in Morocco, and there is a varied choice of cuisine, especially in the larger towns. Some restaurants offer only Moroccan dishes, others a choice of Moroccan or international food, and there is a growing number of Vietnamese and Chinese restaurants.

Most of the larger hotels are open to non-residents for lunch and dinner, but beware the big resort hotels catering for groups with indifferent pastas and lasagnes. There is a wide range in price and quality (which are not necessarily connected); you can pay very dearly at a 5-star hotel for an indifferent meal from a grandiose menu, or you can try out one of the hundreds of **café-restaurants** around town centres—which are often remarkably cheap—and discover gourmet food.

Appearing on nearly every 'international' menu will be various salads (often huge and constituting a meal in themselves), steaks, brochettes, and omelettes, followed by the ubiquitous crème caramel and fruit. Along the coast, and particularly the west coast between Casablanca and Agadir, there is a feast of **fish restaurants**, most good and some exceptionally good. Here again the cheapest can sometimes be ambrosial—it would be hard to beat a platter of sardines straight off the grills in the port of Essaouira, or the freshest of oysters at Oualidia, available for just a few dirhams.

Except when on holiday themselves, by the sea or at a resort such as Ifrane, Moroccans rarely eat out. **Traditional restaurants** are almost exclusively for foreigners. They are often housed in sumptuous palaces where a floor show may be included. For between 200 and 500dh a head you can feast the night away to the accompaniment of Andalusian or Berber music and exotic dancing (and increasingly wine is available to go with the meal). If you hope to experience the full gamut of dishes, it is necessary to order in advance and to go in a party of not less than four. It is always necessary to book ahead through your hotel and it is not uncommon for such restaurants to be taken over by large tour groups, especially in Marrakesh. Since the restaurants are often located deep in the medinas, guides are provided, on request, to take you and bring you back again. Selected traditional restaurants include the following.

Fes

Al Fassia, in the *Palais Jamai* hotel. ☎ (05) 637 415. Faultless Moroccan cooking, at a price.
Les Remparts, Bab Guissa.☎ (05) 637 415. Almost as good as *Al Fassia*, and a bit cheaper.
Dar Saada, 21 Attarine. ☎ (05) 633 343. Deep in the medina. Wonderful *pastilla*.
Dar Tajine, 15 Ross Rhi. ☎ (05) 634 1167. Also in the medina. Good.
Palais M'Nebhi, 15 Souiket Ben Safi. ☎ (05) 633 893. In a fine medina palace.

Marrakesh

La Maison Arabe, 5 Derb Ferrane. ☎ (04) 423 604. In the medina. Excellent.
Restaurant Ed Douira, 14 Derb Jdid Hay Salam. ☎ (04) 442 802. A little cheaper.
L'Oasis de Marrakech, Route de Casablanca. ☎ (04) 430 3368. The Berber floor show is fantastic, the food maybe less so. Expensive, but worth it.

Casablanca

Al Mounia, 95 Rue du Prince Moulay Abdallah. ☎ (02) 317 878. Very good.
Le Tajine, Centre 2000. ☎ (02) 276 400. By the port. Delicious food.

Tangier

Hôtel El Minzah, 85 Rue de la Liberté. ☎ (09) 935 885. Outstanding. Worth saving up for.
Restaurant Raihani, 10 Rue Ahmed Chaouki. ☎ (09) 934 866. In the medina.
Restaurant Marhaba Palace, 67 Rue de la Kasbah. ☎ (09) 937 643. In an atmospheric old palace. Good Moroccan food.

Vegetarians can have a hard time in Moroccan restaurants, especially if they exclude fish as well as meat from their diets. Soups, couscous made only with vegetables, salads and omelettes are usually available, but may well contain a meat-based stock. Vegetarian dishes as such are hard to find. Vegans should bring their own food supplies.

You are advised to read the section on food and drink below.

General information

Climate

Morocco is characterised by a great diversity of climate, as might be expected in view of its unique position facing two seas and backing on to the Sahara. One of the unique attractions of the country is that the traveller can go from the snow of the Atlas to the Saharan desert in a single day. The one thing all areas have in common is sunshine, and that in abundance: annual sunshine levels are more than 8 hours a day at Agadir, Fes, Marrakesh and Ouarzazate, with average temperatures above 21°C. The country can be divided roughly into three climatic zones.

The coastal zone extends across the north and west of the country. Summers are moderately hot and winters fairly cold. Rainfall is quite scarce in summer but plentiful during the rest of the year, and there is a high level of humidity at all times on the north Atlantic coast. The area east of Tangier has a typical Mediterranean climate with hotter, drier summers but cool winters. The best months for visiting this zone are April to October, although the region from Agadir southwards can be visited at any time of year, remaining very warm even in winter and escaping excessive heat in high summer because it is open to the sea.

The mountain ranges include the Rif, the Middle Atlas, the Jbel Ayachi, the High Atlas, the Anti Atlas and the Jbel Sarhro. All have hard, cold winters (the last three on the northern slopes only) with heavy snowfall in the highest parts lasting three to four months, and fairly hot, very dry summers. The best season for visiting depends on what you want to do. For walking and trekking, fishing, wild-flower observation, and so on, April to September are the best months. In winter the roads are often closed by snowfalls, avalanches, or floods, although those leading to ski resorts are usually well-maintained whatever the conditions. The best skiing months are December to February.

The interior encompasses the rest of the country and has a continental climate which becomes drier the further south or east you go. The northern region, which includes Fes and Meknes, is very hot and dry in summer, rather cold and damp in winter. It is not advisable to go south of Marrakesh during the months of July or August when the heat can become intolerable to anyone who is unaccustomed to it. Even Marrakesh can overwhelm you at that time unless you are provided with air-conditioning and go out only in the early morning or late at night.

The best seasons for exploring the interior are March to May or September to October. Marrakesh itself and other southern towns are popular throughout the winter months but exploring the countryside around them can become difficult once the rain or snow has started to fall in the mountains. The dry river beds (*oueds*) which cross and re-cross the desert tracks frequently originate in the mountains and can suddenly become rushing torrents, making the tracks impassable. Such conditions do not usually last very long as the water soon disappears into the thirsty river bed, but they can lead to delays. It is also worth remembering (especially if you are camping or staying in the cheaper hotels) that winter nights in the desert can be very cold.

Average temperatures (°C)

	Jan	Mar	May	Jun	Aug	Oct	Dec
Agadir	20.3	22.5	24.1	25.0	26.9	25.9	20.6
Al Hoceima	16.3	18.2	22.6	25.5	29.2	23.3	17.3
Casablanca	17.2	19.5	22.1	24.1	26.7	23.9	18.0
Ifrane	8.5	12.9	18.3	24.8	30.1	18.7	9.5
Errachidia	17.2	22.8	30.3	35.7	39.1	26.9	18.2
Marrakesh	18.1	23.0	28.7	32.9	37.5	28.1	18.3

	Jan	Mar	May	Jun	Aug	Oct	Dec
Meknes	14.9	19.1	24.5	29.6	33.7	25.0	15.5
Ouarzazate	17.3	23.0	30.8	36.0	38.4	27.0	16.7
Rabat	18.4	21.2	25.9	28.8	31.6	26.5	19.0
Tangier	15.4	17.4	21.4	24.2	26.8	22.1	16.0

Average daily hours of sunshine

	Jan	Mar	May	Jun	Aug	Oct	Dec
Agadir	8.0	9.7	10.0	10.0	10.5	8.0	6.4
Casablanca	5.3	6.9	9.3	9.7	9.7	10.6	5.6
Fes	5.1	7.6	9.3	10.9	10.8	9.6	4.4
Ifrane	4.1	7.6	9.3	12.1	11.4	8.0	4.3
Marrakesh	6.7	8.5	9.5	11.1	10.8	8.0	6.3
Meknes	5.1	6.7	9.7	10.3	11.2	7.9	5.6
Ouarzazate	6.9	9.4	11.0	12.0	9.4	7.9	6.9
Rabat	5.9	7.0	9.9	10.6	10.9	8.5	6.1
Safi	6.0	7.9	9.3	10.6	10.1	7.6	6.0
Tangier	5.3	6.9	10.0	10.9	11.5	9.4	5.3
Tetouan	4.9	7.4	9.5	11.8	11.2	7.8	4.4

Consular contacts in Morocco

The Foreign and Commonwealth Office in London publishes a useful leaflet on what British consuls can and cannot do for British tourists: to receive it contact the FCO Travel Advice Unit, ☎ (0171) 238 4503/4. Briefly, they *can* issue an emergency passport to get you back to the UK, contact your family and advise you about local lawyers. They can *not* get you out of prison or give legal advice, pay hotel or other bills, get you accommodation, work or work permits.

UK

British Embassy, Consular Section, 17 Blvd de la Tour Hassan, BP 45, Rabat. ☎ (07) 720 905.
British Consulate-General, 43 Blvd d'Anfa, BP 13762, Casablanca. ☎ (02) 221 653.
British Consulate, 41 Ave Mohammed V, BP 2122, Tangier. ☎ (09) 941 557.
Honorary Consul, Mr Zkhiri Mohammed, Residence Taib, 55 Blvd Zerktouni, Marrakesh. ☎ (04) 436 078.
Honorary Consul, Mr Oukrim Benlahcen, Agadir Beach Club, Secteur Balnéaire, Agadir. ☎ (08) 844 343.

USA

United States Embassy, 2 Ave de Marrakesh, Rabat. ☎ (07) 762 265.
United States Consulate, 8 Blvd Moulay Youssef, Casablanca. ☎ (02) 224 149.

Canada

Canadian Embassy, 13 bis Rue Jaafar Assadik, Rabat. ☎ (07) 672 880.

Citizens of Australia, **New Zealand** and **Ireland** should use UK consular facilities.

Crime and personal security

Petty **theft** is, unfortunately, growing, particularly in the big medinas and other tourist areas, as it is in resorts throughout the world. Never carry large sums of money with you; wear a money belt for what you do need. Most hotels have safes where you can deposit money and valuables. Campsites can be more of a problem, although many are made secure at night. It goes without saying that you should never leave anything of value in a parked car, although car theft as such hardly exists because very few Moroccans would know what to do with a stolen vehicle. If you are simply walking through a busy medina at night it is quite a good idea to take no money at all, so that you can convincingly declare this to would-be guides and hustlers; if the worst comes to the worst, you can always take a taxi back to base and pay for it on arrival.

Hustlers *are* a nuisance, but not much more if you tell them firmly, and loudly, to go away. They may want to sell you drugs, especially in Tangier or Ketama, but usually they just want to show you around and earn a few dirhams (see the section on guides, below). Most will give up quite quickly, if only because they fear disapproval from other Moroccans immediately around them. The authorities see persistent hustlers as a serious threat to tourism (the second largest earner of foreign currency in the country) and are currently making a major effort to clear them off the streets of major resorts.

Small **children**—sometimes swarming like flies around you—can also be a nuisance because they have learned to beg, for dirhams, *bonbons* or *stylos*. The more sophisticated ones may even try to dip into your pockets. If they offer some service (like 'guarding' the car), fine; if not, simply refuse and chat about something else. They too will eventually disappear, or alight on some other victim.

Inevitably you will meet people who have tales to tell: we met an Englishman travelling alone who was invited to someone's house 'to take tea and meet the family', stayed on for a meal, was offered drugs (but refused) and, when he woke up next morning, had been relieved of all his money, his passport and his shoes. But that sort of thing can happen to the naive traveller anywhere in the world.

Violent crime, however, is very rare indeed. Moroccans are not violent people. Women in particular can feel safer walking alone through a medina in Morocco than in almost any Western city.

If you do need to report a crime, go immediately to the local gendarmerie, who will give you a form to fill in, and register the crime, especially if you have lost an official document. There is not a lot else they can do, but you, or your insurance company, will need a **police report** before taking any further action. Moroccans will quite genuinely be shocked by any crime they see or hear about from you, and will almost certainly help to find the appropriate authorities.

Currency and banks

The Moroccan currency is the **dirham** (dh), which is divided into 100 centimes. There are 10, 50, 100 and 200dh notes, 1 and 5dh coins and 5, 10, 20 and 50 centime coins. At time of writing, there are 15.22dh to the pound sterling, 9.81dh to the US dollar, and 6.75dh to the Canadian dollar.

Dirhams can only be obtained in Morocco: it is forbidden to import or export them. This can often mean a long wait at the bank or *bureau de change* at your entry or exit port. On departure, dirhams are usually exchanged back for US dollars or French francs, rather than pounds sterling. It is illegal to change money in the street. The best place is at a bank or approved *bureau de change* (indicated by a golden sign). No commission is charged and you will be given a slip which until recently was always required at the end of your stay in order to change any remaining dirhams back. This last rule seems now to have eased. Scottish notes and Irish currency are not recognised by Moroccan banks. Dirhams are not accepted by duty-free shops; some other shops will accept francs or pesetas instead of dirhams.

You can withdraw money with major credit cards in banks or directly from a cash dispenser in some large towns. Credit cards are generally accepted in hotels, shops and restaurants, and sometimes even in the souks. Travellers cheques and Eurocheques are accepted at most major banks, but the paper work can be very slow, especially in rural areas.

The following banks are represented in most cities and towns throughout Morocco. They tend to be located in the modern sections of town and invariably on the main street, which is almost sure to be called Avenue or Boulevard Mohammed V or Hassan II.

BMCE (*Banque Marocaine du Commerce Exterieur*)
BCM (*Banque Credit du Maroc*)
Wafabank
Credit Agricole
Banque Populaire
Banque al Maghrib

BMCE is usually the best for the purposes of exchanging money, as it accepts Visa/Mastercard, traveller's cheques, Eurocheques and most currencies.

Customs regulations

You may temporarily import most of your personal effects—in quantities consistent with normal tourist activity, such as two tennis racquets, two pairs of skis, one tent and camping equipment, a camcorder, a camera, a Walkman, a pair of binoculars—into Morocco without any formalities. Restrictions apply to:

alcohol—one litre bottle of wine and one litre bottle of spirits or three bottles of wine per adult

tobacco—200 cigarettes or 50 cigars or 250g of tobacco per adult

arms and ammunition for hunting (shotguns are prohibited)

photographic equipment—one camera and 10 rolls of film, or 24 cartridges, for tourists (professional equipment has to be declared)

If you bring your **pets** with you, obtain for them a health certificate no more than ten days old, as well as an anti-rabies certificate less than 6 months old.

Moroccan law forbids the possession, sale or purchase of **drugs**, even though hashish *(kif)* is legally cultivated in the Rif mountains, and always has been. There is a commitment to stamp out the drugs trade, the more so because of Morocco's wish to integrate more closely with the European Union. To emphasise this point, foreigners are often targeted, particularly when passing through northern ports such as Tangier. Penalties are severe. Even possession of a small amount could earn you a prison sentence, a stiff fine and confiscation of your vehicle. A special danger period is September and October when the *kif* is harvested and dealers are particularly anxious to get rid of it.

Disabled travellers

There are really no facilities for the disabled (*handicapés*) in Morocco, although some of the larger hotels do have entrance ramps. Pavements, even in some of the big cities, tend to be potholed and it is not unusual to see wheelchair-users having to take to the roads. The organisations listed below may be able to give specialist advice.

UK

RADAR, 12 City Forum, 250 City Road, London EC1V 8AS. ☎ (0171) 250 3222

Holiday Care Services, 2nd Floor, Imperial Building, Victoria Road, Horley, Surrey RH6 9HW. ☎ (01293) 774 535.

Ireland

Disability Action Group, 2 Annadale Ave, Belfast BT7 3JH. ☎ (01232) 910 11.

USA

National Tour Association, 546 East Main St, PO Box 3071, Lexington, KY 40596. ☎ (606) 226 444.

Society for the Advancement of Travel for the Handicapped (SATH), 347 Fifth Ave, Suite 610, New York, NY 10016. ☎ (212) 447 7284.

Australia

Australian Council for Rehabilitation of the Disabled (ACROD), PO Box 60, Curtin ACT 2605. ☎ (06) 682 4333; 55 Charles St, Ryde. ☎ (02) 9809 4488.

New Zealand

Disabled Persons Assembly, PO Box 10–138, The Terrace, Wellington. ☎ (04) 472 2626.

Flora

With its great variety of climate and topography, from sandy desert to perpetual snow and from the low coastal plains to the Atlas mountains, Morocco has a rich and varied flora, attractive to the layman for the beauty of the vast spreads of colour painted by meadow flowers in spring and summer, and of interest to the botanist because so many of the species are narrowly endemic and often unique, particularly at high altitudes.

Meadows in spring and early summer look like oriental carpets, woven with species of pot marigold (*Calendula*), cornflower or knapweed (*Centaurea*), stock (*Matthiola*), lupin (*Lupinus*), echium, lavender (*Lavandula*) and members of the chrysanthemum family (*Dendranthema*). A taller accent is given by the asphodels (*Asphodelus*), mignonette (*Reseda*), alkanet (*Anchusa*), fennel (*Foeniculum*), and the century plant (*Agave americana*), so-called because it produces a magnificent spike of a flower from its prickly rosette only once every 100 years or so. Many species of convolvulus decorate the roadside. In lightly wooded country there is a wealth of orchids. The narcissus family is represented, especially by some of its miniature members. The vast spurge genus (*Euphorbia*) is found particularly in arid areas, and the country is rich in prickly, thistly plants, such as the globe thistle (*Echinops ritro*) and the holy or milk thistle (*Silybum marianum*) with its white-mottled, deeply cut leaves. The iris family is also widespread, especially in coastal regions.

Trees of particular interest are the cedars (*Cedrus libani* and *C. atlantica*), especially the blue variety (*glauca*) found in the Middle Atlas and the Rif; the cork oak (*Quercus suber*), widespread in the regions bordering the north and northwest coasts; ancient olive trees (*Olea*), particularly around Meknes; date palms (*Phoenix dactylifera*), very beautiful in flower, in the pre-Saharan oases, and the curious argan (*Argania sideroxylon*) along the southwest coast around Agadir, into which goats climb in search of the olive-like fruit, and later deposit the stones from which is extracted a useful oil much prized in the region.

Shrubs and small trees are mostly of the maquis type: many varieties of rock rose (*Cistus*) with its crumpled petals and sticky aromatic foliage; brooms, of which one endemic variety, *Cytisus battandieri*, is very popular in English gardens; the wattles or mimosas (*Acacia*); oleanders *(Nerium oleander)* flowering from April to September along dried-up water courses and, occasionally to be seen in some sheltered valleys, the strawberry tree (*Arbutus unedo*).

Guides

It is an unfortunate fact that wherever you go in the larger Moroccan towns, and particularly in the tourist-frequented medinas, you will be accosted by aspiring guides—old and young, official and unofficial, honest and not-so-honest. However confident and independent you may be feeling, you will at some point decide it is better to engage a guide, if only to be left in peace by the other aspirants who will then recognise you as 'won' and magically melt away. Your chosen guide will also discourage the multitudes of children who hold out their hands for dirhams, *stylos* and *bonbons*, encouraged no doubt by the large tour groups with bulging purses. (It is noticeable that, as tourism has grown, more and more children have found it profitable to beg.)

Official guides, usually wearing white djellabahs and badges, charge a set rate (currently 150dh per half day) and are obliged to conduct themselves responsibly or they will lose their official status. They know the history of the country and its monuments in some detail and often speak several languages. On the other hand, official guides are occasionally quite obviously bored and blasé, and make it plain that they deserve a better life (and many do, having at some time been writers or teachers). This is particularly so in big resorts like Tangier where they have evidently said the same thing to too many tourists too many times.

If he makes a good first impression you can consider sometimes taking one of the **unofficial guides**, who have nothing to recommend them but their bright, and usually honest, faces, but may be just as good. Moroccans are by nature very friendly people and when your guide tells you he wants to practise his English, he probably means it. There are, sadly, a lot of educated young men who are unable to find work. They welcome the opportunity to talk to foreigners and generally relieve the boredom of hanging around, and often make excellent companions. They sometimes have interesting tales to tell, and are more amenable than the official guides. They also badly need your money to supplement their income (or lack of it).

Both sorts of guide tend to hang around outside hotels and near medina entrances. There are a few golden rules which should help avoid disappointment and/or embarrassment on both sides:

Agree the price before you start. If you engage an official guide for less than half a day, you can often persuade him to lower his price. With unofficial guides it is best to negotiate a lower rate, perhaps promising something on top if you enjoy your tour. Never leave it open. *C'est comme vous voulez* usually leads to arguments in the end.

Control your route. Plan your trip beforehand, with the aid of a guide book or map. Tell the guide what you want to see, what you want to buy (if anything) and what time you want to be back. Try to avoid admitting that this is your first visit. Never appear flustered.

Do not be deflected from your original plan. The guide may try to take you to his own contacts, such as carpet co-operatives. This is fine if you have already said you want to look at or buy carpets, but remember he may have in mind the commission he will get from his friend should you be persuaded to make a purchase.

Do not let the guide hurry you. If you want to stop and look at something on the way, do so. The guide will always wait.

The best guides of all are the old men in country districts: friendly, dignified in their striped djellabahs and yellow babouches, and full of fascinating anecdotes, they unwittingly speak a unique mix of English, French and German. They are usually quite incapable of answering questions but their flow of information is well-presented and the nuggets of wisdom they produce are often memorable.

Health

Inoculations are not obligatory unless you are arriving from a declared infected area. It is wise, however, to have your typhoid, cholera, tetanus and polio immunisation up-to-date; some people consider hepatitis is also advisable. There are mosquitoes in the south but these are said not to be malarial. Cautious travellers may still wish to take a course of anti-malarial tablets, while insect-repellent creams or sprays and some form of anti-histimine cream are useful and are available locally if needed.

Morocco is, on the whole, a healthy country and standards of care are high. There are plenty of French-speaking doctors around: hotels, tourist offices and pharmacies will have lists of them. **Pharmacies** should be your first port of call if a problem arises; their staff are well-trained and their shelves will be well-stocked with drugs, many of which would be available only on prescription in the UK. They will also recommend doctors if necessary. Modern, privately owned clinics and state-run hospitals are available to visitors should the need arise. Emergency telephone numbers (for ambulance services) are usually written up on hotel doors, or are available at hotel reception.

The most likely ailment to befall foreign visitors is **diarrhoea**, so always take supplies of your own preferred remedy. Even this can be avoided if you make it a rule never to drink, or brush your teeth with, **water** from the tap, except in the main towns in the north. There is excellent bottled spring water to be had, including *Sidi Harazem*, *Imouzzer* and *Sidi Ali* (still) and *Oulmes* (sparkling). Large bottles can be bought at supermarkets or corner shops quite cheaply. Top hotels provide complimentary bottles in the rooms. Bilharzia is believed to lurk in pools and rivers in the south, so it is best not to have any contact with water in oases, however tempting it looks.

Change of **diet**, or quite simply over-indulgence, can also cause problems at first. Hotels and restaurants tend to produce full and tempting menus for lunch and dinner. It takes a degree of will-power to insist on just a salad or an omelette for lunch, but this is certainly a good idea, especially if travelling in the heat of the day. Charcoal-grilled meats and fish from market stalls, ice cream from street vendors, fly-blown dates and other fruits which have no peel are best avoided, at least until you have had time to adjust.

Your own travel insurance is of course advisable.

Holidays
Secular holidays

1 January, New Year's Day

11 January, Independence manifesto

3 March, Throne Day (*Fête du Trone*). The anniversary of King Hassan's accession to the throne in 1961 and the most important national holiday in Morocco, it is enthusiastically celebrated throughout the entire kingdom with fireworks, singing, dancing and parades.

1 May, Labour Day

23 May, National Day

9 July, King's birthday; Young People's Day

14 August, Allegiance Day

20 August, Anniversary of the King's and People's Revolution

6 November, Anniversary of the Green March

18 November, Independence Day

Religious holidays

These are public holidays throughout Morocco. Note that the dates are approximately 10 days earlier each year. It is not possible to predict the exact dates, which depend on the lunar calendar and are set by the Islamic authorities in Fes each year.

In 1998 the approximate dates of these festivals will be as follows.

29 January, Aid el Fitr (or Aid el Seghir), end of the month of Ramadan

8 April, Aid el Kbir (or Aid el Adha, 'the feast of the sheep'), commemorating Abraham's sacrifice of his son Isaac

28 April, first day of the month of Moharem, the Muslim New Year

8 July, Mouloud, celebrating the birth of the Prophet

Newspapers

The three main French-language newspapers are *Le Matin du Sahara*, *L'Opinion* and *Al Bayanne*. The main Arabic titles are *Al Alam*, *Al Muharnir* and *Al Djemaa*. The best-known foreign newspapers are usually available at larger kiosks and shops.

Opening hours

Opening hours can vary, especially in rural areas, but for the main cities and towns they are generally as follows.

Banks. 08.15–11.30 and 14.15–16.30 Mon–Fri.

Post offices (*PTTs*). 08.30–11.45 and 14.30–18.30 Mon–Fri.

Shops. 08.30–12.00 and 14.00–18.30 Mon–Sat. Shops in the medinas make their own rules, frequently closing on Fridays for religious reasons, sometimes opening on Sundays, and often staying open till very late in the evening. Food shops in the medinas will usually open on Friday mornings only.

Offices. 08.30–12.00 and 14.30–18.30 Mon–Thur; 08.30–11.30 and 15.00–18.30 Fri.

Museums. Generally open every day except Tuesday. A few are open every day. Their hours are roughly the same as those for banks, with a long period of closure in the middle of the day.

Note that banks and shops close for both secular and religious holidays.

Passports and formalities

A full valid passport is required to enter Morocco. British Visitors' Passports are not valid. If a child is travelling on a parent's passport, his or her photograph must be stamped in by the passport office next to the name. No visa is necessary for nationals of the United Kingdom or the United States but you will be required to complete a standard form giving personal details (profession, passport number etc.) on entry to the country, and on arrival at each hotel. You can stay in Morocco for up to three months and should apply to the local police department (*Bureau des Etrangers*) if you wish to stay longer.

Note that items of photographic equipment, such as video cameras, are entered on your passport and presumed sold if not with you on departure, leading to a charge of duty.

Photography

On the whole, Moroccans are getting used to the sight of camera-laden visitors and some do not hesitate to profit from it, coming up and demanding dirhams if they feel the camera has been pointed in their direction. Water-sellers, bedecked with brass cups and colourful robes, probably make more money from posing than they do from selling water. Camel and goat boys also have the whole business refined to a delicate art and should not be begrudged their few coins.

Ordinary people going about their business should always be asked if they mind being photographed: this applies especially to **women** in rural areas who often cover their faces and run away in fear.

Photography of **holy places** such as the white-domed *koubbas* can cause offence and one should firmly resist the temptation to point a camera towards the interior of a mosque, however inviting the open doors may appear.

As in most countries, photography anywhere near a military installation is highly unwise.

Public toilets

On the whole these are better left well alone. They are usually of the squat variety and often filthy. If caught short, either look for a hotel or restaurant, or get out into the country as soon as possible.

Telephone and postal services

To telephone inside Morocco. If calling a number within the same area, simply dial the six-digit number you want. If calling from one area to another, dial the area code (see below) then, without waiting for another tone, the six-digit number you want. To call a mobile phone, the code is always 02.

The area codes are:

Casablanca 02
Settat 03

Marrakesh 04
Fes 05
Oujda 06
Rabat 07
Laayoune 08
Tangier 09

To make international calls from Morocco dial 00, wait for the tone, then dial the international country code followed by the number you want. Warning: before making an international call from your hotel room, check the rates. Some hotels impose a 'minimum charge' which can make even a short call very expensive. International calls are charged per three-minute period.

To call Morocco from abroad dial the international code for Morocco (212), then the area code but omitting the initial zero, then the six-digit number you want.

Telephone boxes (*cabines*) use both coins (1dh and 5dh pieces) and cards. There are phone boxes in all major towns. If you have difficulty finding one, make for the cental post office (*PTT Centrale*) where there will be several. Failing this, go to a hotel, but check beforehand that it will not make an exorbitant surcharge. Phone cards are available at post offices and in some tobacconists.
A call to Europe will cost at least 20dh, and to North America at least twice that amount.

Useful numbers
Police 19
Fire service 15
Highway emergency service 177
Directory enquiries 16
International directory enquiries 12

Letters take between one week and ten days to reach Western Europe from Morocco, and about two weeks to reach North America. Stamps (*timbres*) can be bought at tobacconists or at post offices. There are post boxes scattered around towns and at post offices; if you cannot find one, you can mail letters through a hotel. Parcels should be taken unwrapped to the post office, as officials sometimes ask to examine the contents.

Tipping
Restaurant waiters expect around 10%–15%. Hotel porters expect about 5dh per large item for loading and unloading luggage. Taxi drivers do not expect tips.

Women travelling alone
Women need not feel threatened when travelling alone in Morocco as long as they respect local customs. Firstly, this means you should **dress suitably** and not wear shorts, mini skirts or minuscule singlets in town. This is particularly important if you are anywhere near holy places (as in Fes or Moulay Idriss or the new Hassan II Mosque in Casablanca). The beach is a different story and anything goes, but for getting there and returning, the above rule applies. Secondly, it is not the custom when speaking to unknown men (particularly older men) for women to look them directly in the eyes. This is perhaps difficult

for Westerners constantly reminded of the need for eye contact, but in Morocco, as in other Arab countries, a direct gaze could be treated as a 'come on' by men. Moroccans, particularly young ones, are naturally inquisitive. They may call out questions as you walk past: 'what's your name' or 'where are you staying' or 'where do you come from?' This is usually just curiosity and has little to do with the fact that you are a woman. Just walk past and, if necessary, tell them sharply to go away. In town, older men will very often move forward and see off the questioners in no uncertain terms, but rarely hang around to be thanked.

It cannot be denied that Morocco is a man's country. What else can you expect when the Koran says 'Men have authority over women because God has made the one superior to the other....'(sura 4, verse 34). No wonder women are not allowed in the holiest places of the mosque but are confined to their own special area; no wonder the cafés are all full of men with never a woman in sight (unless she is a foreigner); and no wonder it is still quite common in country districts to see a man riding a donkey and the woman (with a load of firewood on her back) walking along behind.

This is their culture and we should not presume to interfere. Moroccans will always say, if challenged, that they have the greatest respect for women (especially their mothers) and this is certainly true, even if their way of showing it is somewhat strange to Western eyes.

Moroccan women, who usually go around in groups of two or three, love to talk with foreign women who are not accompanied by men, but are probably too shy to approach you, and may only speak Arabic. A smile and a phrase such as 'your kaftan is beautiful' ('*Votre kaftan est belle*', '*Kaftan dyalek zouin*') will amuse and delight them. They might invite you back for tea in their homes where there will be lots of children and where other women will appear, as if by magic, to meet you, manifesting the very same curiosity about your lifestyle as the men but in a gentler and less irritating way. If you have time and are keen to know more, show an interest in their cooking, which is their pride and joy. You might even learn to make a *pastilla*.

Another place in which to meet women is the hammam or public baths (even the smallest town will have at least one, usually in the medina). Whether sitting around and steaming or having a massage, the setting is ideal for relaxed and sometimes completely uninhibited chatter. Again, the curiosity factor will come into play and you are highly unlikely to be ignored. There are always different hours, and sometimes different hammams, for each sex, and your hotel should be able to provide all the necessary information, particularly if it is also in the medina.

Ironically, there are occasions when travelling with a man can be more frustrating to the modern Western woman than going it alone, or travelling with another woman, insofar as all decision-making and serious conversation will automatically be directed at *him*, even if the question emanated from you, the woman, in the first place. *Plus ça change ...*

Museums

Morocco is rich in museums, many of them housed in splendid **palaces** which are objects of great beauty in their own right. The four Imperial Cities are particularly well endowed. There is a standard **entry fee** of 10dh per person. (For opening times, see above.)

Rabat

Oudaias Museum, Kasbah des Oudaias. ☎ (07) 731 537. Located in one of Moulay Ismael's palaces. Best for carpets, Rabat and Berber; also costumes, pottery, musical instruments, jewellery.

Archaeological Museum, 23 rue el Brihi. ☎: (07) 701 919. The prehistoric section brings together human remains from the middle Palaeolithic to the Neolithic periods. Also an outstanding collection of Roman artefacts from Volubilis, Sala Colonia, Banasa and elsewhere.

Fes

Dar Batha Museum, Pl. du Batha. ☎ (05) 634 116. A Hispano-Moorish palace dating from the late 19C, built by the Sultan Moulay el Hassan to join Fes el Bali and Fes el Jdid. Noted for its fine collection of ceramics (for which Fes is especially famous), for its astronomical instruments created and perfected by learned Arabs, and for its embroidery, coins and jewellery.

Bordj Nord Museum, Ave des Merinides (close to *Hôtel des Merinides*). ☎ (05) 645 241. A museum of weaponry in a 16C fortress close to the ramparts. Includes everything from the prehistoric axe to the modern rifle. Many civilisations are represented but the finest exhibits are Moroccan, with daggers encrusted with stones, and an amazing cannon 5m long and weighing 12 tons, used during the Battle of the Three Kings in the 16C.

Marrakesh

Dar Si Said Museum, Riad Ez-Zaitoun El Jdid. ☎ (04) 442 464. A 19C palace with fine, painted cedarwood ceilings, built around a courtyard. There are carpets from all regions, a collection of wooden children's toys, jewellery, weapons and kaftans. Upstairs a family reception room is arranged as for a wedding with a traditional marriage chair and table used for displaying presents.

Maison Tiskiwin, Rue de la Bahia. A small 19C palace with some beautiful ceilings, housing a collection of carpets, jewellery, costumes, etc., put together by Bert Flint, a Dutch anthropologist resident in Morocco for 40 years.

Majorelle Museum, Majorelle Gardens, in the new town, north of Bab Doukkala. Situated in the former studio of the French painter, Jacques Majorelle, the museum houses a collection of Islamic art. The gardens are exceptionally beautiful and full of birdsong. The whole is now owned by French couturier, Yves Saint Laurent. Entry fee for gardens 15dh and for museum a further 15dh.

Meknes

Dar Jamai Museum, Pl. el Hedim. ☎ (05) 530 863. Another 19C palace, once the residence of the grand vizier of Sultan Moulay el Hassan. It contains fine wrought-iron work, wooden sculpture, leather, brass and copper wares, and beautifully simple Andalusian-style tiles. Best of all are the Berber carpets, mainly from the Middle Atlas. Upstairs rooms are furnished in the traditional 19C style.

Tangier

Museum of Moroccan Arts/Antiquities Museum, Dar el Makhzen, Pl. de la Kasbah. ☎ (09) 932 097. Dominating the Tangier kasbah, this was formerly the governor's palace, laid out around a splendid patio decorated with mosaic floors and marble columns. There is a good collection of weapons, ceramics, carpets, jewellery, etc. Also, accessible via the former kitchens, there are Roman artefacts from Lixus, Banasa and Volubilis. Next door to the museum is the former treasury containing a number of huge wooden chests.

The Forbes Museum, Palais Mendoub, Rue Shakespeare. ☎ (09) 933 606. A unique and fascinating collection of 115,000 military miniatures, put together by the American millionaire, Malcolm Forbes. These figures re-enact the major battles of history from Waterloo to Dien Bien Phu, not forgetting Morocco's own Battle of the Three Kings of 1578.

The American Legation, 8 Zankat America. ☎ (09) 935 317. A rare collection of old maps and correspondence between George Washington and Sultan Moulay Abdallah. Morocco was the first country to recognise the independent United States of America in 1776 and this palace was presented as a gift to the US government for its new diplomatic representative. Open only Mon, Wed and Thur, or by appointment.

There are also museums in Tetouan, Chaouen, Larache, Safi, Essaouira and Agadir.

Souks and shopping

Morocco is a treasure house of traditional **crafts** or *artisanat* and the handicrafts industry plays an important part in the national economy, employing one third of the active population. These crafts reflect centuries-old skills and use local materials such as cedarwood, leather, clay, wool, vegetable dyes, and copper (see *Traditional crafts*, below). The goods are available in all medinas and it is often possible to see them being made. Sometimes the abundance is almost overwhelming, and it is advisable to prioritise in advance what you really want to buy, and how much you are prepared to spend.

There are two methods of acquiring craft items. You can first make for one of the government-controlled **craft shops** (there is one in every main town) known as *centres d'artisanat* or *ensembles artisanals*, where the price is fixed—probably a little higher than you would pay in the souks—but where the quality is reliable and there is no pressure on you whatsoever. A visit to such a place is in any case an essential preliminary to any successful foray into the souks thereafter, for it gives you an idea of the range of goods available, and the sort of price you should be paying.

The word **souk** can mean a stall in a market or a whole market of stalls. In major cities, the souks are to be found in the medinas, usually in groups according to their particular product (for example, the spice souk—*Souk el Attarine*—in Fes).

In the countryside, each market town within a given agricultural area has its souk or market on a different day of the week. This day is fixed and it is often possible to tell from the name of a town the day on which it holds its souk. In Maghrebi Arabic, the days of the week are denoted by numbers: Sunday is Day 1 (*el Had*); Monday is Day 2 (*et Tnine*); Tuesday is Day 3 (*et Tleta*); Wednesday is Day 4 (*el Arba*); Thursday is Day 5 (*el Khemis*); Friday, the only day which is not numbered, is above all the day of prayer, so it is called quite simply *el Jamai* ('the mosque'); Saturday is Day 7 (*es Sebt*). For example, the town of Souk el Arba on the Tangier–Rabat road, does indeed have its souk every Wednesday.

These weekly **country souks** are most entertaining. Family groups, complete with children and donkeys, walk long distances to buy and sell. For them it is a social occasion as well as a commercial one. The tents are set up, often just outside the town, and the produce is displayed. Mint tea is brewed, and various unidentifiable delicacies are put to sizzle over the charcoal. You can buy anything from a couple of eggs and a kilo of oranges to a richly woven Berber carpet, or perhaps the latest thing in sun hats, made out of local reeds. Tailors set up their sewing machines and make kaftans out of customers' own materials; cobblers hammer soles back on to worn-out sandals; sometimes there are acrobats and musicians. It is always a scene of animation and colour.

Bargaining. The joy of a bargain cunningly and painstakingly acquired, and the satisfaction felt both by the buyer and the seller after the game has been well played, are experiences not to be missed. The rules are simple: when asked to name the price you are prepared to pay, pitch it at about half the figure you would expect finally to pay, for the seller will quote you twice as much (at least) as he will settle for. He will no doubt tell you several times that you are ruining him but, in the end, that he will make an extraordinary concession *'parce que vous êtes mon premier/dernier client aujourd'hui'*. You, having exclaimed several times that you are *'un pauvre étudiant'*, will forage around and find the money somehow. If, at any point, this well-oiled ritual appears to stick, then simply turn to walk away, apparently no longer interested. You will undoubtedly be called back with the cry *'mais qu'est ce que vous voulez payer?'* At the end of all this, once money has been exchanged, there will be much handshaking and exchange of goodwill and you may well be invited to take mint tea, depending on the significance of the purchase. Above all, do not be in a hurry. Traditional Moroccans find the western speed of living hard to comprehend and will often quote a proverb—in French—*un homme pressé est un homme presque mort* ('a man in a hurry is a man almost dead'), and they could well be right. (For an account of a timeless shopping ritual in Tiznit, see page 280.)

In some medinas, Fes in particular, old palaces are being taken over by **co-operatives** making carpets, kaftans, jewellery or leather goods and presenting them for sale in a very professional way. The foot-weary visitor will be invited to sit down and take tea, and be regaled with a story (in English, French, German, or Spanish) of how the items are made, whilst prime samples are put before his eyes. There is often high-pressure salesmanship here and nothing is too much trouble, no export order too difficult to fulfil or too far to send. Co-operatives will always tell you that the price is fixed, but that is not necessarily so, particularly at the end of the day and most particularly if you happen to be a member of a large group. Quality is usually high here, prices vary but are certainly lower than you would pay in hotels or shops (because there is no middleman) and the process can be less of a strain—but also less fun—than the one-to-one bargaining ritual.

Sport and leisure activities
Trekking. There are magnificent opportunities for trekking in the High Atlas (especially around Jbel Toubkal), the Jbel Sirwa, the Jbel Sarhro and the Middle Atlas. The possibilities of these vast and little frequented areas are only just being recognised and represent a challenging and most welcome addition to well-worn itineraries in the Alps and Pyrenees. The **best season** for the High

and Middle Atlas ranges is April to October. In mid-summer it is advisable to stay in the upper valleys where water is always available. On the south-facing slopes of the pre-Saharan massifs of Sirwa and Sarhro, November to May is the best period: these become very hot in summer, when it is better to move to the northern slopes.

Transport to the main towns and large villages is by coach or by *grand taxi*. The heart of the massif can then be reached on rough tracks using local 4WD taxis or trucks going to local markets, or mules (always available for hire in villages). It is also, of course, possible to hire self-drive 4WD vehicles (addresses given below).

Mountain escorts belonging to the National Association of Guides and Mountain Escorts in Morocco (ANGAM), which has existed since 1992, have had training comparable to that of their Alpine counterparts. They are autho-rised to lead trekkers on high mountain paths and normal access routes to summits and passes, with the exception of itineraries requiring rock-climbing, alpinism or skiing techniques. Specially trained mountain escorts can supervise mountain skiing, canyon descent and rock climbing. Lists of such escorts, with their telephone numbers, are published each year in a free guide to trekking by the ONMT, and are available in local offices. The guide is published in English and French as *The Great Trek through the Moroccan Atlas* or *La Grande Traversée des Atlas Marocains*.

Porterage: baggage mules can be hired in all mountain villages, particularly in those where the road ends. One animal can carry about 100kg, corre-sponding to the baggage of roughly four trekkers.

Three types of **accommodation** are progressively being set up: mountain inns, overnight stops in the homes of local people (*gîtes d'étapes*), and mountain refuges. These too are listed in the OMNT publication mentioned above.

Basic **provision**s should be prepared before departure. However, every village has small grocery stores where additional supplies can usually be bought. In addition, keep an eye out for local weekly markets. It is also possible to buy chickens, eggs, meat and sometimes vegetables from local people. Drinking water should be taken exclusively from springs and either boiled or else disin-fected with tablets, as a precaution against giardiasis.

Having the right **clothing** is obviously crucial: walking-boots are most suit-able though good trainers might suffice in summer. Warm sweaters are advis-able, even in summer, as early mornings and nights on the mountains can be very cold. Some form of head-covering is necessary as protection from strong sunlight.

Altitude sickness is always a possibility for even the fittest of trekkers, espe-cially if they are climbing fast. It manifests itself as increasing breathlessness, headaches and, ultimately, vomiting. If this happens, stop all exertion and rest, drink plenty of fluid and take aspirin. If symptoms persist, descend to a lower altitude as soon as possible. Official help, particularly by helicopter, can be a long time arriving, because of communication difficulties and the remoteness of some areas. Trekkers are advised to be as independent as possible in **first aid**. The presence of a mountain escort qualified in first aid and familiar with the lie of the land is obviously an important safety factor.

The following **guidebooks** should be available in main bookshops in Morocco and in specialist shops in Europe and North America:

Le Haut Atlas Central: Guide Alpin, A. Fougerolles (Éditions CAF, Casablanca, 1981)

La Grand Traversée de l'Atlas Marocain, Michael Peyron (Éditions Auteur, 1988)

Le Maroc: Les Plus Belles Courses et Randonnées, Bernard Domenech (Éditions Denoel, 1989)

Le Massif du Toubkal: Guide Alpin, J. Dresch and J. de Lepiney (Éditions Belvisi-Edisud, 1993).

Useful addresses
General
Ministry of Tourism (*Ministère de Tourisme*), 64 Ave Al Amir Fal Ould Oumeir, Agdal-Rabat. ☎ (07) 770 686 fax (07) 770 626.

National Association of Guides and Mountain Escorts in Morocco (*Association Nationale des Guides et Accompagnateurs en Montagne du Maroc*, ANGAM), B.P.47, Asni par Marrakech-42150. ☎ (04) 444 979 fax (04) 433 609.

Royal Moroccan Ski and Mountaineering Federation, Parc de la Ligue Arabe, B.P. 15899, Casablanca 01. ☎ (02) 203 798 fax (02) 474 979

Club Alpin Français, B.P.6178, Casablanca 01. ☎ (02) 270 090 fax (02) 297 292.

Club Alpin Français, Rue Jaafar Es Sadik, Agdal-Rabat.

Topographical maps
Division de la carte, 31 Ave Hassan 1, Rabat. ☎ (07) 705 311 fax (02) 705 885.

Meteorological information
Centre de Marrakech, ☎ (04) 430 409 fax (04) 430 566.

Centre de Ouarzazate, ☎ (04) 882 320.

Centre de Casablanca, ☎ (02) 913 329 fax (02) 913 682.

Centre d'Azilal, ☎ (03) 458 236.

Mountain bike hire
Le Sportif, Residence Al Manzah, Oukaimeden. ☎ (04) 447 047.

Lune Car, 111 Rue de Yougoslavie, Marrakesh. ☎ (04) 447 743 fax (04) 437 354.

Four-wheel drive hire
Nomads Land 4x4, 34 Blvd Zerktouni, Casablanca. ☎ (02) 202 682 fax (02) 202 582.

Afoud Transport, 43 Rue de Mauritanie, Marrakesh. ☎ (04) 449 767 fax (04) 434 387.

Inter Rent Europ Car, 63 Blvd Zerktouni, Marrakesh. ☎ (04) 431 228.

Desert Adventure, 5 Pl. du 3 Mars, Ouarzazate. ☎ (04) 884 943.

Specialised agencies
Adrar Adventures, 111 Quartier Essaada, Marrakesh. ☎: (04) 439 388 fax (04) 435 682.

Dynamic Tours, 34 Blvd Zerktouni, Casablanca. ☎ (02) 202 682 fax (02) 264 851.

Ribat Tours, 3 Ave Moulay Youssef, Rabat. ☎ (07) 700 395 fax (07) 707 535.

Tigouba Adventures, Bab Targhount Imm.1. Taroudannt. ☎ (08) 853 122.
For UK agencies running trekking holidays in Morocco, see the list of tour operators, above.

Skiing

Morocco's main ski resort is **Oukaimeden**, 70km and about a 2h drive from Marrakesh, at an altitude of 2650m. The season is roughly (and somewhat unreliably) December to May. There are three hotels in Oukaimeden, the *Hôtel Imlil*, *Chez Juju*, and *Le Chouka*, and also a refuge belonging to the Club Alpin Français. The one big ski-lift, with a gradient of 400m on a run of 1100m, services five slopes with a marked run and costs 2.50dh per person. A smaller lift, with a gradient of 150m over a run of 296m, costs 0.40dh per person; there is also a small ski-lift for beginners on a gradient of 50m. The Moroccan Centre of Skiing and Alpinism runs courses for beginners and advanced skiers.

In the Middle Atlas, near Ifrane, the **Mischliffen**, a huge crater situated at an altitude of 2000m within the cedar forest, is the second skiing resort in Morocco, with snow for between 40 and 60 days a year. There are two ski-lifts: one has a gradient of 193m on a run of 463m, going from the bottom of the crater and serving the 'red' run at its highest point; the other has a gradient of 54m on a run of 232m and is most suitable for beginners. There are 'black', 'red', 'blue' and 'yellow' runs, and cross-country skiing around the rim of the crater and further afield is also possible. Accommodation in the Mischliffen itself is poor, comprising a few shelters and mountain lodgings, but in nearby Ifrane and Azrou it is much better. There are two other ski stations in the Middle Atlas, Jbel Habri (15km from Azrou) and Jbel Hebri (20km from Azrou), connected by a road. They are extremely basic but very suitable for beginners, with one small ski-lift serving the main track.

At **Jbel Toubkal** in the High Atlas there is also skiing, mainly cross-country, from December to May. Many varied tracks begin close to the Neltner Refuge (3207m, recently renamed Toubkal Refuge) and there is one (Tizi n Ouagane) which is suitable for beginners, having a gradient of 540m. The rest tend to be steeper (attaining gradients of 1300m) and very long. This is wonderfully challenging, remote country for advanced skiers. Further details are available from the Royal Moroccan Ski and Mountaineering Federation, at the address given above.

Golf

Golf was first played in Tangier in 1917. It is now one of Morocco's most popular sports (and is the favourite sport of King Hassan II) and there are fourteen splendid golf courses around the country. All the golf clubs mentioned below are open to the public, even if access to them is sometimes limited to players possessing a handicap card. The green fee varies between 100 and 500dh. Most courses offer club-hiring facilities as well as caddies or electric carts. Some are closed one day a week.

For more **information** contact The Royal Moroccan Golf Federation, The Royal Dar Es Salam Golf Club, Rabat. ☎ (07) 755 960 fax (07) 751 026.
Agadir Royal Golf Club, km 12, Route Ait Melloul, Agadir. ☎ (08) 241 278 fax (08) 844 380. 9 holes, 3600m, par 36.
The Dunes Golf Club, The Dunes Club Med Golf Course, Agadir. ☎ (08) 834 690

fax (08) 834 649. Yellow course, 9 holes, 3050m, par 36; blue course, 9 holes, 3174m, par 36; red course, 9 holes, 3204m, par 36.

The Marrakesh Royal Golf Club, BP 634, Ancienne Route de Ouarzazate, Marrakesh. ☎ (04) 444 341 fax (04) 430 084. Built in the 1920s by the Pasha of Marrakesh. 18 holes, 6200m, par 72.

The Palmeraie Golf Club, Marrakesh, Les Jardins de la Palmeraie, Circuit de la Palmeraie, BP 1488, Marrakesh. ☎ (04) 301 010 fax (04) 302 020. Designed by Robert Trent Jones. 18 holes, 6214m, par 72.

The Ouarzazate Royal Golf Club, BP 83, Ouarzazate. ☎ (04) 882 653 fax (04) 883 344. 9 holes, 3150m, par 36.

El Jadida Royal Golf Club, km 7, Route de Casablanca, El Jadida. ☎ (03) 352 251. Designed by Cabell B. Robinson. 18 holes, 6274m, par 72.

The Mohammedia Royal Golf Club, BP 12, Mohammedia. ☎ (03) 324 656 fax (03) 321 102. 18 holes, 5917m, par 72.

The Anfa Royal Golf Club, Casablanca, Anfa-Casablanca Racecourse. ☎ (02) 365 355 fax (02) 393 374. 9 holes, 2710m, par 35.

The Ben Slimane Royal Golf Club, Ave des F.A.R., BP 83, Ben Slimane. ☎ (03) 328 793. Designed by David Coen. 9 holes, 3100m, par 36.

The Dar Es Salam Royal Golf Club, Rabat: Dar Es Salam, Rabat. ☎ (07) 755 864 fax (07) 757 671. Designed by Robert Trent Jones. The Hassan II Trophy competition tales place here each year. Red course, 18 holes, 6702m, par 73; blue course, 18 holes, 6205m, par 72; green course, 9 holes, 2170m, par 32.

The Meknes Royal Golf Club, Bab Belkari Jnane Lbahraouia, Meknes. ☎ (05) 530 753 fax (05) 550 504. Located in Moulay Ismael's *Ville Imperiale.* 9 holes, 2707m, par 36.

The Fes Royal Golf Club,Route d'Ifrane-Imouzzer-Ain Chegag. ☎ (07) 763 849. Designed by Cabell B. Robinson. 9 holes, 3168m, par 37.

The Tangier Royal Golf Club, BP 41, Tangier. ☎ (09) 944 484 fax (09)945 450. Inaugurated by Sultan Moulay Abdel Aziz in 1917. 18 holes, 5545m, par 70.

The Cabo Negro Royal Golf Club, BP 696, Tetouan. ☎ (09) 978 303 fax (09) 978 305. Conceived by Hawtree & Sons and revised by Cabell B. Robinson. 9 holes, 3087m, par 36.

Fishing

The numerous streams and rivers rising in the High and Middle Atlas and the many lakes to be found on the high plateaux are naturally rich in **trout**. (There is no salmon fishing in Morocco.) The best stretches of water are often those which are least accessible, for example,the headwaters of the river Oum er Rbia in the thickly forested area between Ain Leuh and Khenifra in the Middle Atlas, or Lake Isly on the Imilchil plateau. Local village shopkeepers and hotel patrons are often ardent fishermen themselves, and can advise on routes of access and sometimes offer guides. There are tackle shops in Rabat and Casablanca but the fly fisherman would be well advised to bring his own supplies.

The more accessible rivers and lakes tend to be heavily over-fished. The Moroccans are aware of this problem and have created special, artificially stocked lakes—mostly in the Middle Atlas—which are open only for about three months each year, usually in the spring and summer. The fish are counted and weighed before you leave. The season varies but usually starts in April.

The season for **coarse fishing** is from May to June according to species. Pike, black bass, perch, roach, carp, eels and barbels abound in the natural and artificial lakes of the Middle and High Atlas and, notably, in the reservoirs of El Kansera (near Khemisset) and Bin el Ouidane (south of Beni Mellal). There is also a ring of natural lakes in the Imouzzer–Ifrane area which are particularly rewarding, including Dayets Hachlaf, Ifrah and Aoua. Aguelmane Azigza, near Khenifra, is particularly good for pike and bass.

For both trout and coarse fishing **permits** are required.These are available from the Administration des Eaux et Forets, 11 Rue Revoil, Rabat, or from hotels or the local ONMT.

Several ports are equipped for **deep-sea fishing**, notably Mohammedia near Casablanca and Ad Dakhla in the Western Sahara. Tuna, swordfish, marlin, grouper and barracuda are said to be plentiful. **Underwater fishing** is possible all along the Mediterranean and Atlantic coastlines.

For further information on freshwater fishing, contact the Administration des Eaux et Forets at the address given above, or the ONMT. For more information on deep-sea fishing, contact the National Fisheries Office, BP 20300, Casablanca. ☎ (02) 240 551 fax (02) 242 305

Game hunting
Quail, woodcock, turtle dove, snipe, teal, grouse, pheasant and wild boar flourish in vast reserves, the largest and best known of which is the Arbaoua Game Reserve, some 121,410ha of land between Ksar el Kbir and Souk el Arba. The season runs from October to March for most species, but June and July are the months for turtle dove. Visitors to Morocco may only hunt in official reserves and must pay 500dh for a licence, which is obtainable from the Royal Moroccan Hunting Federation, corner of Ave Mohammed V and Rue Alkhil, Rabat. ☎ and fax (07) 707 835. Further information is obtainable from the Federation and from the ONMT.

Riding
The horses of Morocco are superb and the country wonderfully varied, whether you want to gallop along the beach or ride through forests or over mountains. Many hotels provide horses and run trekking expeditions, notably *La Roseraie* at Ouirgane in the High Atlas. For countrywide information about stables, polo, racing, etc., contact the Royal Moroccan Federation of Riding, Dar es Salaam, BP 742, Rabat. ☎ (07) 754 424 fax (07) 754 738.

Surfing and windsurfing
Possibilities for these sports are endless on both the Mediterranean and Atlantic coasts. Essaouira is a particularly good resort. For general information contact the Royal Moroccan Surfing Federation, ☎ (02) 259 530 fax (02) 236 385.

Sailing, yachting and water skiing
For information contact the following:
Royal Moroccan Sailboat Federation, B.P. 30032, Rabat. ☎ (07) 670 956.
Royal Moroccan Water Skiing and Jetski Federation, Jetée Delure, Casablanca. ☎ (02) 274 938 fax (02) 474 979.
Royal Moroccan Yacht Club, Rue Tarik-el-Massa, El Oudaia, Rabat, ☎ (07) 720 264; Mohammedia, ☎ (03) 322 331.

White-water sports

There are many good descents to be had down the rivers of the High and Middle Atlas. You can descend the river Oum er Rbia for 60km by raft at any time of year. For information contact the Royal Moroccan Federation of Canoeing, National Sports Centre, Ave Ibnou Sina, BP 332 Rabat. ☎ and fax (07) 770 281.

Swimming and tennis

Morocco has 3800km of coastline, much of it unspoilt sandy beaches which are perfect for sea-bathing, though dangerous outside the bays on the Atlantic side. Most large hotels have swimming pools and many will permit non-residents to swim if they are also eating in the hotel restaurant, or on payment of an entrance fee (usually 10dh). Otherwise, all major towns have municipal swimming pools which are clean and well kept.

Most large hotels also have tennis courts which are sometimes available for use by non-residents for a fee of 10dh, including the hire of tennis balls, though not usually racquets.

Aerial sports

Aviation, parachuting, gliding, deltaplane, parachute gliding and hot air ballooning are all possible. For information contact the Royal Moroccan Federation for Light Aviation and Aerial Sports, ☎ (07) 708 347 fax (07) 706 958.

The Historical and Cultural Background

The history of Morocco

The Berbers

Since the beginning of history there have been Berbers in North Africa and they were already well established when the Phoenicians made their first incursions in 1200 BC. Their **origins** are uncertain but thought to be Euro-Asiatic, as their high cheekbones and light skin colour would seem to indicate. The generic name 'Berber' was imposed on them by the Arabs and meant (in a derogatory sense) those who were not Arab, probably following the Greek word *barbaros*, which was used to mean those who were not Greek. In reality they have never been one homogeneous racial group but three—Sanhaja, Masmouda, and Zenata—and their loyalties have always been to their tribal origins and not to one amorphous mass known as Berber.

The **Sanhaja**, from which sprang the Almoravide dynasty (the founders of Marrakesh), were nomads who conquered the desert and much of the region to the south of it for Islam in the 11C. The **Masmouda** were quiet farming people who lived in the north and west and in the High and Anti Atlas mountains, and it was they who gave rise (from out of Tin Mal, south of Marrakesh) to the Almohade dynasty which displaced the Almoravides. The **Zenata** were tough, horse-riding nomads of the cold, high plateaux of the interior. The Beni Marin, a sub-group of the Zenata, swept in from the empty region between the Tafilalet and Algeria and became the great Merinide dynasty.

Linked to the Arabs only by Islam, the Berbers have always held themselves proudly separate in all matters other than religion, especially in the rural and mountain areas where there are still families who would not dream of inter-marriage with Arabs. There is no standard form of Berber **language** since each tribal group has always used its own version, and there is no recognised Berber script or literature. Their strongest form of self-expression is **music** and dancing—the former is rhythmic and with little harmony, compelling, loud and often quite intoxicating.

The proudest claim of many Berbers is that they have never been conquered, and this is no idle boast. The Phoenicians and Carthaginians did not try. The Romans finally left, not only because they had pressing matters elsewhere but also because Berber **uprisings** in the Rif and Middle Atlas were proving too troublesome and to expensive to put down. Berbers lived alongside the Arabs, after being initially quelled, and Islam was not so much imposed as welcomed, insofar as it represented a clearly defined way of life to which they could imme-diately relate (albeit with some admixture of their own brand of animism) in place of Christianity, which they had toyed with and discarded.

The ruthless, driving expansionism of the first Arab arrivals in the late 7C and early 8C appealed to the spirited Berbers who gladly joined in the early invasions of **Spain** (though they were somewhat chastened when the Arabs allotted to them the poorer regions such as Extremadura). Subsequent expansion into Spain was Berber-led (by the Almoravides and Almohades) and its conquest, frequently and mistakenly referred to as Arab, is more correctly termed either Moorish or Muslim.

From the mid-11C until the arrival of the Saadians in 1554, Morocco was ruled by Berber dynasties, and even during the Arab years Berbers retained their strongholds in the mountains, particularly in the High Atlas and the Rif, where they were wisely left alone. These lands were officially termed **Bled es Siba** ('land which is not governed'). Nor did the French or Spanish 'protectors' succeed totally in quelling their ardour, and the greatest Berber leader of all, Abd el Krim (1882–1963), was finally put down by the combined Spanish and French forces only because he over-reached himself by venturing out of his mountain fortress to try to take the traditional capital of Fes.

The Phoenicians and Carthaginians

The first invaders are believed to have been the **Phoenicians**, coming in the 12C BC from the land known then as Canaan, in the Eastern Mediterranean. Gradually they established **trading posts** along the north coast of Africa and traces of their occupation have been found at Liks (Lixus), which was probably the earliest settlement, Tingis (Tangier), Russadir (Melilla), Chellah (part of Rabat), and Tamuda (near Tetouan). These traces are usually in the form of fish-salting factories and are often heavily overlaid by Roman remains.

The Phoenicians were essentially a maritime people, uninterested in conquering or colonising, and paying scant attention to the primitive Berber tribes and poor agricultural land of the interior; therefore, their colonies were little more than enclaves along the coast, separated by great open spaces of wasteland which they did not need. Their main centre of influence was **Carthage** in Tunisia and later, when Carthage became an independent state, the more civilised Carthaginians arrived and turned the north coast settlements into prosperous towns; they are known to have developed fish-salting and preserving into a major industry and their anchovy paste, called *garum*, was widely exported. They also grew wheat and probably introduced the grape.

The Carthaginians exercised a considerable cultural influence on the Berbers—even outside their small enclaves and certainly in the prosperous region around Volubilis—and this continued long after the Sack of Carthage in 146 BC; indeed it probably increased at that moment as hundreds of Cathaginians fled westwards and took refuge from the Romans in the friendly enclaves along the coast.

The Romans

By this time there were two Berber kingdoms, **Mauritania** (to the west) and **Numidia** (roughly where Algeria is now), with the Moulouya river forming a boundary between the two.

After they had taken Carthage the Romans moved westwards into Mauritania and Numidia, which became part of the Roman Empire. In 25 BC the Emperor Augustus granted the kingdom of Mauritania to the young Berber prince, **Juba**, son of Juba I of Numidia who had committed suicide 21 years earlier after defeat by the Romans at the Battle of Thapsus. In the same year the emperor added the whole of Numidia to Juba II's realm. Educated in Rome and married to the daughter of Mark Antony and Cleopatra, known as Cleopatra Silene, Juba's pedigree was impeccable and he ruled wisely, probably from **Volubilis**. This had already become a Berber town of some standing before the Romans arrived, due, in part, to the natural fertility of the region surrounding it and in part to the teaching of the Carthaginians, which enabled the Berbers to get the best out of the land.

Juba reigned for 48 years and was succeeded by his son, **Ptolemy**, whose life ended abruptly when the Emperor Caligula, half-mad and obsessively jealous of Ptolemy's success with the populace, had him quietly executed. This infamous act marked the end of the Mauritanian kingdom. Caligula himself was murdered the following year and his successor, Claudius, transformed the kingdom into two provinces of Rome, for easier administration and greater control: **Mauritania Caesariensis** stretched from eastern Morocco across Algeria; **Mauritania Tingitana** (named after Tingis) extended as far west as the Atlantic coast. This gave rise to furious and bloody **Berber uprisings**, led by Aedemon, the late King Ptolemy's minister, which took 20,000 Romans three years to put down.

Thereafter peace and prosperity reigned for a time. Tingis was the capital but Volubilis was the seat of the provincial governor. Roman rule stretched as far west as Sala Colonia (Chellah) and not much further south than Volubilis, where the Middle Atlas formed a natural barrier. The Berbers of the high mountains and the south were little affected and led their lives as before, only occasionally riding northwards to claim new pastures. It was about this time that the desert Berbers discovered the use of the camel, which made them far more mobile and ready for aggression. The Romans built aqueducts and reservoirs and brought water into regions which had hitherto been drought-ridden. But they had little desire to move into the wild south. In one of his letters, **Pliny the Younger** (AD 62–c 112) describes the region south of Sala Colonia as being 'deserted and the home of elephants'.

After some 300 years of civic and engineering improvements and fairly half-hearted city building, though very little of a cultural nature (Volubilis was the main contribution), the Romans began to lose interest in Mauritania Tingitana, which, after all, produced little more than elephants and an almost inex-haustible supply of citrus wood, which was used to make decorative tables for wealthy patrician families. Uprisings of Berbers (who had been ignored rather than subdued) continued and increased, ranging from minor irritations to deeply damaging and costly battles, and the Romans compromised by moving the seat of their administration northwards to Tingis (Tangier) c AD 250. Shortly afterwards they abandoned Sala Colonia and Volubilis and maintained only a small presence in an area bounded by Tingis, Lixus and Tamuda, which looked to Roman Spain for its administration and was probably deemed necessary only for the purpose of guarding the Strait of Gibraltar.

The next 400 years formed Morocco's **Dark Ages**: very little is known about this period. The Vandals and Goths who were sweeping through Spain may have touched the northern tip of Morocco on their way eastwards to Carthage but there are no traces of their having stayed. The Berbers in the mountains and the desert continued life much as before. The Romanised, part-Christian, Berber-Mauritanians of the cities of Volubilis, Sala Colonia, Tingis and elsewhere held on to their mixed cultural heritage and maintained a degree of Roman civilisation, as evidenced by one or two Latin inscriptions, found in several places and dating from as late as the mid-7C. But the weak and divided nature of the country was to prove no match at all for the next wave of invaders.

Islam

The Idrissides

By the 7C AD the Arabs were in full expansion. They were inspired primarily by their fierce desire to spread their own religion of Islam throughout the world. But they were doubtless particularly attracted to North Africa by the endless stretches of desert sand which were to them like home. The first Arab invasions of the North African coastal plain took place in 670 under **Oqba ibn Nafi**, a commander of the Ummayed dynasty in Damascus. He is best known for having founded the city of Kairwan (south of Tunis) and for having built the first mosque in North Africa. He swept with his army into what is now Morocco in the year 683, and history records that he was so triumphant at finally reaching the Atlantic overland that he spurred his horse on into the water, shouting that only the ocean prevented him from carrying his conquest even further, 'preaching the unity of Thy holy name and putting to the sword the rebellious nations who worship any other gods but Thee'. He called this territory *el Maghreb* ('the West'), and that part which is now Morocco he called *el Maghreb el Aqsa* ('farthest West').

The main part of Morocco had still to be conquered. There followed a period of great violence, and Oqba ibn Nafi himself was quickly dispatched by the warlike Berbers. But the absolute and dynamic religion of the Arabs eventually appealed to the Berbers, the majority of whom had been little moved by the Romans' Christianity. When a second Ummayed leader, **Musa ibn Nasir**, arrived in 703, they were not unwilling to participate in the Islamic expansion into southern Spain and into the more southerly areas of Morocco. However, the progress of Islam remained patchy and small enclaves of Christians still existed in the interior (though many fled to Spain).

This lack of national unity persisted until the arrival of **Idriss ibn Abdallah**, a descendant of the Prophet Muhammad, in 788. There are very few original Arab sources about this early period but that which is most frequently cited by historians is the *Raoud el Kartas*, a chronicle by the 13C writer from Fes, Ibn Abi Zar el Fasi. From this we learn that Idriss ibn Abdallah had fled the Abbasides, who had earlier displaced the Ummayed dynasty in Damascus and against whom his own father had led an unsuccessful uprising. Idriss was accompanied into Egypt by his faithful companion **Rachid** (about whom almost nothing is known) and the two arrived, by way of Kairwan, first in Tangier and then in the former Roman city of Volubilis, where they were received by Berbers already fully converted to Islam by the earlier Arab arrivals. The Berber chief Abd el Majid proclaimed Idriss king and pledged the support of his own and neighbouring tribes. It seems that he welcomed the arrival of an assured leader who would guide the country out of the spiritual uncertainties which had increased since the death of Oqba ibn Nafi. Moulay Idriss's power increased daily, and more and more tribesmen bowed to the inevitable and allied themselves to this new and formidable group of believers. So powerful did Idriss become that the infamous and jealous Abbaside caliph, Haroun er Rachid of Baghdad, sent a representative to poison him in 791. His body was taken to **Moulay Idriss**, a town he had founded alongside Volubilis, and it lies there still in what has since become one of the great shrines of Islam.

Fortunately for posterity, Idriss had married and made pregnant a Berber servant girl called Kenza. Idriss ibn Idriss (soon to be Moulay Idriss II) was born after his father's death and was educated and prepared for his awesome task by Rachid, his father's faithful friend, who acted as regent until Idriss was proclaimed king at the age of 12 in 804. Arab historians relate that he was a remarkable child, able to read at four years old and to recite the entire Koran at eight. He was wise and well-loved throughout his reign of 21 years and his faith in Allah as the one and only true God and in the teachings of the Prophet Muhammad through the Koran was exemplary.

Moulay Idriss II was an ambitious and energetic leader and he needed a capital city; Volubilis (now called Oualili by the Arabs) was too small, and anyway it was essentially Roman in character. So he founded (or may have built on what his father had already founded) the city of **Fes**. Historians disagree as to who actually laid the first stone of this historic city but today it is generally acknowledged that Fes began to prosper only from the time of Idriss II. It was ideally sited in the centre of a fertile, well-watered region and at the crossroads of the natural east–west and north–south routes through the mountains. In 818, as if to confirm the significance of Fes, 8000 Arab families arrived there after being expelled by the Christians from the Emirate of Cordoba in Spain. Seven years later 2000 families came from Kairwan, the city which Oqba ibn Nafi had founded and which was by now the most advanced centre of Arab culture in the eastern Maghreb. These 'refugees' were welcomed and installed, respectively, on the right and left banks of the river that divides the town. It was largely as a result of the coming of these people, with their refinements and skills, that Fes became a great spiritual and intellectual centre whose influence very soon reached to the far north of the country, and later beyond. Moulay Idriss II, a charismatic and unequivocal leader, united the warring tribes in a general allegiance to Islam, and to himself as a direct descendant of the Prophet. Thus he created the first Arab kingdom of Morocco. But the oases in the south, and probably much of the great mountain ranges of Atlas and Rif, remained outside his grasp, still uncharted and breeding future dynasties which would wrest his kingdom away.

When Idriss II died in 828 the kingdom was divided between his eight sons and confusion followed. Berber tribes, sensing a lack of firm direction and unity, grew rebellious once more and tried to displace their royal masters; amongst them were the unruly Meknassas who surged in from the east and founded Taza and **Meknes**. The newly established Fatimid dynasty entered the country from Tunisia and the Ummayeds arrived from Cordoba to rid the country of the Fatimid threat. In the event neither stayed long: the Fatimids succeeded in conquering Egypt in 969, moved their capital from Kairwan to Cairo and lost interest in the far west. The now weak caliphate of Cordoba collapsed and Spain became a collection of small autonomous units known as *taifas*, which made for ineffectual government; it became necessary for the wandering Ummayeds to return to Spain to strengthen the cause of Islam. Into this vacuum came the next dynasty, from the south.

The Almoravides

The Almoravides were camel-riding Berber nomads of the Sanhaja tribal group, to whom cultivation of the soil was unknown and who lived off the meat and milk of the camel. They have always been referred to as 'the **veiled ones**' because they wound a length of cloth around their faces as protection against the sand (as their descendants still do today). For a century or more they had been conquering and converting to Islam the black countries to the south of the Sahara, inspired by their search for the source of large quantities of gold which were flowing into Morocco from somewhere in the region of the Niger river. The emir of one of these tribes had been to Mecca and returned convinced of the need to reform his fellow men and particularly his warlike and greedy kinsmen. Other penitents joined him and this large band of pious and fanatical Berbers roamed the south, forcing into repentance and submission the Souss valley (an extensive sugar-growing area on the west coast) and the oases, particularly Sijilmassa, the rich market on the crossroads of the camel caravans, which received most of the gold.

The golden trade

The Arabs had been aware of the existence of gold in the general region of the Niger since they first arrived in North Africa. Certainly, at the time of the foundation of Fes the exchange of **gold for salt** was well under way. Arab historians and travellers throughout the ages have agreed that the 'silent trade' was enacted as follows. The people of the Niger region, it seems, suffered from a permanently unsatisfied craving for salt, and just south of Sijilmassa there were salt mines. Arab merchants set off across the desert, their camels laden with vast loads of salt, and when they reached a certain river on the far side they arranged the salt in heaps on the ground and retired out of sight to wait. A crowd of black men would then arrive in boats, deposit a quantity of gold beside each salt heap and retire, leaving both salt and gold. If the merchants were satisfied with the amount of gold, they would take it and journey back across the Sahara to Sijilmassa; if not, they would go away again and wait for the men to add a little more. Both sides were usually well pleased but never met. Lurid tales are told by travellers about the silent black men: that they lived in holes in the ground, were completely naked, and so on. But no one, neither Berber nor Arab, discovered the source of the gold despite expensive and perilous expeditions over the centuries. For a colourful account of this period read *The Golden Trade of the Moors* by E.W. Bovill.

The campaigns fought by the Almoravides were violent and successful and they soon controlled the whole of the south, under **Youssef ibn Tachfine**, one of Morocco's greatest leaders and the founder of Marrakesh. As nomads, the Almoravides had never been used to settling in one place, much less building a city, but as their power increased so did the need for a central store of weapons and food and, it goes without saying in view of their new-found religious fervour, a mosque. So, after their exhausting crossing of the High Atlas, what more natural than that they should want to stop a while on the vast empty plain immediately to the north, where the mountains offered both protection from sandstorms and an ample supply of spring water. Thus in 1062 the building of **Marrakesh** began and the mosque was erected on the spot where the Koutoubia stands today.

Having established their base the Almoravides went further north to conquer Fes and force submission on the remains of the Idrisside dynasty. This they did without much difficulty, and hugely enriched the city thereafter. From Fes they flowed over the rest of the country and turned everybody, at least superficially, towards their particular version of strict orthodox Islam; this done they began to venture further afield, and by 1080 Youssef ibn Tachfine's Almoravide **empire** stretched as far east as Algiers. His reputation as a formidable fighter had reached the much beleaguered Muslim leaders in Spain who invited him, now a very old man, to lend a hand against the advancing Christians who had just taken Toledo. In 1086 he took his armies across the Strait, regained lost ground and took the important city of Valencia; much of Spain became part of the Almoravide empire. A period of peace and prosperity followed, enriched by the refined culture of the Andalusian courts to which had been added a healthy dose of Berber virility and discipline.

Youssef ibn Tachfine, a legend in his own lifetime, died in 1107 at well over 100 years old. He was succeeded by his son **Ali**, whose mother had been a Christian slave from Andalusia. Ali's reign of 37 years was unremarkable, though he is credited with having built the first enclosing ramparts around Marrakesh, and with much of the city's embellishment, some of this during the absences of his father in Spain. But he did not continue the policy of expansion abroad and pacification at home. Born and brought up in the luxurious atmosphere of the Andalusian court and never having known the hard life of the desert, he was too irresolute and too spoilt to command the necessary respect and allegiance from the tough Berber leaders. He chose advisers of the same origins as himself and latterly, as he became increasingly religious, he turned more readily to spiritual guides than he did to the well-tried and trusted counsellors who had surrounded his father. Unrest began to spread throughout the country. Ali died in 1144 and was succeeded by three rulers who were even more ineffectual. By this time general dissatisfaction was making itself felt amongst the tribes, whilst in the cities the strict orthodox religious code of the first Almoravides had become almost unrecognisable.

The Almohades

A new power was emerging. The Almohades were Masmouda Berbers from the High and Anti Atlas mountains who had long looked down on the once nomadic Sanhaja Almoravides. They had endured 85 years of Almoravide rule, but now that the once vigorous leadership had become effete and aimless they saw their chance to leave their mountain strongholds and take over.

The first Almohade leader, **Mohammed ibn Tumart**, claimed not only Arab descent but descent from Ali, the Prophet's son-in-law. He was a man of extraordinary power and his supporters proclaimed him 'the promised one' of Islam and called him *Mahdi* ('Messiah'). He spoke both Arabic and Berber, and was even more determined in his desire to stamp out weakness and corruption than the early Almoravides had been. The foundation of his doctrine was absolute unity with God, from which stemmed the name *Muwahhadin* ('Unitarian'), which was applied to the followers of this doctrine; Almohade is a European version of this word. In 1107 Ibn Tumart went to Mecca, where he spent ten years deepening his knowledge of divine matters, and it was on his return that he began gathering up large numbers of disciples including **Abd el Mumene**, who would eventually succeed him. Son of a simple potter living in eastern Algeria, Abd el Mumene is said to have attracted the attention of the Mahdi by his intelligence, piety, and good looks, and was persuaded to leave his family with promises that he was the 'chosen one' who would guide the Muwahhadin to victory through faith. The two men, with a huge band of supporters, re-entered Morocco from the east, leaving behind them a path of undying love, or vehement hatred, as the case might be: for Ibn Tumart would unhesitatingly attack any deviation from the strict creed of the Koran and himself abhorred music and even the company of women which, he maintained, could only divert the soul from its true religious path towards God.

In 1118 Ibn Tumart began to preach openly and to appeal to dispirited Arabs and Berbers alike, who were more than ready for another strong leader to replace the irresolute Almoravide, Ali. Tribe after tribe of Berbers were impressed by the depth of his understanding of holy matters, his singleness of purpose and his superb skills as an orator. Still, many a bloody battle had to be fought with the Almoravides themselves and in 1130 Ibn Tumart attacked their great citadel of Marrakesh, unsuccessfully in the first instance as its defences were too strong.

At this moment the Mahdi suddenly died and Abd el Mumene (1133–63) took over quietly, lest news of the sudden death of 'the one exempt from sin' should cause panic and despair. It was to take him another 17 years to put down remaining Almoravide resistance: the final blow was a decisive victory in Tlemcen in 1144, followed within the next three years by the total surrender of Fes and Marrakesh.

Morocco was once more pacified and attention turned again to Spain. Abd el Mumene, now called Emir el Mumenin ('Commander of the Faithful'), reigned for 30 years during which time the Moorish (now Almohade) empire reached its furthest limits, deep into Spain and eastwards as far as Kairwan. He was succeeded at his death by his son **Youssef**, who took greatest pleasure in philosophical discussion and for a time removed to Seville so as to be part of the more developed intellectual life there. It is arguable that much of his father's hard-won territories abroad would have begun to fall away had he not died young (killed in northern Spain in a battle against Alfonso IX of Leon in 1184).

Youssef's son **Yacoub**, whose mother was a negro slave woman, was to become as great an empire-builder and as wise a ruler as his grandfather. He was soon honoured with the proud title of El Mansour ('The Conqueror') but he is chiefly remembered as a builder of mosques. As he pushed further and further into Spain it was his custom not to execute his captives but to bring them back as slave labour for his mighty building projects, the greatest of which was to have been the Mosque el Hassan ('the Beautiful') in Rabat. The town of **Rabat** was founded at this time as a convenient *ribat* (camp), for use by Yacoub and his army as a launching point against southern Spain. Later it was called Ribat el Fath ('Camp of Victory') and the great mosque-building project began. Yacoub died before the Mosque el Hassan was finished and all that remains of his unfulfilled dream are the stumps of pillars which would have supported the roof, and an incomplete minaret known today as the Hassan Tower. He also completed the Koutoubia Mosque in Marrakesh and the Giralda in Seville (both begun by his father).

Yacoub el Mansour was above all a great statesman, deeply concerned with adherence to Islam but not a fanatic, a brave warrior but with an understanding of the arts and sciences, a just and tolerant man, probably one of the most balanced rulers Morocco has ever had. The whole country prospered at this time, spiritually, intellectually, economically and architecturally. Marrakesh (still the capital) and Fes flowered as never before or since and the end of the 12C is generally regarded as the apogee in Morocco's history. Yacoub died in 1199 and was succeeded by his son, **Mohammed el Nasir**, who, like so many sons of great men, turned out to be a weakling (though, in fairness, he was only 17 on his accession). Enemies of Morocco were quick to exploit this, especially in Spain where kings and princes lost no time in regaining much of their land, and the empire began to break up. In desperation Mohammed collected himself and announced he was going to make a supreme effort to 'overwhelm all Christendom'. It is interesting to note that **King John of England**, who was engaged in trying to regain Normandy from the French at the time, was much alarmed by this threat and quickly sent envoys to Morocco to plead for co-operation between the two countries against the French. History might have been very different had he not been refused, but this is nevertheless a fascinating moment of contact between two dissolute monarchs with pressing problems abroad and the threat of civil war at home. In the event, the Almohade army reached no further north than Las Navas de Tolosa, a town on the borders of Castile and Andalusia, where they suffered a gruelling and decisive defeat at the hands of the Christians in 1212, which proved to be the turning point in the Muslim occupation of Spain. In shame Mohammed el Nasir crept back to Marrakesh where he died the following year, having already abdicated in favour of his 16-year-old son, **Youssef el Mostansir**. This pleasure-loving youth had little chance of regaining control of the resentful and increasingly ungovernable tribes in Morocco. He reigned for 10 years and was followed by a string of equally unsuitable monarchs.

After such a major reversal in Spain and a succession of weak rulers at home, chaos inevitably broke out once more. Throughout the early years of Morocco's history, the multifarious and high-spirited tribes had been held in check by one or both of two things: religious fervour and merciless control by the sword. When both these elements were missing, high spirits would naturally erupt and disorder turn quickly to anarchy, until the arrival of the next strong ruler. None was forthcoming at this time from the Almohade camp and a new and threatening force was gathering in the east.

The Merinides

The Beni Merin, or Merinides, were a tribe of nomadic Zenata Berbers who came from the empty area between Taza and Algeria and had been edging their way westwards for some time as they sought pasture for their flocks. Unlike all their predecessors their driving force was not fanatical desire for religious reform but greed for land and, latterly, as success whetted their appetite, for conquest and power. They had no particular creed to preach and were content to comply with the orthodox Islamic faith which had returned to the country after the militant expansionism of the early Almoravides and Almohades. Their leader, **Abd el Hakk**, was a wise and pious man whose father had fought in the war against Spain. He was quick to sense the absolute disarray of the Almohades, and in 1213, one year after their demoralising defeat at Las Navas de Tolosa, he slipped quietly into Fes and was enthroned there with very little ado, and with hardly any effect on the rest of the country, which remained in a state of dissent and inter-tribal violence for some years to come. He died soon after his enthronement and his successor, **Abou Yahya**, a man of little sensitivity, aroused such fury in that proud city that he did not finally take it until 1248, after nine months of siege.

Abou Yahya was succeeded by his brother **Youssef**, who occupied the Almohade capital of Marrakesh without too much difficulty and put an end to the last Almohade ruler, Abu Dabbus, in 1269. By this time virtually all of Morocco had been won over and the tribes were ready, as before, to fall in with a new and forceful leadership which had gained their favour by winning back some territories in Spain. Youssef was a wise and forward-looking monarch who set out to calm the bitter resentment in Fes by firmly making it his capital and then, in 1276, founding a new city, **Fes el Jdid**, alongside the old one, which had already filled its ramparts and could expand no further. Fes el Jdid was essentially a royal city consisting almost exclusively of palaces and military buildings set in vast open spaces. It also became an administrative centre and the Merinides go down in history as having been the first Moroccans to introduce a simple form of **civil service**. Moreover they saw to it that the posts of caids and regional authorities were filled by leading local figures who had proved their worth rather than by members of the royal family, and many influential positions were allocated to Moors returned from Andalusia.

It is often said that the Merinides lacked the panache and passion of either of the preceding Berber dynasties, and that their conquests abroad were not remarkable. But their policy at home was enlightened. One example of their imaginative domestic measures was the introduction of the **mellah** or Jewish quarter in all the major towns, Marrakesh and Fes in particular, where Jews could live secure and unmolested. Hitherto Jews had been scattered throughout the old cities in isolated groups, officially tolerated by Muslims but not welcomed, often abused and frequently made scapegoats. Nevertheless, it is recorded that many Jews converted to Islam at this time rather than be forced to leave their homes and move to the *mellah* and today some of Morocco's most distinguished families have Jewish origins.

Youssef's successor, **Yacoub**, was a philanthropic man, one of the first Berber sultans to seek to improve the lot of the disadvantaged—the blind, the sick, and, above all, the impoverished students who often walked vast distances to their university or other place of learning. The **medersa**—an elaborately ornamented students' lodging hall with one or two lecture rooms—probably originated in Baghdad in the 11C and later found its way into Egypt (see *Moroccan architecture*). The Merinides were certainly the first to introduce the concept to Morocco, and Fes in particular is liberally scattered with fine examples within easy walking distance of the Karaouyine mosque. No expense was spared. **Sultan Abou Inan** (1351–58) who built the Bou Inania Medersa in Fes, the most famous *medersa* of all, is reported to have said upon being told how much it cost, 'what is beautiful is not expensive however great the price', summing up the Merinide belief that gold was of no value unless converted into beauty. Every town was enriched. Certainly the later Merinide sultans much preferred the ornamentation of their environment to the waging of endless and costly holy wars against the Christians in Spain.

Within their extravagant setting Merinide sultans surrounded themselves with scholars who could talk not only about the Koran but about science and law, poetry and geography. The well-known traveller **Ibn Batuta** (1304–78) was an honoured member of the court of Abou Inan, who gave him a secretary to write down stories of his travels as far afield as the Black Sea and Timbuktu. The 14C historian **Ibn Khaldoun**, a Spanish Muslim brought up in Seville, spent many years as an adviser and close associate of Merinide sultans.

The **cultural prestige** of the court in Fes was further enhanced by the arrival, in 1268, of some 13 mule-loads of ancient Arab manuscripts, Korans, and other documents, which Spanish Muslims had lost to the Christians over the years and which were now being returned as part of a former peace treaty with the King of Castile. Moreover, the Merinides were the first to impose a set of secular laws on a relatively unpolished populace who had hitherto deferred solely to the laws dictated by the Koran. To these laws were added rules of **courtesy** and hospitality which are still an integral part of the Moroccan character and which strike a charming—if slightly anachronistic—note upon the Western ear: upon meeting a friend or acquaintance, and after the traditional greeting of *Salaam aleikum* ('Peace be with you'), a ritual of questions and answers as to the health of each member of the family and the state of the harvest or business of each will be enacted before any objective conversation can begin; and the visitor should be aware that even today admiration expressed for one of your host's possessions puts him under an obligation to present it to you as his guest.

The great and beneficial ruler Abou Inan was murdered in 1358, seven years after he had come to the throne, by which time he was reputed to have fathered well over 100 sons. He was succeeded by a series of less worthy rulers and pretenders, including some from Moorish Spain, who fought amongst themselves for power. Almost exactly 100 years after its arrival from the east, the Merinide dynasty began to lose its grip, while its leaders were obsessed by personal advancement and by the pleasures of the court and the harem within it. By now only the kingdom of **Granada** remained as a Moorish enclave within Christian Spain and even that was to go in 1492. At the height of their power the Merinides had raised the spiritual and cultural levels of Moroccan society to new and dazzling heights; their eye for architectural beauty was astounding (it is a sad fact that virtually all of their graceful palaces were destroyed by succeeding jealous rulers, only their *medersas* remaining as a legacy). Their military achievements, however, were negligible and towards the end of their time the empire was actually in a state of reversal.

By the turn of the 14C the dynasty was feeble and its sultans gorged with too much luxurious living. The empire had all but slipped away and Spain and Portugal, encouraged by their recent successes, were now beginning to turn envious eyes on Morocco itself. Moreover, hordes of Christian merchants were spreading throughout Morocco, bringing with them outrageously liberated views which must have horrified strictly orthodox Muslims.

The Wattasides

Upon hearing of the death of one of the last Merinide sultans, **Abd Allah**, in 1398, another ruler, **El Wattas**, who was of the same tribe but not of the same family, left his home town of Asilah on the north coast and came to Fes to avenge his kinsman—unwisely as it turned out, for the Portuguese, who quickly sensed a weakness in their hitherto indomitable enemies, invaded Asilah and carried off 5000 of its inhabitants as slaves, including the son of El Wattas and other members of his family. Understandably enraged, El Wattas was forced to make a treaty with Portugal ceding not only Asilah but also Tangier and Ceuta. Afterwards he turned once more to Fes, besieged it for a year, ousted the killers of Abd Allah and proclaimed himself king.

The minor dynasty of El Wattas is remembered now for the apparently easy way in which it gave up large portions of Morocco to **Portugal**. Portuguese interest in the west coast of North Africa had started back in the 12C, inspired not only by a compulsive urge for expansion and exploration but also by the quest for the gold-producing areas south of the desert and a desire to divert at least some of the gold trade northwards towards Lisbon. El Wattas' son and successor, **Mohammed**, had developed a sympathy for the Portuguese during his enforced stay in Lisbon and he allowed them to settle in Mogador (Essaouira), Mazagan (El Jadida), Azemmour, Safi and Agadir. So, for a time, almost the entire west coast of Morocco became a separate Portuguese colony, to which the remaining castles, ramparts and huge bastions against the sea bear witness today. Chaos was evident throughout the country, with the Portuguese in the north and west, and rebellious Berber tribes trying to take control in the interior. The Merinides were confined to Fes and Marrakesh—the two traditional strongholds in time of unrest. The country was felt to need a new strong leader whose right to rule would appear incontrovertible, and holy men were asked to pray for such a man to come forward.

The Saadians

The Saadians, who were descended from the Prophet Muhammad, came originally from Arabia in the 12C and settled in the valley of the Draa in the south of Morocco. They had lived a quiet and isolated existence, with apparently no thoughts of expansion until the mid-16C, when Morocco was manifestly crumbling away in the hands of the incompetent Wattasides. Their leader, **Mohammed esh-Sheik** (1540–57), was a much loved and brave man, and it was under his guidance that the Saadians first moved northwards in a bid to restore order and the observance of Islam, to oust the Christian invaders and to take the throne from the Wattasides. With their energy and singleness of purpose they achieved all this without much difficulty. By 1541 they had retaken Agadir from the Portuguese, who were beginning to lose interest in Morocco and elected to withdraw from Mogador, Azemmour and Safi, leaving only Mazagan as a token foothold.

Mohammed marched on Fes and was given access by the last of the Wattasides, who offered little resistance. But the people of Fes were shocked by these seemingly coarse and primitive people straight from the desert, who paid scant respect to their traditional and cultured way of life. They were duly pacified by the Saadians who decided that they could not live in an atmosphere of profound hostility and in the 16C rebuilt the 12C Almohade town of

Taroudannt (just east of Agadir) as their capital. Mohammed was succeeded by two unremarkable sons and then by his grandson, **Abd Allah** (1574–76), a man described later as 'not a sultan but a saint', though it was noted that he did put 10 of his 12 brothers to death as potential rivals. One of those who escaped being murdered—**Abd el Malik**—succeeded to the throne and marched victoriously on Fes in 1576, having enlisted the help of Turkish troops from neighbouring Algeria to do so. Following this the Turks were persuaded—with copious rewards no doubt—to return home promptly, and Fes became once more the rightful capital of Morocco, to the evident relief of all concerned, especially the Fassis themselves.

In 1577, another Saadian, a dispossessed nephew of the sultan, secretly applied to the king of Portugal for help in securing the throne for himself. King Sebastian did not need much persuasion as he already dreamed of regaining Portuguese territories in Morocco. He landed in Asilah with a massive force of soldiers including the cream of Portuguese aristocracy and, incidentally, some 700 English troops under Thomas Stukeley, who had been blown off course *en route* for Ireland and had landed in Lisbon. There followed a memorable battle in 1578 at Ksar el Kbir, which resulted in a decisive and terrible defeat for the Portuguese. It came to be known as the **Battle of the Three Kings** because King Sebastian, the Saadian pretender, and Sultan Abd el Malik all died there. After this mortal blow to the Portuguese at the hands of the Moroccans, the whole of Europe began to take notice of the Islamic country's remarkable recovery: ambassadors were exchanged and visitors poured into Morocco, returning home bearing exotic gifts and tales of unbelievable riches.

Glorious in their victory, the Saadians under their new sultan, **Ahmed** (1578–1603), settled down in Fes to continue the process of extravagant embellishment their predecessors had started. As they modified their customs and interests they were gradually accepted by scholars, religious leaders and ordinary people alike. A period of peace and considerable economic expansion followed. But Ahmed was an ambitious and energetic man and he began to look towards the gold-producing areas of the Niger. In 1590 he mounted an expedition of some 3000 men—many of them drawn from the ever restless Berber tribes—across the Sahara. The journey was a terrible one, across the desert and then through dense tropical regions, and many died on the way, but the survivors had little difficulty in subduing the totally unsuspecting and defenceless black tribes who were deprived of both their gold reserves and their liberty. Indeed it is the descendants of these slaves who form part of the Royal Guard today. Gold became a passion for Ahmed, who took upon himself the title Edh Dhahabi ('The Golden One'). Not only gold but also ebony, rhinoceros horn, ostrich feathers and slaves found their way northwards. The whole area of Western Sahara, Mauritania, Timbuktu and southwards to the Niger became a protectorate and was administered by Saadian pashas from Timbuktu, whence tobacco was first introduced into Morocco. At this time many British and Portuguese explorers were also trying to find the source of the gold by working their way up the Niger from the coast. These expeditions usually failed as the sailors fell prey to disease or to hostile local tribes.

Not everyone benefited from the wealth of the Saadians. There was still great poverty amongst the ordinary people, especially in the south, and the Saadians paid far less attention to the plight of the mass of the population than the early

Merinides had done. Most of the gold was spent on prestigious royal **palaces** such as the Badi in Marrakesh (begun 1580), for which 50 tons of marble was brought from Italy and which was later all but destroyed by the Alouites, and the extravagant mausoleum—the Saadian Tombs—built in Marrakesh by Ahmed edh Dhahabi to contain his own body and those of his descendants.

By this time the Saadians had turned their attention away from Fes, which has only the resplendent pavilions in the court of the Karaouyine Mosque to show for all that incoming wealth. So total was the involvement of Ahmed in his quest for enrichment that he began seriously to neglect domestic affairs and the people grew restless and started to look for alternative rulers. When he died in 1603 his three sons fought for the throne and countless pretenders appeared and joined in the fray. The army lost control and a period of **civil war** followed during which Fes was sacked again and again. Even the call to prayer from the minarets was suspended.

During this period, Fes, Meknes and the surrounding countryside also had to contend with a politically ambitious religious sect known as the **Dila**. They were Berbers who had set up a *zaouia* or religious centre near Khenifra in the Middle Atlas at the beginning of the 17C and who became ruthless in their efforts to take over and rule that part of the country.

The Republic of the Bou Regreg

In the north even stranger things were happening: a large band of Spanish Muslims, who had at one time been converted to Christianity but had subsequently been expelled from Spain and so did not know where they belonged, settled on either side of the river Bou Regreg in Rabat and Salé. They were known as the **Sallée Rovers**. In 1627 they formed their own republic which they managed to hold on to for some 14 years. Their chief activity was 'trading', a polite term for **piracy** in which they successfully indulged for many years. Their exploits were primarily directed against Spain, but later they grew bold and extended their attentions as far as the English Channel. Despite this intrusion many Englishmen considered using this wild but excessively brave gang of renegades against Spain, although King Charles I would not recognise the independence of the 'Republic of the Bou Regreg'. The 'republic' was eventually invaded and subdued by the dreaded Dila Berbers. Piracy continued however, much to the impoverishment of European traders, until action to put an end to it was finally concerted at the Congress of Vienna (1815).

Before the fall of the now decadent Saadian dynasty, there was just one more enlightened ruler, **Mohammed**, who came to power in 1637. He ruled for 18 years in Fes in a little pocket of comparative calm but could do little about the fierce rivalries raging elsewhere throughout the country. He was murdered in 1655 and his untimely end heralded the return of strife and killing in the city itself. No other capable Saadian leaders presented themselves and the people of Morocco were faced, once more, with the almost total disintegration of their state.

The Alouites

The Alouites were also descended from the Prophet. They had arrived from Arabia some three centuries earlier to settle near Rissani in the Tafilalet region of the south. (It is for this reason that they are sometimes referred to as the Filali.) Unlike preceding dynasties they did not seize power but were formally invited by the people of Fes to come to the capital and take over the throne of Morocco. Thus in 1666 the first Alouite ruler, **Moulay Rachid**, was welcomed into the city. He restored order with a firm hand, revived the life of the mosques and drove out all pretenders, including the Dila Berbers, whose *zaouia* in the Middle Atlas he went on to destroy. He also occupied Marrakesh and brought much of the south of the country under control. His reign, however, was short: he died in 1672. According to Arab historians he was a brave and wise ruler intent on restoring some form of sanity and faith to the country as a whole, but he was also a cruel tyrant. His life ended abruptly when he was caught by the neck in the fork of an orange tree as he drunkenly spurred on his horse in the Aguedal Gardens of Marrakesh.

His brother **Moulay Ismael** (1672–1727) introduced a period of greater tyranny. He has been described both as a great and wise monarch and as one of the cruellest rulers that Morocco has ever known, the latter view emanating mainly from escaped slaves who were able to produce first-hand evidence of his excesses. It is indisputable that he made an indelible impression during his reign of 55 years and succeeded in creating stability out of chaos. He was tireless in his efforts to pacify the whole country, including its most isolated corners, and it was not long before every tribe paid him homage.

He recovered Tangier from the British (it had been part of the dowry of the Portuguese Catherine of Braganza when she married Charles II in 1661); he also wrested back Larache and Mehdia from the Spaniards; he reduced the enclaves of Ceuta and Melilla to their present modest dimensions; and he made it crystal clear to the Turks occupying Algeria that they should not even consider moving any further westwards.

Undeniably Moulay Ismael made Morocco great again and ensured that the world knew about it, exchanging ambassadors with many leading powers. To reflect his glory and to have somewhere suitable to receive and impress foreign envoys he built 12 palaces in Meknes, which he enclosed within 25km of ramparts to form the '**Imperial City**', no doubt modelling it to a large extent on the Versailles of Louis XIV, who was already on the French throne when Ismael came to power and by whose friendship and respect he set great store. It is interesting to speculate on why he should have chosen Meknes, a town of only minor importance so far, rather than Fes, the traditional centre of cultural and spiritual matters.

The answer is probably that he mistrusted the Fassis, and particularly the many hundreds of Saadians who still lived in and around the city: in any case there would have been no space for him to build there on such a massive scale. Today the miles of ruined walls, palaces, and stables bear witness to his enormous energy and ambition, and to the scale of his success. It is not so much the size of the buildings as the method of building them which shocks posterity: his labour force consisted of at least 2500 Christian slaves and some 30,000 Moroccan malefactors (including, no doubt, many Saadians and rebellious Berbers), hundreds of whom died horribly in the construction process. He also had a harem of around 2000, which included at least one English woman. (We are indebted to the writings of an English prisoner in Morocco, Thomas Pellow, whose *Adventures* were published in London in 1890, for some colourful revelations about this feature of the court. Pellow had apparently escaped death by embracing the Muslim faith and by attracting the attentions of the favourite queen, who put him in charge of her apartments and the 37 concubines who lived therein.) And yet Arab historians relate that Moulay Ismael prayed hard and lived plainly.

Moulay Ismael died in 1727 at the age of 81 and was succeeded by a series of quarrelling and incapable sons. The real power at this time was in the hands of the **Black Guard**, which the sultan had built up for his own protection. They were descendants of slaves taken by the Saadians during their gold-plundering expeditions in the Timbuktu area, and after the death of their master they felt they owed loyalty to no one. For 30 years they rampaged across the country, raising up and then destroying sultans for their sport.

In 1757 a wise and strong Alouite ruler came to the throne once more. This was **Mohammed ibn Abdallah**, who by some means not fully explained brought the menace of the Black Guard under control; it is probable that by this time an excess of power was causing them to degenerate. Mohammed was a good man and sought first to lift the spirits of the people of Fes, who had been sorely tried by Moulay Ismael's cruel 'governors' to the point where many eminent citizens had left; he even built some new *medersas*, as effective a way as any of showing his goodwill. He also founded the modern town of **Essaouira** (formerly Mogador under the Portuguese), inviting English, French and Jewish merchants to settle there and import tea, cloth and other commodities in exchange for the exotic items such as ivory, ostrich feathers and gold still coming out of the sub-Saharan region.

Mohammed's son, **Yazid**, who succeeded in 1790, was a cruel ruler who undid much of the spiritual and material reparation undertaken by his father, until he was put down by his brothers two years later. Those two years were enough to plunge the country once more into misery, and a line of indifferent successors could do little to stop Morocco falling once more into a state of **war** with France and Spain. In 1844 Algiers was lost to the French, after the Moroccan army was humiliatingly defeated by General Bougeaud and whilst French ships were simultaneously bombarding Tangier. In 1860 the Spaniards entered Tetouan from Ceuta and were prevented from continuing to Tangier only by the British, who were unwilling to tolerate any strong European force installed on that side of the Strait of Gibraltar. Peace was achieved on terms proposed by the Spaniards, which involved payment of a huge indemnity by the Moroccans. At this time the **European powers** strengthened their diplomatic representation in Tangier and together set up and managed the Cap Spartel lighthouse.

This unsatisfactory state of affairs continued until 1873 when another capable monarch appeared. He was **Moulay el Hassan**, who tackled the awesome task of pacifying the tribes with undoubted effectiveness and was the first monarch to enter the wild Souss area (inland from Agadir) where the tribes had not hitherto acknowledged the central authority of the State; to maintain control he built the town of Tiznit as a permanent centre for his garrison. He even went as far south as Goulimine and eastwards to the Tafilalet. But his methods were still those of his ancestors: he would mount a *harka*, an 'expedition of pacification and tax-collecting', keeping the destination as secret as possible and then setting forth equipped with battering rams, boulders and sometimes dynamite to bear down on some unsuspecting tribe. The unfortunate villages on his way would be utterly despoiled by his unruly entourage, and a wide swathe of countryside would be quite literally eaten up, as by a swarm of locusts. Sometimes the village caid would hear of the oncoming threat and manage to muster some gifts of slaves, cattle, camels and sometimes even his own daughters with which to meet and please the sultan. Sometimes this worked well enough to save the village from total devastation and the expedition would turn away, satiated, to descend elsewhere. The immediate result would be despair and humiliation for the village, which sooner or later would turn into bitterness and a burning desire for retribution. Thus in the long term these primitive attempts at pacification were doomed to have the opposite effect. The methods had not changed or progressed in hundreds of years and it is tempting to conjecture how much longer they would have continued had the European powers not stepped in.

The death of a sultan

Eventually the unceasing struggle to unite the country wore out the sultan, who died in 1894 whilst leading another *harka* into the Tadla region northeast of Marrakesh. His death had to be kept secret for, as Walter Harris wrote in *Morocco That Was*, 'any inkling of the Sultan's death would have brought the tribes down to pillage and loot the Imperial camp ... nor could the troops themselves be trusted not to seize the opportunity to murder and loot.' Only his personal slaves and his chamberlain, Bou Ahmed, knew of his demise and had to maintain the charade of waiting on the sultan as usual, until such time as the fleetest of runners could reach Rabat to break the news to the royal successor, his son **Moulay Abd el Aziz** (not yet 13 years old), and have him proclaimed sultan. 'Two days later, the body of the dead Sultan, now in a terrible state of decomposition, arrived at Rabat ... the hurried arrival of the swaying palanquin bearing its terrible burden, five days dead in the great heat of summer; the escort, who had bound scarves over their faces, and even the mules that bore the palanquin, seemed affected by the horrible atmosphere. No corpse is, by tradition, allowed to enter through the gates into a Moorish city, and even in the case of the Sovereign no exception was made. A hole was excavated in the town wall, through which the procession passed direct into the precincts of the palace, where the burial took place. Immediately after, the wall was restored.'

Abd el Aziz might, under normal peaceful circumstances, have achieved some success, but he stood little chance with the rumblings of rebellion ever present, and growing louder. He was not helped by the sporadic but well-meant attempts by European governments to suggest ways of reforming the administration, such as fixed salaries for civil servants and a more structured method of tax collection, because although he supported those methods he was manifestly incapable of applying, far less enforcing them. After a few years he allowed his courtiers to persuade him to give up the struggle and turned instead to a life of **decadence** amongst his young friends, many of them European and offering the latest in sophisticated distractions. 'There were bicycle races with ladies of the harem in fancy dress, miniature rifle ranges, balloons and fireworks; even though there was no road in all Morocco, transport of a billiard table, lurching on camel-back from Larache to the royal palace at Fez, was but one of a thousand bizarre extravaganzas devised by the courtiers in their efforts to divert the Sultan's attention from the terrible state into which his country had fallen.' Meanwhile, European financiers and traders were moving in fast, anxious for the rich pickings which would surely soon come their way.

Attacks on foreigners were frequent and the tribes began to take power into their own hands, as did the Europeans. Britain allowed the French to occupy Tunis in return for their agreement to British occupation of Cyprus; later, Britain raised no objection to French action in Morocco, in exchange for British intervention in Egypt. Now it was the turn of the Spanish who, for historic reasons, insisted on a share of influence in Morocco, and this was duly agreed. Not to be left out the German Kaiser visited Tangier and offered his help to the sultan. The 30-nation **Conference of Algeciras** (1906) was called to put an end to all this uncoordinated interference, which was potentially damaging to European peace as well as threatening to the sovereignty of Morocco. The resulting treaty had the effect of internationalising the whole affair, making it illegal for anyone to take bilateral action whilst at the same time affirming the independence of the sultan. It made Tangier into an **international free port** and granted France and Spain a mandate to restore order (thereby implicitly preparing the way for the Protectorate should it become necessary).

Morocco's own despair was exacerbated when the sultan's brother, **Moulay Hafid**, governor of Marrakesh, declared publicly that Abd el Aziz was unfit to reign, on the grounds that he had become an extravagant wastrel. The two brothers marched towards each other with their respective armies but, in the event, no battle ensued and the young sultan fled to his French friends. Moulay Hafid took over the throne in 1908 but could do little to improve his country's position. The French occupied Casablanca, the Germans took a warship into the harbour of Agadir and similar incidents occurred all round the coastline. In 1912, Sultan Moulay Hafid signed the **Treaty of Fes** which relieved him of his power to govern and declared the greater part of the country a Protectorate under a French Resident-General. Simultaneously, the Spaniards signed a treaty which allocated to them the protection of what was left—a small zone to the north. Tangier remained an international city (even though geographically it fell within the Spanish zone) and was controlled by the signatories to the Treaty of Algeciras through their diplomatic representatives. Even the sultan was represented there by his own delegate, the Mendoub. Four months after the signing of the treaty Moulay Hafid abdicated, understandably appalled by what he had allowed to happen, and another of his brothers was placed on the throne by the French. This was **Moulay Youssef** (1912–27), a suitably virtuous and aquiescent man, who was allowed to live in the traditional style of a Moroccan sultan and was treated as the sole spokesman for the Moroccan people whilst retaining no governing power.

The Protectorate

The first French Resident-General (later Marshal), **Louis Lyautey**, aimed not only to pacify but also to construct. His attitude towards the country he was sent to protect, and later learned to love, was positive. He was scrupulously careful not to undermine Islam nor to destroy any of its monuments. He built the ports of Casablanca and Kenitra and the new towns of Rabat, Fes, Meknes and Marrakesh, whilst leaving the old medinas quite untouched. The French arrived in large numbers to live and work in this land of opportunity. A modern educational system was introduced, the administration was modernised and the legal system reformed; roads and railways were built, and phosphates were discovered in the area south of Casablanca and later exploited to become Morocco's main export. The list of achievements was impressive and the benefits incalculable; Morocco was pulled abruptly into the 20C. Development was essentially along French lines, however, and lessons in schools were always in French; French became the language of learning, and of progress, and of power.

The **Spanish zone** was not developed so rapidly, partly because it comprised the more lawless and remote parts of the country, including the Rif mountains, and partly because the Spaniards were preoccupied with their own domestic problems, which were to culminate in the devastating Civil War. Fewer Spaniards settled in Morocco and there was greater tolerance of Moroccan culture, which was already so closely linked with their own.

For the first few years there was relative peace in the cities, as if the people were stunned by what had happened and thought it best to bow to the inevitable, although this was not so in the dissident areas of the south, where tribes were traditionally very rebellious. By c 1920 there were signs of the more structured resistance to come, particularly in the Rif mountains where the very adept Berber leader, **Abd el Krim**, a caid in the Melilla area and a highly respected scholar, gathered a huge following and won a massive victory against the Spaniards near Al Hoceima. El Krim went on to proclaim an independent **Rif Republic**, with himself as president. He was a formidable adversary—seen as a potential focus for national resistance and therefore a major threat to any hopes of peace—and it took the combined strength of the French and Spanish forces five years to put him down.

The French began to drive a wedge between Arabs and Berbers by playing on their differences. In 1930 they even persuaded the sultan to sign a decree upholding Berber law which it was hoped would perpetuate separation. But this was a serious miscalculation, for it served merely to draw the two races, both fearing they were being manipulated by a common enemy, closer together. A new prayer was heard in the mosques: 'Oh God, separate us not from our Berber brothers.' When, after a few months, the decree was amended there was great celebration; the cause of nationalism had been well served.

In the cities, particularly in the new administrative capital of Rabat and the traditional capital of Fes, young intellectuals began to meet together to formulate plans for ridding Morocco of the foreign yoke, and a serious national **independence movement** was born. It had to contend with the powerful caids in the south, however, whose strength had if anything been increased by the French who saw them as a means of controlling the High and Anti Atlas tribes. These traditional leaders feared that a nationalist government would cut them down to size and so they favoured the *status quo*, doing their best to discredit the independence movement.

In 1927 Sultan Moulay Youssef died and was succeeded by his son **Mohammed V**. At 17 years old Mohammed V had a quiet and friendly disposition and the French assumed he would be as amenable as his father had been. In fact his modest exterior concealed an iron will. But it was not until after World War II that the independence movement really gathered momentum. By this time Moroccans held their heads high again: the troops they had provided for the French army had conducted themselves with honour; President Roosevelt had talked with the sultan; and Morocco was no longer the isolated and ungovernable country she had once been. At this time an official independence party was formed, called **Istiqlal**, whose first act was to send a memorandum to the sultan and the French authorities asking for independence and a democratic constitution. The immediate reaction to the memorandum was the arrest of several Istiqlal leaders on blatantly trumped-up charges, and the replacement of a mild Resident-General with the formidable figure of **General Juin**. The new Resident-General, whilst appearing to accede to some of Istiqlal's demands, actually stiffened French control throughout the land by allowing city councils to be elected but at the same time ruling that half their membership should be French.

The sultan began to exercise the only power he really had—to refuse to sign any more decrees concerning his people. This seriously alarmed the French, who invited him on a State visit to Paris in the hope of flattering him into greater cooperation. The sultan, however, took the opportunity to propose some very radical changes to the Moroccan–French relationship. These were not even considered, but the fact that they had been publicly requested ensured a triumphant return home for Mohammed V, now a national hero.

Istiqlal grew stronger by the week and the notorious Pasha of Marrakesh, **Thami el Glaoui** (1886–1956), accused the sovereign publicly of being sultan of Istiqlal rather than sultan of all Morocco. Already a powerful man, and with the support of all those who lived off the fat of the land at the cost of the majority of the poor, El Glaoui plotted with the French Government to discredit Istiqlal and particularly the sultan who openly supported it, even to the extent of collecting hundreds of signatures in support of the deposition of 'this dangerous man'; it was suggested that he was not only a bad sultan but a bad Muslim because he allowed his daughters to go out in the street unveiled.

In August 1953 the palace was surrounded by French soldiers and the sultan and his family were deported, first to Corsica and then to Madagascar, and an elderly, frail, and completely harmless relative was put on the throne in his place. The reactions to this were predictable. In his absence Mohammed V rapidly became an idol, and sympathy for him crystallised into intense longing for his return. Moreover, there began a period of overt violence towards French officials, to the point where they no longer felt safe anywhere in Morocco. It is remarkable that the Spanish Government had not been consulted at all about the removal of the sultan, and it was extremely irritated by this omission. A rift began to develop between the two 'protecting' powers.

Security within Morocco deteriorated fast over the next two years and there was a bloody massacre of French officials at **Oued Zem**. This led to the French Government to depose the ineffectual token sultan with a view to replacing him with a Crown Council. It was whilst plans for this were being drawn up that Thami el Glaoui returned to centre stage. Realising the way events were inexorably leading, he publicly denounced the Crown Council as illegal and allied himself to the people's call for the return of the rightful monarch. Within a week Mohammed V was taken to France, much to the relief of all concerned, who had feared a prolonged period of rioting and bloodshed. There, in December 1955, he signed a declaration promising that there would be a **constitutional monarchy** which would move towards a democratic state.

Independence and after

In March 1956 an agreement was signed by the French which granted full independence to Morocco. In April a similar agreement was signed by the Spanish Government and the old frontier post between the two zones was destroyed. In October the same year Tangier lost its international status and became just another independent Moroccan city. The sultan formed a government and French officials were gradually replaced by Moroccans, though many stayed on as advisers. The change-over was quick and smooth, and any dissident elements in the south who continued to attack French outposts were gradually absorbed into the new Moroccan army. Schools turned towards **education in Arabic**— though there was at first a desperate shortage of teachers—a university was established in Rabat, the Karaouyine in Fes was given more up-to-date premises, and newspapers in Arabic appeared almost overnight. Amongst the more dramatic innovations was the building, by volunteers, of the **Route de l'Unité** (begun 1957) to unite Fes with the Mediterranean across the Rif, which had always been a dangerous and uncharted barrier between the two regions. The sultan changed his title to that of king, an act intended to demonstrate his desire to rule along progressive lines; and he appointed a fully representative National Consultative Assembly. The country was divided into regions which were based on economic rather than tribal boundaries and these were represented by elected regional and municipal councils.

King Mohammed V died unexpectedly in 1961, after a minor operation, and was succeeded by the then Crown Prince, the present **King Hassan II**. In 1962 the monarch presented a new constitution to the people which was ratified after a referendum. It declared Morocco to be a social, democratic and constitutional monarchy, and the first elected parliament assembled on 18 November 1963. This was a coalition of pro-monarchy parties: the main opposition parties, Istiqlal and the Union Nationale des Forces Populaires (UNFP) were excluded from any hope of legitimate power under the new constitution, even though they were supported by a significant proportion of the electorate. Social unrest grew, particularly amongst disillusioned young Moroccans in Casablanca unable to find work, and was exacerbated by the growth of socialism in neighbouring Algeria. The troubles came to a head with the notorious **Ben Barka affair**, when the leader of the UNFP, Mehdi Ben Barka—who had previously been implicated along with other UNFP leaders in an attempted coup against the king—was assassinated in France. Student riots followed, particularly in Casablanca, and in 1965 the king declared a **state of emergency**, in which he suspended parliament and ruled directly without any democratic institutions.

This situation was brought to an end in 1970 by a new constitution that gave the king greater control over parliament than he had had in 1962. There followed several unsuccessful attempts on the king's life, the two most notorious of which were masterminded by army generals: in one, in 1971 during a lunch party at the royal palace on Shkirate beach, many guests were killed; in the second, in 1972, the king was returning from a visit to France when his aircraft was attacked by Moroccan Air Force fighters—his quick-thinking pilot announced over the radio that the king was already dead and the fighters withdrew.

There then came the **Green March**, which, whatever its political implications in the eyes of the rest of the world, had the effect of uniting the country once more around its monarch, rather as the struggle for independence had done in the early '50s. On 6 November 1975 the king led 350,000 unarmed Moroccans, preceded by the army, south into the desert in order to reassert Rabat's sovereignty over what was then the Spanish Sahara, a sovereignty which, it was claimed, went back to the conquests by the Saadian dynasty in the 16C. General Franco was dying at the time and the Spanish withdrew, but the **Polisario**, (created in 1973 by Moroccans of Saharan origin and militant students, who also wanted to oust the Spanish from the area, and armed by Algeria and Libya) was revived, once more with Algerian and Libyan support, to oppose Moroccan rule and to fight for self-determination of the native Saharan population, the Saharwis. The vicious and costly **Saharan War** started, in which Polisario guerillas were ranged against sometimes inexperienced Moroccan soldiers, and many lives were lost on both sides. Many Saharwi were displaced and ended up in refugee camps in Tindouf, Algeria (where many still remain).

Much of the world was deeply affronted by this apparently imperialistic move, and in 1984 Morocco left the Organisation of African Unity because it had offered a seat to the Polisario. That same year, however, saw a **Treaty of Union** between Morocco and Libya, which formally withdrew its support for the Polisario, and relations between the two countries significantly improved. The war had changed character by this time and the killing almost stopped when the Moroccans completed a most astonishing 2092km **defensive wall** around the disputed territory as far south as Dakhla. This denied the Polisario access to the sea, which they had previously used for mounting attacks on shipping off the west Saharan coast, and meant that the immediate hinterland could be declared safe again and cautiously opened up. For a time in the late 1970s visitors were unable to travel much farther south than Goulimine; now people are actually being encouraged to visit the new resorts of Laayoune and Dakhla, although there is still a formidable military presence throughout the region.

Internationally, the incident diminished in importance though occasional skirmishes would bring it back into the headlines. Now the UN has decreed that the matter must be settled once and for all. Morocco, anxious to improve its trade with Europe and keen to increase international tourism, agreed to hold a **referendum** which would decide whether the Western Sahara should be Moroccan or independent. Those entitled to vote would be authentic Saharwi people, who numbered 73,000 according to a Spanish census held in 1974. The referendum was scheduled for January 1992 but did not take place and the UN Secretary General noted that it would be necessary to delay it for some time because of administrative difficulties on both sides. In other words, there had been a failure to agree the eligibility criteria. By the beginning of 1997, nothing much had changed except that many of the UN officials had gone home and the situation was certainly less tense. The UN's special envoy, James Baker, former US Secretary of State, continues to mediate between Morocco, Algeria, Mauritania and the Polisario in an effort to reach consensus but the main stumbling block is still eligibility to vote, with claims and counter-claims flying back and forth, and the thorny question of the Saharwis in Tindouf still unresolved. No one knows their exact number and Algeria will not allow either the UNHCR or the Red Cross to conduct a census. In the meantime, 12 African countries have publicly renounced their support for the Polisario, which has in any case been greatly weakened by current troubles in Algeria itself. The solution may lie in the division of Morocco—from Spring 1997—into 16 regions. The plan is to move away from centralisation towards **regional government**, with each area gradually achieving greater autonomy within the overall framework of the constitutional monarchy. One of the regions is the Western Sahara.

Two more factors adversely affected tourism in Morocco in recent years. The first was the **Gulf War**, which turned out to be only a temporary setback, arising out of a situation which forged many strange alliances and swiftly destroyed many others. The second, the crisis in neighbouring **Algeria**, gave rise to fears of similar Islamic violence next door, fears which have not been justified, and one hopes never will be. The border with Algeria was closed in 1994 and remains closed at the time of writing. Although a small fundamentalist Islamic movement does exist in Morocco, it is unlikely to increase because of the religious role of the king. As 'Commander of the Faithful' and 'Defender of the Faith', he takes his religious duties very seriously indeed and no one can challenge his religious legitimacy. He will be succeeded, when the time comes, by his son the Crown Prince, who is fully prepared for his role, has some very definite ideas about modernising the country, and is highly regarded by the people. (It is worth noting here that the Sunni–Shiah schisms so prevalent throughout the Muslim world—see *A note on Islam*—have never caused problems amongst Moroccans, who are Sunnis, largely because the country's geographical location at the very western end of the Maghreb has distanced it from the centres of conflict.)

A great deal has changed since the turbulence of the 1970s. Morocco is now a stable nation, thanks to its astute and much-respected monarch, its press freedom and a genuinely democratic political system—the latter created by the new constitution introduced in September 1996. This now centres around two chambers of government, in which the 300 members of the larger House of Representatives are directly elected by the people for a five-year term. Thus, it is hoped, the demands of opposition parties that the chamber accurately reflect the wishes of the whole electorate will be satisfied. The 255 members of the second, smaller chamber, the House of Advisers, are indirectly elected through municipal councils, professional bodies and trade unions.

This stability has been greatly enhanced by the signing of an association agreement with the **European Union** (February 1996), under which a free trade zone for goods and services will be established between Morocco and the EU by 2010. This agreement is the crowning achievement of Morocco's foreign policy to date and a clear sign that it intends to become integrated within the world economy.

Chronology

1200 BC	Phoenicians set up trading posts along north coast.
500 BC	Carthaginians arrive.
25 BC	Romans establish Kingdom of Mauritania under Juba II.
44 AD	Direct rule from Rome.
250	Romans begin to withdraw.
3C–7C	Dark Ages: Vandals and Goths sweep through country.
683	Arabs arrive, led by Oqba ibn Nafi.
711	First Muslim invasion of Spain.
788	Arrival of Moulay Idriss, founder of Idrisside dynasty.
799	Foundation of Fes.
1062	Almoravides invade under Youssef ibn Tachfine and found Marrakesh.
1147	Fes and Marrakesh surrender to Almohades.
1195	Yacoub el Mansour extends Muslim conquest to Spain and starts to build the Mosque el Hassan in Rabat.
1212	Battle of Las Navas de Tolosa reverses Muslim fortunes in Spain.
1248	Merinides conquer Fes and found Fes el Jdid alongside it.
1399	Wattasides attempt to rule. Portuguese begin settling along west coast.
1492	Muslims finally expelled from Granada.
1540	Saadians arrive and found a new capital, Taroudannt.
1578	Defeat of Portuguese at Ksar el Kbir. Saadians move capital to Fes and extend empire southwards to Timbuktu.
1627	Spanish Muslims set up pirate 'Republic of the Bou Regreg'.
1666	Alouites arrive under Moulay Rachid.
1672	Moulay Ismael begins to build imperial city of Meknes and creates the Black Guard.
1790	Morocco relapses into chaos. European powers attempt to intervene.
1873	Moulay el Hassan pacifies tribes in south and builds Tiznit.
1906	Conference of Algeciras affirms independence of the sultan and makes Tangier an international free port.
1912	Treaty of Fes declares most of country a Protectorate under France. A similar treaty grants northern zone to Spain. Rabat and Tetouan are respective capitals.
1953	Sultan Mohammed V sent into exile.
1956	Full independence granted to Morocco. Sultan returns and forms government. Tangier loses its international status.
1961	King Hassan II accedes to the throne.
1975	Green March: 350,000 people march into Western Sahara to claim it for Morocco
1996	Morocco signs an association agreement with European Union.

Chronological table of Moroccan dynasties

Idrissides
788–791 Idriss I
791–804 Rachid (regent)
804–828 Idriss II
828–836 Mohammed I
836–848 Ali I
848–923 (sons and grandsons of Ali)

Almoravides
1062–1107   Youssef ibn Tachfine
1107–1144   Ali ibn Youssef
1144–1145   Tachfine ibn Ali
1145   Ibrahim ibn Tachfine
1145–1147   Ishaq ibn Ali

Almohades
   –1133   Ibn Tumart
1133–1163   Abd el Mumene
1163–1184   Youssef
1184–1199   Yacoub el Mansour
1199–1213   Mohammed el Nasir
1213–1223   Youssef el Mostansir
1223–1248   sons of Youssef
1248–(Fes lost to Merinides)
1248–1266   El Murtada
1266–1269   Abu Dabbus
1269–(Marrakesh lost to Merinides)

Merinides
1244–1258   Abou Yahya
1258–1286   Youssef
1286–1307   Yacoub
1307–1308   Abou Rabia
1308–1331   Uthman
1331–1351   Abou el Hassan
1351–1358   Abou Inan
1358–1396   (sons and grandsons of Abou Inan)
1396–1398   Abd Allah
1399–1554   Wattasides

Saadians
1554–1557   Mohammed esh-Sheik I
1557–1574   sons of Mohammed
1574–1576   Abd Allah
1576–1578   Abd el Malik I
1578–1603   Ahmed edh Dhahabi

1603–1628	Moulay Zaidan
1628–1631	Abd el Malik II
1631–1637	El Walid
1637–1655	Mohammed esh-Sheik II
1655–1660	Ahmed el Abbas

Alouites

1666–1672	Moulay Rachid
1672–1727	Moulay Ismael
1727–1757	sons of Moulay Ismael
1757–1790	Mohammed ibn Abdallah
1790–1792	Yazid
1792–1822	Sulaiman
1822–1859	Abd er Rahman
1859–1873	Mohammed
1873–1894	Moulay el Hassan
1894–1908	Abd el Aziz
1908–1912	Moulay Hafid
1912–1927	Moulay Youssef
1927–1961	Mohammed V
1961–	Hassan II

A note on Islam

To come anywhere near understanding the Moroccans (all of whom are Muslims, with the exception of a very small minority of Jews), it is necessary to know something of Islam, which to them is much more than a religion: it is the guidance provided by God (Allah) to all mankind. In short, it is a way of life.

The Koran

The word Islam means 'submission to the will of God' as revealed by the Angel Gabriel to Muhammad, the last in a line of prophets (which included Jesus Christ). These revelations, memorised and written down during Muhammad's lifetime, collectively form the **Koran**. The Koran is regarded as a transcript of a tablet preserved in heaven, in which is written all that has happened and all that will happen—the authoritative word of God. Except in the opening verses and a few passages in which the Angel or the Prophet speak in the first person, the speaker throughout is God Himself, communicating directly with humanity without intermediaries. The 'one-ness' of God constitutes one of the main differences between Islam and Christianity (with its Holy Trinity): indeed, the Koran chides Christians for worshipping Jesus as the Son of God, even though God has expressly commended them to worship none but Himself.

The word Kuran (Arabic, *Qur'an*) means 'the Recital'. The book consists of 114 chapters (*surahs*) and 6236 verses (*ayahs*). For the pious Muslim it is a profoundly holy book, which must never rest beneath other books. In times past, children under ten years old were required to learn by heart all of its verses. Today this extraordinary feat of memory is not expected but Koranic schools still exist and the sound of young voices chanting the Koran is common throughout towns and villages.

The art of Islamic **calligraphy** developed out of the need to produce a form of writing beautiful and elaborate enough to represent the Holy Word of the Koran. The first forms of Islamic calligraphy were angular, and came to be known collectively as 'Kufic' scripts, which were soon the chosen medium for transcribing the Koran. By the 11C the various Islamic countries were developing their own decorative forms of calligraphy, and Maghrebi script is that which is most widely used today in Morocco in a religious context. It is elegant and flowing, with rounded loops and strong verticals, and is frequently seen transcribing passages from the Koran on to the walls of mosques and *medersas*. The Koran is not illustrated (and religious buildings contain no figurative art), for it is generally believed that Islam forbids any form of figurative representation. Debate continues, however, as to whether the Prophet himself actually disapproved of images, or whether attitudes hardened after his death, leading to the doctrine that the representation of animate beings was an attempt to usurp the creativity of God.

The Messenger

Muhammad was born into the Quraysh tribe in Mecca (Arabia) c AD 570. His mother, Amina, died when he was a child and he was brought up first by his grandfather and then by his uncle, Abu Talib, a leader of the Quraysh and a merchant. When he was 25, Muhammad married Khadija, a rich widow 15 years his senior who had employed him to look after her camels. She died 24 years later, after bearing him six children.

Muhammad's first visionary experience did not occur until he was around 40 years old, by which time he had become a deeply religious man, profoundly influenced by Jewish and Christian teachings and by monotheism in particular. The revelations to Muhammad by the Angel Gabriel are said to have followed each other at intervals over a period of 22 years and five months. They were memorised by professional 'remembrancers', *huffaz* (singular, *hufiz*) and also written down by the Prophet's secretary, Zaid ibn Thabit. The work was finally compiled into one volume around 644, some 12 years after Muhammad's death, and it is this original version that is still regarded as the authoritative word of God.

Islam's early years

The first absolute date in Islamic history is that of AD 622, the year when Muhammad moved with his followers from Mecca to Medina. By then he had become deeply critical of the existing heathenism of the Meccans and his doctrine of the unity of God and the wickedness of idolatry made him many enemies. The Medinese, on the other hand, welcomed him principally as an arbitrator to settle their internal disputes, and were prepared to accept the religious implications so long as these agreed with their social and political needs. The migration from Mecca to Medina is known as the **Hegira** and Muslims date their new era from this date. Support for the Muslims in Medina grew steadily and they were joined by many other Arab groups, whom Muhammad authorised to attack Meccan caravans. Finally, in 630, Mecca itself was captured and purged of its idols. Above all, the **Ka'ba** (House of God), a cube-like structure in the centre of the mosque in Mecca, was purified and dedicated to God. The Prophet died two years later.

Muhammad was succeeded by his devoted friend, Abu Bakr, who thus became the first Caliph (leader) of the Muslims. He fell ill and died after two years and was succeeded by Umar, who captured for Islam vast areas of the Roman and Persian empires and the whole of Egypt. He was murdered by a Persian slave whereupon a committee of six members of the Quraysh tribe debated whether Uthman, a member of the Umayyad branch of the Quraysh, or Ali, the Prophet's son-in-law (husband of his daughter Fatima), should succeed. They chose Uthman, who ruled for 12 years before he was murdered by rioters. By this time the expansion of the empire had slowed down and discontent was growing at home as people had more time for internal politics. **Ali** was chosen to succeed Uthman but was opposed by many people including Muawiyah, governor of Syria and a member of the Umayyad family, who demanded vengeance upon the murderers of his cousin Uthman. Ali was duly killed and succeeded by Muawiyah. By now a major rift had developed between the supporters of Ali (the *shi'at Ali*), who believed in succession through the lineal descendants of the Prophet, and the supporters of Muawiyah, who claimed to follow the *sunnah*, or ways of the Prophet (and were known as *sunnis*). This marked the beginning of bitter rivalry between the two factions, both religious and political, which still continues to this day in parts of the Muslim world, though not in Morocco, geographically distant as it is from mainstream Islamic feuding. Morocco is predominantly Sunni.

Islam in practice

Today the devout Muslim can apply the principles of the Koran to almost every moment of his life. In particular there are the five Pillars of the Faith, five rules which he must keep if he is to be saved on the Day of Judgement.

Profession of faith (*shahada*). To believe and to testify that there is no God but Allah and that Muhammad is his prophet. This declaration, called *kalima tayyiba*, summarises the whole of Islamic belief.

Prayer (*sala*). To say prayers five times a day: the prayers are *fajr* (from dawn until just before sunrise), *zuhr* (after midday until afternoon), *'asr* (from late afternoon until just before sunset), *maghrib* (after sunset until daylight ends), and *'isha* (night until midnight or dawn). They can be said wherever the Muslim happens to be, though he must always face Mecca, and the ritual must always be preceded by purifying ablutions and accompanied by a fixed number of genuflexions and prostrations. When the hour of prayer is nigh the chanting voices of the muezzins ring out from the tops of the minarets calling the faithful to prayer with the words: 'God is most great. I testify that there is no God but Allah. I testify that Muhammad is God's Apostle. Come to prayer, come to security. God is most great.' The call at daybreak adds the admonition that 'prayer is better than sleep.' Sadly, the muezzins calls are now mostly amplified recordings. Friday prayer (Friday is the holy day) in the mosques is led by the imams (prayer leaders) who give sermons which generally keep very closely to the text of the Koran.

Payment of alms (*zakah*). This welfare contribution is paid once a year at the rate of two-and-a-half per cent of income. Whereas in times past *zaka* was a compulsory payment collected by civil servants and spent under fixed headings for the poor and needy, it is now left to the conscience and circumstances of the individual, and in some cases he may actually give more. There is no shortage of elderly, blind beggars in the medinas of the big cities, usually chanting verses of the Koran, who are accepted as part of the Moroccan scene. Young people, sleeping rough on the streets as in European cities are, thankfully, a rare if not unknown sight in Morocco. Family values are very strong and children are rarely abused.

Fasting (*sawm*). The fast is observed during Ramadan, the ninth month of every Muslim (Hegiran) year, which means that it moves forward 10 or 11 days in every Christian year, as the latter is that much longer. The exact date is determined by the night on which the thin crescent of the new moon of Ramadan is first perceived by the religious elders (*oulemas*). On a cloudy night it may well not be seen at all so the date can never be fixed absolutely.

Fasting, which involves no eating, drinking, smoking or conjugal relations, begins in the morning when the sun rises and continues until darkness falls. The fast is quite bearable when the hours of daylight are short, but in the summer, when there may be 12 hours of burning sunshine, it can be a hard sacrifice indeed. Sick people are exempt, as are travellers and pregnant or menstruating women, but they are expected to make up the days of fasting when they are able to do so. The moments of beginning and ending the fast are announced each day by the firing of a cannon in large towns, elsewhere by the voice of the muezzin or by the head of the family. At the moment of sunset the streets throughout the whole country are empty because everyone is at home or in an eating-house breaking his fast with the traditional soup, *harira*. The night passes in feasting and prayer and, for those who must work next day, in sleep. A last meal is usually eaten just before sunrise, until the moment when (as the Koran says) you are able to distinguish the difference between a white and a black thread.

The Koran was first revealed during Ramadan, which is why it is a holy month. The last and most holy night of all is the 27th—the Night of Destiny. Muslims believe that on this night there is a spiritual bridge between heaven and Earth and the mosques are crammed with the faithful.

The night of Destiny is worth more than a thousand months.
In this night the angels of the Spirit descend to earth with the permission of God to settle all things. Peace accompanies this night until the break of day.

The next day is a national holiday, Aid es Seghir (also called Aid el Fitr), a day of family rejoicing, giving gifts and visiting friends. Feasting and celebration may continue for several days afterwards.

Pilgrimage (*hadj*). The Muslim should make the pilgrimage to Mecca to visit the Ka'ba—and also, strictly speaking, the Prophet's tomb in Medina—at least once during his lifetime. The *hadj* is performed during the twelfth month of the Islamic calendar. It involves a number of rituals including the wearing of *irham* (two sheets of unsewn white cloth), walking round the Ka'ba seven times and kissing a black stone (said to be that given to Abraham by the Angel Gabriel) set in the wall, and the sacrifice of an animal.

Nowadays, with the help of air travel, the pilgrimage presents few problems except financial ones. In the past it could mean a hazardous expedition by camel across Algeria, Tunisia, Libya and Egypt and might take months. Up to the late 19C pilgrims from Maghreb countries would foregather in Cairo whence they proceeded through Sinai to the Hijaz and south along the coast of western

Arabia, a journey of some 40 days. From the 1880s, they could take a steamer on the Red Sea.

On his return from Mecca the pilgrim is given the title of *Hadj*. Thereafter, however lowly his social status, he is treated with the utmost deference, as if he had brought back with him some of the holiness of Mecca. Increasingly, a pragmatic attitude is taken towards those who cannot afford to go to Mecca, and five pilgrimages to Moulay Idriss are now said to equal one to Mecca.

Women

The position of the Koran on women is highly controversial from a Western point of view.

> Men have authority over women because God has made the one superior to the other, and because they spend their wealth to maintain them. Good women are obedient. They guard their unseen parts because God has guarded them. As for those from whom you fear disobedience, admonish them and send them to their beds apart and beat them. Then if they obey you, take no further action against them.

This attitude has for some time been liberally interpreted in the non-fundamentalist countries including Morocco. It does, however, raise the absorbing question as to how much the Koran was intended to bind Muslims for ever more and how much it applied to circumstances pertaining in Arabia in the 7C.

These divine laws—and much else besides, such as the ban on the consumption of pork and alcohol, are obeyed in principle by everyone from the king himself down to the most humble of his subjects, at least in public and, by the older generation, in private as well. There are those, of course, who know how to adapt and modernise even the five 'Pillars', but on the whole, and most particularly during Ramadan, submission to discipline is unquestioning. The Moroccan does not feel the need to write or speak about religion; he observes its rules according to his degree of faith, his theological knowledge, and the time at his disposal. In the towns religious life is regulated by the mosque, particularly on Fridays when everyone is expected to attend Friday prayer, an occasion not only for worship but also for discussion of communal problems. In the countryside, however, belief is somewhat less orthodox and life is often punctuated by colourful festivals known as *moussems* which provide an opportunity for ritual devotion as well as music, dancing and general merrymaking (see below, page 71). Belief in local saints and their capacity to heal the sick, or ensure good harvests, is strong, and many of these saints have their own annual *moussems*. There is no doubt that many of the ceremonies enacted are linked with pre-Islamic beliefs of the Berbers rather than to the Koran, which expressly forbids the worship of the individual.

It could be said that since every moment of his life is guided by the Koran, a devout Muslim can neither think nor act freely. But there is no doubt that the discipline imposed by Islam in Morocco, and particularly during the fast of Ramadan, builds a benign but unbreakable bond between all layers of society, rich and poor, young and old, Berber and Arab—a kind of solidarity and unquestioning unity which the Western world can only envy.

Moussems, festivals and fantasias

A **moussem** is a religious festival, usually held annually, in which pilgrims and believers assemble around the tomb of a saint or **marabout** to do honour to his memory and to ask his blessing on themselves, their families and their crops. If they are sick, they will ask him for a cure. (For some holy men genealogies have been produced to prove their descent from the Prophet Muhammad himself.) The tombs, also known as *marabouts* or **koubbas**, are contained within small, square, white buildings with domes, which are to be found all over Morocco, sometimes isolated in the countryside, sometimes wedged in amongst the already crowded houses of a village or medina. As they are holy places, close examination by non-Muslims may not be welcomed. The pilgrims often travel many days to a *moussem* and bring with them their families, tents, animals and other possessions. The occasion is a joyful one—intended to break the monotony of daily life and provide relaxation for those who work hard—and devotions alternate with songs, dances and general merry-making.

These activities form the core of the *moussem*. Other people from the neighbourhood will arrive with no particular interest in the saint but with donkey-loads of wares to sell: fresh meat and vegetables, pots, straw hats, carpets and cloth. Tents are pitched, couscous is made in industrial quantities and mint tea is brewed. Troops of dancers arrive in rich costumes and add to the colourful spectacle. (For typical dances, see below.) Some *moussems* may be small affairs involving only two or three villages. Others may be of national importance. Indeed some grow so big that the central theme of devotion to a saint is lost in the general festivities and folklore. Others, such as that at Moulay Idriss near Fes (the most famous of all) manage to retain their essential religious flavour because the onlookers are far outnumbered by the pilgrims. Needless to say all this frantic activity and exotic spectacle is very attractive to foreign visitors who are tolerated as long as they show respect and are discreet with their cameras.

Zaouias are educational institutions, mainly rural, which roughly correspond to the urban *medersas*, the principal difference being that whereas the *medersas* are directly linked with nearby mosques, *zaouias* tend to be associated with holy men or *marabouts*, and perhaps were even founded by them. Moreover, unlike *medersas*, many *zaouias* in remote places are still active.

In more extreme cases believers would form **brotherhoods**, each with its own unique practices based on the perceived magical powers of its chosen saints. One colourful example is the Assouia whose founder, Sidi Mohammed ibn Aissa, who is buried in Meknes, was said to be immune to fire, snakes and other dangers. His followers consequently underwent appropriately life-endangering rituals to show that they, too, were immune. In the past, brotherhoods sometimes wielded considerable political power: in the case of the Tabiya in Ouezzane, every Alouite sultan up to the end of the 19C paid them a courtesy visit.

A **festival** is exactly similar in content to a *moussem*, except that it celebrates a harvest or a local event rather than the life of a saint, and so the devotional aspect is lacking. Once the music and dancing start up, it is difficult to tell a *moussem* from a festival.

Typical dances

Ahouach, performed in the valleys of the High Atlas: the women form a circle around the men and play tambourines.

Ahaidous, from the Middle Atlas: men and women form a circle and beat out the rhythm in turn by stamping on the ground.

Guedra, from southern Morocco: the dancer is on her knees, totally covered by a black veil. A throbbing rhythm builds as the dancer's arms and fingers weave in the air and transfix the audience.

Tissint De Tata, women and men dressed in indigo perform the dance of the dagger.

Taskiouine, also from the High Atlas, close to Ouarzazate, a dance of warriors. Dressed in white tunics, a powder flask on their shoulders, the dancers beat out the rhythm with their feet and clap their hands energetically.

A **fantasia** is an important part of traditional events and usually even the most modest *moussem* or festival will manage to raise one. Lines of horsemen thunder across an open space, brandishing their powder-charged rifles (*moukhala*) in the air and, at a given signal (of which the onlooker is not aware), fire into the air. The riders, nobly and colourfully dressed and on magnificent horses, shout wildly with the intoxication of it all and charge over and over again, with no apparent object but to fire their rifles at precisely the same moment. The sight of them through clouds of dust or sand has inspired many Moroccan artists over the years, notably the painter Hassan el Glaoui, whose atmospheric works have become justly famous throughout the world. Seen against a boundless desert landscape, this age-old Berber spectacle is quite breathtaking.

Anyone travelling extensively across the country, using side roads as well as principal routes, will probably come across at least a minor *moussem* or *fantasia* without even having to look for it. The exact dates for *moussems* should be ascertained from the local tourist office, but approximate times are given below.

Tan Tan: end of May
Goulimine: beginning of June
Moulay Abdeslam Ben M'chich Alami, Beni Arous, near Larache: June
Moulay Idriss: August
Moulay Abdallah, on the coast 10km west of El Jadida: August
Sidi Ahmed Ou Moussa, Tiznit: end of August
Sidi El Gandouri, near Khemisset, south of Rabat: August
Moulay Idriss Al Ashar, Fes: September
Moulay Abdelkader, near Khemisset: September
Sidi Yahia, Oujda: September

Festival of camel racing and folklore, Laayoune: 23 February–1 March
Almond Blossom Festival, Tafraout: February
Festival of Roses, El Kelaa des M'Gouna: May
National Folklore Festival, Marrakesh: 5–14 June (varies slightly from year to

year). This is a truly spectacular event, held in the grounds of El Badi Palace, and includes dancers, horsemen, singers, and acrobats from all over the country.

Cherry festival, Sefrou: June
Honey festival, Imouzzer-des-Ida-Outanane (near Agadir): July
Arts festival, Asilah: August
Marriage festival, Imilchil: September
Date festival, Erfoud: October

Moroccan architecture

Within the overall framework imposed by Islam, Moroccan architecture reflects the origins and general characteristics of each successive Muslim dynasty. Unlike Algeria and Tunisia, Morocco was never invaded by the Turks (nor, until relatively recently, by any other foreign power) and dynasties have always sprung up from within the country itself. Morocco therefore has a remarkably homogeneous architectural heritage which remains faithful to the basic tenets of Islamic practice and resists the temptations of modern design. Techniques may have improved but form has changed very little over the centuries. A worthy example of this is the prestigious Hassan II Mosque, recently completed in Casablanca, which is a model of traditional design and craftsmanship at its finest.

The only outside influence—but strictly speaking not 'outside' at all—has been that of **Muslim Spain** (*el Andalus*), first brought back into Morocco by the Almoravide sultan Youssef ibn Tachfine in the late 11C. From Spain came the horseshoe arch, stucco carved into fine lacey patterns, and glazed decorative tiles, to name but a few distinctive forms.

The **French**, who administered the country for 44 years, maintained an enlightened policy of building European-style towns alongside existing medinas, leaving religious buildings, palaces and defensive walls intact wherever they were. Rabat, where Almohade walls weave picturesquely amongst enclaves of sleek, white administrative buildings, is the supreme example of this approach.

Non-religious architecture reflects two Moroccan priorities. One is the constant need for **defence**, which continued until well into the 20C. Fortifications and massive ramparts pierced by monumental gateways (*babs*) surround all the ancient cities, each of which has its defensive stronghold, or kasbah, within. In rural, mainly Berber, areas there is the fortified walled village (*ksar*; plural *ksour*), also with its kasbah. (In the south, *ksour* and kasbahs defend against the burning sun as well as hostile tribes.) The second priority is personal to every devout Moroccan and relates to his deep-felt need to turn away from the outside world and look in upon his own **personal oasis**. Hence the extensive areas of blank, unpromising-looking walls in medinas, hiding within them often sumptuous family homes built around patios containing fountains and shady trees. Royal palaces demonstrate the same inward-looking characteristic, only rather more extravagantly.

Mosques

The principal form of religious building in Morocco is the mosque (a Europeanisation of *masjid*, a word of pre-Islamic origin meaning a place of prostration), modelled on the prototypes of Cordoba in Spain and Kairwan in Tunisia, which in turn were inspired by Syrian examples.

Moroccan mosques are generally plain on the outside but have a decorated entrance and minaret. Traditionally, five times a day the muezzin ascends to a gallery in the **minaret** to call the faithful to prayer (although nowadays the calls of the muezzin are usually amplified recordings). Moroccan minarets are square in section, unlike the cylindrical minarets of the Middle East, and are usually five times their width in height. They have windows—often differently placed on all four sides—and are surmounted by domed turrets. The masters of minaret design were the Almohades and the most glorious examples of their artistry are the Koutoubia in Marrakesh and the Hassan Tower in Rabat.

The interior of a mosque comprises a **courtyard** (*sahn*) with a fountain, or basin, for ritual ablutions. The **prayer hall** (*haram*) is located alongside and is divided into transversal aisles, intersected by a broad central aisle leading to a niche in the wall, the mihrab, which indicates the direction of Mecca (*qibla*). To the right of the mihrab is a pulpit (*minbar*) from which the prayer leader (*imam*) reads the Koran and delivers his Friday sermon. The minbar is said to have originated from the fact that Muhammad addressed his followers from a high seat with three steps, set in the courtyard of his home. After his death this feature came to be seen as the perquisite of the community leader, and later as an important element of all mosques. In this connection, the layout of a mosque is analagous to that of a Christian church, the mihrab taking the place of the altar (which also faces east) and the minbar that of the pulpit.

The oldest surviving mosque in Morocco is the **Karaouyine** in Fes, founded in 859 by the daughter of a wealthy merchant from Kairwan (Tunisia). It started as a simple rectangle comprising four aisles parallel to the *qibla*, and 12 bays wide. The present minaret was completed in 956 and is of Cordoban style except for its dome and parapet. The prayer hall was extended at about this time. The Almoravides enlarged the mosque still further and added fine stalactite vaulting (*muqarnas*) and a minbar thought to have been made in Cordoba.

By 1146 Fes had fallen to the pious Almohades who abhorred excessive ornamentation. So they plastered over much of the Almoravide artistry, including the *muqarnas* (much of which has been uncovered recently). The Saadians were the last people to contribute to the mosque, in the late 16C adding to the courtyard two highly ornate pavilions, said to be copied from the Alhambra's Court of Lions, and much criticised subsequently.

All of this is, however, academic to the non-Muslim who may not enter the Karaouyine, or any other mosque. The exceptions to this rule are the Almohade mosque at Tin Mal (off the Tizi-n-Test road), the huge and never completed Hassan Mosque in Rabat, also Almohade, and the new mosque in Casablanca mentioned above. Other religious buildings open to non-Muslims are the Mohammed V Mausoleum in Rabat (completed in 1967) and the Moulay Ismael Mausoleum in Meknes, as well as the *medersas* (see below).

Tin Mal offers a unique opportunity for the non-Muslim to study the interior of a mosque, albeit roofless. Completed in 1154 (and therefore slightly predating the other famous Almohade mosques of Koutoubia and Hassan), it has nine aisles of four bays perpendicular to the transverse *qibla* aisle. The *muqarnas* have survived remarkably well, displaying the strong geometric patterns typical of the Almohades, rather than the intricate exuberances of the Almoravides. (See page 245 for more detail.)

Medersas

The *medersa* is an Islamic college with lodgings for students. The idea probably originated in Baghdad in the 11C and was introduced to Morocco in the 14C by the Merinides, who wanted to create an intellectual élite. Despite the ostentatious splendour of many *medersas*, it has to be said that the students themselves lived a frugal and often unhealthy life, as indicated by their cell-like rooms. Sometimes two or more would share a room which was dark, often damp, and certainly ill-ventilated, and there they would sleep, cook, eat and study. But their lodging was free, and they also received drinking water and bread daily from the town. Anything else, such as books, meat or vegetables, they had to finance themselves: some lectured in the mosque, some acted as temporary servants in rich houses, and others were forced to beg for charity, though this was not too difficult since Muslims must give a proportion of their income to the poor and there were enough wealthy citizens who were happy to support the cause of knowledge.

A *medersa* comprises a central courtyard which always contains a pool or fountain for ritual ablutions. Around it is a colonnade or gallery leading to students' rooms (usually little more than cells), and there may be a second floor of rooms above. There is also a large hall which would be used for both prayer and lectures. An exception to this is the huge **Bou Inania Medersa** in Fes, which seems to have been intended for use as a mosque as well as a college, and has a separate prayer hall, as well as an imposing minaret. In contrast with the frugality of the students' rooms, the walls, columns and doorways of the courtyard and halls are extravagantly decorated in minutely worked *zellige*, delicate lace-like stucco combining geometric designs with floral and palm motifs, and magnificently carved cedarwood. This is Hispano-Moorish craftsmanship at its most breathtaking—each design a point of visual repose in its exquisite symmetry.

The Attarine Medersa in Fes is slightly earlier, smaller and, some would say, more perfect than the Bou Inania. Other *medersas* in Fes include the Seffarine, the Es Sahrij and the Es Sebbayine. There are also *medersas* in Marrakesh and Meknes. They are no longer used as religious colleges (though the Bou Inania still holds Friday prayers and is therefore closed to visitors on that day). Today's students are housed on modern campuses and the *medersas* have become a part of Morocco's rich architectural heritage. Most have been well restored and are open to visitors in the same way as any other historic monument.

Koubbas

A common sight throughout Morocco is the *koubba* or *marabout*, a small, white, domed building containing the relics of a saint or holy man (also called a *marabout*). Most villages have at least one and cities will have several. *Koubbas* are visited by pilgrims and supplicants at certain times of year in celebration of the saint and his good deeds, or by the sick in search of restored health (see the description of *moussems*, above). It is not wise for non-Muslims to approach too close to *koubbas* at any time of year: they are regarded as very holy places.

A famous exception to the above rule is the **Koubba el Baadiyin** in Marrakesh, which was rediscovered as recently as 1952. It is the only Almoravide building remaining intact in the city and would originally have covered an ablutions pool probably connected with the nearby Ibn Youssef

Mosque. It has simple pointed-horseshoe and lobed arches, with windows above and stepped merlons on top, surrounding a dome decorated with interlaced arches. The interior is richly decorated with floral and pine cone motifs. This *koubba* is no longer regarded as holy and can be visited by anyone, on payment of 10dh. It is a very compact, early (11C) demonstration of classical architectural forms which were to become so familiar later on.

Much simpler in design and still imbued with a strong sense of mystery are the seven small Merinide *koubbas* clustered around the sacred Pool of Eels at Chellah in Rabat.

Ramparts and babs

City walls are everywhere and reflect the seige mentality (quite justified in the circumstances) of each successive dynasty. Not only did they help to keep out invaders—who nevertheless managed to enter and sack the cities with astonishing regularity, either through trickery or by diverting river water to weaken the foundations—but they were useful for displaying the heads of vanquished enemies.

The first energetic wall-builders were the Almoravides, in the person of Ali, son of Youssef ibn Tachfine, who surrounded the newly founded capital of Marrakesh with 8km of high walls made of local pink mud reinforced with lime.

The Almoravides also built walls around Fes but these were demolished by the Almohade leader, Abd el Mumene, saying 'only justice and the sword shall be our ramparts'. He was proved disastrously mistaken and his successors quickly built them up again, stronger than before. The old city of Fes el Bali is still enclosed by what is left of the Almohade walls, albeit much repaired and restored. A drive around the city walls in both cases is highly recommended.

The Almohades also built many *babs*, including the very simple **Bab Agnaou** in Marrakesh, with fine carving on the stone arches in the manner of the Koutoubia minaret. The most monumental of all is **Bab Oudaia** in Rabat, believed to have had a ceremonial rather than a defensive function since it has three interior chambers and would have stood at the centre of the royal kasbah, subsequently destroyed by the Alouites. Both of these survive in good condition.

The Merinides enclosed their necropolis in Rabat—Chellah—in fine castellated walls with a powerful stone gateway flanked by monumental **towers**. In his book *Islamic Architecture*, John Hoag draws attention to 'the projecting corners of the towers which are supported by corbels of *muqarnas*, one of the rare instances in North Africa or Spain where this motif was translated into stone, perhaps under Egyptian influence'.

The most notorious wall-builder of all was the second Alouite sultan, Moulay Ismael, who enclosed his 'Imperial City' in Meknes in 25km of walls within walls, conceiving it as a mighty fortress to protect him from hostile tribes. The effect today is breathtaking (and exhausting if you happen to be on foot). He was also a great builder of *babs*, the most famous being **Bab el Mansour**, massively constructed, perfectly proportioned and minutely decorated with green and white *zellige*.

Kasbahs and ksours

In the north of Morocco, kasbahs are defensive **strongholds** within Arab cities, built to house and protect a chief or royal person and his family, his harem and his retainers. On principle, a conquering dynasty would seek to destroy the kasbah of its vanquished predecessors and not many survive intact. The Almohade Kasbah of the Oudaias in Rabat retains only its ceremonial gateway, that of Tangier only its palace, built by Moulay Ismael and now a museum. Both these kasbahs were subsequently rebuilt and greatly changed in character by Muslim refugees fleeing from Spain in the 16C and 17C, and have more recently been 'enhanced' and turned into fashionable and atmospheric residential areas for rich expatriates and artists.

In the south, Berber kasbahs remain largely intact, or, if they have suffered from rain erosion, have been replaced by newer versions of the same. This is because the need for defence amongst Berber tribes continued well into the 20C. Their kasbahs are made of *pisé* (mud and straw), usually set on a foundation of mud and stones, and have a watch tower at each corner and splendid decoration incised into the *pisé* walls, often recalling black African rather than Islamic designs.

Ksours are a phenomenon of southern Morocco and are essentially **fortified villages** behind *pisé* walls. Many have kasbahs within, or adjoining, them. Sometimes it is difficult to tell where one starts and the other ends. They are a distinctive and picturesque sight in the south: the best ones are to be found in the Draa, Dades and Ziz valleys, as well as on the southern slopes of the High Atlas (the former territory of the Glaoui and other powerful Atlas tribes).

For a fuller description of kasbahs and ksour, see page 249.

Family homes

Walking through the Fes medina (or any other medina, for that matter) you pass unpromising stretches of blank wall with no windows and nothing in the way of decoration. Only the occasional well-hidden doorway betrays that you are walking past a house, or *dar.*

Supposing you were to be invited inside, you would walk through a narrow, convoluted corridor which still gives nothing away, finally emerging into a square or rectangular **courtyard** or patio, with fountains, alleyways often lined with *zellige* and, in the richer houses, one or more pavilions. It is open to the sky and full of flowers and citrus and palm trees, the whole reflecting the traditional Muslim concept of paradise as a place of abundant water and shade. The courtyard (known as a *riad*) is bordered by colonnades inside which are galleries to shelter the family from sun and rain. The *riad* is the unifying centre of the house, the place of passage and of meeting. It serves the function of both circulating air and diffusing light into some, at least, of the surrounding rooms, recalling the Roman atrium.

Giving on to the galleries are the **main rooms**—reception rooms, family salons and bedrooms. Kitchens and bathrooms tend to be located in corners where light does not penetrate. Upstairs are more bedrooms and private areas, particularly women's rooms with *mushrabiyya* windows, wooden screens with complex interlaced patterns through which women can look out without being seen. The reception rooms are particularly ornately decorated using traditional forms such as *zellige*, sculpted plaster and carved wood. Always there is continuous repetition of design (as with *medersas*) and every space is filled. The furnishings are integrated into the architecture with divans and cushions lining the walls.

The size and degree of luxury of family dwellings will obviously vary but the principle remains the same; even nomadic encampments have tents arranged in a circle and looking inwards, thus excluding the outside world and creating a tranquil, separate environment within.

A **palace** is but a multiplication of all the above elements, with many court-yard leading one into the other. The El Badi palace in Marrakesh had over 100 fountains and many extravagant pavilions until it was wantonly destroyed by Moulay Ismael. Many other palaces do survive and have been turned into museums. It is worth looking beyond the exhibits at the structure of the build-ings themselves, always positioned around courtyards. Dar Jamai in Meknes and Dar Batha in Fes are two good examples.

Traditional crafts

The traditional crafts of Morocco have kept their identity for over 1000 years—unlike many Western countries where special efforts must be made to ensure the survival of old skills. The most important influence on Morocco's crafts is, and has been since the 7C, **Islam**. For a Muslim, Islam is a way of life which finds expression in everything he does, and most evidently in his creative and artistic pursuits. However, many **Berber products** reflect much older, pre-Islamic beliefs and animism, symbolism and magic can often be detected in Berber work, particularly in the carpets. Sometimes these influences will interact with the geometric patterns, flowing arabesques and calligraphy of Islamic designs.

The two main geographical influences are those of **black Africa** and Andalusia. The Saadians, coming originally from the Draa valley, were the first Moroccan dynasty to spread southwards into Mauritania, Mali and beyond, in their quest for gold, ebony, ostrich feathers and slaves. Since their time (1554–1660), there has been a constant flow of people and ideas across the Sahara, with consequent enrichment of art forms, particularly jewellery and ceramics.

Moorish Spain (*el Andalus*) was renowned for the richness and variety of its culture, and its influence over music, literature, architecture and art was bound-less. After the fall of Granada in 1492 and the subsequent expulsion of Muslims and Jews by the Inquisition, many thousands fled to Morocco, bringing with them their traditions and art forms. The Andalusian architectural influence in the medinas of northern towns such as Rabat and Chaouen, for example, is most striking.

A distinction can be made between rural and urban crafts. The **rural tradi-tion**—most likely Berber and tribal—reflects the fact that its creators have always lived close to nature, in the mountains or the desert: to animals and insects, to the sun, moon and stars, and to the agrarian cycle. Berber designs are generally less abstract and less ordered than those of the urban Arabs, displaying a wonderful spontaneity and exuberance. They use whatever mate-rials are most accessible—sheep's wool, goat and camel hair, home-made vegetable dyes, clay and semi-precious stones. On the whole, their craftspeople are not professionals, though this is beginning to change now.

Urban work, mainly Arab, *is* carried out professionally and craftsmen belong to guilds according to their skill. It is normal to find, for example, all the carpenters together in the Fes medina. Moreover their progress from apprentice to fully-fledged artisan is very carefully supervised, and they can only set themselves up independently with the consent of their master craftsman. This custom, still rigidly observed, is responsible for the preservation of age-old skills and the generally high standard of work.

A recent phenomenon beneficial to both rural and urban workers is the growth in mass **tourism**. Whereas hitherto, rural Berbers would make carpets for their own tents and jewellery for weddings and other ceremonial occasions, and the urban Arabs would be paid to produce carved woodwork, glazed tiles and stucco for palaces and mosques (and still are), there is now the additional and insatiable tourist market. It is interesting to note that some Berber women in the south, who have always woven carpets in their own villages or tents, now buy modest houses in town in which to work, because carrying carpets to market across the desert or mountains is simply too slow and arduous. And they perceive that demand is growing.

Inevitably there is beginning to be some compromise of traditional designs and materials, in favour of modern taste. A delicate balance has to be struck between traditionalism, on the one hand, and improved opportunities for Morocco's craftsmen and women, on the other. In December 1996 it was reported that the handicraft sector employs one third of the active population and, together with agriculture and tourism, accounts for more than 25 per cent of gross domestic product.

Carpets

Carpets form a large part of Morocco's craft production. They fall into two main categories, Rabats, which are knotted, and Berbers, which are woven. **Rabat** carpets are certainly the most valuable and are thought by many to be the most beautiful, and they contain the greatest density of threads (up to 150,000 per square metre). Based on a design introduced by Turkish merchants in the 18C, they bear a central diamond-shaped or hexagonal medallion and a wide border consisting of between three and seven bands—the greater the number, the greater the value of the carpet. The whole is covered with animal, geometric and floral motifs, these last intended to symbolise the Muslim paradise of well-watered gardens. The colours are harmonious and range through reds, blues, beige, and oranges, and the most frequent ground colour is a soft pinkish red. The quality of workmanship and the softness of the colours, particularly those of the old carpets which are made with vegetable rather than chemical dyes, is outstanding.

Rabat carpets are on the whole solid and hardwearing, but care should be taken when choosing an old one: look for holes and worn places, and ensure that any fault or repair is reflected in the price. Old Rabats are expensive and are becoming quite hard to find, though some of the merchants in the Rue des Consuls in Rabat will undoubtedly have good examples tucked away in the back of their shops. New ones are priced per square metre, according to the quality of the wool and the amount of work which has gone into their making; the accuracy with which old designs have been reproduced also counts.

Apart from Rabat carpets and those known as 'royals' or 'orientals' in rich blues and reds, based on Rabat designs but usually simpler and therefore cheaper, all the others are **Berber**. These can be found in an infinite variety of texture, colour, mood and quality, and they are much cheaper than Rabats. Generally colours are muted and designs are often asymmetrical, with geometric shapes interspersed with symbols and stylised animal forms. There may or may not be a border. No two Berber carpets are ever alike. This is because the weaver feels she has total freedom to express herself (only Berber women weave) and she may even incorporate her own tattoo to give an added personal touch. Women who weave are highly respected in Berber society and command a higher bride price than those who do not.

Pre-Islamic superstition, animism and respect for magic are still strong in Berber culture, even though they have been superimposed by Islam. (An analogy can be drawn with the Bolivian Altiplano Indians, who still place a llama foetus under the foundation stone of a new house, whilst inviting the Catholic priest to bless their home.) The most frequently used **symbols** include the hand of Fatima (the Prophet Muhammad's daughter), supposed to ward off malevolent spirits and the evil eye; an eight-pointed star which is a fertility symbol, as are snakes, lizards and scorpions; camels signifying bride wealth; and crosses, which are believed to have the power first to draw in, and then to disperse, evil in the six directions of the Berber universe—north, south, east and west, above and below.

Each tribe produces its own carpets, the designs passed down through generations, and the expert can tell at a glance from which region, or even which tribe, a carpet comes. Those from the Middle Atlas tend to be worked in beiges and browns, often undyed natural sheep's wool, with a simple design in one corner in deeper brown, reproducing exactly that of the tattoo worn by the carpet-maker; or they may be in rich combinations of red and ochre covered in diamond patterns. Those from the High Atlas, the Jbel Siroua and the Ouarzazate regions, woven by women of the Ait Ouaouzguite and Ait Haddidou tribes, are amongst the most beautiful. These are often referred to as 'Glaoua' carpets because of the dominance of El Glaoui over the area. They are usually in soft reds, ochres, orange or black, with diamonds, stars, and lozenges arranged in bands.

Some Berber carpets are too thin to put on the floors of Western houses. They will have been made to hang inside tents to give warmth and—if sequinned—light at night. When Moroccans do put carpets on the floor they tend to overlap them, thus providing a soft, rich surface to walk (in slippers or barefoot), sit or lie on. Their most appropriate use in a Western household is probably as a blanket or bedspread, and they can transform an otherwise dull bedroom.

The best place to look for Berber carpets, old and new, is undoubtedly in the very regions where they have been made. You may find them in some country souk or small town shop (Agdz is good for Glaoua carpets). You certainly pay far more in the medinas of the big cities. Take the opportunity to visit museums such as the Dar Batha in Fes or the Dar Jamai in Meknes to accustom your eye to the vast range of design and colour available.

Jewellery

Moroccan women like to adorn themselves with jewellery at all times of day. It denotes their social and marital status, the wealth of their husband and—for Berber women—their tribal identity and religious and/or superstitious beliefs.

Most Moroccan jewellery is made of silver or has at least a silver base. Berbers traditionally believe that gold is evil and always wear silver; gold is worn only by rich Arab women in the towns, usually in the form of bracelets or heavy ornate belts, often studded with emeralds and worn tight over the kaftan. Nowadays, gold jewellery is increasingly made for the tourists.

Jewellery making is done almost exclusively by men, and the skills are passed on from father to son. Originally most silversmiths were Jews who had fled from the Spanish Inquisition in the 16C and 17C. They settled initially in the northern towns but soon made their way south and eventually passed on their techniques to the Muslims, especially the Berbers, who preserve them to this day in the old *mellahs* and *kasbahs*. (The Kasbah des Juifs in Zagora is a good example.)

There are two basic **techniques**. One is to pour molten silver into moulds, the other is to pound it into sheets, flattening it to the desired thickness before cutting, soldering or bending. It can then be filigreed, enamelled or dotted with semi-precious stones or pieces of coloured glass.

Different regions of Morocco specialise in different techniques. Tiznit is one of the best places to see the art of filigree—usually carried out by young boys because they have thin enough fingers to twist the silver wire into delicate shapes. Enamelling—and particularly the technique of pouring enamel into a design which has been dug out of the silver base—is most commonly practised in the Middle Atlas.

Jewellery comes in many forms. **Necklaces** are worn by all women. Berbers in the south wear heavy and ornate combinations of amber, filigree balls, enamelled eggs, glass and coral, or sometimes just massive chunks of amber or multiple strings of small coral beads. Amber is believed to be an aphrodisiac and is also worn as protection against evil spirits; coral is mentioned in the Koran as a precious substance, but Berbers were using it for curative purposes long before the arrival of Islam. It is no uncommon sight to see a Berber woman working in the fields, her neck weighted with heavy necklaces. The influence of black Africa is very strong in the south and legend has it that massive bejewelled necklaces were once an expression of joy on the part of freed slave women. More delicate necklaces have what look like old silver coins suspended from strings of coral beads, sometimes with beautifully filigreed or enamelled Koranic boxes added.

Fibulas or brooches, which represent fertility, are a very important form of jewellery to Berber women. They are necessary to fasten draped garments at the shoulder. They can come in the simplest of triangular forms or in the more decorative jackal's paw design (to which magical qualities are attributed), often engraved or filigreed. **Bracelets** tend to be worn in great quantity, on wrists or ankles. They are often heavy and may well be hinged, or simply left open. One kind, originating in the Draa region, has protruding knobs and was undoubtedly intended for self defence. **Head-dresses** or diadems can be very ornate and are usually reserved for weddings and other festivals. They are usually made of silver, possibly filigreed and inlaid with gems, and fixed on to a leather base. There are also brooches, rings, earrings, pendants and silver 'hands of Fatima'.

The Koran forbids the wearing of jewellery by men but tolerates unlimited luxury in their weapons. Thus another important activity of the silversmith is to make weapons—ceremonial rifles for use in *fantasias*, pistols, sabres and daggers, finely ornamented in silver or gold and often encrusted with semi-precious stones. These are very popular with tourists.

All these items are very collectable and can look quite irresistible in the Aladdin's cave atmosphere of a Fes souk. Be aware that fastenings on old necklaces nearly always need attention once you get them home. Modern jewellery, using the same basic designs as antique examples, varies greatly in the quality of both material and execution and therefore in price. Antique jewellery commands higher prices but anything can happen if you are a skilful bargainer. Obviously the souks in the large medinas make good hunting grounds, and all sizeable towns have their own jewellery souks (*souks de bijoux*), Tiznit and Agdz being particularly recommended. In the south, you may be fortunate enough to find a knowledgeable guide who will take you to an old kasbah where silversmiths still work in the traditional way or, better still, to meet a merchant who has just returned from the Sahara where he has exchanged grain, flour, sugar and salt for trinkets, boxes and jewellery of great beauty. This all takes time but is immensely rewarding (see the section on Tiznit for the story of such an encounter).

Pottery and ceramics

There is a marked distinction to be made between rural **Berber pottery** and urban ceramics. The Berbers use local deposits of natural clay to make mainly unglazed, utilitarian objects for the home. They cook on clay braziers and eat and drink out of clay vessels. The familiar *tajine*—the shallow stew pot with a conical lid—is a Berber creation, as is the *guerba*, a jar into which milk is poured and then swung about, using string and sticks, to make butter. Both men and women produce pottery, but it is interesting to note that women's pots are used at home whereas men's creations are taken to the souks for sale. Pottery is sacred to many Berber tribes and is thought to ward off evil spirits in the home. It is also quite common to see shards of pottery scattered over cemeteries, for the same purpose. Berber pottery comes in simple, satisfying, even voluptuous shapes and experts compare it with that of ancient Greece and Carthage. In the south (for example, at Tamegroute), however, the influence of black Africa is perceptible.

Urban ceramics come in the form of painted or glazed tableware and utensils, green roof tiles and *zellige*. The art of glazing with the use of lead oxides originally came from Moorish Spain, around the year 818, when 8000 Arab families arrived in Fes from Cordoba. The technique of making **architectural mosaics** from glazed tiles, known as *zellige*, probably originated in Fes between the late 12C and 15C and then crossed over to *el Andalus*. Indeed, ceramics owe more to the cultural cross-fertilisation between Morocco and Andalusia than any other traditional craft. The glazed tiles are best seen in the *medersas*, fountains and palaces of the great medinas of Fes, Marrakesh, Meknes and Rabat, but the Moroccan government is to be congratulated for preserving this distinctive art form by commissioning traditional *zellige*-makers to line the walls of modern ceremonial buildings such as the magnificent Hassan II Mosque in Casablanca.

Much urban domestic ware is based on the extravagant eating habits of rich families in the past, with huge bowls, soup tureens and jugs, glazed and painted with ornate patterns in soft greens, browns, yellows and blues. These continue to be produced, but mainly for decorative purposes. Fes, Meknes, Marrakesh, and Safi are the great pottery towns, each with its own recognisable style, and it is a good idea to visit a museum so as to learn to distinguish one from the other. You can also visit the potters at work. A particularly good and relatively tranquil place to do this is Salé, which has its own pottery industry on a smaller scale than those of the 'Imperial Cities'. Salé pots are fresh and uncomplicated in design and look well in contemporary homes. Particularly charming are the coffee services with tall narrow jugs, and the soup bowls with conical lids. Safi, too, has an attractive and easily accessible potters' quarter, though many people find the heavily glazed and decorated objects too much orientated towards mass tourism.

Leather goods

For centuries the tanning and dyeing of animal hides to make leather has been an important part of Moroccan life, both rural and urban. Goatskin is the material most commonly employed and the traditional method of tanning by immersion in animal urine, and dyeing in huge vats sunk into the ground, is still in use in the medinas of the great cities and—on a smaller scale—in rural areas. (See page 208 for a description of the process.) However, such is the popularity of, and demand for, Moroccan leather, both within the Islamic world and outside it, that the old methods are beginning to give way to more modern industrial ones. (The Fes tannery was almost deserted when the writer last visited it, albeit out of season.)

Utilitarian articles such as saddles and bags, scabbards for swords, belts and boots have been part of the Moroccan scene for centuries. In towns, *babouches*—the pointed slippers worn by both men and women—are everywhere. These shoes are easy to slip off when entering the mosque or home, and immensely comfortable to wear (if you can master the art of keeping them on in the first place).

In recent years the repertoire has been extended to meet the taste of the Western world: cigarette boxes, desk sets, wastepaper baskets, wallets and pouffes (these last in astonishing variety, gold-tooled if coming from Fes, embroidered with silk if from Marrakesh). A desk set in fine black kidskin, discreetly tooled in gold, can make a handsome present,and it is quite satisfying to see an exactly similar article for sale in a London department store for six or seven times as much as you have had to pay, by dint of skilful bargaining. The medinas are the best places to look. Leather goods in tourist shops should be examined carefully because the quality of skins varies considerably; the more ornate the decoration, the less fine the quality of the skin is a fairly safe rule.

One very ancient branch of the leather trade is book-binding. The finest goatskins and most delicate skills have always been reserved for binding sacred works, the Koran in particular. You only have to look at the Nacyrin library at Tamegroute (see page 262), where the earliest Koran dates back to the year 1063, to see examples of this. And the trade continues to prosper. 'Bound in Morocco leather' is no idle term and, with the increase in the paperback industry throughout Europe, the Moroccan book-binder is finding his supreme skills very much in demand, particularly amongst visitors from overseas.

Woodwork

Morocco is rich in timber, particularly cedarwood which comes from the Middle Atlas, but also thuya and argana from the west coast region, palm, citrus and tamarisk. All these woods are used in furniture making, cedar and thuya being the most prized. Traditional woodwork is seen at its best as part of architecture—in the mosques, *medersas* and ancient palaces where it forms part of the classic Islamic trilogy together with *zellige* and plaster stucco. What visitor has not admired the magnificent carved and painted cedarwood ceilings in some of the great palaces, the Dar el Makhzen in Tangier, for example? Then there are the carved canopies such as that over the north portal of the Andalous Mosque in Fes, and the ancient doors, often painted with symbols to protect the inhabitants from evil spirits, many now displayed in museums because they have outlived the buildings they once guarded.

Part of both Arab and Berber culture are the massive cedarwood **marriage chairs**. In the tradition of the Arabs, the chairs are usually held high off the ground, allegedly to discourage the bride from escaping; in the Berber tradition they take the form of elaborate tubs in which the bride is ceremonially carried around. More easily collectable are the smaller items such as chests, tables—including those delicately carved and balanced to carry brass tea trays—bowls and chessboards.

The very distinctive **marquetry** and woodcarving of Essaouira can be observed in workshops within the old ramparts. The trunk and root of the hardwood thuya tree (which grows locally) is inlaid with ebony, mother-of-pearl, walnut or even copper or silver wire to make table tops, chests, musical instruments and every kind of ornament. Or it may be used on its own, highly polished to bring out the fine grain of the wood. These articles, all made in the one region, can be found all over Morocco.

Miscellaneous crafts

Apart from jewellery there are many kinds of **metalwork**, such as the big brass lanterns with insertions of coloured glass to reflect the light, or little ones meant to take a candle. There are heavy copper urns; superbly engraved brass and silver tea trays; and six-sided caskets of silver, or rather, silver-plated copper, which are part of the tea-making paraphernalia and make attractive ornaments in their own right, ranging as they do from the size of an egg-cup to rectangular ones some 30cm long (they are found most readily in Marrakesh). There is also the distinctive damascened work, made only in Meknes, where silver wire is hammered into patterns scratched out of ironwork to form vases and all sorts of other containers.

Traditional **tailors**—all men—are to be found making kaftans and djellabahs in their tiny shops in the medinas, often surrounded by young apprentices. The best places to see and buy from a wide range of these clothes are the big city medinas, particularly the cooperatives often to be found in old palaces in Fes and Marrakesh, or in *kissarias* (covered markets). Bargains can often be found in less obvious locations, such as Salé, Ouezzane, Chaouen and some of the southern towns. Fine **embroidery** is still being done by hand, mainly in Fes and Meknes. This is remarkable for having no 'wrong' side and was originally taught by Catholic nuns to girls preparing for their wedding days. It is now used mainly to ornament tableware and is a very attractive, non-bulky item for the tourists to take home.

Morocco is also a treasure-house of **semi-precious stones**: amethyst, topaz, cobalt, and so on. These should be bought, if possible, in the High Atlas mountains where they originate. You do not have to search very far for they are displayed in stalls or on makeshift tables on all the high passes, wherever there is space. Be careful of imitations and do not hesitate to apply a wet finger to a doubtful 'amethyst' to see if the purple paint rubs off.

Food and drink

Moroccans are amongst the most hospitable people in the world. Their heart-warming courtesy and the lavishness of the food provided, as much to a near stranger as to a family friend, is often quite out of proportion to their means. A guest in a Moroccan household is someone to be honoured, someone to partake of the best that can be offered. A Moroccan is deeply hurt if you refuse his **hospitality**, even if he can ill afford to give it to you. He will share his last crust with his guest.

Taking tea

Mint tea is the staple drink all over Morocco and is drunk at any time of day, before or after a meal. It is traditionally very sweet, but recently people have taken to asking foreigners whether they want it with or without sugar—*sucré ou non-sucré?* It is a refreshing and thirst-quenching drink in hot, dry weather, and a warming, revitalising one on cool, wet days. It is also an excellent digestive. The tea used is green tea and it comes from China. Tea as drunk in the West is called black tea (*thé noir*) or, if you prefer it with milk, *thé avec du lait*. It is obtainable in the larger towns and hotels but otherwise may be difficult to come by.

The tea-making **ceremony** is an ancient and dignified one. The host usually invites a close friend or an important guest to prepare it. This person sits cross-legged on the most honoured seat in the room and is brought a round tray, usually silver or brass, about a metre in diameter and standing on its own legs. On the tray is a silver teapot with a conical lid, glasses, coloured and decorated to a high degree and usually far more numerous than the guests, and three silver boxes, one containing green tea, one irregular chunks of white sugar and one sprigs of mint. A steaming copper kettle, often with its own charcoal brazier, is brought in. There is also a silver spoon and a sharp instrument for hacking the sugar into more manageable pieces.

Slowly, and in silence, a quantity of tea will be put in the pot. Boiling water is added. Then a large amount of sugar and a handful of mint are crammed in, the lid is pushed down and the mixture is left to infuse for some minutes. Then the tasting begins. The tea-maker, profoundly aware of his responsibilities, pours a little tea into his own glass, tastes it with all the concentration of a wine connoisseur, pours it back, perhaps adds more water, sugar or mint, leaves it a little longer, tastes it again, and so on until he is quite satisfied that it is good enough. He then pours a little tea into each glass, holding the pot high in the air and affecting a masterly flourish. The glasses are then filled and passed round on the tray. They are often so full and so hot that the only way to hold them is with the thumb on the brim and the second and third fingers underneath. Greatest pleasure will be given by allowing the glass to be filled at least twice more, unless you know that this is just the preliminary to a meal. It goes without saying that if you are casually offered some tea whilst, say, negotiating for a carpet in the medina, the whole process will be greatly accelerated.

A festive meal

A full meal in a well-to-do Moroccan household can be a delicious and quite formal affair, and it is worth noting that appreciation of the food is on the whole deemed far more important than conversation. Indeed, a lack of conversation means that you are dedicating yourself to enjoying the meal, and this is appreciated. Moroccans often eat in friendly silence. The time for talk is before or after. There is always an atmosphere of well-being and warmth and this is what matters.

You will be ushered to a seat on the narrow, padded divan, which lines the walls of all Moroccan living-rooms, and cushions will be thrust behind your back to ensure your total comfort. A round low table will then be brought up to you, as yet with nothing on it but a richly embroidered linen tablecloth, or perhaps a more practical plastic one, and a number of very large napkins. Your host and those of lesser importance than yourself will group themselves around the table against the wall or on cushions and pouffes. A servant with a towel over his arm will then bring a kettle of warm water and a metal bowl with a raised disc in the middle which holds a cake of soap. You must wash your hands because you will be eating with your fingers—or, more precisely, with the thumb and first two fingers of your right hand only. (In restaurants, however, it will be expected that you use the Western-style cutlery provided.)

After this procedure has been completed by everyone the first course is brought in, probably **mechoui**, a whole lamb roasted in a special oven and served on a heavy round platter. Or it may just be part of a lamb, according to the number of guests or the status of your host. Round loaves of unleavened bread, nutty and granular, are liberally scattered on to the tablecloth and little dishes containing salt and ground caraway seed are put around. There are no plates. Your host will murmur *bis m'Allah*, which means 'with the blessing of God', and invite you to start. The meat is so tender that it comes away easily in the hand. The fat, browned and crisp, peels away easily to reveal the succulent flesh underneath, and experienced *mechoui*-eaters know just where to look for the most tender morsels. If you appear at any time to hesitate or to have difficulty in extracting your meat, juicy portions will be held out to you by your host or anyone wishing to give you pleasure. This may well be the first of some four or five meat courses, but it is entirely up to you to take as much or as little as you like, although it is difficult in fact to avoid taking more than enough. Do not be surprised if, after you have munched solidly for half an hour or so, your host says to you, *'Mais vous ne mangez rien Monsieur/Madame'*. He does not mean it. He just needs you to reassure him that it is good.

A **pastilla** may come next, or it may come instead of the *mechoui*. This is the most calorific part of the Moroccan menu and should be eaten sparingly by the weight-conscious. It consists of wafer-thin layers of flaky, feather-light pastry, usually made by your host's wife, filled with a mixture of pigeon meat (or, increasingly, chicken), almonds, hard-boiled eggs and an assortment of herbs and spices. It is served very hot and usually has icing sugar sprinkled on top. Hardened *pastilla*-eaters quite ruthlessly fold back the layers of pastry in order to get at the spicy meat inside, but be careful not to burn your fingers for the contents retain their heat long after the rim has cooled down. This is the glory of Moroccan cuisine. If offered a *pastilla*, you know that you are being truly honoured. Countless hours will have been spent in its preparation; indeed it is said that a guest can measure his standing with a family by the number of layers of pastry in the *pastilla*.

Next may come chickens, slow-cooked with saffron and either pickled lemons and olives, or dates and nuts, and served—usually three or four to a dish—in a delicious aromatic sauce. This is known as **tagine de poulet**. The chicken meat is easily removed from the carcass and the sauce can be mopped up with bread. In the Mediterranean area, instead of chickens there might be a fish baked whole (usually bream or sea bass) and stuffed with either tomatoes and herbs or raisins, honey and almonds.

After all this there will probably be a stew of tender mutton, **tagine de mouton**, cooked with onions, prunes, and nuts, and often decorated with hard-boiled eggs. *Tagines* are served in a heavy earthenware dishes with a conical lid which is whipped off at the last moment so that the food can be served at maximum heat. (The vessel itself is also called a *tagine*.) It is perfectly understood if, at this stage, you feel that you have eaten just about enough meat and prefer to soak your bread in the sauce, where much of the flavour is anyway, and pick at the prunes and the vegetables.

Finally comes the **couscous**, and when this appears you know you are approaching the end of the road. This is Morocco's national dish. It is served at all tables, from the richest to the poorest, and on all occasions. A veritable mountain of white granular semolina hides within it carrots, turnips, courgettes and, usually, pieces of mutton. The dish will probably be moistened by a thin piquant sauce poured over it at the last moment. The semolina may also be served plain, as a dessert, with milk, cinnamon and sugar. It varies widely from region to region and each of your hosts will think that his is the best. It is all a matter of personal taste and one can quite quickly become a couscous connoisseur while travelling across the country.

Whichever way it is cooked, couscous is very light and digestible, and the right way to eat it is to pick up a small quantity of the grain in the fingers and, by applying gentle pressure, shape it into a perfect spherical ball. This is then tossed delicately into the mouth. Unless you have had time to practise in private, this can be a very messy business. Even with the protection of your napkin over your knees, couscous has a way of seeping down your chin and into your shoes or up your sleeves. Spoons will probably have been put around at this stage and it is not at all shaming to pick one up and use it. It will certainly be kinder to your host's carpet to do so.

Now you are nearing the end of the meal. You may be presented with a dish of typical **sweetmeats** including the famous *cornes de gazelle*, tiny croissants stuffed with ground almonds and honey and rolled in sugar and chopped nuts. Or you may go straight on to **fruit**: peaches, grapes, oranges, cherries, apples, bananas, dates, melons or iced watermelon, according to the season and where you are. Look particularly for cherries in the Middle Atlas, bananas in the Souss valley around Agadir, and dates in the south. Fruit in Morocco is cheap, of high quality and plentiful.

The meal is over when the hand-washing apparatus reappears. Some of the guests may wash their faces as well. At this stage you can relax back against the cushions and even go to sleep if you wish. It is a relief to have room to spread out after the rather cramped eating position when you are bent over the low, round table and your legs, if they happen to be long, tend to be rather in the way. Tea, or the possible alternative of thick black **coffee**, will be served, and as soon as you have had your two or three glasses it is permissible to leave.

The meal described above is a formal, traditional Moroccan meal, called a *diffa*, and is served when a festival is being celebrated. The repertoire of dishes is fairly predictable and there is no reason to over-eat if you can master the technique of appearing to be permanently busy either choosing a morsel or consuming it. The custom of crouching over a low table around a common platter stems, of course, from earlier life in tents in the desert. The meal is taken very seriously but a warmth and friendly intimacy is generated which is often lacking around the Western dinner table with its carefully positioned chairs and place-settings.

You will doubtless be surprised by the vast quantities put in front of you; seemingly far more than is necessary. In fact, there is no waste. Moroccan households take the form of large family conclaves and each dish, as it leaves the principal guests, goes straight on to other members of the family, or to the children, or to the servants. But Moroccans do not normally eat on this scale. They live modestly and a simple meal of *tagine* or couscous with fruit to follow will usually suffice. The quantity and the general splendour of presentation is put on for you, the guest. It is quite unthinkable for a Moroccan to ask a guest to take pot-luck as Westerners might do if taken unawares by a sudden arrival.

Other dishes and drinks

Two more typical dishes deserve mention: one is the delicious **harira**, a soup which comes into its own during Ramadan, when it is used to break the day-long fast. Imagine virtually the whole of Morocco poised around the soup tureen waiting for the magical hour of sundown when consumption may begin. It is an appetising and nutritious soup made of chickpeas and lentils slow-cooked in stock, with or without the addition of mutton or chicken, and flavoured with lemon and fresh tarragon. Then there are the ubiquitous **brochettes**—kebabs of grilled mutton—and spicy meat balls, known as **kefta**, which turn up on all occasions and in all settings, from road-side stalls to 5-star hotels, often smelling better than they taste.

A variety of drinks, usually non-alcoholic, will be on hand to accompany the food. Coca-cola is universal, and so is locally-produced **mineral water**—*Oulmes* (fizzy), *Side Harazem* or *Sidi Ali* (both still)—which is good and healthy. Fresh orange juice will probably be available and there may also be **almond milk** (made by adding milk to ground almonds), a dry, refreshing drink which blends well with the quantities of meat one consumes.

In households accustomed to receiving foreign guests, and nowadays in all hotels and restaurants, Moroccan **wine** will be offered. Wine is produced in three districts: Berkane (near Oujda), Boulaouane (Casablanca) and Meknes. Local wines include Cabernet du President, Guerrouane, Beni Snassen and Valpierre (reds); Coquillages, Valpierre blanc de blanc, Oustalet and Chaudsoleil (whites); and Gris de Boulaouane (rosé). The whites in particular are very drinkable, and the best of the reds is Cabernet du President.

The best way to enjoy Moroccan food is in a family home. Failing that the various dishes may be sampled in the traditional Moroccan **restaurants**, notably in the medinas of Fes and Marrakesh or, to a limited extent, in tourist hotels and restaurants. (See the discussion of traditional restaurants on page

19). If you hope to sample the full gamut of dishes, it is necessary to order in advance and to go in a party of not less than four.

Another way of appreciating the food is, of course, to **cook it yourself**. Most dishes involve subtle blends of herbs and spices, such as coriander, cinnamon, cumin, ginger, fennel, sesame, thyme and cloves, all of which should be readily available wherever you are. There are now a number of good cookbooks dealing with Moroccan cuisine, enabling you to do just this; they include Robert Carrier's *A Taste of Morocco* and Mme Zette Guinaudeau's *Traditional Moroccan Cooking: Recipes from Fez*, which is available from Central Books, London E9 5LN, ☎ (0181) 986 4854.

Typical dishes

Mechoui, whole lamb roasted in a special oven (or on a spit if outdoors), served with spices and Arab bread.

Pastilla, a pie of flaky pastry containing pigeonmeat or chicken, almonds and hard-boiled eggs.

Poulet au citron (also called *tagine de poulet*), chickens casseroled with salted lemons and olives and saffron.

Tagine de mouton, mutton stew, with either prunes and nuts, or dates and almonds.

Chermoula, or *poisson à la Marocaine*, the marinade commonly used with fish, made with peppers, cumin, saffron, coriander, and parsley.

Couscous, granular semolina served in a mound and containing courgettes, carrots, turnips and, usually, mutton. Can also be served without vegetables or meat but with sugar and cinnamon added.

Kefta, spicy meat balls, usually mutton but can also contain offal.

Harira, thick creamy soup of chick peas, haricot beans and either mutton or chicken, often flavoured with lemon and tarragon.

Cornes de gazelle, delicate pastries stuffed with honey and almonds.

Select bibliography

History and general interest

Barbour, Neville, *Morocco* (Thames & Hudson, London, 1965). A readable and thoroughly reliable history of Morocco up to 1965. Particularly interesting on the country's struggle for independence.

Bovill, E.W., *The Golden Trade of the Moors* (second edition, Oxford, 1968). A colourful account of the 'silent trade' between Arab merchants from Morocco and the people of the Niger region during the 12C and 13C, when salt from the north was exchanged for gold from the south (see *The history of Morocco*, above).

Gaillard, Henri, *Une ville d'Islam: Fes* (Paris, 1905). Anyone seriously interested in Fes and its beginnings should read this scholarly book. Gaillard uses sources, mainly early Arab historians, to throw some light on the origins of this mysterious and highly complex city.

Bowles, Paul, *Their Heads are Green* (Jonathan Cape, London, 1963). Bowles vividly describes Moroccan souks and the art of bargaining.

Harris, Walter, *Morocco That Was* (Eland Books, 1921). Anyone visiting Morocco for the first time should read this book if nothing else. Harris was correspondent of the British newspaper *The Times* and lived in Morocco during the chaotic pre-Protectorate period at the turn of the century, managing to sustain the role of adviser and friend to no less than three sultans, Moulay el Hassan, Moulay Abd el Aziz, and Moulay Hafid. His insights into court life with its extravagances and unspeakable cruelties make compelling reading. It is true that subsequent writers have sometimes questioned the authenticity of his more outrageous first-hand accounts, particularly that of his imprisonment in Asilah by the legendary Berber chief, Raisuli. He does seem to have had an astonishing propensity for getting himself into trouble and escaping virtually unscathed.

Harris became particularly close to the young sultan, Abd el Aziz, who was catapulted into power at the tender age of 13. In referring to the sultan's miserable treatment of his soldiers, he blamed him to his face, risking instant dismissal or some far more grisly fate. The sultan's first reaction was one of anger. 'Remember,' he said, 'you are speaking to the Commander of the Faithful.' 'I do,' Harris replied. 'It is your majesty who forgets that these men *are* the faithful.' The sultan's look of anger passed into one of great sadness and he said, with tears in his eyes, 'You don't know how weary I am of being sultan.'

Hassan II, *Le Défi* (Michel, Paris, 1976). A justification of the Green March of 1975 (see *The history of Morocco*), written by the King of Morocco himself.

Herbert, David, *Second Son: An Autobiography* (Peter Owen, 1972). The author was a leading light in the expatriate social scene of Tangier. The book gives rare insights into the lives of the rich and famous of the 1920s and '30s but only the last chapter is about Tangier, in its days as an International Zone.

Landau, R. and Swaan W., *Morocco* (Elek Books, London, 1967). Rom Landau is always readable on Morocco and the photographs by Swaan are outstanding, including some of the mosque interiors that are forbidden to Western visitors.

Landau, R., *The Kasbahs of Southern Morocco* (Faber & Faber, London, 1969). A detailed study of life in an Atlas community.

Lane-Poole, Stuart, *The Barbary Corsairs*, (London, 1890). Adventurous and bloodthirsty account of the infamous Sallée Rovers.

Le Tourneau, Roger, *Fes avant le Protectorat* (Casablanca, 1949). A vivid and very informative description of life in Fes before the arrival of Western influences and the construction of the modern town by the French.

Le Tourneau, Roger, *La Vie Quotidienne à Fes en 1900* (Hachette, Paris, 1965). In similar vein to the above, with memorable descriptions of the domestic life of ordinary people at the turn of the century.

Lewis, Bernard, *The Arabs in History* (Oxford University Press, 1947). Effectively follows the Arabs through their turbulent history and successful expansionism, up to 1945.

Maxwell, Gavin, *Lords of the Atlas* (Longman, London, 1966). This book tells the story of the all-powerful Berber chieftains, the M'touggi, the Goundafi and, most notably, the Glaoui, who dominated the High Atlas up to and during the years of the French Protectorate. As far as the French were concerned, these legendary figures were performing the extremely useful task of keeping the unruly southern tribes in some sort of order. Thami el Glaoui caused the removal of the sultan, Mohammed V, into exile in 1953 and became known himself as 'the uncrowned king of the real Morocco', but he died in 1956, an exhausted and defeated man.

This work quotes heavily from first-hand accounts by Walter Harris and is compulsive reading particularly for anyone intending to visit Ouarzazate and the legendary Glaoui kasbah of Telouet nearby.

Mayne, Peter, *The Alleys of Marrakesh* (Penguin, 1953). Peter Mayne's account of his life with ordinary Moroccans in the heart of the Marrakesh medina in the early 1950s is quite delightful. The atmosphere, the smells and the sounds of the place are vividly recalled, and his one encounter with visiting English aquaintances in a smart hotel merely reinforces his desire to be back with his Moroccan friends, despite the living conditions. 'Derb esh-Shems—the alley of the sun—is not a very smart address, though one of the neighbours is said to have a lady relative who was once a Court favourite. There are no drains or piped water. The public water-point is in a main road that runs at right angles to our alley, near the ramparts. The pump is generally surrounded by neighbours' womenfolk, Berbers mostly, wives and daughters. It is an exclusively Muslim quarter and inhabited by poor people. The women at the water-point chaff me good-humouredly. Am I not married? Then why don't I get a *fiancée*? Then she could look after me. Who looks after me, who cooks? Must I really fetch the water myself? Why don't I get the water-carrier to bring me a skinful each day with his donkey?'

Mayne takes each day as it comes and manages to attain an enviable level of contentment. 'I am resolved never to run, not to walk always with a slow, measured tread, and that when I choose, or am actually compelled, to look to right or left, I shall do so calm and tranquil. I shall gear down my jittery European reactions to those of a Blue man riding his camel across the desert. I shall refuse to be hustled—why hurry? All the evidence about me points to the fact that it is for ever NOW. You can't go skipping into the future, however much you hustle. I shall be content, as the Moors are, with me in the centre of my universe and leave the universe to do the spinning.'

Meakin, Budgett, *The Moorish Empire* (London, 1899). One of the earliest English-language books on life in Morocco, this makes fascinating reading.

Mernissi, Fatima, *Doing Daily Battle*, translated by M.J. Lakeland (Women's Press, 1988). This book consists of interviews by a Moroccan sociologist with 11 very different Moroccan women, revealing the injustices they suffered at the hands of husbands, employers and officials. During the 1930s two of them lived in Fes in a prosperous harem, which is revealed 'not as a place of eroticism or pleasure but as a power structure which holds young girls prisoner'. A fascinating insight into an unknown world.

Pellow, Thomas, *The Adventures of T. Pellow* (Brown, London, 1890). Pellow was an English prisoner held in Meknes by the tyrannical sultan, Moulay Ismael. He escaped death by becoming a Muslim. Though probably exaggerated, his accounts of life in the royal apartments (after he had won the protection of the favourite queen), and of the fearful fates of fellow prisoners who did not renounce their religion, make gripping reading.

Porch, Douglas, *The Conquest of Morocco* (Jonathan Cape, 1986). This is a serious but most readable account of the years leading to and during, the French Protectorate. History is lightened by one or two vivid quotes from earlier writers such as Gerhard Rohlfs, on his first visit to Morocco in the 1860s, describing the Rif as 'a naked, steep, savage-looking rocky wall'.

Rogers, P. G., *A History of Anglo-Moroccan Relations to 1900* (London, Foreign & Commonwealth Office). A serious, factual, and somewhat dry, account of relations between England and Morocco in the early years, including the period covered by Rowth (see below).

Rowth, Emily, *Tangier, Britain's Last Outpost* (London, 1910). Few people know that Tangier was British for 22 years in the latter half of the 17C. This is a colourful account of the English army's occupation of the city and of its deprivations and suffering in the face of determined—and eventually successful—attacks by Moulay Ismael's forces.

Saint-Exupéry, Antoine de, *Courrier Sud / Southern Mail*. The author describes his experiences as a pilot for the French *Service Aéropostale* delivering mail to and from West African countries in the 1920s. Cap Juby (Tarfaya) and Villa Cisneros (Ad Dakhla) were important staging posts and Tarfaya commemorates Saint-Exupéry with a memorial on the beach.

Fiction

Bowles, Paul, *The Spider's House* (Arena/Black Sparrow Press, US). A political novel set in Fes in the last days of the French Protectorate, and a wonderful read.

Bowles, Paul, *The Sheltering Sky* (Granada/Ecco Press, 1955). Set in Algeria, and recently made into a film by Bernardo Bertolucci.

Choukri, Mohammed, *For Bread Alone. An Autobiography*, translated by Paul Bowles (City Lights, US)

Freud, Esther, *Hideous, Kinky* (Penguin, 1992). Another account of life amongst ordinary people, mainly in Marrakesh, and written from a child's point of view. The writer and her sister are dragged by their hippy mother from one house to another as she seeks the perfect place to live, and the perfect person to live with. An amusing and evocative read.

Mrabet, Mohammed, *Look and Move On*, translated by Paul Bowles (Peter Owen, London, 1989)

Mrabet, Mohammed, *The Big Mirror*, translated by Paul Bowles (Black Sparrow Press, US)

Islam

Koran, translated by N.J. Dawood (Penguin Books, London, latest revision, 1997) The intrinsic beauty of the word of God as revealed to Muhammad is apparent in this translation. There is a brief but useful introduction for the beginner and the chapters have been rearranged so that the shorter and more poetic surahs come before the longer, more complex ones that presuppose familiarity with events in the early days of Islam.

Guillaume, Alfred, *Islam* (Penguin Books, London, 1954). A straightforward account of the life of Muhammad and the expansion of Islam during his life, this book is particularly interesting regarding the holy revelations and the creation of the Koran, its philosophy and its creeds. Modern Islam (as at 1954) and its relation to Christianity are also treated.

Hamidullah, Muhammad, *An Introduction to Islam* (MWH Publishers, London, 1979). A useful book for all students of Islam.

Sarwar, Ghulam, *Islam. Beliefs and Teachings* (Muslim Education Trust, London, 1980). An attractive text book for young Muslims living in Britain. It deals with basic beliefs and duties of Islam, the life of Muhammad, sharia law and much else. An excellent primer for any beginner.

Savory, R.M., *Introduction to Islamic Civilisation* (Cambridge University Press, 1976). A scholarly and readable exposition of Islam.

Art and architecture

Hoag, John D., *Islamic Architecture* (Faber & Faber/Electa, 1975). Essential for anyone with a serious interest in religious architecture and the early influence of the Islamic countries on each other. The book is well illustrated and the close connections between architecture and Islam itself are clearly expounded.

Jereb, J.F., *Arts & Crafts of Morocco* (Thames & Hudson, 1996). An expensive but lavishly illustrated book containing fascinating insights into the origins of this important aspect of Moroccan life, and into the meaning of symbols as manifested particularly in Berber carpets.

Terrasse, C., *Medersas du Maroc* (Paris, 1928). A serious architectural study of the discovery and restoration of numerous *medersas* throughout the country.

Food

Carrier, Robert, *A Taste of Morocco* (Arrow Books, 1989). The most accessible and complete book of Moroccan recipes around.

Guinaudeau, Zette, *Traditional Moroccan Cooking: Recipes from Fez* (Serif, available from Central Books, London; see page 89).

Trekking

Smith, Karl, *The Atlas Mountains. A Walker's Guide* (Cicerone Press, 1989). Good walks in the Toubkal region, the M'Goun Massif, and Jbel Sarhro, described in detail.

Brown, Hamish, *The Great Walking Adventure* (Constable, 1987). A personal account of walking in the Atals mountains.

The Great Trek through the Moroccan Atlas (Moroccan National Tourist Office, Rabat, 1996). A very useful booklet, full of detailed itineraries, useful addresses and even names of mountain escorts. Available free of charge from OMNT offices abroad or in Morocco.

See also the list under *Sport and leisure activities*, above.

Language
Moroccan Arabic Phrasebook (Lonely Planet, Australia)
An Introduction to Moroccan Arabic (University of Michigan Press)
Breakthrough Arabic. The Complete Introductory Course for Colloquial Arabic (Macmillan, London, 1992)
Teach Yourself Quick and Easy Arabic (Langenscheidt/Hodder, 1992)

Flora and fauna
Polunin, O. and Huxley, A., *Flowers of the Mediterranean* (Oxford University Press)
Heinzel, Fitter and Parslow, *The Birds of Britain and Europe with North Africa and the Middle East* (Collins, UK; Stephen Green Press, US)
Bergier, Patrick and Fédora, *A Birdwatcher's Guide to Morocco* (Prion Ltd)
Haltenorth, T., and Diller, H., *A Field Guide to the Mammals of Africa* (Collins, UK; Stephen Green Press, US)

Language

Although **classical Arabic** is the language of education, the civil service and the media, the everday language of Morocco is dialectal, similar to that of Algeria and Tunisia, and is known as **Maghrebi Arabic**.

Berbers, who form 60 per cent of the population, speak one of three **Berber dialects**—Rifian, Braber or Chleuh—which are said to be mutually incomprehensible. Most Berbers also speak some Arabic.

Nearly all Moroccans, with the exception of the very old, the very young or the very isolated (desert nomads for example), speak some **French**, a legacy of the Protectorate, since when it has been taught in all schools, even the most remote. However, many people in the old Spanish Zone around Tetouan prefer to speak **Spanish** as French has only been taught there since Independence in 1956.

All the larger hotels and most of the tourist shops and restaurants are equipped with **English**-speakers. Many young people speak amazingly correct English which they probably pick up from watching television as much as they do from school. All official, and many unofficial, guides speak some English.

Although it is not strictly necessary for the short-term visitor to know any Arabic, an attempt to recognise and speak a few words of greeting can be rewarding and will undoubtedly give great pleasure.

Hello (informal)	*Labas*	
Peace be with you (formal hello)	*Salaam aleikum*	
Good morning	*Sbah l'khir*	
Good afternoon	*Msah l'khir*	
How are you?	*Ash h'barak?*	
Very well	*Mezian*	
Welcome	*Marhaba*	
Thank you (informal)	*Shokran*	
May the blessing of God be with you (formal thank you)		*Barak'allah oufik*
With God's blessing (often said before starting a meal)		*Bis m'allah*
Praise be to God (upon hearing good news)		*El hamdu lilla*
God willing (after expressing an intention)		*Insh'allah*
Goodbye		*B'slama*
Have a good journey, bon voyage		*Treq slama*
Sir		*Sidi*
Madam		*Lalla*
Yes, OK		*Waha*
No		*La*

Other useful words

good, nice, beautiful	*mezian*
not good, bad	*ma shi mezian*
little, small, a few	*chwiya*
a lot	*bezzef*
big	*kbir*
little	*sghrir*
more	*zid*

money	*floos*
I don't understand	*Ma f'hemshi*
What is this?	*Shnoo hada?*
How much?	*Bish'hal?*
today	*lyoom*
tomorrow	*ghedda*
watch out!	*balak/andak!*
one	*wahad*
two	*juge/tnine*
three	*tleta*
four	*arba*
five	*khamsa*
six	*setta*
seven	*sebta*
eight	*tmenya*
nine	*tse'ud*
ten	*achra*

Sunday	*el had*
Monday	*et tnine*
Tuesday	*et tleta*
Wednesday	*el arba*
Thursday	*el khemis*
Friday	*el jamai*
Saturday	*es sebt*

(equivalent months for 1998)

Mouharram	April–May
Safar	May–June
Rabai al Awal	June–July
Rabai Attani	July–August
Joumada Aloula	August–September
Joumada Attania	September–October
Rajab	October–November
Chaaban	November–December
Ramadan	December–January
Chaoual	January–February
Dou al Kida	February–March
Dou al Hijja	March–April

Glossary

AGADIR, a fortified grain silo

AGDAL, garden

AGUELMANE, lake

AID, feast

AIN, source, fountain, eye

AIT, sons, tribe

ALLAH, God

AZROU, rock

BAB, monumental gate

BABOUCHES, leather slippers with pointed toes and no heels

BALI, old, as in Fes el Bali

BARAKA, blessing, mystical power

BIT, room

BLED, countryside

BLED EL MAKHZEN, land under government control

BLED ES SIBA, land outside government control

BORDJ, fort

CAID, government official, district officer

CALDARIUM, hot room in Roman bath (Latin)

CHERIF, descendant of the Prophet Muhammad

COL, mountain pass (French)

DAR, house, dwelling arranged around a central patio

DAYET, lake

DIFFA, traditional Moroccan meal, usually at a festival

DJELLABAH, long, hooded outer garment

DJMAA, mosque or assembly; also Friday (as the day of prayer)

DOUAR, village or group of tents

FANTASIA, colourful display of Berber horsemanship

FASSI, someone born in Fes

FONDOUK, lodging house with space for livestock

FRIGIDARIUM, cold room in Roman bath (Latin)

FOUM, mouth of a river

GNAOUA, a religious brotherhood descendants of slaves brought back from sub-Saharan Africa—often seen in Marrakesh

HADJ, pilgrimage to Mecca; also a title for someone who has made the pilgrimage

HAIK, garment used by women to cover themselves in public

HAMMADA, stony desert

HAMMAM, public bath

HARAM, prayer hall in a mosque

HARKA, a tax-collecting raid carried out by sultans on towns and villages, especially in the south where rebellion was suspected

HEGIRA, flight of Muhammad from Mecca to Medina in 622, and the start of the Muslim era, reckoned in lunar years of twelve months

IBN, son

IMAM, a Muslim prayer leader

JBEL, mountain

JDID, new, as in Fes el Jdid

JORF, cliff

KASBAH, a chief's fortified residence in the south, a fortress of an Arab town

KHETTARA, irrigation channels underground

KIF, hashish, cannabis

KORAN, the word of God, dictated to the Prophet Muhammad

KOUBBA, small, white, domed building, tomb of a saint; see *marabout*

KSAR (pl. KSOUR), fortified village, houses clustered round a kasbah, especially in the south

KUFIC, Arabic script named after the town of Kufa, in Iraq

LALLA, term of respect for a woman, 'madam'

MA, water

MAGHREB, west, often used to describe North Africa

EL MAGHREB EL AQSA, furthest west, i.e. Morocco

MAKHZEN, government

MARABOUT, a saint or holy man, or his shrine

MECHOUAR, assembly area, space around a royal palace

MECHRA, dam

MEDERSA, religious college or students' boarding house

MEDINA, town: now used for the original, pre-Protectorate town, often medieval

MELLAH, Jewish quarter; literally 'salt', with which Jews dressed the heads of vanquished enemies

MENDOUB, representative of the sultan

MIHRAB, niche inside a mosque showing the direction of Mecca

MINARET, a mosque tower, used by the muezzin (see below)

MINBAR, pulpit in a mosque

MINZAH, pavilion, usually in a garden

MOULAY, descendent of the Prophet

MOULOUD, birthday of the Prophet

MOUSSEM, festival and/or pilgrimage in honour of a saint or holy man

MUEZZIN, prayer caller, usually from minarets

MUQARNAS, stalactitic vaulting, in mosques or palaces

MUSHRABIYYA, an interlaced wooden screen, used wherever privacy is required, particularly in mosques so that women can see but not be seen

NYMPHAEUM, Roman pleasure house, usually containing fountains and pools

OUED, stream or river

OULEMA, religious elder

PASHA, governor of a city

PISÉ, mud mixed with straw or rubble for building purposes (French)

PISTE, rough track (French)

RAMADAN, month of fasting

RAS, source or head

RIAD, an internal garden

SAHN, courtyard in a mosque

SHEIK, leader of a religious brother-hood

SIDI, term of respect for a man, 'sir'

SOUK, a stall in a market, or a whole market of stalls

TEPIDARIUM, warm room in a Roman bath (Latin)

TIZI, mountain pass

VIZIER, prime minister

ZAOUIA, religious retreat or cult centre

ZELLIGE, mosaic made of intricate ceramic or enamelled shapes, tile work

THE GUIDE

The North and West Coasts

Tangier

Tangier, so close to the southernmost tip of Europe, is for many tourists the first point of contact with Morocco. Its eventful history and its years as an International Zone have left it the most cosmopolitan and atypical of Moroccan cities. No longer the centre of political intrigue, Tangier now dedicates itself to tourism. Its advantages are a climate that is exceptionally temperate and sunny; beaches that face both the Mediterranean and the Atlantic; an atmospheric medina; and a flourishing modern town with graceful boulevards, good shops and restaurants. Its disadvantages are a somewhat bored attitude on the part of guides and some hotel and restaurant staff, who all too frequently give the impression that they have long since stopped trying to please; and a greater concentration of hustlers than any other Moroccan town. Nevertheless, Tangier is a good starting-point for journeys to Fes and Meknes to the south and the Rif mountains to the east.

History of Tangier

Tangier's origins are steeped in legend. One of the Labours of Hercules was to fetch a golden apple—guarded by the daughters of Atlas—from the Garden of the Hesperides, which was believed to have been near Lixus. In doing this Hercules managed to kill the evil giant Antaeus and then married his widow Tinge, in whose honour he built a city, which he named **Tingi** after her.

Tangier is one of the oldest urban settlements in Morocco. It was probably founded as a trading post by the Phoenicians c 1100 BC, along with Liks (Lixus), Russadir (Mellila), Tamuda, Chellah, and others. The Carthaginians turned all these into prosperous colonies, and some of them, Tingi in particular, built up sizeable fish-salting industries.

The Romans arrived after the destruction of Carthage in 146 BC and Tingi became **Tingis**. In AD 40 Tingis was made the capital of the province of Mauritania Tingitana, which was named after the city. Later, the seat of provincial government was moved to Volubilis where it remained until the end of the 3C, when the Romans returned in force to Tingis after abandoning Volubilis, probably in order to distance themselves from increasing pressure from Middle Atlas Berbers. This was, in fact, the first stage in their complete withdrawal from the province.

In the 7C Tingis was one of the first towns to fall prey to the unstoppable wave of **Arab invaders** who, in 683, under the leadership of Oqba ibn Nafi, began surging into Morocco from Kairwan in Tunis. It was from Tingis, now renamed Tangier, that Muslim armies departed soon after to begin the conquest of Spain. They were commanded by the man who was to give his name—Tarik—to the rock that stood between him and the mainland, and which is today known as Gibraltar (deriving from *jbel*, which means mountain, and Tarik). In the 11C the Almoravide sultan Youssef ibn Tachfine (1062–1107) also used Tangier as a base from which to cross the straits in order to pacify Andalusia. Four centuries later, Arab refugees chased out by the now victorious Spaniards returned through Tangier.

At the end of the 15C Tangier became Portuguese, then Spanish, then Portuguese again, until Princess Catherine of Braganza married Charles II of England, at which point the city was handed over, as part of her dowry, to **England**. From 1661 to 1683 the English flag was raised over Tangier, though the Alouite sultan Moulay Ismael tried, without success, to storm the city in 1679 and repeatedly thereafter. By 1683 the English soldiers had become so weakened by poor diet, insanitary conditions, lack of money and, above all, the frequent and determined attacks by Moulay Ismael, that they withdrew, but not without first destroying a large part of the port installation and the famous mole, the remains of which can still be seen, it is said, at low water. For a fascinating account of this period, read Emily Rowth's book, *Tangier, Britain's Last Outpost* and *A History of Anglo–Moroccan Relations to 1900* by P.G. Rogers.

In 1906, under the Treaty of Algeciras, Tangier was once again separated from the rest of the country and made an **international port**. It was governed by a legislative assembly of 27 members, of whom only six were Moroccan and the rest European, and each country brought with it its own currency and banks. It followed that Tangier gained a reputation—a shadow of which still remains thanks to the cinema—for smuggling, political intrigue and espionage. It also became exceedingly prosperous. Its international status lasted until 1956 when the French and Spanish Protectorates ended. The city's prosperity diminished but it became an attractive bolthole for the slightly tarnished élite of many nations. Now Tangier flourishes once again: this time it is the tourists who are bringing prosperity and hotels have sprung up everywhere to accommodate them.

■ Practical information

Tourist information. **ONMT**. 29 Blvd Pasteur. ☎ (09) 938 239.
Banks. Blvd Pasteur/Blvd Mohammed V.
Post office. 33 Blvd Mohammed V.
Air transport. Boukhalef Souahel Airport is 14km west of town. ☎ (09) 935 129. Flights to London, Montreal, New York, Paris, Madrid, and Gibraltar. There is no regular airport bus, but a *grand taxi* to the town centre costs 100dh, less if you share and negotiate.
Trains. The station is in Pl. de la Marche Verte (close to ferry terminal). ☎ (09) 934 570. Trains to Asilah, Rabat, Casablanca, Meknes, Fes, Marrakesh, and Oujda.

Ferries. Regular sailings to Algeciras and Tarifa (Spain), Gibraltar, and Sète (France). Tickets and timetables are available from travel agents in town or direct from the companies concerned, *viz.*:

Comanav, 43 Ave Abou Alla El Maari. ☎ (09) 932 649 (Algeciras).

Limadet, 13 Rue du Prince Moulay Abdallah. ☎ (09) 933 621 (Algeciras).

Comarit, 7 Rue du Mexique. ☎ (09) 931 220 (Algeciras).

Transtour, 4 Rue Jabha Al Ouatania. ☎ (09) 934 004 (Tarifa, Gibraltar).

Transmediterranea, 31 Ave de la Resistance. ☎ (09) 936 745 (Sète).

Buses and taxis leave from Sahat Al Jamia Al Arabia. ☎ (09) 946 682. Bus services to Rabat and Casablanca, Tetouan, Ceuta, Meknes, Fes etc.

Hotels

Hôtel El Minzah, 85 Rue de la Liberté. ☎ (09) 935 885 fax (09) 934 546. *****L (100 rooms). The best, if you can afford it, combining sea views with proximity to both the medina and the new town. It has a lovely Andalusian-style interior courtyard and an excellent Moroccan restaurant (see below).

Hôtel Les Almohades, Ave des F.A.R. ☎ (09) 940 026 fax (09) 946 371. *****A (150 rooms). Typical of the huge, palatial hotels on the seafront. Fine for package tours wanting instant access to the beach.

Hôtel Solazur, Ave des F.A.R. ☎ (09) 946 897 fax (09) 945 286. ****B (360 rooms). As above, but even bigger. A sumptuous interior with a resplendent spiral staircase.

Hôtel Tanja Flandria, 6 Blvd Mohammed V. ☎ (09) 933 279 fax (09) 934 347. ****A (151 rooms). In the centre of the new town, 10min walk from the beach and 15min from the medina. Has a pool on the roof.

Hôtel Rembrandt, corner of Blvd Mohammed V and Blvd Pasteur. ☎ (09) 937 870. ***A (80 rooms). Equally central but more modest in size and price. No pool, but recommended.

Hôtel Continental, 36 Rue Dar El Baroud (medina). ☎ (09) 931 024. **A (57 rooms). This stylish, turn-of-the-century hotel was once the best in Tangier. The rooms are a little shabby now but the service is good and there is still a grand piano in the hall. It has a terrace overlooking the port, which it stands just behind.

Restaurants

Unlike the imperial cities of Marrakesh, Fes and Rabat—or even Casablanca—Tangier has very few memorable restaurants. The following are cautiously recommended.

Restaurant Raihani, 10 Rue Ahmed Chaouki (opposite the Mirador by Place de France). ☎ (09) 934 866. Good Moroccan food, moderately priced.

Restaurant Romero, 12 Ave Prince Moulay Abdallah. ☎ (09) 932 277. A Spanish fish restaurant. Paella and lobster.

Restaurant Matisse, 10 Rue Velasquez. ☎ (09) 330 128. French food. A sophisticated atmosphere with music. Pricey.

La Grenouille, 3 Rue El Jabha El Ouatania (ex-Rue Rembrandt). ☎ (09) 936 242. Very French.

Hôtel El Minzah (see above) The Moroccan restaurant, *El Korsan*, in particular is outstanding and worth saving up for.

Restaurant Andalos, 7 Rue du Commerce (medina). This unlikely-looking place near the Petit Socco serves some of the best grilled fish in town and is extremely cheap (see below).

Restaurant Marhaba Palace, 67 Rue de la Kasbah. ☎ (09) 937 643. An atmospheric old palace serving good Moroccan food.

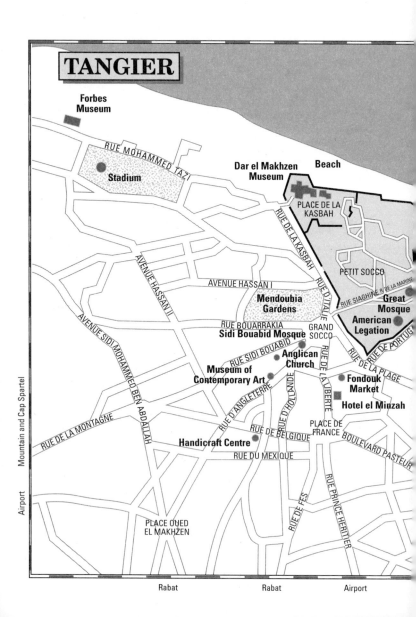

TANGIER

Forbes Museum

Stadium

RUE MOHAMMED TAZI

Dar el Makhzen Museum

Beach

PLACE DE LA KASBAH

AVENUE HASSAN II

AVENUE HASSAN I

RUE DE LA KASBAH

RUE D'ITALIE

PETIT SOCCO

RUE SIAGHINE

RUE DE LA MARINE

Great Mosque

Mendoubia Gardens

RUE BOUARRAKIA

Sidi Bouabid Mosque

GRAND SOCCO

American Legation

RUE DE PORTUG

AVENUE SIDI MOHAMMED BEN ABDALLAH

RUE SIDI BOUABID

Anglican Church

Museum of Contemporary Art

RUE DE

RUE DE LA PLAGE

Fondouk Market

Hotel el Minzah

RUE D'ANGLETERRE

RUE DE HOLLANDE

RUE DE LA LIBERTE

PLACE DE FRANCE

RUE DE LA MONTAGNE

Handicraft Centre

RUE DE BELGIQUE

BOULEVARD PASTEUR

RUE DU MEXIQUE

Mountain and Cap Spartel

Airport

PLACE OUED EL MAKHZEN

RUE DE FES

RUE PRINCE HERITIER

Rabat   Rabat   Airport

Campsites

Camping Tingis, on the way to Cap Malabata alongside the Oued Moghoga lagoon, 2km from the beach. Snack bar, restaurant, swimming pool, showers, and laundry.

Camping Sahara, 300m from beach. Facilities as above.

Camping Miramonte, 1km from beach. Snack bar, pool, showers, and laundry.

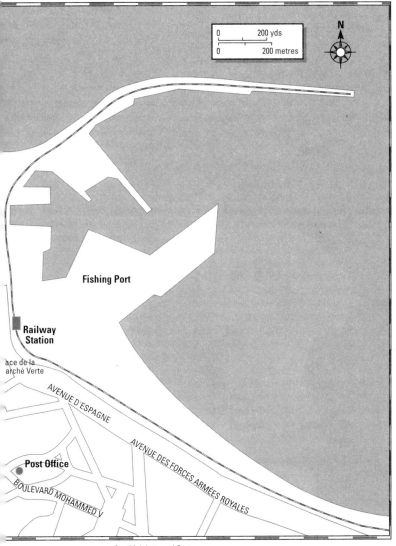

Cap Malabata and Ceuta

A tour of the city

The best place to begin a tour of Tangier is the **Grand Socco**—a large and very busy open square which is supposed to have been the site of the Roman forum and now occupies a strategic position between the new town (*ville nouvelle*) and the medina. There are two main objects of interest here: one is the distinctive multi-coloured minaret of the **Sidi Bouabid Mosque**; the other is the extraordinary **banyan tree** just inside the Mendoubia gardens, which is thought to be 800 years old.

The **Mendoubia Palace**, once the residence of the sultan's representative (*Mendoub*), now houses the tribunal (lawcourts) and cannot be visited. The gardens, however, are open when the court is not in session. It is worthwhile going in to take a look both at the tree and at the broad view of the medina and fishing port from the terrace. All but two of the fine 17C and 18C cannons—Portuguese, Spanish, Dutch and French—which once rested here have been moved to the Mirador just off the Place de France (see below). **Open** after 15.00 Mon–Thur, Sat, all day Sun; closed Fri.

To enter the **medina**, leave Grand Socco at its northern end via Rue Semmarine.

Turn immediately right and continue downhill along the Rue Siaghine ('Street of the Silversmiths') to a small, busy square flanked by café terraces and known as the **Petit Socco**. This has become a place where enterprising street traders creep up behind you as you sip your expensive Coca Cola and whisper 'Look—Woolworth's price!' in perfect English. Just go a few metres up one of the narrow side streets to escape them. These side streets contain the cheaper and more authentic restaurants (such as the *Restaurant Andalos* in the Rue du Commerce), where freshly-caught fish will be charcoal-grilled to perfection and served up with a crisp green salad at less than half the price you would pay at one of the more sophisticated fish restaurants in the centre or by the beach.

Tangier – the medina

If you cross the Petit Socco and take the Rue de la Marine northeastwards, you will find the **Great Mosque**, with its fine green-and-white minaret. It was built by Moulay Ismael at the end of the 17C to celebrate the withdrawal of the English from the city. Continue down this street and you come to **Bab el Moussa**, where the terrace has a very fine view over the port towards Cap Malabata.

Return to the Petit Socco and turn up one of the narrow and enticing alleyways which lead towards the heart of the medina. These streets are crammed with every kind of shop and bazaar, selling ornaments in silver, gold, brass and copper, or silks and wools, or leather goods. Here and there, in quiet contrast with all the commercial bustle, are Berber women wearing traditional costume—red-and-white striped skirts and straw hats decorated with plaited wool and pom-poms—sitting alongside their wares of goat cheese, brooms and onions, which they have brought by donkey from the mountain villages. Then there are bakers crouching in the shadows over their wood-fired ovens: customers bring their own dough to be baked. The round, flat loaves are quite delicious and the ideal accompaniment to Morocco's rather spicy food. You will also notice old men sitting against the walls twisting strands of brightly coloured silk or wool, ready to be woven into kaftans.

One of the great charms of the medina in Tangier is the opportunity it affords for glimpses of bright blue sea between white and shadowed walls; another is the preponderance of very beautiful old mosques (the one in Place Aissaoua dates back to 1263), with minarets that are miniature replicas of Sidi Bouabid on the Grand Socco.

If you keep on going uphill, you will eventually arrive at the **kasbah**—the fortified part of the medina and now one of the most sought-after residential areas of Tangier, where traditionally-styled modern mansions, looking almost too perfect to be true, are packed comfortably in amongst older buildings. The **Place de la Kasbah** is the highest point in the medina, and its terrace faces the sea with good views of Jbel Tarik (Gibraltar) and the Spanish coast.

The square is dominated by the great white bulk of the **Royal Palace (Dar el Makhzen)**, built by Moulay Ismael. It was occupied earlier this century when the deposed sultan, Moulay Hafid, was allowed to live here after signing the Treaty of Fes in 1912. It now houses a **museum** which has good examples of 17C and 18C craftmanship and marble columns from Volubilis in the courtyard. The rooms around the courtyard contain the museum and have some particularly fine, hand-carved cedarwood ceilings painted in soft colours. The mosaic floors, marble columns and bare white walls are a perfect background to the display of old carpets, traditional furniture from Fes, ceramics, jewellery, leather, and ornamented daggers. Behind the museum, the sultan's garden is open to visitors and is full of orange and lemon trees, jacarandas, palms, and strongly perfumed datura. Overlooking the garden is the somewhat over-priced *Café-Restaurant Detroit* which offers exceptional views of the sea on one side and of the medina on the other. **Open** every day except Fri; entry 10dh.

Next door to the museum and accessible from the Place de la Kasbah through a separate entrance is the former **Treasury** (*Bit al Mal*), very recently restored and containing a number of large wooden chests, an 18C balance and a heavy door with three separate bolts.

Whilst in the area, you may wish to continue westwards along the coast road (15min on foot, 5min by car or taxi) to a very different sort of museum established by the late millionaire publisher, Malcolm Forbes, for his unique collection of over 100,000 military miniatures. In the **Forbes Museum** are re-enacted the Battle of the Three Kings (1578) at Ksar el Kbir, in which the Portuguese suffered a major defeat, and the battles of Waterloo (1815) and the Somme (1916), amongst others. The more recent Green March (1975), when 350,000 Moroccans marched into the disputed Western Sahara, is also featured. This exhibition is highly recommended, particularly since it is housed in a sumptuous palace set in delightful gardens. There is no entry charge, the collection having been bequeathed to Tangier by Forbes before his death in 1990. **Open** 09.00–17.00; closed Sat, Sun.

Five minutes' walk along the coast road from the Forbes Museum is the remote **Café Hafa**, perched on a terrace halfway down the cliff and a romantic spot, if ever there was one, in which to take a mint tea overlooking the ocean. The American writer Paul Bowles is said to have come here quite often. (Do not make the mistake, as we did, of driving down; there is nowhere to park and nowhere to turn either.)

For a different—and quicker—route back to the Grand Socco from the Place de la Kasbah, take the Rue de la Kasbah which skirts the medina. The street descends in steep steps and becomes the Rue d'Italie, which has more fine sea views and glimpses of ancient minarets. It is lined with typical Mediterranean houses with wrought-iron grilles over the windows.

The **Ville Nouvelle** (new town) begins at the southern end of the Grand Socco. Walk down Rue de la Liberté towards **Place de France**, the busy, café-strewn town centre. On the way, notice the stepped street on the left, just before the *Hôtel El Minzah*. This leads to a **fondouk market** consisting, it seems, of stalls selling everything from fruit and vegetables to radio parts. Take the second turning on the right to find a real *fondouk*—a former lodging-house for visiting merchants (pack animals were accommodated below and people on the first floor) built around a central patio. Push your way through the crowds to the centre for some real atmosphere and maybe a bargain or two.

If you continue on down the stepped street over a square and into the Rue de Portugal, you come to a fascinating relic of the past—the old **American Legation**, now a museum. Turn left through a white arch opposite a taxi rank and you are suddenly in a maze of narrow, uncrowded alleyways, discreetly signposted to *Zankat America*. Morocco was the first country to recognise the independent United States of America in 1776 and this former palace was presented by the then sultan as a residence for the new diplomatic representative. The museum contains correspondence between George Washington and Sultan Moulay Abdallah and a rare collection of old maps, and the building is worth a look in its own right. **Open** 10.00–13.00 and 15.00–17.00 Mon, Wed, Thur, or by appointment. ☎ (09) 935 317.

Return to Rue de la Liberté, cross it and continue up the road facing you to reach Rue d'Angleterre and the strikingly English sight of the **Anglican Church of St Andrew**, still used for Sunday morning worship by a much-diminished

British colony. The cemetery is the final resting place of Walter Harris correspondent of *The Times* newspaper at the turn of the century, leading authority on pre-Protectorate Morocco and author of *Morocco That Was*, essential reading for any serious student of the country. Here too is the grave of Sir John Drummond Hay, a distinguished Consul General (1845–86). Just up the road is the old British Consulate General, which has recently been turned into Tangier's **Museum of Contemporary Art**. It is devoted exclusively to Moroccan art, and is well worth a look. The building has sadly decayed since its heyday, though the gardens retain a certain dishevelled charm. **Open** 09.00–12.00 and 15.00–18.00 daily; closed Tues; entry 10dh.

Next door is the *Grand Hôtel Villa de France*, a somewhat faded palace set in romantic gardens and currently closed for refurbishment. Its quality of peace coupled with its relatively central position within easy walking distance of the medina made it the author's preferred hotel, but who knows what 'refurbishment' will bring. Opposite, at No. 42 Rue d'Hollande, is a new and glistening white hotel, the *Ziryab*, which is part of a complex of shops and restaurants. There is a *salon de thé* above the hotel with a terrace offering a splendid view over the medina and all its minarets, and the somewhat incongruous-looking tower of the Anglican church on the left.

A short distance west of Rue d'Hollande (about 5min by car along Rue de la Montagne) is the fashionable and sought-after residential quarter known as the **Mountain**. Here are elegant houses built to every kind of fantasy and design, well spaced between masses of shrubs and beautiful gardens. The Mountain is in fact just a small hill with a superb sea view. Many rich Europeans retire here. Amongst the many sumptuous residences are a palace of King Hassan II, occupied by his mother until her recent death, and a palace newly created for the Saudi royal family; both are heavily guarded and unapproachable. The Mountain can be included as part of an excursion to Cap Spartel (see below).

To reach the **old fishing port**, return to the Grand Socco and leave it by the steep and narrow Rue de la Plage (Costa de la Playa). This animated street is packed full of restaurants and cheap pensions. The elaborate *art deco* façades of the *Hôtel Familiale de Talavera* and the Gran Teatro Cervantes (1913) give it an unmistakably Spanish flavour. The port is extremely colourful and lively, often crowded with hundreds of small craft, particularly at 05.00, when the boats come in, or at sundown, when they prepare to leave.

Next to the port is the town **beach**—a vast expanse of fine sand—which is very safe because it is in a bay. During summer it becomes extremely crowded. It is backed by a seemingly endless complex of cafés, changing cabins, casinos, and so on. In the season you are obliged to change in a cabin (there are policemen who check that this rule is complied with). For more isolated bathing you can go west or east and still benefit from the calming influence of the bay. Outside the bay, however attractive and peaceful the beaches look, the Atlantic becomes a treacherous enemy with strong unpredictable currents, undertows and rough breakers. Behind the line of cafés is a promenade, behind this the railway line, then the Avenue des Forces Armées Royales, and then the hotels—tall white giants, impersonal, expensive and largely designed for group tourism.

Take any street away from the beach and you will find yourself once more back in the new town in the general area of Place de France or Boulevard Pasteur which runs off it, and contains not only the ONMT but also a range of useful shops, travel agents, car-hire firms and the main post office.

Excursions from Tangier

About 14km east of Tangier lies **Cap Malabata** with good beaches and exceptional views of the Rif Mountains on one side, of the Spanish coast and the Rock of Gibraltar on the other, and back towards Tangier nestling in the bay. This once peaceful, gorse-covered spot is now undergoing major **tourist development** with holiday villages, hotels, apartments and a marina in various stages of completion. The Moroccan government also has grandiose plans for a bridge connecting the cape with Tarifa in Spain. We are assured by the Tourist Board that feasibility studies have been carried out and that now it is 'simply a question of money'. In connection with this a motorway network is planned to link the main cities of Tangier, Rabat, Casablanca, Marrakesh, Fes and Meknes.

East of Cap Malabata a picturesque and still unspoilt road winds its way to the old Portuguese fishing port of Ksar es Srir (Little Fortress), and continues on to Jbel Moussa and Ceuta.

Cap Spartel lies 11km west of Tangier. It is accessible either by continuing along the road over the Mountain (see above), or by making a short detour from the main Tangier–Rabat road. Known in Roman times as Ampelusium or 'Cape of the Vines', Cap Spartel has an impressive lighthouse (entry prohibited) with a beacon that can be seen at a range of 80km. All around the lighthouse are stalls selling tourist trivia and there is a somewhat sad café-restaurant which has definitely known better times. The fine sandy beaches around the cape are now backed by an assortment of holiday villas but very little in the way of cafés or bars.

A further 4km brings you to the **Caves of Hercules**, a series of natural caves famous for the production of millstones, which have been quarried there since prehistoric times. Despite their name, the caves have nothing to do with the mythical 'Pillars of Hercules': it is now commonly held that the two 'pillars' are the Rock of Gibraltar and Monte Hacho at Ceuta, although some identify Jbel Moussa as one of them, especially as it has a similar form to the Gibraltar rock.

It is possible to enter the caves—with a guide—to study the weird formations of stalactites and stalagmites and to gaze into the deep pools of black water far below. It is all rather eerie, and sometimes beautiful as you catch a glimpse of the raging sea through a jagged opening. Outside the caves men chip at hunks of stone to fashion crude figures of animals and birds for sale. Quite a little resort is growing up around the caves, with shops, hotels, apartments, a campsite and even a health farm.

A little further along the road (a 15min walk from the car park at the caves) a track bears off right towards the beach and the ruins of **Cotta**, a 3C Roman settlement built over a Phoenician fish-salting factory. Like so much of Morocco's earliest heritage, this site stands neglected, seriously overgrown and unsignposted. Little boys will undoubtedly appear out of nowhere to indicate a temple arch (lying on the ground), a small courtyard, an olive press, fish storage tanks and a watercourse.

Hotels
Hôtel Robinson, near the Caves of Hercules. ☎ (09) 938 765. ***A (116 rooms). A lovely sea view and a good restaurant, *Le Mirage*.

Restaurants
Le Mirage, part of the *Hôtel Robinson* (see above). Good Moroccan or international food in a lovely setting.

Campsites
Robinson Plage, in a woodland setting, close to the Caves of Hercules and the hotel of the same name.

The road from Tangier to Rabat
The **main road** (P2) leaves Tangier from the Place de France, passing turnings to both the international airport and the Cap Spartel coast road mentioned above. The total distance between Tangier and Rabat is 277km, less if you take the new motorway which starts at Larache and continues as far as Kenitra, with one exit *en route* for Moulay Bousselham. The intention is that it will one day start in Tangier itself and eventually join up with the existing motorway from Rabat to Casablanca. It is a toll road (*péage*) and, at time of writing, almost completely empty. Nevertheless there are radar traps at both ends to catch anyone travelling over 120kph.

Asilah
Built on the foundations of the old Phoenician city of *Silis*, Asilah lies 46km southwest of Tangier. Today it is a charming white town by the seashore. The old part is enclosed within 15C Portuguese-built walls with two fine gates, the **Bab el Bahar** (Sea Gate) and **Bab el Jbel** (Mountain Gate). If you follow the signs for the *Centre Ville* you will come to Bab el Bahar where there is a convenient car park. Walk through the *bab* and along the path that follows the shore as far as the pier, from which there is a good view back over the ramparts and, in the foreground, the ancient cemetery and the **Koubba of Sidi Marzouk**, a local saint. Before reaching the pier, you pass on the left the **Palace of the Caid Ahmad er Raisuni** (who was also known as Raisuli), overlooking the sea.

A Berber tyrant
Raisuli was a legendary figure in his own time. He was so powerful that, at the beginning of their Protectorate, the Spanish deemed it wise to leave him alone and allowed him to retain his authority over the wild Berbers of the Western Rif, who without him would doubtless have become quite uncontrollable. He was a very cruel leader and allegedly forced malefactors to jump to their death from the windows of his palace on to the jagged rocks 30m below. One of his victims is said to have cried, 'Your justice is great, Sidi, but these rocks will be more merciful.' Raisuli was eventually taken prisoner by the much more progressive and less self-indulgent leader of the Rif Berbers, Abd el Krim, who for a time seemed to be succeeding in forcing the Spaniards back into the sea.

Raisuli's palace was built in 1908 and has two storeys of richly decorated rooms around a central courtyard. It is now used every August for an arts festival featuring music, painting and poetry. The murals that somewhat surprisingly decorate much of the medina have been created in the past by grateful artists connected with the festival. The **medina**, which stretches behind the palace, is charming: small, clean and full of local activity; the *trompe l'oeil* effect of doors and windows painted on blank white walls makes for added interest.

The **beaches** of Asilah are tempting, with immense stretches of sand as far as the eye can see, and there are numerous organised campsites.

The **Cromlech de M'Zorah** lies some 16km south of Asilah. It is—or once was—a prehistoric burial mound encircled by standing stones; since its excavation in 1935 it is now little more than a series of holes, though the tallest stone of all still stands, and it is arguably not worth the effort. It is not at all easy to find: take a side road off the P37 to Tetouan (a short distance from the junction with the P2) signposted to the village of Souk el Tnine Sidi Yamani; from here a rough track leads to the site and local people are usually happy to guide you to it.

Lixus

The important archaeological site of Lixus is located at the mouth of the river **Loukkos**, 2km northeast of Larache (see below). Since it is not signposted at all, many people drive straight past it. Look for a right-hand turn off the P2 marked *Plage Ras R'Mal* and pull off the road by some green railings on the right. Lixus lies above you.

History of Lixus

Like Tangier, Lixus is connected to the legend of **Hercules**, for the Garden of the Hesperides, to which the hero was sent—as his penultimate labour— in search of the golden apples (perhaps to be interpreted as tangerines), is thought to lie somewhere in the fertile region behind the site.

Lixus is one of the best-preserved of the trading posts set up along the coast of North Africa by the Phoenicians around 1100 BC. Lixus (or **Liks** as it then was) developed a thriving fish-salting industry. The Carthaginians later refined the salting process and produced a fish paste known as *garum*. The Romans came in the 1C BC, chased the Carthaginians into the sea, and probably took over the factories, the remains of which can be seen today right by the road, comprising 147 storage vats and sundry wells and water cisterns. Below them would have been the port, for in those days the sea came right up to this part of the promontory.

The main evidence of Roman occupation lies up the hill, and it is well worth scrambling up the rough path to see it. (It takes about 1hour to cover all the sites.) There are traces of Phoenician building—huge, very carefully cut rectangular stones—and the Roman remains include, notably, an amphitheatre and a bath with a well-preserved **mosaic** depicting a wild and glaring figure of Neptune. The **amphitheatre**, the only known example of this kind of structure in Morocco, would have been used for gladiatorial contests either between men or between men and wild beasts, probably including lions from the Middle Atlas. Above the amphitheatre is a confusion of walls and foundations which seem to include a forum (with stumps of columns), several temples, a single-naved Christian church and a mosque. A few solitary cypresses lend the scene a romantic air but one is struck by the all too obvious neglect of this interesting site. Many of the artefacts have been taken to museums, in particular the Archaeological Museum in Tetouan, but there must be much more to discover. Lixus lies uncared for, except by one or two devoted but very nearly incomprehensible 'guides', one of whom will certainly appear the moment you arrive. He will at least ensure that you leave nothing out.

Larache is a pleasant fishing town with strong Spanish overtones and a stormy history. Today it is an important port for tuna fishing, but once it prospered from the construction of pirate ships for the infamous Sallée Rovers based in Rabat and Salé, using wood from the Forest of Mamora to the south. The Spaniards occupied Larache for a time in the 17C, and they built the **Château des Cigognes** (Castle of the Storks) which so picturesquely dominates the town.

The Alouite sultan Moulay Ismael reclaimed the town in the early 18C and much of the small medina was built at that time, as was the kasbah which crowns the town on the seaward side. When the Spanish returned in 1912 Larache became an important port for the Protectorate and it was at this time that much of the Spanish character was added, including many hotels and bars, the cathedral and the main square, once Plaza de España, now Place de la Libération. There is a fine **beach** to the north of the town, much used by Moroccan holiday-makers.

Larache marks the beginning of the new **motorway** towards Rabat, mentioned at the beginning of this section.

Accessible from the motorway or by several minor roads from the P2, **Moulay Bousselham** is worth visiting not so much for the village itself—which only comes to life every July for its annual religious festival—as for the lagoon it overlooks which adjoins one of Morocco's richest protected wetlands, known as **Merdja Zerga**. Go down a track marked '*Camping-Caravanning*' to reach the mudflats and reedbeds, where a host of tiny blue boats compete to take you out to islands to see colonies of flamingoes, terns and the rarer sorts of gull. Closer at hand egrets, often roosting in the oleanders, herons, oyster catchers and black-winged stilts. The whole extensive area is a delight and the blue boats are part of the picture, which can be observed in comfort from the terrace of a brand new café-restaurant called *Izaguirre*. Better still, spare half a day and go out in a boat. There is a small hotel in the village called *Le Lagon*.

Inland from the lagoon is a game reserve of 34,805ha, a third of which is accessible to tourists. There is wild boar, hare, pheasant and, above all, snipe; locals claim that this is some of the world's best snipe shooting. The reserve is best approached from **Arbaoua** to the east (on the P2). The hotel-restaurant there—*Hostellerie Route de France* (13 rooms)—provides hearty, reasonably priced food and exudes a strong French hunting-lodge atmosphere with its dark panelled dining-room and trophies all around. There is also a campsite.

Ksar el Kbir

Ksar el Kbir lies 12km northeast of Moulay Bousselham. It was built on the foundations of the Roman settlement of Oppidum Novum by the the Almohade sultan Yacoub el Mansour in the 12C. He gave it its Arab name, which means 'Great Fortress'. Both Spain and Portugal coveted this town, and the famous **Battle of the Three Kings**—in which the Portuguese suffered a major defeat, losing the cream of their aristocracy at a stroke—took place here in 1578. Ksar el Kbir flourished proudly until, in the 17C, Sultan Moulay Ismael was annoyed by the local caid and sent his troops to destroy the walls, a sad insult to a town which for centuries had held an honoured place in Morocco's history.

It never prospered again though the Spaniards injected some fresh life during the Protectorate. Today it is an active market town living off the produce of the fertile agricultural land which surrounds it. The main street is always animated and full of heavily laden donkeys, of men arguing about prices, and of women moving stealthily, covered from head to foot in white robes, often with only one eye showing. The town is now bypassed by the P2 but can make an interesting stopping-place on the long journey between Tangier and Rabat for anyone taking that route, especially on Sunday, which is market day.

Between Ksar el Kbir and Arbaoua is the old **frontier post** which used to separate the French and Spanish zones during the years of the Protectorate. It was only partially destroyed in 1956 when Independence was granted to Morocco and it stands as a depressing monument to those difficult days, surrounded by a posse of basketware and pottery stalls.

Souk el Arba du Gharb, 37km south of Ksar el Kbir, is a sprawling market town, particularly busy on Wednesdays when it has its weekly souk. Its produce comes from the great Gharb plain, one of the most fertile areas in the whole of Morocco, producing cereals, oranges, olives, rice and tobacco.

More Roman remains

The Roman site of **Banasa** (established 3C BC) is to be found—with difficulty—some 16km south of Souk el Arba. Follow the P2 as far as Souk Tleta du Gharb and then turn left on to a minor road which soon crosses the river Sebou. At a T-junction 2km further on, turn left and after 2.6km turn left again along a track, which is signposted '*Ruinas*' only to those coming in the

Roman site at Banasa

opposite direction. Carry on towards a clearly visible white *koubba*: the ruins lie below it.

The site is very extensive. A 'guide' will appear, as if by magic, as soon as you arrive, and will point out in a mixture of languages the scant remains of arches, millstones, hypocausts and so on. There are also traces of mosaic, but anything worth seeing has recently been removed to museums. One is little the wiser at the end of the tour and saddened by evident neglect. Information on Banasa can be found in the various museums to which its artefacts have been removed (the Museum of Antiquities in Rabat in particular), but none is available on site.

Another Roman site, probably contemporary with Banasa but even less interesting to the general visitor, is **Thamusida**. It too is hard to find and arguably not worth the effort except to a specialist. It lies some 12km north of Kenitra and can be approached by way of the P2. Coming southwards, turn right at a petrol station at El Khemis. After about 2km follow the middle one of three tracks and look, once more, for a *koubba* which overlooks the site. Here again, anything of value has been removed and you are left with almost unidentifiable remains of walls and baths.

Kenitra, 39km north of Rabat, is a noisy, rather untidy industrial town with little of aesthetic or historical interest. Developed and modernised by the French at the beginning of the Protectorate, and known then as Port Lyautey, it is now very much second in importance to Casablanca as a port. Its main function is as an outlet for the produce of its hinterland—fruit, wine (from the Meknes region), vegetables and cereals. It also has a large fish cannery. Until the onset of the Gulf War, it was used by the Americans as a naval and military base.

Lying just 12km north of Rabat at Sidi Bouknadel, the **Plage des Nations** is easily the most spectacular beach in the region. Indeed it looks from above like a whole coastline, with virgin sand and Atlantic rollers as far as you can see. It is a refreshing experience to walk along the sand in the cool season and in high summer it is much frequented by the international set keen to escape the city heat. However, there are treacherous undercurrents and swimming is really only for the brave. The *Hôtel Firdaous*, which overlooks the beach, has a pool which is open to non-residents for a small charge.

Les Jardins Exotiques lie between the Plage des Nations and Rabat and should not be missed: they make a pleasant excursion from Rabat, if there is no time *en route*. In the early 1950s an enterprising Frenchman struck water here and decided to create an area of tropical rainforest with paths, wooden huts on stilts and swinging bridges at tree-branch level. The gardens were somewhat neglected during the 1980s but have recently been revived and improved by the government. There is much of serious interest to botanists and children find it endlessly fascinating to follow the discreetly marked paths through the various gardens. Every space is miraculously filled to overflowing with lush growth—a satisfying contrast with the generally arid landscape surrounding the Tangier–Rabat road. **Open** 09.00–18.30; entry 10dh.

Rabat

Rabat is both an ancient imperial city and a modern administrative capital, and manages to combine the trappings of both with remarkable success. It is the permanent residence of the monarch, the seat of government and home to over 80 foreign embassies. Its remarkable historic treasures, which are to be found both inside and outside the ancient ramparts, are well cared for, and from the visitor's point of view Rabat is small and easy to get around. Its main attractions are the Kasbah of the Oudaias, the medina, the Hassan Tower and Chellah. The Museum of Antiquities in the new town (the *ville nouvelle*) should not be missed and the Mechouar is a bonus if time permits.

History of Rabat

The first occupants of Rabat are believed to have been the Phoenicians, closely followed by the Carthaginians who established trading posts in the estuary of the Bou Regreg river. In the 1C AD the Romans built a port on the site today known as Chellah (see below), which they called **Sala Colonia** and which became one of the southernmost outposts of their empire in North Africa.

After the departure of the Romans, the **Berbers** set up an independent state here that reached its apogee in the 8C and which was perceived as a threat to orthodox Islam at a time when the Idrisside dynasty was establishing its power base in Fes. The Idrissides accordingly moved in and set up a fortified camp—a *ribat*—on the site of the present-day Kasbah of the Oudaias, from which to control the Berbers. This led to the eventual demise of the Berber state, many of whose inhabitants moved across the river to **Salé**. Their departure coincided with the arrival of the first Almohade sultan, Abd el Mumene (1133–63), who rebuilt the original *ribat* and used it as a base from which to conduct his campaigns into Andalusia. His grandson, Yacoub el Mansour, later made the *ribat* his capital, extending it and erecting ramparts around it, some of which still exist, and the town became known as **Ribat el Fath** (Camp of Victory).

In thankfulness for his splendid victory over the Spaniards at Alarcos in 1195, Yacoub el Mansour (*el Mansour* means 'the Conqueror') started to build in Rabat a mosque which was to have been of such vast dimensions that his whole army could pray inside it at one time. But he died before it was finished and today only stumps of the columns bear witness to the enormity of his dream. However, the mosque's minaret, known as the **Hassan Tower** ('Beautiful Tower') remains a worthy and impressive monument to this great sultan. Although it was never completed (it lacks a top storey) and despite its rather squat appearance it has considerable charm and commands a superb view. Yacoub el Mansour and his father also built some five kilometres of walls, fortifications and monumental gates which the great city was to have filled.

With the death of Yacoub el Mansour in 1199 the Almohade dynasty began to decline and Rabat dwindled in importance, particularly when the rulers of the succeeding Merinide dynasty chose Fes as their capital (although they did build a necropolis and a *zaouia* alongside the original Roman site of Sala Colonia, which they called **Chellah**). It even became second in importance to Salé and was known for a time as Salé el Jdid (New Salé) to distinguish it from its more prosperous neighbour across the river. At this time only the Kasbah of the Oudaias was inhabited.

In the 17C both towns were settled by Andalusians escaping from the intolerant Philip II of Spain, who issued a decree in 1609 expelling Moors from his kingdom. The refugees brought new life and energy and rebuilt much of the Oudaias and the medinas, replacing crumbling Almohade structures with their own. At this time the river Bou Regreg became a haven for pirates—the **Sallée Rovers**—who infested northern waters, lying in wait for Christian ships and particularly for Spanish and Portuguese men-of-war returning from the New World or West Africa laden with gold and silver. Their adventures also provided Morocco with an almost unlimited supply of Christian slaves—a cruel irony (and satisfying revenge) at a time when Muslims were being driven out of Christian Spain. The independent **Republic of the Bou Regreg** was formed in the Kasbah of the Oudaias, by now seemingly impregnable with ramparts and cannons, and flourished there until put down by Moulay Ismael in the early 18C.

Rabat became the capital of the country for a short time in the second half of the 18C, under the Alouite sultan Mohammed ibn Abdallah. It has been Morocco's capital city again since 1912, when the French Resident-General, Louis Lyautey, made it his administrative centre and built what is now known as **La Ville Nouvelle** alongside the old town, which he was careful to preserve.

▨ Practical information

Tourist information **ONMT**. Angle Ave Al Abtal, Rue Oued Fes, ☎ (07) 775 171 and 22 Ave d'Alger, ☎ (07) 730 562.
Banks. Ave Allal ibn Abdallah/Ave Mohammed V.
Post Office. Ave Mohammed V.
Air transport. Royal Air Maroc, Ave Mohammed V. ☎ (07) 769 766. The nearest international airport is at Casablanca and there are regular buses to and from there, departing from the *Hôtel Terminus* by Rabat railway station. The journey takes about 90min. Alternatively, there are frequent trains.
Trains. The main station—Rabat Ville—is on Ave Mohammed V, in the centre of the new town. ☎ (07) 772 385. Trains to Tangier, Casablanca, Meknes, Fes, Marrakesh, and Oujda.
Buses. The main bus station is on Pl. Zerktouni, on the Casablanca road. Buses to Casablanca, Tangier, Meknes, Fes, Ifrane, and Azrou.
Taxis. *Grands taxis* can be found outside the rail and bus stations. *Petits taxis* are all over town.

Hotels
Hôtel La Tour Hassan, 26 Ave Abderrahman Annegai. ☎ (07) 726 307 fax (07) 725 408. ***** (157 rooms). Traditionally Moorish in style, built around a large, flower-decked patio. Its Moroccan restaurant is good and it is five minutes' walk from the Museum of Antiquities.
Hôtel Safir, Pl. Sidi Makhlouf. ☎ (07) 734 747 fax (07) 722 155. ***** (197 rooms). Huge and modern. Well placed for visiting the medina and the Hassan Tower.

Hôtel Chellah, 2 Rue d'Ifni. ☎ (07) 700 209 fax (07) 702 365. ****A (117 rooms). Comfortable with a good restaurant. Close to the Museum of Antiquities.

Hôtel Sheherazade, 21 Rue de Tunis.☎: (07) 722 226. ***A (80 rooms). Good value.

Hôtel Balima, Ave Mohammed V. ☎ (07) 707 755 fax (07) 707 450. ***A (71 rooms). Probably the best of a number of modest hotels in the centre of the new town, convenient for the railway station, the museum, and good shops and surrounded by a plethora of restaurants and bars. Has character and memories of the French Protectorate years, when it was the best hotel in town. It still retains some faded grandeur. The terrace bar is lively but the restaurant inside is disappointing and somewhat over-priced.

Restaurants
La Tour Hassan (see above). The best Moroccan food in town, but pricey.

Restaurant Saidoune, 467 Ave Mohammed V. ☎ (07) 709 226. Quite good Moroccan food, and cheaper than *La Tour Hassan*.

Au Vert Galant, Angle Rue Atlas and Sebou. ☎ (07) 774 247. Good international cuisine.

L'Eperon, 8 Ave Al Jazair. ☎ (07) 725 901. French. Quite expensive.

La Bamba, 3 Rue Tanta. ☎ (07) 709 839. Spanish food. Atmospheric and very moderate in price. Just behind the *Hôtel Balima*.

La Mamma, 6 Rue Tanta. ☎ (07) 763 729. Italian. Serves pizzas with excellent salads. Close to *La Bamba*.

La Caravelle, Plage des Oudaias. ☎ (07) 723 148. Housed in an old Portuguese prison overlooking the beach, it serves very good fish.

For restaurants on the Rabat–Casablanca road, see the section on beaches, below.

Campsites
None in the town; the nearest is at Salé, and there are two at Temara beach (see below).

Golf
Dar Es Salam Royal Golf Club, Dar Es Salam, Rabat. ☎ (07) 755 864.
Red course, 18 holes; blue course, 18 holes; green course, 9 holes.

A tour of the town
The oldest part of Rabat—the point on the bank where Abd el Mumene first pitched his camp—is that which is known today as the **Kasbah of the Oudaias**. (Oudaias was the name of one of the Arab tribes that invaded North Africa in the 11C.) The kasbah is visible from the general area of the Hassan Tower as a promontory, a mass of flat-roofed houses and occasional minarets, held up out of the sea by massive ramparts. A grand stairway rises to the massive ochre-coloured gateway, the **Bab Oudaia**, the noblest of five surviving Almohade gates in Rabat. Considered by experts to be the finest Almohade gate in Morocco, it was built by Yacoub el Mansour in the 1190s within walls already created by his father, and was intended as the centre of the royal kasbah, the three spacious interior chambers of the gate functioning as staterooms attached

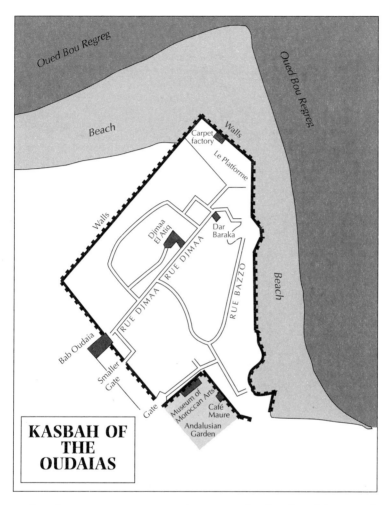

KASBAH OF THE OUDAIAS

to the palace. Its purpose was entirely ceremonial rather than defensive and today it is all that is left of the Almohade kasbah, the rest having been destroyed by the Alouite sultan Mohammed ibn Abdallah in the late 18C. To the left of and slightly below the gate would have been the main wool and slave market—the Souk el Ghezel—and this name is still used for the square.

Nowadays the Bab Oudaia is opened only for festive occasions: you usually enter the Oudaias through a smaller gate on the right, which leads into the one main street, **Rue Djmaa** (Street of the Mosque). Follow one of the alleyways on your left uphill and you are immediately in a different world—a world of white walls and deep blue shadows—where little has changed for centuries. The buildings are largely the work of Moriscos (Muslims forced to leave southern Spain by intolerant Catholic monarchs), which accounts for the distinctly Andalusian appearance of the place. Today the Oudaias is inhabited by some 3000 people, a few of whom are foreign artists or teachers who have chosen to immerse themselves in this uniquely evocative atmosphere and seem to have been completely accepted. Because there are no shops the whole area is uniquely clean and has a rare tranquillity.

Back on the Rue Djmaa, notice the many heavy and beautifully carved Andalusian doors, and the mosque—**Djmaa El Atiq**—founded in 1050 and said to have been rebuilt in the 18C by an Englishman, Ahmed el Ingles, who joined the Sallée Rovers. You may also spot the **Dar Baraka** ('House of Blessings') which has a golden cat depicted on the wall to the left of the door: the story goes that a cat was taken in by the owners during a siege; it quickly lead them to a treasure-filled coffer in the house, and so presumably escaped ending up in the pot.

Continue seawards along the Rue Djmaa and you come to a wide jetty (known locally as **le plateforme**) high above the open sea with an exhilarating view of Rabat and Salé to your right. According to local guides many of the forts visible from here were also the work of Ahmed el Ingles. The 17C Portuguese prison which overlooks the somewhat grubby beach is now a popular fish restaurant, *La Caravelle*.

The pink building on the jetty is a **carpet factory** where young girls, guided by older women, use nimble fingers to make carpets of modern or traditional design. You are welcome to look around: comments that these children should really be in school or at play are met with inscrutable smiles and assurances that they do have time for that, too, although the children's tired eyes belie this. There is usually a good stock of carpets for sale, but the medina is a better place to find an old Moroccan carpet.

If you return along the Rue Djmaa and take the last turning left before the Bab Oudaia, down a winding alley, you reach an open-air Moorish café, *Le Café Maure*, which looks out over the estuary. Painted a soft blue and decorated with colourful mosaics, it provides a delightful setting for mint tea and pastries stuffed with almonds and honey. Geraniums and morning glory cascade over the walls. From the far side of the café you can look back up at the vertical cliff into which houses of all shapes have been wedged.

On the opposite side of the street from the café, withdrawn into the niches in the wall, old men make wrought-iron work, tool in leather, paint intricate designs on wood or shape mysterious musical instruments.

Continuing your tour of the Oudaias, leave the café through a small archway and you will find yourself in a walled garden of great peace and enchantment and known as the **Andalusian Garden**, with paths that wander through beds of hibiscus, datura, roses, lilies, poinsettias and plumbago. Rabatis love to come here to walk and meditate, watched by the storks which build their nests on top of the walls. The storks spend spring and early summer in Morocco and are generally regarded with much affection. Their untidy nests can frequently be seen crowning minarets in the city.

At the top of the garden is the **Museum of Moroccan Arts**. It is housed in one of the many palaces that Moulay Ismael built in Rabat. Although he created Meknes as his capital, Moulay Ismael kept a garrison in the kasbah of Rabat in order to exact tribute from the pirates whose infamous trading he publicly condemned but privately espoused for his own ends; for example, his palaces in Meknes were almost exclusively built by Christian slaves brought in by pirates. The museum contains carpets, musical instruments and jewellery; there is also an elegant reception room laid out just as it would have been in the 17C. **Open** 09.00–12.00 and 15.00–18.30; closed Tues; entry 10dh.

A second museum, the **Museum of Traditional Arts** (*Maison de l'Artisanat*) occupies a converted customs house a few metres down on the road that forks left as you look from the Oudaias entrance. The entrance to the museum is down some steps on the right. The exhibition proves the richness of Morocco's folk art, past and present. Here are carpets, leatherwork, pottery, jewellery and embroidery. Official opening hours are the same as for the Museum of Moroccan Arts.

Below the Oudaias is the **medina**, still within its Almohade and Andalusian ramparts. This maze of narrow, winding streets and whitewashed houses was created largely by Muslims returning from Spain and has a distinctly Mediterranean atmosphere: its small buildings are packed tightly together, with few windows but sometimes offering tantalising glimpses of flower-filled patios within. It is dotted with mosques and fountains, and is so small that the visitor can wander round without fear of getting lost and also with remarkably little hassle from would-be guides.

The commercial area of the medina is more lively than the residential part, and the best street for shopping is the **Rue des Consuls**. It is so called because in the days before the *ville nouvelle* was built by the French it was the diplomatic quarter. Its shops often appear dark and dingy but they contain a vast collection of old carpets, pottery, brass, copper and silverware, every kind of antique jewellery, jewelled daggers, dress materials and ready-made kaftans. Notice particularly the **fondouks**, ancient courtyards which once provided overnight lodging for merchants and their livestock and are now often used by groups of artisans: some are full of leather-workers, others of carpenters or goldsmiths. There is very little pressure to buy and most are content to say *Bonjour* and get on with their work. There are at least three major *fondouks* on the left as you walk down Rue des Consuls.

If, going southeast from the kasbah, you turn right towards the end of the Rue des Consuls down Rue Souk Sebbat, you will find scores of tiny shops selling dates, mint, olives and spices in heady profusion. The colours and smells are wonderful, enhanced by the street's roofing of reeds which concentrates the effect and offers shade on a hot day. There are stalls piled high with *babouches*, jewellery, musical instruments and some modern wares. This street becomes the Rue Souika, with more utilitarian goods and fewer handicrafts for sale. Prices tend to be lower here and so, usually, does the quality. Also on this street is the **Great Mosque** which dates from the Merinide period but has been many times rebuilt. Beyond the mosque, there are second-hand goods for sale as well as books and furniture. There is even a flea market (*marché aux puces*) on the right of the street, thought this is of doubtful value. You should emerge into the modern city through **Bab El Had** with the **Central Market** on its medina side. The market is worth a look for its magnificently displayed meat, fish, vegetables and fruit. There are piles of luscious peaches, apricots and melons in early summer and different kinds of grapes later in the year, as well as globe artichokes, aubergines, and red and green peppers. It all seems ridiculously cheap and, because the climate over the vast area of Morocco is so varied, the seasons are long.

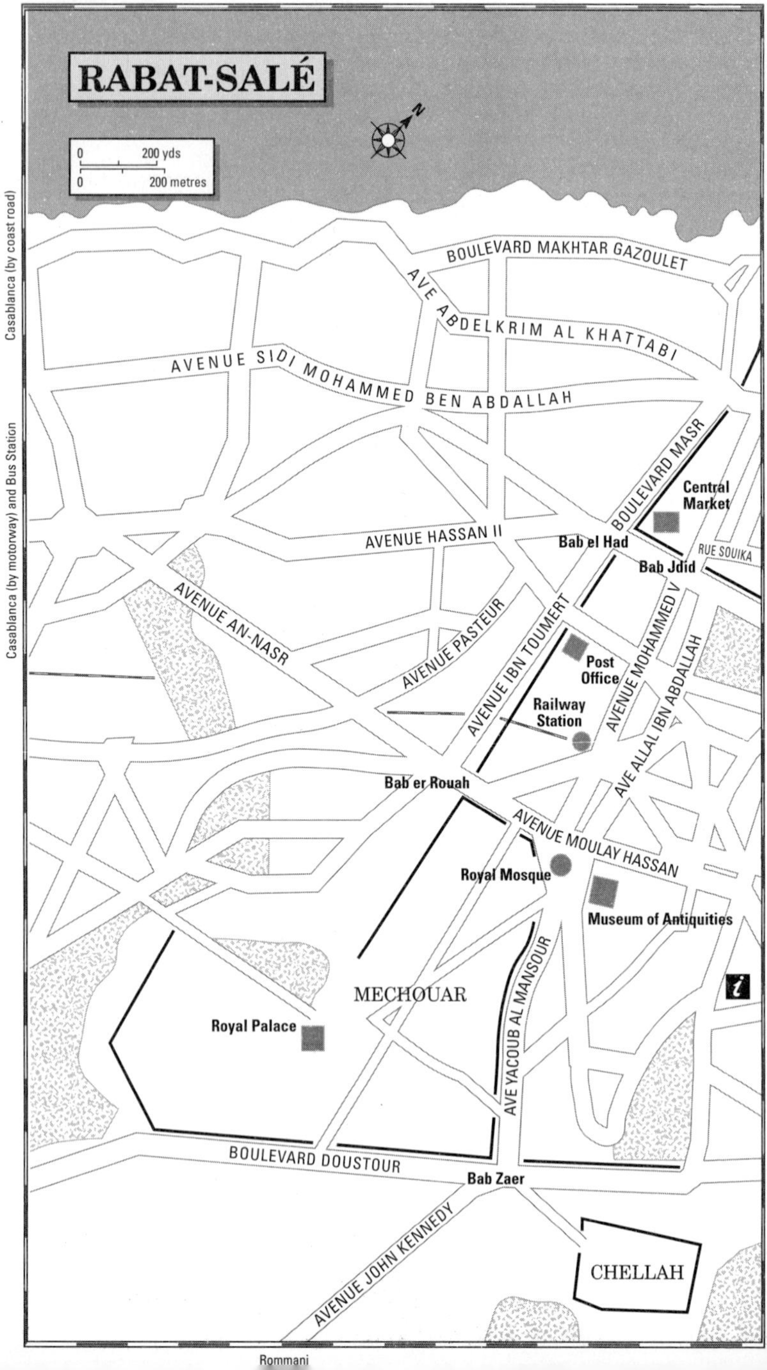

RABAT-SALÉ

N

| 0 | 200 yds |
| 0 | 200 metres |

Casablanca (by coast road)

Casablanca (by motorway) and Bus Station

BOULEVARD MAKHTAR GAZOULET

AVE ABDELKRIM AL KHATTABI

AVENUE SIDI MOHAMMED BEN ABDALLAH

BOULEVARD MASR

Central Market

RUE SOUIKA

AVENUE HASSAN II

Bab el Had

Bab Jdid

AVENUE AN-NASR

AVENUE PASTEUR

AVENUE IBN TOUMERT

AVENUE MOHAMMED V

AVE ALLAL IBN ABDALLAH

Post Office

Railway Station

Bab er Rouah

AVENUE MOULAY HASSAN

Royal Mosque

Museum of Antiquities

MECHOUAR

AVE YACOUB AL MANSOUR

i

Royal Palace

BOULEVARD DOUSTOUR

Bab Zaer

CHELLAH

AVENUE JOHN KENNEDY

Rommani

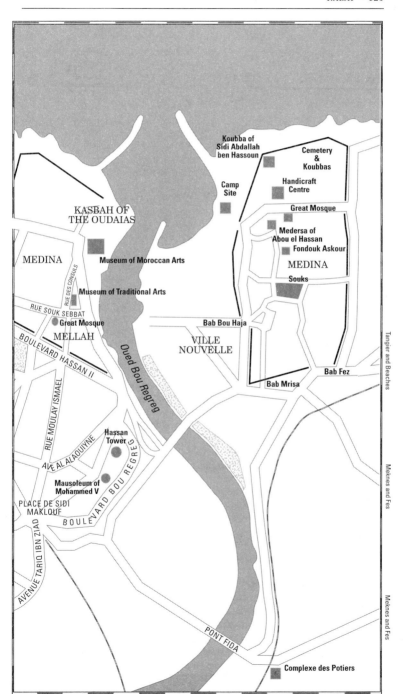

Koubba of
Sidi Abdallah
ben Hassoun

Cemetery
&
Koubbas

Camp
Site

Handicraft
Centre

KASBAH OF
THE OUDAIAS

Great Mosque

Medersa of
Abou el Hassan

MEDINA

Museum of Moroccan Arts

Fondouk Askour

MEDINA

RUE DES CONSULS

Museum of Traditional Arts

Souks

RUE SOUK SEBBAT

Great Mosque

Bab Bou Haja

MELLAH

BOULEVARD HASSAN II

VILLE
NOUVELLE

Oued Bou Regreg

Bab Fez

Bab Mrisa

RUE MOULAY ISMAEL

Hassan
Tower

AVE AL ALAOUIYNE

BOULEVARD BOU REGREG

Mausoleum of
Mohammed V

PLACE DE SIDI
MAKLOUF

BOULEVARD BOU REGREG

AVENUE TARIQ IBN ZIAD

PONT FIDA

Complexe des Potiers

Tangier and Beaches

Meknes and Fes

Meknes and Fes

Bargaining

This medina is as good a place as any to learn the skills of bargaining. If you are interested in something, ask the price and then offer a good deal less than you expect the merchant to accept, for he will have asked you for much more than he expects you to pay. You will compromise at some intermediate sum. This is a **ritual** which Moroccans expect and enjoy. They are apt to look quite disappointed if some unwitting tourist offers the full asking price straightaway. If you are seriously looking for an old Rabat carpet (the most beautiful and most sought after of all Moroccan carpets) you should accept the invitation to sit down—on a pile of rugs—and talk of anything and everything except the one subject which interests you most: you will probably be offered a glass of mint tea which you must certainly accept; crumpled photographs of relatives studying in Europe may be produced. Only after these courteous preliminaries will the merchant seriously begin showing you carpets. You may not be impressed at first but, as time goes on, they will become older, rarer, more soft and delicate in colour. The carpet-seller will enjoy the whole process and savour your growing appreciation, and he will not be too unhappy if, after an hour or so spent in this delightful way, you thank him and gracefully withdraw without buying anything at all.

For a more speedy but less rewarding method of acquiring a carpet, there is an **auction** once a week in the Rue des Consuls, where an always surprising variety of carpets are thrown down and unrolled on the street with amazing skill and speed, sold and whisked away almost before you have time to draw breath. It is amusing to watch but you are unlikely to find any real treasures this way.

It is of course equally satisfactory—and more convenient for anyone staying in the *ville nouvelle* and wanting to start a tour with the medina—to do the above journey in reverse, finishing in the Rue des Consuls. Follow one of the town's main arteries, **Avenue Mohammed V**, straight into the medina through **Bab Jdid** and then turn right into Rue Souika.

One of the most distinctive landmarks in Rabat is the **Hassan Tower**, which is a 15min walk or a short taxi ride along the outside of the medina ramparts down the broad, animated **Boulevard Hassan II**. The tower is almost all that remains of the mosque started by Sultan Yacoub el Mansour in 1194 but never finished. Not only time but also the Lisbon earthquake of 1755 has exacerbated the deterioration of the surrounding mosque walls (a few uneven chunks remain to mark the perimeter, now wisely protected by a modern wall). Some 350 stone column stumps survive, sadly bearing witness to what might have been the greatest mosque in the world, but which has ended up a roofless space. The site forms a rectangle 180m by 140m, and the mosque, with 21 aisles, is believed to have had 14 entrances.

The tower of warm red stone stands 44m high, but it should have been as high as 80m, roughly the height of the Koutoubia minaret in Marrakesh, which it closely resembles but which it is considered to exceed in fineness of detail. Each of the four sides of the minaret is decorated differently. Certainly the delicate, almost lace-like tracery over the windows is comparable with and possibly finer than that of the Giralda in Seville, which was completed by Yacoub el Mansour to celebrate his successful campaigns in Andalusia. Inside the tower are six storeys, each comprising one room with a domed ceiling, and these are joined by a wide ramp by which the sultan had planned to reach the top and address his people without getting off his horse. Until recently visitors were allowed to walk up the ramp to the top of the tower for an inspiring view of both Rabat and Salé, but the passage of so many feet was found to be causing damage to the 800-year-old structure, and it is now permanently closed.

At the opposite end of the mosque site (and actually occupying a portion of it) is a great complex of gleaming white buildings. In front, nearest the road and approached by a flight of steps, is the **Mausoleum of Mohammed V** (begun 1961) which King Hassan II had erected in memory of his father. No expense was spared in the creation of this unique edifice which took more than 200 of Morocco's finest craftsmen (mainly from Fes) over ten years to build, using traditional techniques. Surprisingly, this sacred monument, which is a fine example of modern Alouite style, was designed by a Vietnamese architect living in Paris. Fortunately for posterity, everyone, Muslim and non-Muslim alike, may enter (and take photographs) and gaze down at the white onyx **tomb** of Mohammed V, splendid on its floor of Portuguese black marble, which is polished so brightly that it looks like some unfathomable black lake. In one corner is the slightly smaller tomb of the present king's brother, Prince Moulay Abdallah, who died in 1972. Nearby sits an imam reading the Koran aloud.

Notice the superbly carved **dome** (in mahogany, which resists Rabat's humid climate better than cedarwood) and the incredible delicacy of the stucco-work. The colours and designs of the minutely executed **mosaics** are typical of Moroccan art. Almost 20,000 pieces of burned and glazed clay were needed to produce each square metre: the total area of mosaic is over 1000 sq m. Notice too the bronze lamp, which was made in Fes. It weighs 1500kg and has some 400 bulbs. The bronze doors were also made by Fassi craftsmen.

Some people dislike the fact that any modern building (albeit a royal mausoleum) should be erected on the site of Rabat's oldest and most sacred historic monument. Others consider that the two monuments belong together—the one in memory of the Almohades who built Rabat and made Morocco great in the 12C, and the other in memory of the Alouite king, Mohammed V, who regained Morocco's independence some 800 years later. Behind the mausoleum is the associated **mosque,** which non-Muslims may not enter, though it is possible to peer through the grille. This building is of ochre-coloured stone and forms a quiet contrast with the ornate mausoleum. Adjoining it is a **library** which is sometimes open to visitors. At intervals around the whole complex are posted royal horse guards splendidly arrayed in white robes. The sand boxes in which their mounts are allowed to stand are a surprisingly gentle touch.

Chellah

If you follow the Bou Regreg estuary a little further upstream, via Place de Sidi Maklouf, you will notice, on your left and up the hillside from the river, some of the old, turretted, red walls of the Merinide period, which end with a magnificent gateway flanked by two octagonal towers. This is Chellah. The gate is open every day and entry costs 10dh. Leave your car outside the wall and walk in. At first sight it appears to be just a peaceful, rather untidy garden, full of orange and lemon trees, bougainvillaeas and prickly pears. But here are also the remains of two civilisations, Roman and Merinide.

On the **Roman** site there are traces of even earlier settlement by the Phoenicians, which probably dates back to the 8C BC. Here was the busy Roman river port of Sala Colonia (see *History*, above). In the 1C and 2C AD it exported oil, cereals, wine, pottery and wool to Rome. Much of the port installation today lies buried in the silt of the river but above it are the remains of a **forum** with a **triumphal arch** at one end, and traces of a flagstoned main street (Decumanus Maximus), with an arcaded wall on one side which may have been a row of shops. The arch was built in the style of the reign of the Emperor Trajan and is thought to have been 3.35m high and 4.30m wide; it was probably flanked by two smaller side arches.

Sala Colonia appears to have been built in a series of terraces. The **residential area**, to which the remains of small houses and one or two oil presses testify, was higher up the hill. It was essentially a working port with little in the way of luxury or entertainment. Only one rather poor mosaic (still *in situ* below the main street) has been found, and no traces of noble houses or of an amphitheatre. (The only remains of an amphitheatre in Morocco are at Lixus, near Larache.) There is, however, a round, quite well-preserved **nymphaeum** and a **thermal bath system** with typical Roman hypocaust still in place. The spring that supplied the Roman baths was used later by the Merinides who placed their baths on top of the Roman system, damaging much of it in the process.

The port was abandoned in the mid-12C and the site suffered as stone was gradually removed for incorporation into local buildings: indeed, the two small white columns to be seen in the great Merinide gate are undoubtedly Roman. It was further damaged by the Lisbon earthquake of 1755.

Sala Colonia was rediscovered by the French in 1930. Intensive excavations began in 1960, under the auspices of the Ministry of Cultural Affairs, and many of the treasures, including fragments of sculpture, were removed to the Museum of Antiquities in Rue el Brihi (see below). It is possible that there is much more to be found beneath the river silt, but excavation appears now to have stopped. The site is seriously overgrown and fenced off. The public is not admitted, though there are good views to be had through the wire fence as you proceed, downwards, through Chellah gardens.

In the 14C a **Merinide** sultan, Abou Said (1310-31), decided to build alongside the Roman site a small fortress, which he enclosed with massive walls that still survive today, though severely cracked in places. The **gateway** is truly magnificent and far more intricately decorated than the earlier Almohade gate of the Oudaias. The two great towers either side frame it to perfection. A distinctive feature here is the intricate carved stalactite vaulting which rises out of the octagonal bastions to form bases for the square-turreted upper sections.

Abou Said later built within the ramparts a **necropolis** for the remains of his royal descendants. His son, Abou el Hassan (1331–51), built a **mosque** and a **zaouia** to which holy men came to spend their days contemplating the Koran

The Merinide gate at Chellah

and living off the surrounding land. Today all that remains of the mosque are some arches and the lovely **minaret** with coloured faïence still intact. The walls and arches of the *zaouia* also survive, showing the main hall with its central basin and the tiny cells where the holy men lived. At the end of the hall was the **oratory**, and it is still possible to recognise the **mihrab** at the end where the imam would have stood facing Mecca to lead the prayers. Below the mosque and the *zaouia* are several **royal tombs** (all aligned to face Mecca); the largest and most centrally placed, and contained in a kind of pavilion, is that of Abou el Hassan himself. A short distance away, outside the pavilion, lies the tombstone of his favourite concubine and mother of Abou Inan, Shams ed Doura ('Morning Sun'), who was a convert from Christianity. It is covered in verses from the Koran.

The whole area has now been taken over by families of storks and by fig trees which manage to grow through the walls. Below it is a rectangular garden, somewhat better tended than the wilderness above, where hordes of butterflies play amongst the hollyhocks. There is a real sense of remoteness here, with only the storks for company: below stretches the estuary and above is the wall of the pavilion-mausoleum, beautifully decorated on this side.

Seven domed **koubbas** (containing relics of local saints) also remain from Merinide times and below them, on the right, is a deep **pool** of clear water fed by a spring which was used by the Merinides for their religious ablutions and is believed to date back to Phoenician times (though it was the Romans who built the bath). In those days it was undoubtedly a hot spring, and the 1755 earthquake is blamed for the fact that it now runs cold. Beside the pool sits an old man with a large dish of hard-boiled eggs. Families of well-nourished cats sit at his feet. Peer into the depths of the water and you may just discern the dark shapes of eels. What does it all mean? Moroccan women believe that the magical quality of the water on their skins will prevent sterility. The eels add to the magic. Buy an egg from the old man and throw the white into the water. A dark, writhing shape will slowly emerge from the black depths and swallow it. Throw the shells in too, for they help keep the water clear. Throw the yolks to the cats. Everybody will be well satisfied, including the old man who will tell you that the eels come from the Sargasso Sea by way of the estuary below, which is, theoretically, possible. The eels certainly come and go; for months there may be none at all; then one day they are back.

Modern Rabat, known as the **Ville Nouvelle**, is an efficient, white and airy city which turns its back to the sea. The old city regained some of its former importance when the later Alouite sultans, particularly Mohammed V, made it their imperial residence, but it was General Lyautey, arriving in 1912 at the beginning of the French Protectorate, who made Rabat the administrative capital and planned and built the broad avenues and luxurious residences that we see today. Being a man of imagination and sensitivity, he respected Islam and the traditions of the country in which he found himself. Consequently nothing was destroyed. White office buildings appeared alongside ancient mosques and gateways, and openings were made through the Almohade walls for modern highways to pass. The best example of this is the triple arch through which you enter the city on the main road from Casablanca.

Alongside it is another of Rabat's monumental Almohade gates, the **Bab er Rouah** ('Gate of the Winds'). Every bit as solid as the Oudaias gate, it too contains three spacious chambers. Unlike Oudaias, however, it had a defensive function, forming part of the exterior wall of the Almohade town. Today it is used for art exhibitions and is usually open. Another, less impressive example is **Bab Zaer**, which stands opposite Chellah and leads through the original Almohade wall directly into the centre of town, towards the Royal Mosque.

The focal point of modern Rabat is the **Mechouar**, the royal enclosure containing the Royal Palace, the Royal Mosque, the Prime Minister's office and many other important buildings. Anyone can walk or drive into the Mechouar and there are two entrances: one is directly opposite the Chellah gate, the other runs off Avenue Moulay Hassan in the centre of town. If you enter from the Chellah end, the **Royal Palace** will be on your left. You will be told where you may park and a guide will appear to show you round on foot. No one is allowed inside the palace itself, but a walk in front of the buildings is rewarding and provides a good opportunity to study the splendour of modern Moroccan decorative architecture. The palace was in fact built in the 18C but has been fully restored by the present king.

This is a 'working palace' and behind the three arches to the right of the residential section stands the Royal Cabinet Office. To its right is the Prime Minister's Office. On the left of the palace are the Royal Library, a necropolis of the Alouite dynasty and sundry offices. On the far left is a door behind which is the Throne Room, where foreign ambassadors go to present their credentials to the king on their arrival in Morocco.

The Royal Guard

Perhaps one of the most striking and colourful aspects of this great open space dotted with palaces and fountains is the Royal Guard. Noble of bearing and clad in traditional scarlet uniforms, they are known by the Moroccans as 'Sudanese' which simply means 'black'—their forebears came from south of the Sahara. Moulay Ismael was the first Alouite sultan to surround himself with such guards in his capital city of Meknes, in the late 17C, and the custom has survived to this day in Rabat, though the role of the guards is now purely ceremonial. Very occasionally, on major religious festivals, the Mechouar hosts a splendid spectacle when the king emerges from the Royal Mosque dressed all in white and riding a fine grey, flanked by his colourful guard.

Modern Rabat is crossed by a network of fine wide boulevards, the most important from the visitor's point of view being **Avenue Mohammed V** and **Avenue Allal Ibn Abdallah** which runs parallel to it, north of the Royal Palace and the Royal Mosque. In these two streets and in the little roads which join them are to be found the most interesting shops, restaurants and cafés.

In this general area too is the **Museum of Antiquities**, which is well worth a visit, especially if you have already seen some of Morocco's Roman and prehistoric sites. Like all Moroccan museums this one seems not to want to be found: it hides behind a glass door marked '*Service des Antiquités*' in the Rue el Brihi, which is a turning off the Avenue Moulay Hassan. Within are many treasures of prehistoric and Roman times, and many of the smaller items and fragments of sculpture found at Sala Colonia, Lixus, Volubilis, Banasa and Thamusida have been brought here. There is a good collection of Roman jewellery, oil lamps, cooking utensils, bronze figures, gravestones, millstones, and pieces of central-heating pipe, all of which add up to a fairly complete picture of how the citizens of Mauritania Tingitana lived. The items are well displayed and labelled. Amongst many fine **bronzes** are a wonderfully life-like guard dog and the heads of Juba II and Cato, all three from Volubilis. These are the real treasures of the collection. In the little garden alongside the museum are fragments of marble statues, columns, altars, and other remains. **Open** 08.30–12.00 and 15.30–18.00, in high summer 09.00–15.00; closed Tues; entry 10dh.

Salé

Salé is Rabat's sister town, which achieved prosperity and notoriety in the Middle Ages but is now very much in the shade of its imperial neighbour. With its lively, unspoilt medina, and one of the most beautiful medersas in the country, it is certainly worth a short visit and is accessible by a modern bridge over the Bou Regreg river. There is no accommodation other than a campsite on the beach, *La Plage*, ☎ (07) 782 368, and a very basic hotel in the market square, the *Saadiens*.

History of Salé

The history of Salé is inextricably entangled with that of Rabat; it was founded by the inhabitants of Sala Colonia (now Chellah) who in 1154 abandoned their original home and moved across the river to what they considered to be a better site; by the 13C, with the arrival of the Merinide dynasty, Salé was becoming a thriving port and a place of greater economic importance than Rabat.

Salé's prosperity in medieval times was based on the **export** of goods from all over the country, including skins, fabrics, carpets and spices, and ships bearing English, Italian and Flemish merchants came into the port to receive the goods. This provided rich spoils for pirates who plagued the area for several centuries, menacing the Spanish and French coasts and sometimes reaching as far as England until they were finally cleaned up by Moulay Ismael in the late 17C. (Stories of the exploits of these pirates, known as the Sallée Rovers, have appeared in many adventure books since.) Like Rabat, the town was further enriched by the arrival of hundreds of Muslims fleeing from Andalusia in the 17C, and much of Salé's medina was built at this time.

With the rebirth of Rabat at the time of the French Protectorate, Salé sank into relative obscurity and is now a modest town, a maze of winding streets and picturesque houses. General Lyautey did not build his wide boulevards here.

The Almohade ramparts are pierced by several monumental gates. Having crossed the Bou Regreg river, you will come to a large roundabout. If possible, park your car somewhere in this area (or, better still, take a taxi from Rabat) and walk a short way along the outside of the wall going off to the right. On your left will be **Bab Mrisa**, which is the oldest of the gates. Its name means 'harbour' and it spans a now silted-up canal along which merchant ships used to pass from the Bou Regreg estuary right into the centre of town. Essentially Almohade in the simplicity of its design, and incredibly high to allow access to tall ships, it is thought to have been built by the first Merinides in the late 13C.

Bab Fes—a short distance north of Bab Mrisa and with the main bus station just outside it—leads straight into the busy and colourful **souks**, the Souk el Ghezel (wool market), Souk el Kbir (a large square with a covered market at the centre), and the shops of leather-workers making *babouches* and carpenters making cedarwood table-tops. There are spice markets, second-hand clothes markets and whole sections selling nothing but kaftans. It is all deliciously mixed up and often cheaper than equivalent merchandise in Rabat.

From the souks it is a short walk westwards along the inside of the town ramparts to the **Koubba of Sidi Abdallah ibn Hassoun** (Salé's 16C patron saint), which stands by the road and is visible through the windows of the building that protects it. The origins of Sidi Abdallah's sainthood are unclear, but he is thought to have protected sailors from pirates; when the annual *moussem* takes place, on the eve of Mouloud (the Prophet's birthday), local people dress up as sailors and pirates and process through the streets carrying huge, multi-coloured wax candles which are preserved from one year to the next and can be seen beside the *koubba*. Further on, by the sea, is the very old cemetery which contains the hallowed white **Koubba of Sidi Benachir**, a 14C Andalusian saint. The *koubba* is said to cure blindness and mental illness and is also visited by pilgrims and supplicants on the eve of Mouloud. Surrounding it are the remains of what are thought to have been pilgrims' lodging-houses. Here too, through a large green archway, is a small **handicraft centre** (*ensemble artisanal*). It is worth stopping here to see groups of adolescent boys and girls being taught the traditional crafts of mosaic, carpet-weaving, wood-carving and the weaving of reed mats, a Salé speciality. The apprenticeships are much in demand and are subsidised by the government. Goods are for sale and prices are usually considerably lower than those in Rabat.

Across the road from the cemetery is the very beautiful **Medersa of Abou el Hassan**, founded by the Merinide sultan of that name in 1341, and recently restored. It has a small pillared courtyard with some strikingly delicate, off-white stucco-work above the pillars, dark-painted cedarwood ceilings and a highly ornate mihrab. Your guide will take you up the staircase to the terrace, off which lie the tiny cells which served as accommodation for students of the Koran. From here there is a fine view of old Salé with its blue and white Andalusian-style buildings. As with all significant *medersas*, there is an entry charge of 10dh and the building is open daily except Fridays.

Opposite the *medersa* is the **Great Mosque**, one of the earliest in Morocco, which was founded by the Almohades in the 13C but has many later additions, including the minaret. Sadly, the non-Muslim can do no more than admire the outside, though it is sometimes possible to glimpse the colonnaded interior through one of the entrances. Next to the mosque there is a library containing European as well as Moroccan books, which you may enter. Behind the mosque is the elaborate entrance to yet another saint's shrine, that of **Sidi Ahmed el Tijani**, which is also the subject of an annual *moussem*. All around the mosque are houses once inhabited by aristocrats, markedly whiter and cleaner than those in the rest of the medina, or so it seems.

Walk on down the Rue de la Grande Mosquée and you come back to the souks. On your right at the end of the street you will notice the **Fondouk Askour**: built in the 14C by the Merinides (note the fine doorway), it was first used as a veterinary hospital and two centuries later became a *fondouk*. Our enlightened guide explained that it is now a house for arranging marriages and divorce. Cross the big square and continue in the same direction and you will arrive once more at either Bab Mrisa or Bab Fes.

Courtyard of the Great Mosque

The many potteries which used to cluster along the roadside near the river have now been brought together as the **Complexe des Potiers** in the suburb of Oulja, which is located about 2km southeast of Salé on the Meknes road. (Coming from Rabat, cross the river by the Pont Fida and the complex is on the right just under the railway bridge.) It is usually recognisable from afar by its plume of black smoke. You can wander at will through heaps of raw shapes drying in the sun and see the whole timeless process from treading the wet clay to the delicate hand-painting of the final product. There are many *ateliers* where you can admire—and buy if you wish—anything from a set of spice jars to the utimate garden plant pot. Salé pottery is less ornate and lighter in design than that of Fes, Meknes or (particularly) Safi and, in the author's opinion, fits more easily into a European household. There is also basketry and bambooware for sale, as well as typical Salé reed mats. On a practical note, if you take a taxi there from Salé (or a *grand taxi* from Rabat) it is necessary to ask the driver to wait, as you are unlikely to find another one to take you back.

The road to Casablanca and the beaches

For those who want to cover this rather uninteresting 90km of countryside quickly the motorway is the obvious answer. Alternatively, the frequent and comfortable express train takes under an hour from one central station to the other. A more leisurely alternative for drivers is the old coastal road, which offers fine sea views and gives access to a string of beaches, many with lagoons which allow safe swimming protected from the Atlantic rollers and currents. For some reason this road, which carries very little traffic anyway, has a speed limit of 60kph, which in places drops as low as 40kph. What is more, a number of traffic police—out of all proportion to the importance of the road—patrol hungrily up and down, itching to stop anyone exceeding the limit, however slightly, in order to extract a fine on the spot. Foreigners, it seems, represent fair game.

The coast road passes first through Rabat's least attractive quarter, where tall blank walls hide a shameful area of shanty town and rubbish litters the shoreline. How strange that Rabat appears to turn its back to the sea. Drive on a few kilometres further out, however, and the mood changes as European-style villas, beach clubs and restaurants start to appear and the air becomes distinctly fresher.

Plage Harhoura is closest to Rabat. It is quite small, but it does have a good fish restaurant, the *Miramar.* ☎ (07) 747 656. The first major beach is that of **Temara**—very crowded at weekends and positively humming by night with bars and discos and all the activity which Rabat itself lacks. It has two hotels— *La Felouque Balnéaire*, ☎ (07) 744 388 and *Temara Plage*, ☎ (07) 744 230, as well as a campsite—*La Palmeraie*. The small town of Temara (2km inland from the beach) is worth a look. It has a crenellated **kasbah** built by Moulay Ismael which is now used as a stud farm. The **zoo** has a good range of animals, including elephants and giraffes, living in an environment which is not too seriously depressing. **Open** 09.30–18.30; entry 10dh.

Next come **Plage Contrebandier** and **Sables d'Or**, the latter having a good fish restaurant—*Les Sables d'Or*, ☎ (07) 744 237. A little further on, **Skhirate** is the most sophisticated of all the beaches, and is well-equipped with all possible facilities and at least two notable hotel-restaurants—*La Kasbah*, ☎ (07) 749 133 and *Hotel Amphitrite*, ☎ (07) 742 236. Skhirate owes its up-market atmosphere to the fact that the king once had his summer palace here. It was the scene of the notorious attempted coup by army officers in the summer of 1971, during Hassan's birthday celebrations. Not surprisingly the king no longer comes here but other members of the royal family do, it seems, as there is at least one heavily guarded palatial residence along the roadside.

The last beach of all is Mohammedia (see Casablanca, below).

Campsites
Camping La Palmeraie, Temara, 100m from the beach. ☎ (07) 749 251. Snack bar, restaurant, grocery, showers, laundry.
Camping Gambusias, Temara, 100m from the beach. Snack bar, restaurant, showers.

An excursion from Rabat to Oulmes

The little spa town of Oulmes les Thermes lies at the western end of the Middle Atlas, midway between Rabat and Khenifra as the crow flies. The route from Rabat is, however, the more scenic of the two and returning via Rommani on the P22 makes a very pleasant day-long round trip of some 270km.

Leave Rabat on the Meknes road, and drive through the cork oak **Forest of Mamora** (136,000ha), which is a particularly attractive area for walks and picnics, with a carpet of wild flowers in early spring and only the occasional cow or donkey for company. After 56km you come to **Tiflet**, known for its colourful pompommed hats which are made locally and held out for sale on long poles as you pass through. Just after Tiflet, turn right on to the S209 marked to Oulmes, and then left at the sign indicating the lake **Dayet er Roumi** (about 30min from Tiflet). This is a large natural lake in hilly country which provides swimming and fishing facilities in season and has a restaurant on its shore.

From the lake, rejoin the S209, which takes you some 70km southeastwards to Oulmes in the Jbel Mouchchene. The mountains are thickly wooded and covered with cistus and other aromatic plants which give off a wonderful bittersweet smell in spring. This is wild boar country. **Oulmes les Thermes** is a watering place and you can scramble down from the *Hôtel les Thermes* (***A, 42 rooms, ☎ (07) 552 353) to the point where the water springs from the rocks (Lalla Haya) and becomes a raging torrent. There are no facilities for swimming but the water is delicious and healthy to drink and is sold in bottles all over the country. The area is highly recommended for its truly magnificent scenery, soaring wooded heights, deep ravines and turbulent rivers pouring over the rocks. There are many tracks up into the mountains but their surface condition varies considerably. It is easy to get lost and villages are few and far between.

From Oulmes you could extend the tour still further by returning 56km to **Maaziz** and then turning left and driving 43km to **Rommani**, another charming town in a hilly setting. Rommani is 82km from Rabat along the main P22 road. Otherwise, return to Rabat via Maaziz, or take the *piste* northeastwards as far as **Ouljet as Sultane** and thence the S316 road to Meknes.

Casablanca

Casablanca is Morocco's largest and most sophisticated city, with a population of over 3.5 million. It is the economic capital of Morocco, with well over half the country's industry on its outskirts, and it has the busiest port. Rich, efficient, and streamlined, with boulevards of impressive skyscrapers which could belong anywhere in the world, it is the town which most closely relates Morocco to the 20C. It is not exciting or exotic, or even typically Moroccan, and yet the tourists stream in, attracted no doubt by the well-stocked shops, by its reputation for a lively nightlife, and perhaps by the name itself, which to many spells adventure and romance.

Three sections of the city deserve attention. These are the elegant city centre, the vast new Hassan II Mosque and—in refreshing contrast to the extravagance of both—the old and new medinas. The outer sections of town, particularly the industrial area around the port, are noisy and dirty and traffic there is a nightmare, whether you are driving or trying to cross the road. If you are driving, make for the *centre ville*, leave the car at your hotel or in a car park and take taxis thereafter—or walk. Fortunately, everything worth seeing (with the exception of the mosque, which is a short taxi ride away) is concentrated around the city centre.

History of Casablanca

The origins of Casablanca are in **Anfa**, now a very desirable suburb to the west of the city where the rich and famous have their villas. Anfa was already a significant Berber settlement when the Arabs arrived in 683. The Phoenicians had settled here previously, and it is likely that the beginnings of Anfa are prehistoric.

During the reconquest of the Iberian Peninsula by the Catholics in the 13C and 14C, when the Moorish invaders of Spain returned to Africa, Anfa became a haven for pirates intent on attacking and plundering heavily-laden Spanish and Portuguese vessels. At the beginning of the 16C the **Portuguese** attacked the town several times and finally drove out the pirates. They occupied the town and renamed it Casa Branca ('White House'). They stayed just over 200 years, until the Lisbon earthquake of 1755 damaged the place so severely that they abandoned it. The Alouite sultan Mohammed ibn Abdallah (1757–90) arrived soon after, repaired the town, repopulated it, and named it Dar el Beida (the Arabic for 'white house'). It was then that the various mosques and most of the houses of the medina were built. The town became Casa Blanca when the Spanish obtained special port privileges soon afterwards.

This distinctly un-Moroccan and un-Islamic city was transformed into a modern metropolis by the French Resident-General, General Lyautey, at the beginning of the 20C. Today it is known by the international set quite simply as 'Casa'.

But the story does not end there. Rapid industrial growth has brought with it attendant problems of poverty, overcrowding and consequent social unrest. Shanty towns (*bidonvilles*) ring the city landwards and have also sprung up in pockets along the coast. Not surprisingly, the city became a breeding ground for anti-French feeling in the 1940s and early '50s and for militant socialism thereafter, including the formation of the left-wing party led by Mehdi Ben Barka, the UNFP (Union Nationale des Forces Populaires), and student riots in the mid-1960s and early '80s. Now, in the wake of the creation of the Hassan II Mosque, there exists a programme of urban development and road-building—at least in the mosque's immediate vicinity—and it remains to be seen how much this will do to improve a still-volatile situation.

▪ Practical information

Tourist information. ONMT. 98 Blvd Mohammed V, ☎ (02) 221 524 and 55 Rue Omar Slaoui, ☎ (02) 271 177.
Banks. Blvd Mohammed V.
Post office. Pl. Mohammed V.
Air transport. Royal Air Maroc, 44 Ave des F.A.R. ☎ (02) 311 122. The Mohammed V airport is on Route de Marrakesh, 28km southwest of the city. ☎ (02) 339 100. There is an hourly train to the city centre and also a shuttle bus.
Trains. The Gare des Voyageurs is at the eastern end of Blvd Mohammed V, ☎ (02) 243 818, and the Gare du Port is by the docks,☎ (02) 223 011. Besides frequent inter-city trains between Rabat and Casablanca, there are services to Tangier, Meknes, Fes, Oujda and Marrakesh.
Buses. 23 Rue Mohammed Kamal. ☎ (02) 268 061. Services to all destinations.
Taxis. *Grands taxis* can be found outside the train and bus stations. *Petits taxis* are all over town.

Hotels
There is a vast number and range of hotels in Casablanca, and the tourist office should be able to provide a full list. Because of traffic problems, it is best to stay right in the centre, or right outside, say, on the Boulevard de la Corniche.
Hôtel Royal Mansour, 27 Ave des F.A.R. ☎ (02) 311 130 fax (02) 314 818. *****L (182 rooms). Right in the heart of the city. The ultimate in luxury with a good Moroccan restaurant (*Le Douira*) and a charming 'winter garden'. No pool but just about everything else. A high standard of service.
Hôtel Sheraton, 100 Ave des F.A.R. ☎ (02) 317 878 fax (02) 315 137. ***** (306 rooms). Has a pool, a fine Moroccan restaurant (*El Andalous*), and a night club. Much used by upmarket package tours.
Hôtel Plaza, 18 Blvd Houphouet Boigny. ☎ (02) 221 262. ***B (27 rooms). A comfortable, centrally located, old hotel. Good value.
Hôtel Windsor, 93 Place Oued El Makhazin (just off Ave des F.A.R.). ☎ (02) 200 352. ***B (32 rooms). Another old hotel. Good value.
Hôtel Suisse, Blvd de la Corniche. ☎ (02) 360 202. ****B (192 rooms). Out of town. Fresh air and good service. Very pleasant.
Hotel Bellerive, 38 Blvd de la Corniche. ☎ (02) 391 357. ***A (32 rooms). Comfortable and modest in size. Recommended.

Restaurants
The best Moroccan food is to be had in the big hotels, especially the restaurants of the *Sheraton* and the *Royal Mansour* (see above). Otherwise you could try:

Al Mounia, 95 Rue du Prince Moulay Abdallah. ☎ (02) 222 669.
La Tajine, Centre 2000 (by the port). ☎ (02) 276 400.
The best fish restaurants are on the coast:
A ma Bretagne. ☎ (02) 362 112. Expensive but worth it (see below).
La Mer, Phare d'el Hank (by the lighthouse). ☎ (02) 363 315.
Le Cabestan, Phare d'el Hank. ☎ (02) 391 190.
Le Chalutier, Centre 2000 (by the port). ☎ (02) 203 455.

Campsites
Oasis Campsite, 10km from the beach at Beausejour, on the El Jadida road. ☎ (02) 253 367.
Desserte des Plages, On the Azemmour road (16km from Casablanca)

Golf
Royal Anfa Golf Club, Anfa–Casablanca Racecourse. ☎ (02) 365 355. 9 holes, 2710m, par 35.

A tour of the city
The **city centre** of modern Casablanca and the location of its main administrative buildings is the impressive square, once called Place des Nations Unies, now re-named **Place Mohammed V**. Graced with a huge fountain which becomes multi-coloured at night by dint of skilful spotlighting, it is a magnet for tourists and Casablancais alike, with its water, pigeons, music and general excitement. Standing back, quite modestly, in one tree-filled corner is the French Consulate, in front of which is a fine bronze equestrian statue of General Lyautey. Dominating the square are the **Lawcourts** (*Tribunal*), the **Town Hall** (*Préfecture*), and the **Post Office** (PTT); the Town Hall has a tall, thin tower up which you may climb for a splendid view. The square has space to walk, sit and contemplate the not unpleasing effect of these French-designed Mauresque buildings. Visible down a side street on the opposite side from the Town Hall is the old Catholic **Cathedral of Sacre Coeur**, built by the French in 1930 and remarkable for its unconventional modern design; it is now used as a school. South of the cathedral is the pleasant wooded square known as the **Parc de la Ligue Arabe**.

Whilst in this general area it is worth walking on down the Avenue Mers Sultan, past the 1950s **Church of Notre Dame des Lourdes** with its fine stained-glass windows, to have a look at the **New Medina**, or Habbous district—a French-built urban development in Mauresque style from the 1920s, born of the need to house hundreds of families who came in from the countryside to seek work in the new factories. Better by far than the *bidonvilles*, this district is now full of artisans and souks bursting with all kinds of merchandise. It seems to have taken over the role of the Old Medina, which remains badly in need of regeneration (and may well attain it with the construction of new access roads to the Hassan II Mosque from the city centre). Also here is the **Mahakma du Pacha** (Pasha's Courthouse). Built in the late 1940s as a Muslim lawcourt and reception hall for the then pasha, or governor, of Casablanca, it incorporates in its 60 rooms every possible nuance and decorative motif of modern Hispano–Moorish architecture. It is now a government building and you may or may not be allowed to go in and have a look. Nearby is the **Royal Palace** which is closed to visitors even when the king is not in residence.

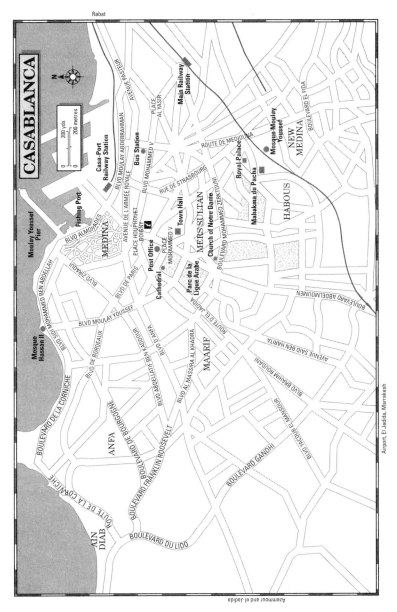

If you return to Place Mohammed V and leave it by way of the tree-lined **Avenue Hassan II** (at the opposite end from the Parc de la Ligue Arabe), you come to a second noble square, recently re-named **Place Houphouet Boigny**, recognisable by its cupola and thoroughly European clock tower; the latter was built by

Architecture of the 1930s in Casablanca

a French army officer to emphasise the need for timekeeping, subsequently demolished and replaced by an exact replica in 1992. Leading off this square to the right is the second prestigious thoroughfare, **Boulevard Mohammed V**. The wonderfully eclectic façades both here and on Avenue Hassan II reflect the energy and determination of the French in the 1930s to make Casablanca the most modern and exciting city in Morocco, incorporating the best of Moorish traditions with those of Renaissance and Neo-Classical architecture. Thus, stucco, *zellige* and carved cedarwood blend comfortably with balconies, pediments, arcades and columns. Here, and on the parallel **Avenue des Forces Armés Royales** (known as Avenue des F.A.R.), are the main hotels, shops and travel agents'offices.

Also on Boulevard Mohammed V is the **Central Market**, its entrance lined on both sides by flower stalls. It is worth a visit for the sheer vibrancy of colour and life it reveals. The section selling fish makes any European fishmonger seem dull by comparison. Close by is the ONMT.

The **Old Medina** represents all that there was of Casablanca before the French came. The best way in is through the decorated *bab* off Place Houphouet Boigny (opposite the *Hyatt Regency Hotel*). This brings you into a small square overlooked by a green-and-ochre minaret, with alleyways off to left and right. The small medina does not have the excitement, the craft workers or the ancient buildings of Fes, Marrakesh or even Rabat, for much of it was destroyed in the 1755 earthquake. Since then there have been various attempts at reconstruction, but people have tended to move out and an air of neglect pervades it. Goods on sale are largely manufactured and are for local people rather than for tourists. One advantage is that you can wander freely, and no-one will try to persuade you to buy anything you do not want. The original west wall is currently being repaired as part of a plan to make a grand avenue between the town centre and the **Hassan II Mosque**.

The east side of the Old Medina is next to the **port**, which occupies some 117ha and is protected from the Atlantic by the immense **Moulay Youssef Pier** (3180m long). It is backed by heavy industry and chemical factories belching fumes into the thickly polluted air. (Casablanca is said to be home to 60% of Morocco's heavy industry.) The **Centre 2000**, next to the port railway station, is worth a visit for its auctions and interesting international restaurants.

The **Hassan II Mosque** lies to the northeast of the medina, overlooking the sea, on the Ain Diab road. After all the hype and astonishing statistics handed out in advance of its completion, the question everyone is bound to ask is 'Does it live up to expectations?' The answer has to be a resounding 'yes'. The mosque is quite simply breathtaking. It is the brainchild of King Hassan II himself, who wanted to build a mosque on this, the most westerley point of the Muslim world.

Fortunately non-Muslims are as welcome as the faithful to enter: **tours** lasting 1h are conducted every day except Friday by English- and French-speaking guides at 09.00, 10.00, 11.00 and 14.00. The tour costs 100dh for adults, 25dh for under-12s, and there is a 5% discount for groups.

Hassan II Mosque

This is money well spent. Within the mosque no written information is available, not even a sketch plan, nor is there even a kiosk outside the mosque precinct. (We were told we would have to go back into town and buy a guide at a bookshop.) Perhaps this will be rectified in time. Photography is allowed but filming is not. (Our guide related that this is because a company recently filmed without permission and subsequently produced anti-Islamic material.) There is ample parking underneath the courtyard.

First, some statistics: building work started in 1980 and the mosque itself was inaugurated in 1994, though much of the surrounding complex of museums, a Koranic school and libraries, and a lift up to the top of the minaret, was only finished in early 1997. The project cost over £500 million and employed 3300 of Morocco's most highly skilled craftsmen although, as in the case of the Mohammed V Mausoleum in Rabat, begun in 1961, the architect came from France. The money was raised from public subscriptions and the mosque caused intense national interest and engendered an increasing sense of pride amongst Moroccans at all social levels.

Much of the building, which covers 2ha in all, has been built over the sea, on the site of the former municipal swimming pool (mindful perhaps of the words of the Koran that God has His throne on water). It is the third largest mosque in the world, after those at Mecca and Medina, and its minaret is 200m high, surmounted by a laser which beams towards Mecca. The prayer hall can accommodate 20,000 of the faithful and the surrounding esplanade a further 80,000.

Before entering the **prayer hall** you must take off your shoes and carry them round in a plastic bag. The hall is splendid with its highly polished marble floor and its finely carved cedarwood roof, which can be retracted in three minutes to permit ventilation for Friday's worshippers. The chandeliers come from Murano in Venice and the fine white marble is also Italian. Everything else is home-produced— cedarwood from the Middle Atlas, granite from Tafraoute and pink marble from Agadir. For all its ornamentation, the prayer hall engenders a sense of great peace which probably has something to do with the near perfect proportions, the satisfying perspectives in every direction, the soft golden light and the floor like some still and fathomless ocean.

There is also an **upper prayer hall** which can accommodate 5000 women who, in keeping with Islamic tradition, must pray separately from men. It is hidden from public view by a *mushrabiyya* screen through which the women can see, but not be seen.

Door of Hassan II Mosque

Reunited with your shoes, you pass on to the **ablutions room**, where worshippers must ritually wash before prayer. Notice the lovely lotus-flower fountains and the magnificent brass chandelier made by Fes artisans. After this you will see the **hammam**, in which the rooms are named—in the manner of Roman Volubilis—as the *tepidarium, caldarium* and so on, and has space for 700 people at any one time.

Between the mosque and the medina is an area of poor housing and general deprivation. There are plans to demolish and rebuild here, which is just as well as the negative effect is greatly magnified by the proximity of so grandiose and extravagant a neighbour.

To the west of Casablanca city and connected to it by the splendid **Boulevard de la Corniche** is the seaside resort of **Ain Diab**, and rising up behind it is the elegant residential area of Anfa, with its fine villas and the 9-hole course of the Royal Anfa Golf Club. Ain Diab is really just a string of exclusive clubs, with swimming pools, and names like *Tahiti, Le Miami* and *Le Sun-Beach*, each endeavouring to outdo its neighbour in tropical luxury. Behind them are the thunderous rollers of the Atlantic, a magnificent sight at any time of year and a formidable and dangerous challenge to even the strongest swimmer. The area is well-served by good hotels and many delightful fish restaurants (see above): the more modestly-priced ones stand back from the shore and serve delicious, freshly-caught *merlan* or *lot*. The best (and arguably the best restaurant in Morocco) is *A Ma Bretagne* which stands on a promontory a little beyond the others. Their *Mousse de St. Pierre, sauce homardine* is memorable.

Visible from the restaurant, on a rocky island, is the white-washed **Koubba of Sidi Abd er Rahman**, a local saint said to have had miraculous powers to cure mental illness. Pilgrims go there once a year to spend the night and to bathe in the surrounding water. At low tide it would be possible to walk out to the *koubba*, but non-Muslims are not welcome at this shrine. It is worth noting that Ain Diab, facing straight out to the Atlantic as it does, enjoys an altogether more bracing climate than slightly humid Casablanca (and Rabat). This probably accounts, at least in part, for its significant expansion along the coast.

Mohammedia

Mohammedia lies 28km to the north of Casablanca, and is accessible from both the coast road and the motorway. It also has its own railway station. Much used as a weekend **resort** by the *Casablancais*, it has some 5km of sandy beach, a yacht club, a race course, a casino, an 18-hole golf course beside the sea, and some pricey hotels. Conditions for sailing and fishing are some of the best on the Atlantic coast. In fact, it is a millionaire's paradise, though many might prefer to go further south for a hotter, dryer climate.

The town has a large **port** which has been active since the 14C when it was visited by ships from Venice, Pisa, Genoa and Portugal. Now Mohammedia has several major industries including a large oil refinery with its own modern port specially constructed to receive shipments of crude oil. International playground and industrial complex co-exist quite happily, neither seeming to encroach on the other's space. Every July there is a **festival**, with activities ranging from *fantasias*, music and dancing to exhibitions of arts and crafts, which is well worth a visit.

Hotels

Hôtel Miramar, Rue de Fes. ☎ (03) 322 021 fax (03) 324 613. *****A (188 rooms). Just behind the beach. Very international.

Hôtel Samir, 34 Blvd Moulay Youssef. ☎ (03) 324 005. ****A (46 rooms). Also near the beach.

Restaurants

There are lots of moderately priced fish restaurants near the beach with not much to choose between them. Probably the best is *Restaurant du Port*, 1 Rue du Port. ☎ (03) 322 466.

Campsites

Camping International Loran, 2km south of the town. ☎ (03) 322 957.

Golf

Mohammedia Royal Golf Club, BP 12 Mohammedia. ☎ (03) 324 656. 18 holes, 5917m, par 72.

The West Coast: Casablanca to Agadir

This section of Morocco's coast is rocky and inhospitable. The deserted sandy beaches, though tempting, are dangerous for bathing unless they are in a bay. With the exception of the busy port of Safi and the once important ports of Azemmour, El Jadida and Essaouira, the coastal strip is little inhabited. The main road runs inland, so if you want a view of the sea you must turn westwards along one of the many tracks, or take the coastal road (where there is one) which is usually deserted except for the odd slow-moving donkey cart. The coast road between El Jadida and Safi is highly recommended.

The major towns are protected by magnificent ramparts built at the end of the 15C by the Portuguese, who braved the rocks and installed their colonies all the way down the coast. They did not evacuate their strongholds until late in the 16C, and in some places later, when forced out by the Moroccans. There is no doubt that these ramparts, heavy and a dark red-brown in colour in contrast to the usually white Moorish houses, add greatly to the charm of the towns.

The advantages of this part of Morocco's west coast have only just been discovered by the world at large, and a controlled effort is being made by the tourist authorities to offer adequate accommodation, sports facilities and entertainment which will fit in with the environment rather than destroy it (the new golf course south of Azemmour is an example of this).

Azemmour

Azemmour, 80km from Casablanca, is a cluster of white, flat-roofed houses along the banks of the river **Oum er Rbia**. Kasbahs and minarets rise up to add a vertical note to the line of flat roofs and the whole is guarded by sentinel ramparts. Time seems to have stopped here and the importance of Azemmour lies in the past, going back to its foundation by the Carthaginians in the 4C BC. Up to the end of the 19C it was an important fishing port and a centre for shoe-makers, weavers and blacksmiths. Now, however, little of these industries survives and Azemmour has been put in the shade by the bigger and more modern El Jadida, 16km away. But it is still a holy town for both Arabs and Jews, and many pilgrims come to pray at the tombs of an Islamic saint (who died here in 1183) and a grand rabbi who was said to have performed miracles.

It is worth spending an hour or two wandering through the narrow byways of the **Medina** (the rather neglected ruins of the old *mellah* and kasbah are less interesting). The main road turns left as soon as it reaches the medina walls; it is worth stopping here for an energetic walk around the top of the ramparts which extend two thirds of the way round the medina, after which you continue at ground level. The walk takes about 1h.

You climb up alongside the main entrance, flanked by a Portuguese tower with distinctive triangular windows out of which boiling oil would have been poured to deter invaders. You will see a mosque which started life as a Portuguese church, and the ruined fortress of **Dar el Baroud** ('House of Powder') with its fine Gothic window, turrets and subterranean passage leading out to the sea, which was an escape route for the Portuguese defenders.

The view from the walls down into the cramped little courtyards of clean white houses is a fascinating one. This is a small and very friendly medina (as you will see when you walk back from the end of the wall), worth stopping for if only because most visitors pass by in their haste to get to El Jadida and Safi. As you leave, notice the **synagogue** and behind it the **mellah**, which has been empty (so our guide said) since 1955. There are no hotels in Azemmour: the nearest are in El Jadida (see below).

Just south of Azemmour is the lovely sheltered beach of **Haouzia**, much appreciated by local townspeople. Alongside it is the new, American-designed 18-hole golf course—the El Jadida Royal Golf Club.

El Jadida

El Jadida is 16km west of Azemmour and beautifully situated in the arms of a bay. El Jadida means 'the new one' and the Moroccans re-named the town when they recovered it from the Portuguese (who had called it Mazagan) in the middle of the 18C. Azemmour (see above) is the Berber word for 'old city', so called because it had already been wrested from the invaders some 200 years earlier. El Jadida therefore bears traces of a more profound Portuguese penetration.

Today, El Jadida is once again an economic success story: its agricultural hinterland and a healthy textile **industry** have caused the population to rise from 90,000 to 120,000 over the last five years. The once decidedly shabby modern town centre has been spruced up quite noticeably and squares and streets (such as Place el Hansali) are animated and full of cafés. The town is also blessed with long stretches of sandy beach and a temperate climate with near-constant sunshine and a good deal of wind, which keeps temperatures down even in high summer.

The most interesting part is the old **Portuguese Quarter**, well-signposted as the _cité portuguèse_. In particular, do not miss the impressive **underground cistern**, an immense square hall supported by 25 columns and lit only by a circular opening in the roof. The Portuguese built it originally as an arsenal but in the mid-16C transformed it into a cistern: a mark on the wall records the water level at that time. It was discovered, quite by chance, in 1916, and Orson Welles used it in his film _Othello_, most of which was shot in neighbouring Essaouira. Now there is just enough water on the floor (carefully controlled) to show a stunning reflection of the arcaded roof. The best time to come, if possible, is when the sun is directly over the illumination hole. **Open** 8.30–12.00 and 14.00–18.30; entrance 10dh.

Nearby is the 16C **Church of the Assumption**, known as _le Cathedral_ and used today as an exhibition hall. The Portuguese built on a lavish scale and much of the town wall (around which there was a moat) and four out of the five great bastions survive. Two of these—known as **Le Saint Esprit** and **L'Ange**—overlook the harbour, which was once of major importance but is now too shallow for more than the sardine fishing-fleet. Walk out to **Porte de la Mer**, the old sea gate, or up to the top of L'Ange, for fine views.

There is a superb beach at **Sidi Bouzid**, a short drive down the coast road, where there are holiday villas and a couple of fish restaurants.

Hotels

Palais Andalous, Rue Curie, Ave Pasteur. ☎ (03) 343 745. ***A (36 rooms). A converted pasha's house in Andalusian style, built around a traditional court-yard. Sumptuous and recommended.

Hôtel Salam Doukkala, Rue de la Ligue Arabe. ☎ (03) 343 737. ****B (81 rooms). Large. Used for tour groups.
Hôtel de Provence, 42 Ave Fquiher-Rafy. ☎ (03) 342 347. **B (18 rooms). Simple but comfortable. The sea is at the end of the road.

Restaurants

Le Relais, 26km out on the road to Oualidia. Good for seafood.
The Safari Pub, 6 Ave Fquiher-Rafy. ☎ (03) 342 886. International.
Restaurant Le Tit, 2 Ave Jamai El Arabia. ☎ (03) 343 908. International.

Campsites

Camping International El Jadida, 500m from beach. ☎ (03) 342 755. Snack bar, restaurant, grocery, swimming pool, showers, laundry.

Golf

El Jadida Royal Golf Club, Route de Casablanca. ☎ (03) 352 251. 18 holes, par 72.

8km along the minor coast road (S1301) is the village of **Mouley Abdallah** with its impressive white *zaouia* surrounded by a crop of *marabouts*, and a fine Almohade minaret with a different design on each side (like the Hassan Tower in Rabat). The **zaouia** was founded by the son of a holy man, Ismael Angher, who arrived from Medina in Arabia with his two brothers in the 11C, during the reign of the Almoravides. Later, the Almohades came and built a *ribat*, parts of whose defensive wall still survive by the shore. The area immediately around the *zaouia* is still a holy place, visited by pilgrims every August when there is a large *moussem*. Casual, non-Muslim visitors simply wanting to look around are not welcome.

On the landward side of the village there is a second, older, **minaret**. It is Almoravide, much simpler, smaller and narrower than the one by the sea: it stands alone and unappreciated amidst ramshackle houses and is accessible by driving away from the sea round the walls and turning left through an opening. 5km further southwest is the village of **Jorf Lasfar**, formerly Cap Blanc and now transformed into an ultra-modern phosphate port with chemical works and a holiday village for the workforce just along the coast. After this the road rejoins the main coastal road (S121) which will take you all the way to Safi, 142km from El Jadida, through a prosperous market-gardening region where tomatoes, peppers, carrots, and other crops are grown.

Oualidia, a small fishing port, lies about half-way between El Jadida and Safi. It is named after a Saadian sultan, **El Oualid**, who, to defend what he saw as a good natural harbour, in 1634 built a kasbah here, one wall of which survives by the road. Today Oualidia is much appreciated by local people for its lagoon beach and for its oysters, which are relatively cheap, always fresh, and available all the year round. Conditions in the lagoon are said to be excellent for raising the shellfish, with constantly changing waters, thanks to the high Atlantic tides, and complete freedom from pollution. There are several good hotel-restaurants where oysters and other seafood can be enjoyed, including *L'Araigné Gourmande*, ☎ (03) 346 447 and *Auberge de la Lagune*, ☎ (03) 346 477. Best of all is the

Ostrea-Restaurant, tucked away below the road and picturesquely overlooking its own oyster beds. There is also a campsite, *Camping Oualidia*.

Safi

Today Safi's economic importance is threefold—phosphates, sardines and pottery. Since the creation of Jorf Lasfar, however, the balance has changed and the bulk of Morocco's phosphate production from the Khouribga area southeast of Casablanca is now processed at the new port. Safi is still one of the busiest sardine ports in the world with a huge fishing fleet and a canning industry to match, but it is now best known for its pottery, which is sold all over Morocco and in many parts of Europe. Some of it may be over-ornate to Western eyes, but much of it is delightful and it is certainly relatively cheap. A visit to the potters' colony behind the medina is not to be missed.

History of Safi

Safi is an historic town dating back to the 12C Almohades who created an important cultural and religious centre here. Some historians give it an older pedigree and claim that it was the point at which the first Arab conqueror, **Oqba ibn Nafi**, reached the sea in 683. The Portuguese devastated the old town in the 15C and built the by-now familiar ramparts to protect their conquest. After they left, the Saadians brought new prosperity to Safi by exporting sugar from Marrakesh. The Alouite dynasty continued the rehabilitation process, rebuilding religious institutions and restoring the ancient medina.

Safi attained brief international fame in the 1960s when Thor Heyerdahl set off from there in his reed boat, the *Ra*, in a bid to prove that Africans in prehistoric times could have reached the West Indies, using favourable currents and winds. He took 57 days to reach Barbados.

■ Practical information

Trains. Station on Rue du Caid Sidi Abderrahman, about 2km south of the medina. Services connect with the main Casablanca–Marrakesh line twice daily.
Buses. 1.5km south of the medina. Regular services to and from Casablanca, Agadir and places *en route*.

Hotels

Hôtel Safir, Ave Zerktouni. ☎ (04) 464 299. ****A (180 rooms)
Hôtel Atlantide, Rue Chaouki. ☎ (04) 462 160. ****B (74 rooms)
Hôtel Assif, Ave de la Liberté. ☎ (04) 462 311. **A (52 rooms)

Restaurants

Not surprisingly there is a good selection of fish eateries in Safi, with the more basic cafés often selling the most delicious grilled sardines. For a more upmarket menu, and a table in a delightful shady patio, go to the *Calypso* (see below).
Restaurant Calypso, on the main square, beside Dar el Bahar fortress. International.
Restaurant Genene, 11 rue de la Marne. ☎ (04) 463 369. Seafood.

Campsites

Camping Sidi Bouzid, 2km north of the town, 1km from Sidi Bouzid beach. Snack bar, grocery, swimming pool.

Park by the 16C Portuguese fortress known as **Dar el Bahar** (or *Château de la Mer*). This was once the Portuguese governor's residence and later became a prison. There is a good collection of 17C European cannons on the platform, but inside there is little to see apart from old prison cells. **Open** 09.00–12.00 and 14.00–16.00; closed Sat, Sun; entry 10dh.

Walk through the very small medina along its main street, Rue du Socco. As you reach the walls on the other side you will see the distinctive beehive kilns on the hill in front of you, **La Colline des Potiers**. More than 850 potters' co-operatives can be found there, using traditional methods to work the clay which is washed downhill by a stream. The craftsmen welcome the opportunity to take visitors round and explain the whole process: the kneading of raw clay, as if it were dough, to get rid of stones and impurities; the skilled fashioning of pots on wheels worked by foot treddles set in the ground beneath them; the laying out of the articles to dry in the sun for a day; the first firing (at 750°C), the painting of the design with fine horsehair brushes; the glaze (which comes from France); and the second firing (at 950°C).

Pots in every imaginable shape and size, as well as tiles (green for use in the mosques) are produced in seemingly endless quantities by this very cheerful band of men and boys, often working in family groups and using methods which have changed little over the centuries. A good selection of their wares is laid out for inspection and sale, but a wider range (and often of better quality) can be had in the pottery souk in the medina, on your right as you return along Rue du Socco.

For a panoramic view of the whole smoky process, walk up to the terrace at the top of the hill. Here too is a view of the **Kechla**, another 16C Portuguese fortress with a palace and chapel, to which the Moroccans later added a mosque and a garden. This rather shabby looking building with a green-tiled roof now houses the offices of local government (Mahkzen).

Close to the Kechla is the **zaouia** of the Hamdouchia brotherhood, where a *moussem* is held every May featuring wild, dervish-style dancing. A second **shrine**, that of the Sufi saint Sidi Bou Dheb (also with a *moussem* in May), can be found at the seaward end of Rue du Socco. Neither shrine is open to non-Muslim visitors but the *moussems* can be fascinating to watch if you happen to be in Safi at this time.

As you walk back through the medina, look out for the **Great Mosque** (17C Saadian with an imposing minaret) and the scant remains (the choir) of a Portuguese cathedral, which is behind the mosque in Rue Cadi-Ayed, off the Rue du Socco.

There are three roads out of Safi, all of which eventually join up with the P8 going south towards Essaouira. One is the road to Marrakesh, the P12 mentioned above, which joins the P8 at Tleta de Sidi Bouguedra (26km). Another is the slightly more southerly route signposted to Sebt-des-Gzoula (20km). The third is a coastal route which takes you through Safi's industrial zone, past the fish canneries and the chemical works, bears left c 15km before the small seaside resort of Souira-Kedima, and rejoins the main road at Tnine-

Rhiate (S6531). Without doubt the last of these three routes is the most rewarding.

The latter part of the road between Safi and Essaouira is wild and mountainous, for you are crossing the outer arm of the High Atlas on its way out to sea. This is wind-swept, olive tree and mimosa country, and the air is scented with aromatic herbs. The final plunge down into Essaouira is triumphal as the road spirals through the dunes to the tiny, sparkling white town at the foot of the cliff.

Essaouira

Essaouira was called Mogador by the Portuguese when they invaded it in the 16C. Later it became Essaouira, deriving from the Arabic *al sawira*, which means 'fortress surrounded by ramparts'. The French rechristened it Mogador during the Protectorate, and now, once more, it is Essaouira.

History of Essaouira

The medina, with its white houses with blue doors, and its narrow, winding streets, is glimpsed through ornately decorated arches. It is one of the cleanest and brightest medinas in Morocco. This is no surprise for it is not old at all but was built in the second half of the 18C by the Alouite sultan Mohammed ibn Abdallah, who needed a southern base from which to counter any possible revolt from Agadir, which was giving trouble at the time. Essaouira, with some fortifications already in place, was ideal for the purpose. So the Sultan commissioned a French architect, Theodore Cornut, to design a port and a town alongside, which explains why the medina—unlike any other in Morocco (except the new one in Casablanca)—is built on a **grid system**. Most of the ramparts also date from this period. Wealthy families from all over Morocco were invited to settle here and a large Jewish community was made welcome, alongside British and other European merchants. Essaouira became extremely prosperous and stayed that way until the French came in 1912 and made Casablanca their centre of commerce and finance. Thereafter Essaouira declined economically and with Independence in 1956 most of the Jewish community left.

Now, the town is thriving once more and is finding its rightful place on the tourist maps. Moreover, not having the glitz or the huge hotels of Agadir, it is largely free of package tours. Main attractions are the medina, the thuya-wood workshops in the ramparts, and the fishing port. There is a car park (with a 24-hour *gardien* who expects 10dh per overnight stay) between the medina and the port. The extensive sandy beaches are somewhat more exposed than those of Agadir, and are good for surfing. The sun shines all the year round and there is a constant wind keeping the temperature down, which is particularly welcome for the people of Marrakesh who come here to escape the midsummer heat.

■ Practical information

Tourist information. **ONMT**. Pl. Moulay el Hassan.
Buses. 2km out of town, northeast of Bab Doukkala.

Thanks to M. Cornut the **medina** is small and easy to navigate on foot. Enter via

Bab es Sebaa, which faces you as you approach from the beach and main promenade, **Boulevard Mohammed V**. Just before entering the *bab*, note Place Orson Welles on the left: the town is proud that much of his film *Othello* was made here. Walk along Avenue du Caire and turn right at the clock tower into the lively main street, **Avenue de l'Istiqlal**. The **food market** in an arcaded square on the right is a particular joy, with all kinds of fish and vegetables interspersed with locally made basketware and bright blue barrels full of olives. The women add a strange enchantment as they dart to and fro, enveloped from head to foot in white *haiks* with only the narrowest of slits left to look through.

The **jewellers' souk** (*Souk des Bijoutiers*) is on the right, just before reaching another *bab*: lots of tiny shops are crammed into a network of cool, tiled streets, and are full of silver filigree bracelets, rings and other goods, either being made or exhibited for sale; this is a refreshingly quiet and unpressurised section. Not so the **spice market** (*Marché aux Epices*) on the left after the *bab*. Here you will certainly be encouraged to go in and look and sniff. Tempting jars will be held out in front of you: 'You know what this is?', 'Smell that?' Go in, if only to escape the attentions of all the others stallholders, sit down and have a rest while your tormentor explains the contents of some 50 or 60 jars around the walls. There are powders to make you slim, and others to make you fat; there are love potions and culinary spices including mixes such as the famous *ras el hanout*, which has 125 different ingredients. You will come out bemused, maybe a few dirhams poorer, and with every exposed part of you smelling quite delicious.

Back on Avenue Mohamed Zerktouni (the name of the street beyond the *bab*), you are now in the old **mellah** or Jewish quarter, which now looks very much the same as the rest of the medina, only rather more shabby. Either return the way you came or take a left turn and another left to come back down a parallel street; at the end make a right turn to arrive in the **Place Prince Moulay el Hassan**—a charming mix of Portuguese and Moroccan architecture lined with small hotels, cafés and coppiced trees, which give it a distinctly French feel.

Essaouira is above all famous for its marquetry and woodcarving and all the serious **wood workshops** are to be found within the ramparts. From the Place Prince Moulay el Hassan, take one of the roads heading towards the sea, and turn right into Rue de la Skala. Here men and boys work with the trunk and root of thuya—a hardwood found in the surrounding countryside. They carve or inlay it with ebony, mother-of-pearl, walnut, citrus wood, or even copper or silver wire. The resulting chests, tables, boxes, animal figures, and ornaments may not be to everyone's taste but one can only admire the skill and artistry of these traditional craftsmen, many of whom work in appallingly bad light within the walls. Their work is highly prized throughout Morocco and beyond, often turning up in the classier European stores at five times the local price.

You can walk back along the top of the ramparts, stopping a moment on the **North Bastion** with its spectacular view of port and town on the left and boiling sea and rocks on the right. Ranged along the walls is a fine collection of 17C and 18C European cannons. Because of repairs to the rampart it is not possible to walk the length of it. At some point you must come down and from there it is but a short walk to the **museum** on Rue Derb Laalouj. It is housed in a 19C pasha's mansion and displays a range of typical handicrafts as well as fine examples of marquetry and carpets. **Open** 08.30–12.00 and 14.30–18.00; closed Tues; entry 10dh.

The ramparts, Essaouira

At the foot of the ramparts, and accessible through a gate on the left of the main Marine Gate, is the fishing **port**—a veritable hive of activity with hundreds of boats bobbing up and down in the shelter of the sea wall. A lot of ship-building goes on here and the jagged, orange-painted wooden hulls in various stages of construction make a colourful addition to the scene. Nets are mended and catches unloaded, sorted and packed with the gulls wheeling excitedly above. Not to be missed if you are even remotely hungry are the **fish grills**, with tables temptingly laid along the quayside, whose owners compete to offer you the best priced, best smelling and best tasting charcoal-grilled fish—sardines (of course), shrimp, sole, red mullet, and shellfish including sea urchins, crab and lobster. A knowing and unhurried wander amongst the tables beforehand, assessing the quality and price, is always respected and can be rewarding. Inevitably the outer tables get filled first (usually by Europeans).

Out to sea are two rocky islands known as **Les Îles Purpuraires**, so named because it was here that, in the 1C BC, the Berber King Juba II of Mauritania is believed to have set up a dyeworks, which was subsequently used by the Romans for their imperial purple cloth. The larger of the two islands—**L'Île de Mogador**—is crowned by a large building, formerly a prison. Nowadays the only inhabitants apart from a *gardien* are birds—some of them rare—including Eleanora's Falcon, which can often be sighted from the mainland in the evenings, wheeling low over the sea. It disappears to Madagascar in October and returns in May. Visitors to the islands are discouraged but permits are sometimes available from the Municipal Offices of the Province.

Hotels
The less pretentious hotels cluster around the Place Moulay Hassan.

Hôtel des Iles, Blvd Mohammed V. ☎ (04) 472 329. ****A (75 rooms). A large modern hotel on the front with a perfect sea view, only a 2min walk from the medina.

Hôtel Villa Maroc, 10 Rue Abdellah ben Yacine. ☎ (04) 473 147. ***B (20 rooms). A special treat. A restored 18C mansion just inside the medina walls, it has a terrace with fine views. Its intimate atmosphere is designed to make visitors feel as if they are 'staying as guests in a private house.' Delicious Moroccan food.

Hôtel des Machouar, Rue Okba Ibn Nafia. ☎ (04) 472 018. *A (27 rooms). Basic but very lively.

Villa Quieta, 86 Blvd Mohammed V. ☎ (04) 783 281. A superb villa by the sea. Not classified but highly recommended by a correspondent.

Restaurants
There is a wide range of good value fish restaurants in the medina and on the sea front.

Chalet de la Plage, Blvd Mohammed V. ☎ (04) 472 158. Opposite *Hôtel des Îles* (see above). Highly recommended.

El Minzah, 3 Ave Oqba Ibn Nafia. ☎ (04) 472 308. Seafood. Expensive.

Chez Sam, Port de Peche. ☎ (04) 473 513. Seafood. Cheaper than above.

El Khaima, Rue L'Aalouj, Place Chrib Athay. ☎ (04) 473 052. Good Moroccan food.

Campsites
Camping Municipal Essaouira, 50m from beach. Grocery, showers, laundry.
Camping Balneaire Essaouira Kedima, next to the beach. Showers, laundry.

Essaouira to Agadir

Two thirds of this 171km-long road passes inland through hills spotted with argan and thuya trees, the latter supplying the raw material for Essaouira's marquetry and woodcarving industry.

The former—*argania spinosa*—is a scrubby, feathery tree which grows only in this part of Morocco, and here in great profusion. It is appreciated most of all by the **goats** which climb right up into it with astonishing agility and devour its leaves and fruit. Bright little goat boys, knowing that tourists will want to stop and photograph this sight, stand well to the fore, quick to ask for a dirham or else push the goats down out of the trees. The tree is useful to humans as well as to the goats: the fruits are harvested in May or June and crushed to yield an orange, nutty flavoured oil which is much prized and used domestically throughout the region. And they provide lively interest through otherwise featureless countryside.

Things improve as the road approaches **Cap Rhir**, an outlying spur of the High Atlas which forms one arm of the Bay

Goat in an argan tree

of Agadir. Here there are lagoons which are perfect for peaceful and uninterrupted birdwatching. 2km north of the village of **Tamri** we saw flocks of flamingoes stamping their feet to stir up crustaceans in the sand, and also herons, cranes, gannets and much else. (Serious birdwatchers may want to go on to the protected reserve of **Oued Massa**, 40km south of Agadir, where the rare bald ibis has been sighted as well as the more usual waders and seabirds.)

Once you have rounded Cap Rhir there are some wonderful stretches of beach, often quite deserted, known collectively (and rightly) as **Paradis Plage**. There is little in the way of hotels or holiday villas but for a picnic on the way down to Agadir it would be difficult to think of anywhere nicer. As you move southwards you will find village shops selling great hands of tiny, pink-tinged bananas. These are quite delicious and are just one of the products of the Souss Valley, which is one of the most fertile areas in Morocco.

12km north of Agadir there is a left-hand turn signposted to **Imouzzer-des-Ida-Outanane**. It is the road itself rather than the destination which is significant, for it follows a green and luxuriant valley alive with cascading waterfalls, which appear in startling contrast to the arid lands behind and to the south. For those who want to go all the way (50km), Imouzzer is a white hilltop village known particularly for its delicious aromatic honey, and for its honey festival each July. There are wonderful opportunities for walking and birdwatching, offering the possibility of sighting golden eagles.

Hotels

Hôtel des Cascades,well sign-posted from the main square in Imouzzer. ☎ (08) 834 705. As near to paradise as one can get, with fabulous views, a path down to the falls, a swimming pool, pony trekking and guides on offer.

Agadir

Agadir's greatest asset is the extent of its beaches—stretches of fine golden sand protected by the arms of the Baie de Ghir and offering some of the best bathing in Morocco. There is also sailing, water-skiing, skin-diving and fishing, not to mention riding, golf and tennis. With an ideal temperate climate (in January the minimum temperature is 16°C, in July the maximum is 27°C), Agadir is Morocco's busiest tourist resort, well set up for group tourism and still growing. There is not much to choose between the huge glossy hotels which line the seafront, with their international menus, swimming pools and night clubs. Everyone seems happy enough, though manners and smiles are sometimes lacking on the part of overworked and bored receptionists.

History of Agadir

The village which became Agadir was inhabited by Berber fishermen and farmers living off the fertile hinterland and using natural caves to store their grain. Portuguese sailors began to arrive and were quick to see the possibilities not only for fishing but for smuggling. In 1513 the Portuguese king, Manuel I, installed a **garrison** which began to control slave routes from Timbuktu and central Africa. In 1540 the Saadians attacked Agadir in force and, after a siege, drove out the invaders. They built the kasbah on the hill overlooking the harbour and were later ousted by the Alouites, who strengthened the kasbah. Agadir prospered as never before with ships arriving daily to take on cargoes of sugar cane, dates, spices, and gold in exchange for European cloth and grain. It came briefly into the limelight in 1911 when the Germans sent a gunboat—the *Panther*—into the bay and shot off a few rounds in protest against French and British plans to divide up the whole of North Africa between them; it had the desired effect and Germany was placated by being ceded territory in the French Congo.

After Independence (1956) trade went into decline but hotels began to be built and the future looked bright. Then, in a mere 15 seconds on 29 February 1960, Agadir was almost completely destroyed by an earthquake; 15,000 people died. King Mohammed V declared, 'If it was Agadir's destiny to be destroyed, its reconstruction will depend on our faith and our determination.' These qualities were not lacking and rebuilding began almost immediately, slightly to the south of the old town and using anti-seismic materials. Today, all that remains of the old town (the ruins were bulldozed to prevent epidemics) is the plateau known as **Ancienne Talborjt**. A garden has been planted over it and Moroccans still come up to sit quietly and to remember.

The **kasbah** is a different matter. After the ravages of time and earthquake, all that remains today of the old Saadian fort are some walls and a *bab*. People are puzzled by the Dutch inscription (which translates as 'Fear God and obey the king') on the *bab*, which dates from the 18C when the Dutch were trading here. The whole site has now become a tourist trap. The coaches roll in and the camels and trinket sellers are there to amuse the crowds. In fact, the only point of driving 8km up the steep road to the top is to enjoy the view, which is superb, and one can do this perfectly well without camel rides or 'guides'.

■ Practical information

Tourist information. **ONMT**. Building 'A', Pl. du Prince Héritier Sidi Mohammed. ☎ (08) 842 894. **Syndicat d'Initiative**. Ave Mohammed V. ☎ (08) 840 307.
Banks. Ave du Général Kettani. and Blvd Hassan II.
Post office. Ave Sidi Mohammed.
Air transport. Royal Air Maroc, Rue du General Kettani. ☎ (08) 880 045. Al Massira airport is 28km out on the Inezgane road. ☎ (08) 839 001. Flights to London, New York, Montreal,and connections with all Moroccan airports. There is no airport bus. *Grand taxis* into town cost 100dh (more at night).
Buses. Blvd Mohammed Cheikh Saadi. Services to Casablanca, Marrakesh, Essaouira, Taroudannt, Goulimine, Laayoune etc.
Grands taxis. Pl. Salam.

Hotels
There are scores of high-rise, luxury hotels vying for space along the seafront, most with their own swimming pools and tennis courts. Most concentrate on mass catering for tour groups. The list below is a very small sample.
Hôtel Europa Safir, Blvd du 20 Août. ☎ (08) 821 212. ***** (137 rooms)
Hôtel Sahara, Blvd Mohammed V. ☎ (08) 840 660. ****A (273 rooms)
Hôtel Adrar, Blvd Mohammed V. ☎ (08) 840 437. ****A (170 rooms)

Hôtel Anezi, Blvd Mohammed V. ☎ (08) 840 940. ****A (257 rooms)
Hôtel Alibaba, Blvd Mohammed V. ☎ (08) 843 326. ***A (105 rooms)
Hôtel el Oumnia, Rue Oued Souss. ☎ (08) 840 351. ***B (180 rooms)
Hôtel Royal, Blvd Mohammed V. ☎ (08) 840 675. **A (98 rooms)
Hôtel Ait Laayoune, Rue Yacoub El Mansour. ☎ (08) 824 375. *A (9 rooms)

Holiday villages
Club Mediterranée, Rue Oued Souss. ☎ (08) 840 542. 375 rooms
La Hacienda, 6km out on the Inezgane road. ☎ (08) 831 847. 51 rooms and an excellent restaurant.

Restaurants
Again, the possibilities are endless. The best fish restaurants are around the port area.
L'Amiral, Port de Peche. ☎ (08) 846 080.
Restaurant du Port, Yacht Club Port d'Agadir. ☎ (08) 843 708.
La Mer, Blvd du 20 Août.
Tafoukt, Pl. Prince Heritier Sidi Mohammed. ☎ (08) 821 491. Good Moroccan food.

Campsites
Camping International Agadir, Blvd Mohammed V. ☎ (08) 840 981. Very central. Snack bar, restaurant, grocery, swimming pool, showers, laundry.
Taghazout, 12km out on the Essaouira road. Grocery, showers, laundry.

A tour of the city
The town itself is made up of broad avenues and refreshing green spaces. Some of the architecture is imaginative, particularly the central post office and the fire station, but the throbbing heart of the medina—so much a part of other Moroccan towns—is of course greatly missed. Restaurants, night clubs, casinos, shops and banks are concentrated along the coastal strip immediately behind the hotels. Further inland is the **Nouvelle Talborjt**—the new city centre—where shops are less tourist-orientated and restaurants serve Moroccan food at reasonable prices.

Apart from the beach, there are two places worth noting in Agadir: one is the **Valley of the Birds**—a kind of open-air zoo right in the middle of town, occupying a gully that runs underneath the main **Boulevard Mohammed V** and **Boulevard Hassan II**. In this strip of lush parkland are aviaries of exotic birds, interspersed with ponds of duck and guinea fowl, and interesting animals such as mouflons, llamas and macaques. Some of the cages are rather small but everything seems clean and well cared for. The whole is a triumph of imaginative planning, if nothing else. **Open** 09.30–12.30 and 15.00–19.00; entry adults 5dh, children 3dh.

In more serious mood, and definitely worth a visit, is the excellent **Folk Art Museum**, which is housed underneath the Roman-style theatre on Boulevard Mohammed V. This collection of southern Moroccan and Saharan crafts was put together by a Dutch anthropologist, Bert Flint, who has lived in Morocco since 1957. (The other half of his collection, covering the rest of the country, is to be found at the Maison Tiskiwin in Marrakesh.) There are costumes, jewellery, pottery, carpets in soft colours and some exceptionally finely carved doors. It is a pleasure to see such beautifully worked and simple folk art, as a change from the more frequently displayed formal and highly ornamented artefacts taken from ancient palaces. **Open** 09.30–13.00 and 14.00–18.00; closed Sun; entry 10dh.

Inezgane

Inezgane is an unaffected, tranquil town 10km south of Agadir, which has two hotel-restaurants serving a range of excellent French food, mainly fish. One can occasionally feel the need to escape from the somewhat claustrophobic atmosphere of tourist-driven Agadir, if only for a few hours, and Inezgane serves this purpose very adequately. Otherwise, for a longer interlude and a complete change of mood, Taroudannt lies just 68km to the east.

Hotels

Hôtel Le Provencal, on the Agadir road. ☎ (08) 832 712. Lovely gardens and a very good restaurant.
Hôtel de Paris, 10 Blvd Mohamed V. ☎ (08) 830 571. Good, and cheap.

Golf

Agadir Royal Golf Club, Inezgane. ☎: (08) 241 278. 9 holes, par 36.

The Rif mountains and the Mediterranean coast

Thought to have been the original natural frontier between Europe and Africa and stretching some 300km from west to east, the Rif mountain range is a formidable barrier by any standards. Throughout history it has been the home of proud and fierce Berber tribes, whom no one ever succeeded in permanently subduing. They were better left alone and the phrase *Bled es Siba* ('Land of the lawless tribes') was used to distinguish this territory—and that beyond the similarly impenetrable barrier of the High Atlas—from *Bled el Makhzen* ('Land which is governed').

This section of *Blue Guide Morocco* follows the road (built soon after Independence) that runs along the backbone of the range from Tetouan through Chaouen as far as Al Hoceima and beyond (P39); it also describes an excursion southwards to Ouezzane. The views and the sheer scale of the mountain scenery are breathtaking; villages are thinly scattered and isolated; life is very hard here and the population is sparse, but wherever the ground is approximately level, it has been minutely cultivated. Also included in this section is the 'Taza Gap', the corridor of land which runs between the Rif and Middle Atlas ranges.

By contrast with the mountains, the Mediterranean coast between Tetouan and Ceuta is a warm and smiling land of sheltered sandy beaches wedged between rocky promontories. One-time fishing villages have been developed as highly profitable tourist resorts, some of which are very attractive. The central crescent of coastline is, however, inhospitable and remains undeveloped and inaccessible as far as Al Hoceima. The road then continues eastwards over the plains as far as Oujda on the Algerian border.

Tetouan

Tetouan, 54km southeast of Tangier, is a white town set on a hillside and surrounded by olive groves and gardens. It has a strong Spanish atmosphere, which is not surprising since it has been intimately connected with that country throughout its history, not least during the Protectorate (1912–56) when it was capital of the Spanish Zone. Even today it is sometimes known as 'the daughter of Granada'.

History of Tetouan

The origins of Tetouan lie in prehistory, in the Berber city of **Tamuda** which was destroyed by the Romans in the 1C AD, probably as part of the campaign to quash the Berber rebellion against direct rule from Rome. The Romans built their own town on the ruins. (The remains of Tamuda are to be found today 5km out of Tetouan off the Chaouen road, by the river **Martil**.)

In the 13C the Merinides founded a new city alongside Tamuda. The kasbah (1286), was a massive fortification intended to protect the important north–south route from Tangier to Fes from marauding Rif Berber tribes. This well-protected town prospered for about 100 years until the Spanish king Henry III of Castile crossed the Strait of Gibraltar and destroyed it, massacring most of the population and leaving only a ruined site behind him.

The medina and kasbah that survive today were built on the ruins of the Merinide town during the 15th and 16C by Muslims and Jews who had fled Spain and Portugal during this period. Later, the Alouite sultan Moulay Ismael surrounded the medina and kasbah with a massive **rampart**, much of which still stands. As relations with Spain improved, and not before time in view of Tetouan's geographical proximity to both mainland Spain and the Spanish enclave of Ceuta, trading links were set up and one or two of the Catholic orders were even allowed to establish foundations within the city walls. It seemed natural therefore—Tangier having been declared an International Zone—that Spain should choose Tetouan as **capital** of the Protectorate in 1912, and it was the Spanish who built the modern city on the west side of the wall.

The Spanish did not have an easy time, however, for just to the south was the great range of the Rif, which harboured some of the fiercest Berber tribes in the whole of North Africa, led by the legendary Abd el Krim. He was imprisoned by the Spanish for a relatively minor matter, managed to escape and, fired with desire for revenge, gathered up a huge army of rebellious mountain Berbers who stood up to Spain in what became known as the **Rif War**, which lasted 14 years. Massive defeats were inflicted on the Spanish, who were almost driven back into the sea in a battle near Al Hoceima (1921), and who lost their mountain stronghold of Chaouen. For a time Abd el Krim was in complete control and declared himself president of an independent Rif Republic, but following his decision to strike southwards towards Ouezzane and Fes (where he planned to have himself

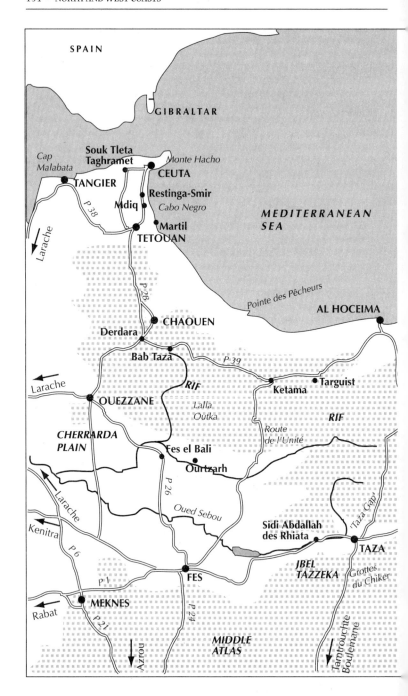

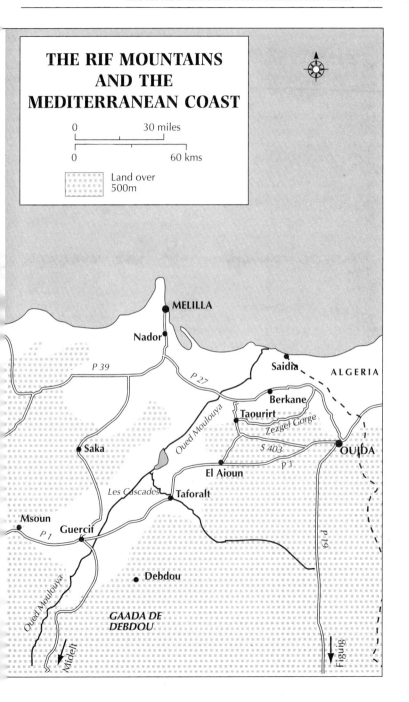

THE RIF MOUNTAINS
AND THE
MEDITERRANEAN COAST

0   30 miles

0   60 kms

Land over
500m

MELILLA

Nador

P 39

P 27

Saidia

ALGERIA

Berkane

Oued Moulouya

Taourirt

Zezgel Gorge

Saka

S 403

OUJDA

El Aioun

P 1

Les Cascades

Taforalt

Msoun

Guercif

P 1

P 19

Oued Moulouya

Debdou

Midelt

GAADA DE
DEBDOU

Figuig

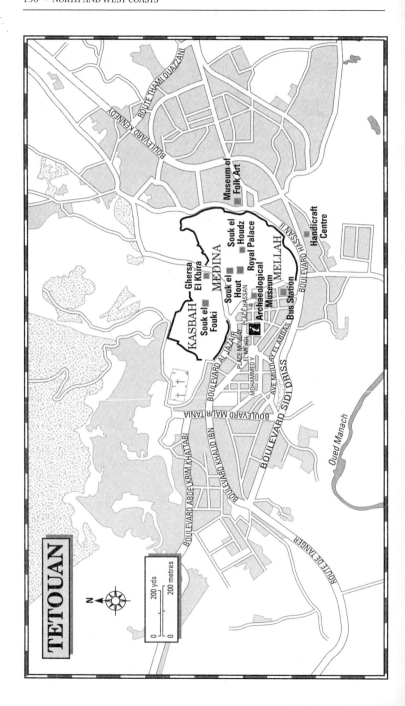

Museum of Folk Art

Souk el Houdz

Royal Palace

Ghersa El Khira

MEDINA

Souk el Hout

Archaeological Museum

Handicraft Centre

MELLAH

BOULEVARD HASSAN II

Bus Station

KASBAH

Souk el Fouki

PLACE HASSAN II

PLACE MOULAY EL MEHDI

MOHAMMED V

AVE MOULAY EL ABBAS

BOULEVARD AL JAZAIR

BOULEVARD MAURITANIA

BOULEVARD SIDI DRISS

BOULEVARD ABDELKRIM KHATTAB

BOULEVARD KHALID IBN

ROUTE THAMI OUAZZANI

BOULEVARD KENNEDY

ROUTE DE TANGER

Oued Manach

TETOUAN

200 yds

200 metres

0

0

N

declared sultan of all Morocco) the Spanish and French formed a somewhat uneasy alliance to get rid of this common enemy. Together they managed to defeat him and he was sent into exile in 1926. With the loss of their leader the Berber resistance dissolved and the Rif War came to an end. There followed a period of peace within the Spanish Zone which was maintained even throughout the Spanish Civil War.

■ Practical information

Tourist office. **ONMT**. 30 Ave Mohammed V (off Pl. Moulay el Mehdi). ☎ (09) 964 407.
Banks. Pl. Moulay el Mehdi.
Post office. Pl. Moulay el Mehdi.
Buses. Bus station off Blvd de Mouquauama—southeast of Pl. Moulay el Mehdi. Services to Tangier, Ceuta, Chaouen, Meknes, and Fes.
Grands taxis. Ave Moulay el Abbas.

Hotels
Hotel Safir, Ave Kennedy. ☎ (09) 970 144 fax (09) 970 692. ****A (96 rooms). 3km out of town and really designed to suit the package tours.
Hotel Chams, Route de Martil. ☎ (09) 990 901 fax (09) 990 907. *** (74 rooms). Also about 3km outside, close to the airport.
Paris Hotel, 11 Rue Chakib Arsalane. ☎ (09) 966 750. **A (40 rooms). Centrally placed and adequate. No restaurant.
Hotel Oumaima, Rue Achrmai. ☎ (09) 963 473. **B (36 rooms). Also central. No restaurant.

Restaurants
The best fish restaurants are on the coast in the Cabo Negro area, and include *Meridiana*, Croisement Cabo Negro M'diq. ☎ (09) 971 514.
In town, try:
Restaurant Zerhoun, 7 Rue Mohammed Ben Larbi Torres. Spanish and Moroccan food.
Palace Bouhlal, Jamai El Kebir No.48. ☎ (09) 974 419. Moroccan food. In the medina.

Campsites
El Fraja, 200m from the beach. Snack bar, restaurant, grocery, showers, laundry.

At the centre of Tetouan, between the medina and the modern city, is **Place Hassan II**, overlooked by the old **Royal Palace**, built by Moulay Ismael in the 17C and restored in the 1930s for use by Mohammed V. It is not, unfortunately, open to visitors. The impressive square used to be dominated by the old Spanish Consulate but in 1988 this was replaced by a new royal palace, and the Spanish-style flowers and fountains have made way for a huge circular pavement of modern Islamic design. Five minutes' walk west of here is the second important square, **Place Moulay el Mehdi**, where the ONMT, the post office and banks are located.

The **medina**, which you enter from Place Hassan II by way of the Bab el Rouah, is quite small and full of interest. Its charm lies in the preponderance of tiny squares, vine-trellissed streets, delicate Andalusian houses complete with wrought-iron balconies, and very small mosques (22 in all), many of which have brilliant white minarets.

Throughout the medina there are souks, among them the **Souk el Fouki** selling both cloth and clothes; **Souk el Hout**, which must be one of the liveliest fish markets anywhere in Morocco (although Tetouan is not on the coast it benefits from the rich waters of the river Martil estuary); **Souk el Houdz**, a Berber market where the women sell the red-and-white striped material from which they make their distinctive skirts (*foutas*); and **Ghersa El Kbira**, which is a market for fruit and vegetables by day, and for second-hand clothes in the evening. The small tanning works is fairly easy to find, if only because of the sickly smell; there, the skins of camel, goat and calf are scraped, cleaned, soaked and dyed in great open-air vats, and then laid out to dry in the sun. There is also a surprising proliferation of barbers, their Sweeney Todd-like chairs gleaming in shadowy rooms awaiting the next victim, and dentists, who announce their trade to passers-by with glass cases full of grinning dentures. This is a very varied medina, and one which seems content, for the moment, to resist the commercial pressures that have affected, for example, Tangier.

There are two museums in Tetouan. The **Museum of Folk Art** (*Musée d'art folklorique*) is in an old palace right up against the inside of the ramparts, near the beautiful **Bab el Okla** ('Queen's Gate'). It exhibits crafts of the region, including some interesting wedding costumes. **Open** 09.00–12.00 and 14.30–17.30; closed Tue, Sun; entry 10dh. ☎ (09) 966 905.

The **Archaeological Museum** is situated on Place el Jala near Place Hassan II; it shows artefacts from Lixus and Tamuda and also some prehistoric megaliths from the once Spanish zone of the Western Sahara. Opening hours as above; ☎ (09) 967 103.

Equally interesting is the **School of Traditional Arts and Crafts** (*École d'arts et de métiers*), which is also near Bab el Okla but just outside the ramparts. Occupying another old palace, this active school is run by the government to teach young people traditional crafts which might otherwise die out. In termtime you may enter the various workshops and see the processes of carpetmaking, cedarwood carving and painting (for ceilings), and the delicate art of inlaying olivewood with silver and fragments of sea-shells to make elegant cabinets and desks. During school holidays it is still worth trying to go in to see the finished articles, even if the 40 or 50 students are not there. ☎ (09) 962 721.

There is also a **handicraft centre** (*centre artisanal*), south of the modern town on Rue Moulay Hassan II. It is certainly worth a visit if you intend to do any serious shopping in the souks. As with so many other centres, it is the craftsmen in the surrounding workshops who prove the most absorbing and informative company. ☎ (09) 967 822.

The **kasbah** lies to the north of the medina and can be reached either by car from outside the ramparts or on foot (a steep climb) from within the medina, going up Rue Tala (near Souk el Fouki). The fortress, built by Muslim refugees from Spain c 1600, is now occupied by the Moroccan army and is not open to visitors. The approach, by car or on foot, is through an uninspiring part of town and can be an anti-climax after the undoubted charm of the medina.

Chaouen

The road to Chaouen, 63km south of Tetouan, climbs gently over cistus-studded hillsides, with enticing glimpses of the high Rif peaks in the distance. The name Chaouen (or Chefchaouen as it is sometimes called) literally means 'the horns' (or 'see the horns'), and the reason for this becomes apparent as you approach the town, which sits dramatically between the twin peaks of Jbel Ech Chaouen ('Horned Mountain')

History of Chaouen

Like Tetouan, Chaouen was built by Muslims and Jews fleeing from Christian persecution in southern Spain in the late 15C and 16C and it too has a distinctive Andalusian atmosphere. But unlike Tetouan, Chaouen remained closed to the outside world for centuries. This was partly because of its physical impregnability, but mainly because of its reputation for being particularly sacred to Muslims (the tomb of an important saint—Moulay Abdessalam ibn Mchich—lies there), and consequently violently anti-Christian. Nevertheless, two eminent explorers and one journalist—Charles de Foucault, William Summers and Walter Harris—are known to have got in: de Foucault spent one night there disguised as a Jew in 1883, Summers was poisoned by the inhabitants in 1892, and Walter Harris relates that he only just escaped with his life in 1889. Even the Spaniards failed to enter Chaouen until the final assault on Abd el Krim, the Berber leader, in 1926. When they did finally succeed in storming the town they discovered, to their amazement, craftsmen using some of the skills last seen in 15C Cordoba, and long forgotten there.

■ Practical information

Tourist office. **ONMT**. Pl. Mohammed V.
Banks. Banque Marocaine and Banque Populaire, both near the bus station.
Post office. Ave Hassan II.
Buses. Station is in the market place west of town (just outside the walls). Services to Tetouan, Al Hoceima, Melilla, Ouezzane, Fes, and Meknes.
Grands taxis. By the bus station.

Hotels

Parador Chaouen, Pl. el Makhzen. ☎ (09) 986 324 fax (09) 987 033. ****B (35 rooms). Recommended for both comfort and location (see below).
Hôtel Asma, Sidi Abdelhamid. ☎ (09) 986 265 fax (09) 987 158. ***A (94 rooms). Overlooks the town from on high (see below).
Hôtel Magou, 23 Rue Moulay Idriss. ☎ (09) 986 257. **A (35 rooms). Overlooks the market outside the medina.
Hôtel Panorama, 33 Rue M. Abderrahmane. ☎ (09) 986 615. *A (20 rooms). A new hotel outside the medina but with splendid views from its terrace.

Restaurants

Al Baraka, Derb M'hatib. ☎ (09) 986 988. Moroccan food. In the medina.
Fuenterrabia, Place Uta Hamam. ☎ (09) 987 221. Moroccan fish. In the medina.
Both the *Parador* and the *Hotel Asma* have good restaurants.

Campsites

There is a campsite right by the *Hotel Asma*.

A stay in this enchanting place is a must. The two principal **hotels**, the *Asma* and the *Parador Chaouen*, are very different from each other in both atmosphere and location. The luxurious *Asma* is easy to find: it stands—a huge, white, unlovely building—on top of one of the hills that dominate the town and so has a superb view, but it is totally dissociated from the life of Chaouen. The more modest *Parador* stands in the main **Place el Makhzen**, with the medina and the kasbah only two minutes' walk away. A room at the front of this hotel affords a view over the red-tiled roofs which range up the hill in glorious disorder and are clustered around a very old brick minaret crowned with a white turret. In the square below are the orderly rows of stalls of various merchants, shoemakers, potters and sellers of Berber magic spells. A room at the back of the hotel looks out over the lower slopes of the mountain, with a rushing stream far below and the white ruins of a one-time Catholic church above.

It is pleasant to walk beside this stream; the abundance of water in Chaouen makes possible a great deal of profitable activity, including at least one very old water-mill still in use for grinding local cereals into flour. There are also several olive-oil presses, unchanged in design for hundreds of years and still in use.

A street in Chaouen

A walk through the **medina** (which comprises most of the town) is a memorable experience, though somewhat less tranquil than before Chaouen was discovered by tourism, which has caused attitudes to change and become more commercial. As everything is on a slope, the walk is quite strenuous. The medina is entered by a path exactly opposite the *Parador* hotel, and has four sections—'Moroccan', Andalusian, Berber, and Jewish—an historic distinction probably dating back to when Berbers (and certainly the Rif Berbers) were not considered to be Moroccan. Originally each quarter was locked up at night behind great wooden doors. Some of these doors still remain (now permanently open), and the one giving access to the Jewish quarter has been well preserved. Only the **Andalusian section** is markedly different from the rest, displaying the *Ajimez* paired windows with delicate wrought-iron grilles so typical of southern Spain. In fact, the whole medina is strongly Andalusian in atmosphere; many of the tiled roofs are outlined in white, and there is only the occasional minaret or rounded *marabout* dome to remind you that you are in Morocco.

The women from the Andalusian section dress quite differently from the rest, enveloping themselves almost completely in white robes. Berber women wear traditional red-and-white striped shawls and skirts, and straw hats and gaiters, the latter designed to protect their legs from mountain thorn bushes. The walls, and also sometimes the steps of the houses, are painted bluish-white, which is said by the locals to keep away mosquitoes. It also produces an effect of coolness. The whole town is immensely picturesque and colourful.

Every Monday and Thursday morning the medina bursts into life when Berbers come in from nearby mountain villages to sell their wares. But there is a lot of quiet hard work going on all the time, much of it based on **wool**, as sheep-rearing is an important part of the Rif economy. You will see wool being spun everywhere, often by quite small children, and groups of men, working in large rooms that open on to the street, weaving lengths of cloth for djellabahs on traditional hand looms; it is usually the older men who sew the woven lengths of cloth into garments. In other rooms women will be knotting **carpets** (this is traditionally women's work, as weaving and sewing appear to be men's). They will probably not mind if you watch them work, but they may well dislike having their photograph taken.

There are many **Koranic schools** in this ultra-traditional town and the muted chanting of children's voices from behind thick walls is one of the more characteristic sounds of the medina. By law all children between the ages of five and seven should attend such a school, where they acquire an early grounding in the essential wisdom of the Koran before going on to primary school. There are also a number of **hammams** in Chaouen, often identifiable by piles of firewood in the street outside; the men usually bathe in the morning, and women in the afternoon; some hammans also have family rooms. There is even a square called **Place Uta al Hammam** (Place of the Bath), an animated spot right in the centre and surrounded by cafés, preserving a 15C bath which still functions (but only for men). Close by, on the south side, is the **Great Mosque**, with a fine octagonal minaret. It was built in the 15C by Cherif Ali ibn Rachid, founder of Chaouen and head of the Emirate of Chaouen and Tetouan, a minor dynasty related to the Wattasides who ruled somewhat disastrously from Fes until ousted by the Saadians in the mid-16C.

Dominating the main Place el Makhzen is the great, aggressive bulk of the **kasbah** fortress. It was built in the 17C by the Alouite sultan Moulay Ismael to keep the Berbers in order; later, in the early years of the Spanish Protectorate, it became the headquarters of the Berber leader Abd el Krim, and was the last stronghold of his resistance; finally, in 1926, it became his prison when the Spanish at last succeeded in taking it. Within the curtain walls remain the house of Abd el Krim (now a museum), a dungeon and a large garden, where there are traces of further building.

The **museum** has some interesting exhibits, including some unique examples of *cajas de boda*, hand-carved and painted wooden carriages in which brides were carried to their weddings. There are two sorts of carriage: one type was pulled by a donkey, and the other carried by men, and both are so incredibly small that you wonder how the bride in her wedding regalia could possibly sit inside. There is also a collection of Berber and Andalusian musical instruments, and a very fine heavy wooden door said to have survived from the original building of the kasbah. The **dungeon**, still dark and miserable, has chains with metal collars and leg-irons still in place to remind one of past barbarities. The gardens outside provide a cheerful contrast and beneath them is an underground chamber which is today filled with water and cannot be entered but which was once connected to the outer walls and beyond by a maze of passages.

Ouezzane

A short visit to the remote hilltop town of Ouezzane is recommended. The road from Chaouen, 60km away, offers an easy mountain drive with sweeping bends and glorious views over the pink oleander-covered slopes of the Rif to the river far below. Here and there a herd of goats, usually guarded by an incredibly small child, will provide a speck of movement in an otherwise lonely landscape. Surrounded by 600,000 olive trees, Ouezzane, when seen from a distance, is a mass of white houses which spread in a kind of orderly chaos over the side of the hill.

History of Ouezzane

The town once marked the boundary between the governed *Bled el Makhzen* and the lawless *Bled es Siba* and, as such, it was a base for influential sheikhs who held the balance of power. These sheikhs, known as the Ouezzani, claimed to be descended from the founding dynasty of Muslim Morocco—the Idrissides—and became influential spiritual leaders, acquiring a great following. In 1727 one of their number—**Moulay Abdallah**—established an exclusive, powerful, and sometimes fanatical brotherhood known as the Tabiya. He built a mosque in Ouezzane where he was buried, and this sanctuary formed a focal point for devout Muslims, and a centre for pilgrims almost as significant as the holy town of Moulay Idriss itself; it was jealously guarded from outsiders such as Christians and Jews. So powerful was the brotherhood in the 19C that each new Alouite sultan would pay a formal visit to Ouezzane to seek its support (without which he would doubtless have been severely hampered). The *cherif* of Ouezzane would in turn pay homage to the sultan, in the name of the Rif tribes.

Transport. Buses and a stand for *grand taxis* at Pl. de l'Indepéndence.

The **Mosque of the Tabiya Brotherhood** stands close to the central square—**Place de l'Indepéndence**—up a small, stepped passageway. It has a distinctive octagonal minaret covered with green tiles which was restored in 1968. All around are the remains of pilgrims' lodgings and a derelict Ouezzani palace. Close by is a lively area of **souks** with carpenters, blacksmiths and weavers hard at work. Painted furniture and heavy woollen rugs are the particular speciality of this town and a good range can be seen in the **Centre Artisanal**, facing Place de l'Indépendence.

Because the town was built on the lower slopes of the **Jbel Bou Hellal**, most of the streets of the **medina** are steep. It is perfectly possible, though tough going, to walk the extent of the medina and emerge into the olive groves on the upper side, where you are rewarded with a fine view back over the town. Tourists seem to be few in these parts and you can wander freely and without hassle. Ouezzane may lack the softening Andalusian touches of its picturesque Rifian neighbour, Chaouen, but its dilapidated streets have a certain raw charm and its people are naturally friendly.

There are no classified hotels in Ouezzane.

The roads from Ouezzane to Fes

There are two ways to get from Ouezzane to Fes. One is the fairly featureless and relatively straight road (P28) which runs directly southwards across the **Cherrarda Plain** (134km). In places the edges of the road have been eroded away and so your speed will depend on whether or not you are the sort of driver who moves automatically on to the soft shoulder when another car approaches. The P26 from Ouezzane is a more easterly and leisurely route along the edge of the Rif foothills, as far as the little village of **Fes el Bali**. 20km further on there is a turning left to Ourtzarh, from where a track leads 37km to a high point in the heart of the Rif known as **Lalla Outka**, with some spectacular mountain views. 30km east from Ourtzarh the road joins up with the Route de l'Unité running between the main Rif west–east road and Fes.

Back on the P26 heading towards Fes, the **Jbel Amergou** (681m) appears to the right of the road. It is crowned with the ruins of an 11C Almoravide wall. The road crosses the river **Sebou** and then climbs in a series of steep curves up the side of the **Jbel Zalagh** (906m), but stops short of the top. The descent into Fes is magical, with a characteristic view of the white medina and the Middle Atlas mountains in the far distance, beyond the **Sais Plain**.

To continue the journey west–east along the Rif, turn left at **Derdara**, which lies 8km south of Chaouen. (It is anyway worth stopping here for a splendid view back over Chaouen.) Soon after Derdara you begin to climb towards **Bab Taza** and, after some breathtaking serpentine bends, you arrive at the **Bab Berred Pass** (1240m).

Ketama, exactly 100km east of Chaouen, lies at the heart of a forest of cedars and pines. The air is fresh and the countryside, dominated by the cedar-crowned **Jbel Tidighine**, is alive with cascading waterfalls and translucent streams. Ketama is now the *kif* capital of Morocco. The smoking of *kif* (hashish) has always gone on amongst the Rif tribes, who used it to mitigate the harshness of their daily lives. Now however, it has become big business. Hashish plants are grown on every available mountain slope and the stuff is processed in Ketama for export to Europe and elsewhere. Dealers are everywhere and many of them can be aggressive and even threatening, especially to foreign tourists. At one time, Ketama looked like becoming Morocco's third skiing centre (after Oukaimeden and Mischliffen, near Ifrane), as well as a popular place in summer for boar-hunting and walking. Nowadays, the wise traveller will pass through without stopping.

Hotels

Hôtel Tidighine. ☎ 16 (through the operator) ***A (64 rooms).

Ketama marks the beginning of the spectacular north–south road which crosses the Rif and goes on to Fes. It is known as the **Route de l'Unité** and was built at the end of the Spanish Protectorate in order to unify the former Spanish and French zones and generally to put an end to the isolation and perceived lawlessness of the Rif tribes. A masterpiece of engineering, it was built by thousands of volunteers under the leadership of the left-wing politician Mehdi Ben Barka. It is 156km long, tortuous, dramatic and very beautiful.

After Ketama the P39 follows the valley of the river Ouringa and climbs up to the **Bab Tizichen Pass**, from which point a track winds steeply down to **La Pointe des Pecheurs**, a little fishing settlement on the coast 61km to the north. 30km east of Ketama is the sleepy village of Targuist with little to recommend it but its eponymous restaurant and its Saturday souk. Historically, it is notable for having been the last stronghold of Abd El Krim.

Al Hoceima

Some 65km east of Targuist, the road suddenly dips and descends very steeply to Al Hoceima, which stands on the west bank of a huge bay protected by three islands and backed by steep cliffs. After hours of hard driving over the dry and dusty Rif road this place looks something like paradise.

History of Al Hoceima

The strategic advantages of this deep and protected natural harbour were recognised by the European powers as far back as the 17C; it was the Spaniards who finally occupied the existing fishing village and obtained trading rights from the then sultan, Moulay Rachid. A Spanish general—Sanjuro—founded the town in 1920 and it was named Villa Sanjuro in the first instance, until the Spaniards re-named it Alhucemas.

▪ Practical information

Tourist office. **ONMT**. Ave Tarik Ibn Ziad. ☎ (09) 982 830.
Bank. Blvd Mohammed V.
Air transport. Royal Air Maroc. ☎ (09) 982 063. The airport is 17km east of town. Flights to Casablanca. Charter flights to and from France and Germany in season. ☎ (09) 982 005.
Buses. Station at Place du Rif. ☎ (09) 982 273. Services to Fes, Casablanca, Nador, Tetouan, Taza, and Oujda.
Grands taxis. By the bus station.

Hotels

Hôtel El Maghrib el Jdid, 56 Ave Mohammed V. ☎ (09) 982 504. ***A (40 rooms). Very central and modern. Good restaurant.
Hôtel Quemado, Plage de Quemado. ☎ (09) 982 371 fax (09) 983 314. ***A (102 rooms). Built on the beach and much used by package tours. Very large.
Hôtel Karim, 27 Ave Hassan II. ☎ (09) 982 184. **B (51 rooms). Comfortable and quieter but quite a way from the beach.

Restaurants

There are a huge number of fish restaurants, mainly in the port area. Of these, try *Kiyossko Port*, ☎ (09) 982 065 and *Karim*, ☎ (09) 982 318.

Campsites

Club Mediterranée, a holiday village 4km east of town off the Melilla road. ☎ (09) 982 222. Wonderfully located and still has its straw huts. Recommended for a sporty, hearty holiday.

Camping Plage el-Jamil, next to the beach. ☎ (09) 984 046. Snack bar, restaurant, grocery, showers, laundry.

Camping Cala-Iris, next to the beach. Same facilities as above.

Over the last 30 years Al Hoceima has been developed as a major holiday resort with endless stretches of fine sand and perfect conditions for water sports. It could so easily have been spoilt but development has been carefully controlled (it had to be because space at the foot of the cliffs is limited) and the result is a harmonious complex with all amenities in a very beautiful setting. The old Spanish town behind the hotels is charming with its palm-fringed avenues and abundant cafés, and a visit to the fishing port to the north of the main beach—**Playa Quemado**—is a must. This beach gets very crowded in high summer, but there are less crowded beaches to the east and west, including **Kalah-Bonita** (which has a good café-restaurant) and **Sebadella**, with 2km of sand. The biggest of the three islands is **Peñon de Velez de la Gomera**. Originally a refuge for pirates, it then became a fortress-prison—a grim reminder that life here was not always so pleasure-bent. The island is still Spanish and is closed to visitors.

East of Al Hoceima

There is little to tempt you east of Al Hoceima. The road climbs inland, following the river Nekor up to the ridge, and then zigzags down in a series of sharp turns, described on the map as 'the toboggan', to the village of **Talamagait**. After 156km it forks left to Nador and Melilla, right for Berkane and Oujda.

Nador is a dull little town, and its development as a port has been somewhat hampered by the fact that the sea in front of it—the **Mar Chica**—is enclosed by a sand spit which no amount of dredging will clear. It has a beach and several recently-built hotels but its importance is economic rather than touristic and it acts as an outlet for iron and steel from the Jerarda district to the south. It also has a cement-works and a sugar refinery.

Melilla

13km north of Nador—half-way along the peninsula—is the Spanish enclave of Melilla. The usual **customs** formalities are necessary to enter Melilla and these can be very time-consuming as you join queues of Moroccan workers either leaving or entering the port to or from Spain. Hire cars are not allowed to cross the border at all, and any foreign car is liable to be thoroughly searched for drugs and/or illegal emigrants.

History of Melilla

Melilla was founded as a trading post by the Phoenicians, who called it **Russadir**. The Romans occupied Russadir for a time and then in 927 it was captured by Abderrahman III of Cordoba, and governed from there until the fall of the Caliphate in the early 11C. In 1492 the Muslim king Boabdil landed in Melilla after being thrown out of Granada by Ferdinand and

Isabella of Spain. Four years later it was captured by a Spanish raiding party and handed over to the Catholic monarchs, and it has remained **Spanish** ever since, despite efforts by several Moroccan sultans to recapture it.

Melilla's population has decreased significantly in recent years as its strategic importance has diminished, and it is now little more than a stopping-point for ferries and flights between the Spanish mainland and Morocco.

The most evocative section (if you must go at all) is the original walled Spanish town known as **Medina Sidonia**, which is right behind the ferry terminal. With its tall white houses and narrow streets, it represents all there was of Melilla until the early 20C. Of some interest is the municipal **museum** housed in the Bastion de Concepcion, which is part of the 16C ramparts. The contents of the museum reflect the various civilisations that have left their mark on the area, going right back to prehistory. **Open** 09.00–13.00 and 15.00–18.30; closed Sat, Sun.

It is also pleasant to walk around the ramparts, noting particularly the splendid **Gate of Santiago** (Puerta de Santiago) which displays the coat of arms of the Emperor Charles V and is next door to the **Chapel of St James the Apostle** (known in Spanish as Santiago).

The modern 20C town behind is unremarkable, though the **Plaza de España** is distinguished by one or two jolly Art Deco façades by Enrique Nieto, a contemporary of the Catalan high priest of Modernism, Antonio Gaudi (1852–1926).

It is possible to reach the tip of the peninsula without going through Melilla by taking the track to **Cap des Trois Fourches** which is met just before the customs post. The cape, which is not part of the enclave, offers some wonderful sea views.

Return southwards for 24km to take a turning left for Berkane and Oujda. The road here is flat and uneventful; about half-way to Berkane it crosses the **Oued Moulouya**, Morocco's longest river (450km), which is controlled for irrigation purposes about 50km upstream by the **Mechra Klila dam**, completed in 1967 and one of modern Morocco's proudest achievements. 20km beyond the river is a turning right to Taforalt and the Beni Snassen Mountains, which offers a short and worthwhile diversion along the Zegzel Gorge with its terraced slopes and orange and olive groves. The mountains are full of caves and there are prehistoric drawings to be found in the **Pombo cave**. The **Tghasrout** or 'Camel' grotto has extraordinary limestone formations. This is a wild and beautiful area to pause a while and explore. There are no official guides but little boys will usually appear from nowhere to 'guide' you. The road (S403) continues south-eastwards to Oujda. But if you want to see Berkane and Saidia, return to the main road.

Berkane is a modern agricultural town which serves the whole fertile Beni Snassen region, rich in vines above all (Beni Snassen is one of Morocco's foremost wine-producing areas), but also other fruit and vegetables, almond trees, and orange and lemon groves.

About 20km to the north lies Morocco's most easterly seaside resort, **Saidia**, with 20km of sandy beach and near perfect bathing conditions. However, it serves a large area and gets very crowded in summer, whilst in winter it is almost deserted. The marshes behind the beach make for good birdwatching and the woods are full of game as well as being ideal for walking and picnicking.

Campsites
Camping Essi, Saidia Place, 200m from the beach, 500 from the bus station. Grocery, showers, laundry

Oujda
Oujda, 58km from Berkane, is a prosperous, lively, modern city with a charming medina which has imposing ramparts and four monumental gates, a fine 13C mosque and a range of colourful souks. However, Oujda's position on the Algerian border makes it extremely tense at the present time.

History of Oujda
Because of its geographical position, Oujda has been much fought over in the past. Founded in the 10C, it was destroyed and rebuilt by the Almoravides in 1070, and then by the Almohades (who built the ramparts) in 1206. In the 13C the Merinides took it and enriched it with mosques, *medersas* and fountains. Later came the Saadians who used it as a base from which to march on Fes and, finally, the Alouites were here. It was the great Alouite sultan Moulay Ismael who was responsible for much of the building that we see today. After his death in 1727 Oujda passed into the hands of the Turks arriving from Algeria (it was the only part of Morocco ever to do so), and was not regained from them until the early 19C. The French, who started infiltrating the country from Algeria, took possession of Oujda in 1907—five years before the official start of the Protectorate. It was, therefore, French longer than any other town in Morocco and was the capital of the French *Maroc Orient*. It was they who built the modern city around the medina walls.

▦ Practical information

Tourist office. ONMT. Pl. du 16 Aout. ☎ (06) 682 036.
Banks. Place du 16 Août/Blvd Mohammed V.
Air transport. Royal Air Maroc. Blvd Mohammed V. ☎ (06) 683 963. The airport lies 15km north of the town. ☎ (06) 682 084.
Trains. Station at Pl. de l'Unité Africaine. ☎ (06) 683 133. Trains run to Taza, or to Algeria.
Buses. Station at 12 Rue Sidi Brahim. ☎ (06) 682 047. Services to Taza, Al Hoceima, Nador, Berkane, and Fes.
Grands taxis. By the bus station.
Handicraft centre. Rue El Mouahidine. ☎ (06) 683 552.

Hotels
Hôtel Terminus, Pl. de l'Unité Africaine. ☎ (06) 683 212. ****A (106 rooms). Opposite the railway station. Good restaurant, nice gardens and swimming pool.
Hôtel Oujda, Blvd Mohammed V. ☎ (06) 685 063. ***A (105 rooms). Central, just outside the ramparts. Has a small pool.

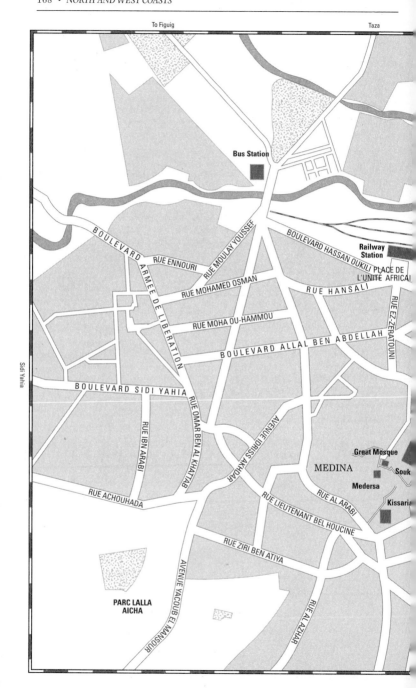

To Figuig

Taza

Bus Station

Railway Station

PLACE DE L'UNITÉ AFRICAI

BOULEVARD ARMÉE DE LIBERATION

RUE ENNOURI

RUE MOULAY YOUSSEF

BOULEVARD HASSAN OUKILI

RUE MOHAMED OSMAN

RUE HANSALI

RUE MOHA OU-HAMMOU

RUE EZ-ZERATOUNI

BOULEVARD ALLAL BEN ABDELLAH

BOULEVARD SIDI YAHIA

Sidi Yahia

RUE IBN ARABI

RUE OMAR BEN AL KHATTAB

AVENUE IDRISS AKHDAR

Great Mosque

Souk

MEDINA

Medersa

RUE ACHOUHADA

Kissaria

RUE AL ARABI

RUE LIEUTENANT BEL HOUCINE

RUE ZIRI BEN ATIYA

AVENUE YACOUB EL MANSOUR

PARC LALLA AICHA

RUE AL AZHAR

OUJDA

0 — 200 yds
0 — 200 metres

N

Oued Nachef

Airport

RUE ABDELLAH CHEFCHAOUNI

RUE ABDELLAH BEN YASSINE

BOULEVARD MOHAMED BEN ABDELLAH

RUE BERKANE

BOULEVARD AHFIR

BOULEVARD MOHAMED DERFOUFI

BOULEVARD OMAR ERRIFI

PLACE DU
16 AOUT

RUE MAS

RUE AL GHAZAWATE

AVENUE MOHAMED V

RUE ASSADIYINE

RUE FIGUIG

RUE RABAT

RUE CASABLANCA

RUE MOULAY EL HASSAN

BOULEVARD AL MAANSOUR ADDAHBI

RUE MOULAY ISMAIL

RUE AHMED BEN DAHI

HASSI BAYDA

RUE MOULAY ABDELLAH SIDI DRISS

Hôtel Angad, Rue Ramdane El Gadi. ☎ (06) 682 892. **A (28 rooms). In the medina. Modest but adequate. No restaurant.

Restaurants

Al Manar, 50 Blvd Zerktouni. ☎ (06) 697 037. Moroccan food.
Restaurant Langouste, 13 Rue d'Alger. ☎ (06) 691 323. Fish a speciality.
For the adventurous there are a number of small restaurants and grills in the space immediately surrounding Bab el Ouahab.

Campsites

Camping Mansour Oujda. For details, call the ONMT. Otherwise, the closest site is at Saidia, 58km away (see above).

Not surprisingly for a town that has passed through the hands of so many civilisations, there is a great variety of architectural styles in Oujda. The **medina** still contains much that is Merinide, including the Great Mosque and the 14C *medersa*. The principal gate is the 17C **Bab Sidi Abdelwahab**, known also as 'Gate of the Heads' because, until the beginning of the 20C, the heads of enemies were hung from it in time of war. The area around the gate has become a centre for story-tellers and players of traditional instruments and is perhaps the most atmospheric spot in the medina today.

There is a wide variety of souks including **Souk el Ma** (straight ahead through the *bab* and past the large **kissaria** or covered market where water used to be rationed and sold in time of drought). Close by is **Souk el Knadsa**, which sells a wide range of traditional items and is worth a look. Ahead of you, in the northwest corner of the medina, is the administrative centre—**Place du 16 Août**—where the post office, banks and tourist office are located. Directly south of Souk el Ma, past Place el Attarin (spice market) are the Merinide **Great Mosque** and **medersa**, neither of which is open to non-Muslims. Further south again you can walk to the very pleasant **Parc Lalla Meriem** via one of the *babs* in the ramparts, whose massive Almohade structure looks particularly impressive from this vantage point: there is a **Museum of Traditional Arms** in the park.

Embracing the medina on all sides is the French-built modern town—the **Ville Moderne**—with wide leafy avenues and rather anonymous, box-like buildings. The busiest part is **Place de l'Unite Africaine**, to the west of the medina, wherein lie the railway station and customs sheds and Oujda's best hotel, the *Terminus*.

6km out of Oujda is the **Oasis and Mausoleum of Sidi Yahia**, a saint whom Muslims and Jews identify with John the Baptist. This is a weird and haunting place made beautiful and fertile by an abundance of springs, and shaded by palm trees and ancient banyans. Amongst the trees is a village of saints' white-domed *koubbas*, and under one of them, you will be told, Sidi Yahia's body reposes. The other *koubbas* belong to lesser saints who followed him to this peaceful place. There is a holy well which is believed to have been Sidi Yahia's sole water supply when he stayed here, other water sources having sprung up since his death. There is also a sacred grotto, **Ghar El Hourijat** ('Cave of the Houris'—houris were maidens promised to good Muslims in Paradise).

From Oujda there is a road west to Fes via Taza, and another south to Errachidia or to Figuig via Bouarfa.

The Taza Gap ~ Oujda to Fes

The P1 road from Oujda to Fes passes through the natural corridor between the Rif and Middle Atlas ranges, known as the **Taza Gap**. It is the route by which the invading Arabs first arrived from the east in the 7C. Countless armies have since made use of it, including the Almohades and Merinides who successfully invaded Fes from here. There is a theory that here lies the original frontier between Europe and Africa. Some scientists claim that the Rif range is an extension of the Spanish Sierra Nevada and that the Strait of Gibraltar and the Mediterranean were formed by a chance sinking of the land. It is certainly true that the rock of the Rif to the north is grey-white and that of the Middle Atlas to the south is red and altogether different in shape and texture.

The first part of the road from Oujda is sparsely populated and frankly dull, with nothing but rows of eucalyptus trees—a bid to fix the sand—to break the monotony. **El Aioun** ('The Springs'), 59km away, has a kasbah built by Moulay Ismael. **Taourirt**, a further 50km on, has always been a town of some strategic importance, located as it is at the ancient crossing-place of caravan routes from east to west through the Taza Gap to Fes, and from north to south from Melilla all the way to the legendary city of Sijilmassa, south of Erfoud. It is still regarded as strategically significant and there is a considerable military presence. The town owes its fortifications to the Merinide dynasty.

A road goes south from Taourirt to the little town of **Debdou**, 53km away, where the countryside is much greener. The road rises to a plateau, the **Gaada de Debou**, with splendid views, and then disappears into the desert wilderness. Debdou is not on the way to anywhere but it makes a pleasant diversion. Another rewarding diversion can be made by taking the track that turns north 6km west of Taourirt to a series of waterfalls, **Les Cascades** (5km). Another 50km along the main road, **Guercif** is a rather dull market town situated at the confluence of the Moulouya and Melloulou rivers. **Msoun**, 37km further on, has a fine kasbah built by Moulay Ismael in the 17C and worth visiting, for much of the building is still intact, as are the grain stores and water cisterns.

Taza

Taza is one of Morocco's oldest towns founded, like Meknes, in the 10C by the Meknassa tribe on a site undoubtedly inhabited since prehistoric times, as evidenced by the quantity of fossils and bones found there. It was also, in its day, of major strategic importance to every invading dynasty coming from the east and making for Fes, and it bears the mark of them all, particularly the Almohades who built the defensive outer walls in the 12C.

Today Taza is a somewhat underrated and neglected place. Like so many of Morocco's historic cities, it is split into two parts, medina and modern town, the latter built alongside the medina by the French during the Protectorate (and in this case a discreet 3km away).

■ Practical information

Tourist office. **ONMT**. Ave Tetouan (behind Pl. de l'Indépendance).
Trains. The railway station is at the north end of the new town. Trains to Fes, Oujda and Al Hoceima.

Buses. Buses leave from outside the railway station to the destinations above, plus stops in between.
Grands taxis. Also depart from the railway station.

Hotels

Hôtel Friouato Salam, Ave de la Gare. ☎ (05) 672 593. *** (58 rooms). Located between the two halves of the town. Has a pool.
Hôtel de la Poste, Place de l'Indépendance. ☎ (05) 672 589. Unclassified (20 rooms). Seven years old. Good value.
Hôtel du Dauphine, Ave Prince Heritier Sidi Med. ☎ (05) 673 567. **B (26 rooms). Located near Pl. de l'Indépendance. Art Deco in style and evidently quite grand at one time.

Restaurants

There is nothing remarkable. The choice is one of the hotels, or the *Restaurant Majestic*, 26 Ave Mohammed V.
Otherwise, try your luck around Place de l'Indépendance.

Campsites

The only campsite is now closed.

The **medina**, which is at the west end of the town and stands on the edge of the plateau, has one or two interesting features. If you walk down the main street, the **Mechouar**, you will see the best of the souks, which are Berber in character and refreshingly free of tourist-orientated wares, and several Merinide *medersas*, the best amongst them being the **Bou Abou el Hassan Medersa**, which is worth visiting if you can find anyone to open it and take you in; it has a lovely courtyard. At the end of this street is the **Great Mosque** built by the Almohade ruler Abd el Mumene (founder of Rabat) in the 12C. It is one of the oldest mosques in the country, but sadly the non-Muslim may do no more than peer in. Nearby is the lovely Almohade **Bab er Rouah** ('Gate of the Winds'), which was originally the only entrance to the town but now, like its namesake in Rabat, leads nowhere in particular. At the other end of the Mechouar is the **Andalusian Mosque** with its unusual 13C minaret. Taza has now dwindled in importance and the *ville nouvelle*, at a lower level than the medina, offers little of interest to the visitor apart from one or two cafés and restaurants around its main square, Place de l'Indépendance, at the end nearest the medina.

The Jbel Tazzeka National Park

A recommended excursion takes you along a spectacular mountain road which loops south for about 80km at **Sidi Abdallah des Rhiata** (30km west of Taza) and then returns to Taza just south of the medina. The road runs first through the dark schist ravine of the **Oued Zireg**, then climbs steeply and turns east to loop around the southern slopes of Jbel Tazzeka (1979m). There is a track up to the top for anyone minded to reach the summit and a predictably splendid view of forests and mountains in all directions. This is an interesting region geologically, insofar as it marks the spot where the Rif and Middle Atlas ranges all but merge, with only a narrow gorge between them. Forested with cork oaks and

Miracles and murder

Behind the Andalusian Mosque, and rather difficult to find, is the house of the Pretender to the Alouite throne, **Omar Ez Zarhouni**, an educated and ambitious man who actually had himself crowned sultan of Morocco at Taza in 1902, declaring that he was 'the first born son of the late Sultan Moulay el Hassan and therefore the elder brother of the then reigning sovereign, Moulay Abd el Aziz'. He had a habit of riding a donkey to visit his followers and was popularly known as **Bou Hamara** which means *Father of the She-Ass*. He also performed 'miracles' and is particularly remembered for his 'conversations with the dead': he would bury a servant in a shallow grave, allowing him a straw to breath and talk through; having held audible conversations with the unfortunate man, Bou Hamara would then stamp on the straw so that by the time amazed onlookers got around to uncovering the servant, he was indeed truly dead. This colourful character met his just desserts when Moulay Hafid came to the throne in 1908 and accorded him a suitably dramatic end, parading him through the town in a cage on the back of a camel, and then throwing him to the lions. According to Walter Harris, who describes this incident in graphic detail in *Morocco That Was*, the lions only mauled him, so in the end he was shot and burned. Walter Harris's account is quoted in full by Gavin Maxwell in his book, *Lords of the Atlas.*

cedars and covered in aromatic cistus in spring, it is rich in butterflies and birds such as hoopoes and fully deserves it status as a national park.

The road continues east and passes the **Friouata Caves** (a signpost on the left points simply to '*Gouffres*'). These are worth visiting, though not without a torch or guide as no lighting is provided. They are part of a great network of caverns and are believed to be the deepest in Morocco. The entrance to the caves is over 30m wide. On the opposite side of the road, a little further along, are more caves—**Les Grottes du Chiker**. These are also impressive, especially the one called **Ifri ou Atto**. Next comes the **Dayet Chiker**, a large depression which sometimes fills with water to make a lake. Now the road begins to descend quite steeply, passing the lovely waterfalls known as **Les Cascades de Ras el Ma** (*Ras el Ma* is Arabic for 'head of the water'). Here too the amount of water depends very much on the time of year, and at the end of the dry season the falls can be reduced to a trickle.

For the really adventurous, a track runs southwards from near the lake, passing the villages of **Merhaoua**, **Tamtrouchte** and **Ait Makhlouf** and curving round the southern flank of the **Massif de Tichchoukt**, to join the main Fes–Midelt road a few kilometres south of Boulemane. The Michelin map shows the route as snowbound in the winter, but at any other time of year it is spectacular. It should really be attempted only by four-wheel drive vehicles.

The coast between Tetouan and Ceuta

This beautiful coastline with its miles of clean golden sand and string of creeks, bays, cliffs and crystal-clear waters is a paradise for holiday makers. The

Moroccans have not been slow to realise this and between Martil and the north-ernmost point of Ceuta there is an almost continuous sequence of holiday villages and hotels. On the whole the development has been tastefully done and the region is not yet quite spoilt, though obviously beaches become extremely crowded in high summer.

Martil, a pleasant drive of 12km from Tetouan, is the least developed and tends to cater mostly for local Tetouan residents who have weekend villas here. Anyone prepared to do without mini-golf, organised watersports, and nightclubs will be very happy here. On the seafront is a good hotel, the *Etoile de Mar*, with an excellent fish restaurant, and another, slightly cheaper restaurant opposite called the *Rio Martil*.

Immediately north of Martil is **Cabo Negro** (also known as Taifor), with its modern white buildings facing the sea, dedicated to pleasing the visitor with its hotels, holiday homes, restaurants, night-clubs and disco. There is a jetty allowing anchorage for pleasure boats and an 18-hole golf course—Golf Royal de Cabo Negro—overlooking the Mediterranean. There is also a Club Méditerranée in its own white-washed village nestling amongst oleanders and shady trees.

Further north is **Mdiq**, infinitely preferable for the non-extrovert, which still retains its colourful fishing port while the holiday village is tucked well back on the hillside. Mdiq has a long-established annual *moussem* in praise of the sea.

Next comes **Restinga-Smir**, until recently also a modest fishing village but now one of Morocco's most successful tourist centres. Restinga-Smir is a large and well-spaced complex of well-appointed bungalows, chalets and apartments, two luxury hotels, shops, supermarket, swimming pools, tennis courts and nightclubs. And another Club Méditerranée. The Restinga bay, with its calm, crystal-clear but cold water, is ideal for water-skiing and sailing, and there are plenty of boats and water-skis for hire, and instructors for those who need them. Inexperienced swimmers and children can feel quite safe so long as they swim within the area marked by buoys, which is shallow except at high tide and constantly watched by a *maître-nageur*. Sea-fishing is recommended here and the water is rich in tiny squid, langoustes, crabs, and other shellfish.

Hotels

Hôtel de l'Etoile de la Mer, Ave Moulay El Hassan, Martil. ☎ (09) 979 276. **A (32 rooms). Recommended (see above).
Hôtel Kabila, Restinga-Smir. ☎ (09) 975 013. ****A (96 rooms).
Hôtel Golden Beach, Restinga-Smir. ☎ (09) 975 077. ****B (88 rooms).
Hôtel Playa, Blvd Lalla Nozha, Restinga-Smir. ☎ (09) 975 166. *A (21 rooms).

Restaurants

There is a huge range of fish restaurants in all the resorts.

Holiday villages

Club Méditerranée, Restinga-Smir. ☎ (09) 977 058.350 rooms.
Club Méditerranée, Cabo Negro. ☎ (09) 978 198. 307 rooms. See above.

Campsites

Camping Martil, Martil, next to the beach. Showers, laundry.

Ceuta

The P28 coast road continues north a further 18km, past other, smaller, holiday areas, to the Spanish enclave (with Melilla, one of only two left in Morocco) of Ceuta, which stands on the isthmus of Africa's most northerly promontory, formed by the rock of Monte Hacho (180m). The town is also known as **Sebta**, so named because there are seven points on the **Jbel Moussa** ridge behind it. Ceuta's chief importance today is as a ferry terminal and the Transmediterranée Line has several sailings daily for Algeciras (on the Spanish mainland) and Melilla.

To enter Ceuta means crossing a frontier with the usual passport formalities and sometimes long delays. Note also that to call the enclave from Morocco, you must first dial the international dialling code for Spain (00 34) before the Ceuta number.

History of Ceuta

The Moroccans first lost the town when the Portuguese captured it in 1415. Prior to that the great Almoravide leader, Youssef ibn Tachfine had embarked from here on his numerous Spanish campaigns. In 1580 Portugal and Spain were briefly united under one crown. When they separated 70 years later Ceuta remained under Spanish rule, and has done so ever since, despite several attempts to win it back by various Moroccan sultans.

There is nothing much to see in Ceuta except three very Spanish-looking churches; there is the heavy Baroque **Church of our Lady of Africa**; the **Church of San Francisco**, which contains the body of King Sebastian of Portugal, who died in the Battle of the Three Kings at Ksar el Kbir in 1578; and the **cathedral**, which was built over a mosque in the 15C and later received Baroque additions.

A drive out to the rock of Monte Hacho is worthwhile, if only for the views. The fortress on top has recently been converted to use as a military museum.

A very pretty road turns left off the P28 just before Ceuta and returns inland to Tetouan via **Souk Tleta Taghramet**.

The Interior

Meknes

Meknes is one of Morocco's four 'Imperial Cities'. Situated on the edge of the Middle Atlas mountains, at an altitude of 522m, it enjoys an equable climate and is surrounded by extremely fertile land growing vines, olives, and citrus fruits. It has some small industry on the outskirts centred mainly on fruit and vegetable preserves and wine.

From the visitor's point of view, Meknes is an excellent centre from which to visit the holy city of Moulay Idriss, Roman Volubilis and the Middle Atlas mountains. It also has a great deal to offer in its own right, not least the unique and monumental Imperial City, created on a vast scale in the late 17C and early 18C by the wise but tyrannical sultan, Moulay Ismael, and containing the finest monumental gates (*babs*) in Morocco. There is a very manageable medina (less daunting, but also less magical than that of Fes), and a pleasant new town with good hotels and restaurants, built by the French during the Protectorate years.

History of Meknes

Meknes was founded in the 10C by a Berber tribe known as the **Meknassas**, who decided to settle on the shores of the river Boufekrane. They were succeeded by the Almoravides in the second half of the 11C, and in the 12C by the Almohades, who destroyed most of the monuments of the preceding dynasty. A century later came the Merenides. While Fes was chosen as their capital, the Merinide dynasty did build a number of mosques in Meknes and, most notably, the Bou Inania Medersa.

It was not until the 17C, however, that Meknes reached its apogee, under the rule of the Alouite sultan **Moulay Ismael**, who reigned for 55 years (1672–1727) and is believed to have had 360 wives and some 800 children. He was without doubt one of the most effective of all Moroccan rulers and also one of the cruellest. His first act on being made sultan was to send the heads of 10,000 members of rival tribes whom he had slain in battle to decorate the walls of Fes and Marrakesh, thus making it clear that he would have neither of these troublesome towns for his capital.

Moulay Ismael built on a gargantuan scale. He enclosed his town—and the medina which pre-dates him—in 25km of massive walls, pierced by monumental gates. He made sumptuous palaces and gardens watered by great reservoirs, stables for his 12,000 cavalry horses, and countless mosques and mausoleums. Despite his cruelty history has judged Moulay Ismael a wise, indeed a great man, because he **united Morocco** and earned the respect of the major European powers for so doing. He also succeeded in driving the British out of Tangier and the Spanish out of Larache. For the first time in centuries all the warring tribes in Morocco were subdued (with the exception of the Rif Berbers whom, arguably, no one has ever succeeded in rounding up, let alone conquering). His philosophy was that people expected to be ruled by the sword and would only relapse into chaos when the yoke of cruelty was lifted. There was no mercy in him, but people are said to have respected his rough justice and it is generally recognised that he created order and stability where before there was widespread disorder.

To make all this possible Moulay Ismael formed an army of some 30,000 'Sudanese' soldiers, mainly descendants from slaves taken by the Saadians from south of the Sahara. ('Sudanese' in Morocco is used to mean, quite simply, black.) Contingents of these men roamed the country, collecting taxes, putting down any signs of insurrection, and meting out punishment generally. In his *Kitab al Istiqsa* the historian Ahmed el Nasiri (1834–97) wrote that by the end of Ismael's reign it was possible for a Jew or a woman to walk from one end of the country to the other without being molested by unruly tribesmen. One supposes they would need to have kept clear of the sultan's army as well.

Today Moulay Ismael is proclaimed above all as the builder of **Imperial Meknes**, which he visualised as a copy of the Versailles of his contemporary Louis XIV of France, for whom he had the greatest admiration and with whom he exchanged ambassadors. He is said to have used some 2500 Christian slaves to build the Imperial city, a number which astonishes until one sees the actual volume and extent of the walls. He also employed large numbers of Berber tribesmen, in the belief that full-time hard labour would keep them quiet. Stories of extreme cruelty, some no doubt exaggerated, were brought back by Europeans who escaped. Whether Moulay Ismael really built a bridge across the river using rushes interwoven with the bodies of prisoners can be neither proved nor disproved; and whether he could be exonerated by the fact that most of his murders of infidels were committed on Fridays (and therefore by divine decree) would have been a point for endless discussion between succeeding generations of devout Muslims. What is certain is that Moulay Ismael himself thought that what he did was right. So sure of himself and of the supremacy of his faith was he that he proposed to Louis XIV that he too should become a Muslim, and also asked for the hand of one of his daughters in marriage: he was politely refused on both counts. Towards the end of his long reign he actually allowed Catholic **missionaries** to minister to the thousands of Christian prisoners still working in Meknes, a strange irony amongst so much savagery. Perhaps the apparently smooth and civilised life-style of *le roi soleil* did have some effect on the excesses of this larger-than-life tyrant. (There are Franciscan nuns in Meknes to this day, running an orphanage and teaching embroidery.)

■ Practical information

Tourist offices. **ONMT**. Pl. Administrative. ☎ (05) 524 426 and Esplanade de la Foire, ☎ (05) 520 191.
Banks. Ave Mohammed V/Pl. Administrative.
Post office. Pl. de France
Air transport. Royal Air Maroc, Ave Mohammed V. ☎ (05) 520 963.
Trains. Main railway station, Zankat Amir Abdelkader, is at the eastern end of the new town. ☎ (05) 521 060. There is also a small station—El Amir Abdelkader—nearer the centre, behind the *Hôtel Majestic*. Trains run to Tangier, Rabat,

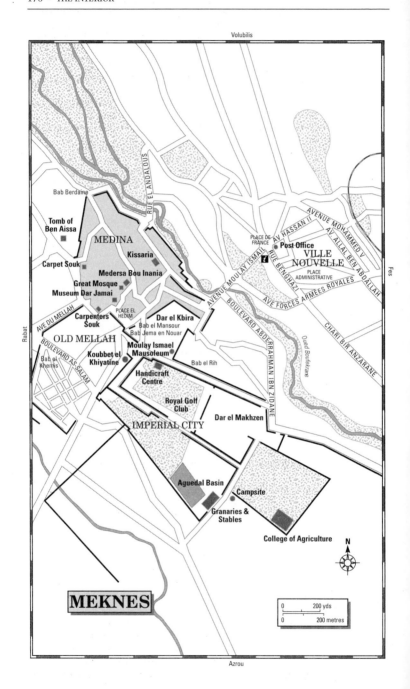

Volubilis

Bab Berdaine

Tomb of
Ben Aissa

MEDINA

Kissaria

Carpet Souk

RUE EL ANDALOUS

Medersa Bou Inania

Great Mosque
Museum Dar Jamai

Carpenters
Souk

PLACE EL
HEDIM

OLD MELLAH

Bab el
Khemis

BOULEVARD AS-SALAM

Koubbet el
Khiyatine

Dar el Kbira

Bab el Mansour
Bab Jema en Nouar

Moulay Ismael
Mausoleum

Bab el Rih

Handicraft
Centre

Royal Golf
Club

IMPERIAL CITY

Dar el Makhzen

AVE DU MELLAH

AVENUE MOULAY ISMAIL

BOULEVARD ABDERRAHMAN IBN ZIDANE

Oued Boufekrane

PLACE DE
FRANCE

AV HASSAN II

RUE BENGHAZI

Post Office

VILLE
NOUVELLE

PLACE
ADMINISTRATIVE

AVENUE MOHAMMED V

AV ALLAL BEN ABDALLAH

AVE FORCES ARMÉES ROYALES

CHARI BIR ANZARANE

Fes

Rabat

Aguedal Basin

Campsite

Granaries &
Stables

College of Agriculture

N

MEKNES

0   200 yds
0   200 metres

Azrou

Casablanca, Fes, Marrakesh, and Oujda. In theory all trains call at both stations.
Buses. Station at Ave Mohammed V. ☎ (05) 522 583. Services to Rabat,
Casablanca, Fes, Errachidia, Erfoud, Ifrane, Volubilis, and Moulay Idriss.
Taxis. Pl. El Hedim and Pl. de France have the main taxi ranks, but there are
others all over town, including the medina.

Hotels

Hôtel Transatlantique, Rue el Meriniyine. ☎ (05) 525 050 fax (05) 520 057.
***** (121 rooms). On the edge of the *ville nouvelle* with a fine view over the
medina. It has a traditional and a modern section, each with its own swimming
pool.
Hôtel Rif, Zankat Accra. ☎ (05) 522 591 fax (05) 524 428. ****A (120 rooms).
More centrally placed in town (close to the Pl. de France). Less luxurious than
the *Transatlantique* and, some would say, more friendly.
Hôtel Zaki, Blvd Al Massira. ☎ (05) 520 790. ****A (163 rooms). A new and very
large hotel just off Ave Mohammed V. Mainly for large groups.
Hôtel de Nice, 10 Rue d'Accra. ☎ (05) 520 318. ***B (33 rooms). An older and
much smaller hotel. Central and with adequate accommodation. Good restaurant.
Hôtel Majestic, 19 Ave Mohammed V. ☎ (05) 522 035. **A (42 rooms). Between
Ave Mohammed V and the railway. Modest but clean and has a restaurant.

Restaurants

Zitouna, 44 Jamaa Zitouna (medina). ☎ (05) 530 281. Good atmosphere and
delicious Moroccan food.
La Hacienda, Rue de Fes. ☎ (05) 521 092. A 10min drive from the town centre.
Spanish, Moroccan and French food, reasonably priced.
La Cuisine d'Or, Zankat Antsirabi. Grills are a speciality.
La Coupole, Ave Hassan II. ☎ (05) 522 483. International cuisine.
Recommended.
Hôtel Transatlantique (see above). A good Moroccan restaurant, but pricey.

Campsites

Agdal, ☎ (05) 538 914. Next to the Aguedal Basin in a shady location.

Golf

Meknes Royal Golf Club, Bab Belkari Jnane Lbahraouia. ☎ (05) 530 753 fax
(05) 550 504. 9 holes, par 36.

A tour of the city

Meknes today is not as prosperous as it once was. Unlike Fes, it has not really
kept up with its history: the vestiges of past splendour remain in the form of
palaces and noble *babs* but few people today know what to do with the spaces
that are left. The walls of the Imperial city are of overwhelming size, but there
are also great **open areas** where nothing has yet been built. (The Lisbon earthquake of 1755 also caused much damage to the city.) Moulay Ismael presumably dreamed of creating even more than he did, for he had unlimited space
when he built Meknes. When the Merinides founded Fes in a narrow crack in the
hills, there was no space to spare and the effect today is infinitely more striking.
To experience the full impact of Moulay Ismael's extraordinary energy, it is a

good idea to drive (or walk) around the **walls** for at least part of their 25km circuit. A good place to start is from Bab Berdaine at the far end of the medina, turning left and going at least as far as Bab el Khemis, thus taking in the most impressive section of castellated ramparts as well as two of the finest of the sultan's gateways (which are described below).

Located between the Imperial City and the medina is **Place el Hedim**, a large and animated square which has recently been 'sanitised': water-sellers, craftsmen and other colourful characters have all been tidied away and replaced by a fruit and vegetable market on one side, and fountains on the other. Once upon a time this formed part of the medina, but Moulay Ismael had houses razed to the ground to make room for a grand, ceremonial **forecourt** to his palace, the Dar el Kbira. The square was also used as a collecting point for all the marble columns and other elements taken from the buildings of former dynasties and civilisations and used to adorn the sultan's own palaces. The Saadian palace of El Badi in Marrakesh and Roman Volubilis were just two of the sites which suffered thus.

At the medina end of Place el Hedim is the Dar Jamai Museum (see below) but the square is dominated by the **Bab el Mansour**, named after its architect, a convert from Christianity. It is the most immense and perfectly proportioned of Moulay Ismael's gateways, decorated all over with minuscule fragments of glazed green-and-white ceramic which shine in the sunlight. Indeed, the French writer, Pierre Loti, said it made him think of a piece of shimmering brocade which had been hung over the ramparts to break up their uniformity. The gate is flanked by square **bastions**, similarly decorated and standing on elegant marble columns brought from Volubilis. It was completed by Ismael's son Moulay Abdallah in 1732, and is now a permanent exhibition hall. The way in to the Imperial City is through **Bab Jema en Nouar** which stands alongside, a small replica of El Mansour.

To appreciate the **Imperial City** fully it is necessary to know that Moulay Ismael conceived it as a mighty fortress with no fewer than four sets of walls, one within the other, surrounding 24 royal palaces in the centre as well as mosques, barracks, stables and ornamental gardens. In his book *Islamic Architecture*, John Hoag writes: 'The Imperial city is a direct descendent of the round city of Baghdad or the Forbidden City of Peking insofar as they were fortified palaces—to protect the ruler—not fortified cities to protect the inhabitants.' To see everything on foot would be exhausting and time-consuming. There is ample parking along the way if you are driving; otherwise, take a taxi from outside Bab el Mansour, once you have looked at the sites immediately inside.

Go through Bab Jema en Nouar, as described above. Just inside, on the right of an open square, is the **Koubbet el Khiyatine** ('Koubba of the Tailors', named after the cooperative which once occupied the square), a pavilion where Moulay Ismael received foreign ambassadors.

Underneath it, and accessible by some steps outside the *koubba*, are the **dungeons** which once housed up to 40,000 prisoners, mostly European Christians (many brought in by the Sallée Rovers) but also Turks and Berbers. There were three exits to the three different sites where the slaves were put to work: one pointing towards Volubilis (the source of marble pillars etc.), one southwards towards the cedar forests, and the other emerging at the far end of the town under construction. A guide with a flickering candle (there is no other source of light and the ground is very uneven) will take you down and assure you that the outer reaches of the maze of **tunnels**—extending over 7km—have been closed since a couple of French journalists strayed too far and got lost, but were eventually found again. In the dim light you can see the marks of chains and even some graffiti. Prisoners were incarcerated here at night and brought out during the day to work on the Imperial City. It is an arresting story, and perhaps a salutory prelude to your tour. **Open** every day except Friday; entry 10dh.

Above ground again, the first significant point of interest, on your left through a triple-arched doorway, is the **Moulay Ismael Mausoleum**. It was restored in 1959 by King Mohammed V and it was he who decreed that non-Muslims should also be given access. (It is now one of only three holy places in Morocco where this is so, the others being the Mosque of Hassan II in Casablanca and the Mohammed V Mausoleum in Rabat.) You will pass through a series of decorated courtyards, each with an ablutions fountain in the centre and, on arriving at the ante-chamber, will need to remove your shoes. You can then stand in front of the railing and peer in at the sumptuously decorated room which contains the sultan's tomb, along with three others—that of Moulay Ismael's preferred wife (Lalla Khnouata) and those of two of his sons. Behind the tomb, looking slightly incongruous and very European as they stand like sentinels guarding the great horseshoe arch, are two very fine French longcase clocks, until recently keeping perfect time but now, it seems, in need of repair. In 1700 these were a gift from Louis XIV, intended to mitigate the sultan's disappointment at not being allowed to marry a French princess. (Two exactly similar clocks stand in the corners nearest to you but you cannot see them since you are not allowed to go beyond the railing.) Muslims are, of course, allowed in to pray by the tomb and to seek blessing (*baraka*) from the holy relics. The ante-chamber where you stand is remarkable in its own right. The pillars are of marble, brought from Italy in exchange for sugar on an ounce-for-ounce basis. The stucco-work is particularly striking. **Open** 08.30–12.00 and 15.00–18.00; closed Fri; entry 10dh.

Behind the mausoleum and accessible through a small gate is the area known as **Dar el Kbira**, once a complex of palaces and evidence of Moulay Ismael's extraordinary energy and ostentation. It was completed by 1677, only to be destroyed 50 years later by his jealous son, Moulay Abdallah. It is now a series of crumbling ruins.

In a building opposite the mausoleum there is a permanent **handicraft centre** (*ensemble artisanal*), most distinctive being the exhibition of vases and figurines made of damascened iron (i.e., inlaid with silver thread), a highly skilled technique which tends to crop up in bazaars all over the country. Craftsmen are happy to demonstrate the delicate work of scratching designs on to the metal surface with a blade, which is followed by an application of silver. Also on show is local embroidery, and here again a demonstration is available if you want it; the fine linen tablecloths and napkins are remarkable for being exactly the same on both sides, a skill that was introduced, and is apparently still taught by, Franciscan nuns. Then there is the usual assortment of Berber rugs, djellabahs, jewellery and cedarwood items. This is as good a place to shop as any because of the broad range and the above-average quality. Prices, said to be 'fixed', often turn out not to be the moment you start walking away.

Now follow the long straight road which runs southeast between high walls for over a kilometre. On the right is an expanse of parkland which was once an ornamental garden for the wives of the sultan; now it has been converted into an 18-hole golf course, the Royal Golf Club. You will pass under **Bab el Rih** ('Gate of the Winds'). This gate is not decorated like the others but incorporates marble columns removed by the sultan from Volubilis and from the Saadian El Badi Palace in Marrakesh. Further on, to the right of the walls, is the **Dar el Makhzen**, the last of the great imperial palaces, completed at the end of the 18C. In recent years painstaking restoration of the palace has made it possible for the royal family to stay here when visiting Meknes, but this means that it is closed to public view.

At the end of the long corridor you turn right into an arcaded square. On the right is the main entrance to Dar el Makhzen and on the left are some botanical gardens now belonging to the College of Agriculture and closed to the public. Straight ahead is the most evocative part of the whole imperial complex—the ruins of the **barracks, granaries and stables**. It was here that the 30,000 'Sudanese' soldiers of the Royal Guard were housed. To feed them, the royal household and the population of Meknes, grain and other foodstuffs were stored in 22 granaries known as **Heri es Souani**. Throughout his life, Moulay Ismael was obsessed with fears of siege, and one of his priorities was always to prepare for that eventuality; in fact, with granaries of this capacity, he could probably have fed the entire population of Meknes for 20 years. The vaulted underground chambers still standing today remain at a constant temperature of 15° C even in the heat of summer, thanks to the thickness of the walls (4m) and the roof (3m). The building survived the 1755 Lisbon earthquake virtually unscathed. You will also see some of the twelve wells (14m deep) which were connected by underground cisterns with the Aguedal Basin alongside (see below). The chain pumps attached to horizontal wheels would have been turned by mules to bring water to the surface. In one of the chambers, propped against the wall, is a door taken from the Koubbet el Khiyatine (see above). An image of the sun has been carved on to it, no doubt in honour of Louis XIV, *le roi soleil*. No one seems to know why the door was removed and brought here.

Up on the roof, accessible by steps alongside the entrance, is a

The stables at the Imperial City, Meknes

pleasant garden with extensive views giving some idea of the immensity of the ruined city. Notice particularly the old and new royal palaces, side by side. There is a small café in the middle of the garden. Next to the granaries are the stables, constructed to hold up to 12,000 horses and consisting originally of 23 naves and 3000 pillars. This roof, obviously less solid than that of the granaries, was totally destroyed by the 1755 earthquake, but what is left is impressive enough. It is rather like standing in some vast mosque (Cordoba comes to mind) with perfect perspectives opening up all round you. The scale is breathtaking.

Outside is the **Aguedal Basin**, some 4ha of water which was fed by a 20km conduit system and which would have provided the town's water supply in an emergency. Today it waters the golf course and the royal gardens. Next to the basin there is an extensive campsite and the large building visible in the distance is a palace which was built by Mohammed ibn Abdallah at the end of the 18C, at the time when Morocco recognised the newly independent United States of America; the palace is named **Dar el Beida** ('White House'), which may or may not have something to do with this fact. It is now a military academy. Of the few other ruins in this area, most are in a sorry state and cannot be identified even by local guides.

At this point, either walk back or drive on until you come once more to the Place el Hedim by way of the **Old Mellah**, once the home of over 3000 Jews, and the very fine **Bab el Khemis**, one of the town gates that bestrides the Rabat road. The original gate was built by the Almohades but it was embellished and refined by Moulay Ismael. Like all *babs*, it is best seen from the outside (looking in towards the *mellah*) from where its green-and-blue ceramic design is particularly striking against the sunburnt colour of the walls. Notice the inscription on the pediment intended by Moulay Ismael to convey his religious tolerance: 'I am the gate of the fifth day, open to all races whether from the east or the west.'

The **medina** pre-dates Moulay Ismael. It is animated and refreshingly intimate after the spacious and somewhat daunting echo of past splendour represented by the Imperial City. Its narrow, winding streets, so typical of the medieval cities of Morocco, are often shaded from the sun by rose- or vine-covered trellises, and the merchandise in the souks is varied and plentiful: Berber rugs, embroidered goods, copper and silverware, pottery and damascened metalwork. Craftsmen are usually grouped together according to their trade and many of them can be found in the *fondouks*, set back from the streets.

The least complicated way in to the centre of the medina is to walk along the street immediately behind the Museum Dar Jamai, at the opposite end of Place el Hedim from the Imperial City. You will shortly come to a T-junction. Turning left brings you to **Souk en Nejjarine** (carpenters' souk); beyond that is the carpet souk. Turning right at the T-junction brings you to **Souk Sebbat** (cobblers' souk) full of *babouches*, the softer versions of which make wonderful bedroom slippers. Continue up this main street to reach the **Medersa Bou Inania**, built c 1350 and named after a Merenide sultan. Of the same period as its namesake in Fes, but slightly smaller, its lovely central courtyard is softly coloured with mosaic, stucco and cedarwood in the usual perfect balance. The mihrab is particularly striking for its highly decorative Andalusian style. From the upper floor of students' rooms there is a close-up view of the minaret of the **Great Mosque** next door, and also over the ruined **Medersa Filada**, which was

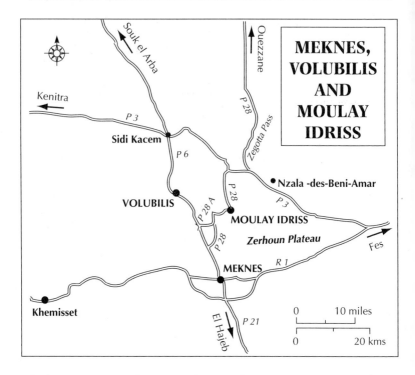

MEKNES,
VOLUBILIS
AND
MOULAY
IDRISS

built some 300 years later by Moulay Ismael, and whose decoration appears coarse by comparison. There are 14 other, smaller, medersas and mosques awaiting discovery in the maze of little streets. You will notice that most of the Meknes minarets are decorated quite simply with bands of green tiles and are altogether less ornate and colourful than those of Fes or Marrakesh.

Continue along the same street to reach the entrance to the 14C **kissaria** or covered market. Inside is the **Souk el Herir** (silk souk) specialising in kaftans, and beyond it are the master tilemakers, chipping away with a hammer at designs drawn on to glazed ceramic. If you carry on northwest (behind the *medersa*) you find yourself in a quieter, more residential area, and will soon reach a large open square at the end of which is the city wall and **Bab Berdaine** ('Gate of the Saddlemakers'). This was created by Moulay Ismael as the principal entrance to the medina and it resembles somewhat the central section of Bab el Mansour, flanked as it is by two massive bastions. Like Bab Khemis, it is best appreciated from outside, where its exterior is decorated in green tiles and patterned with flower-like designs picked out in black. Notice the minaret of the mosque of the same name, visible through the arch and contemporary with it.

A little way west of here (outside the walls) there is a vast cemetery, in the centre of which is the **Tomb of Ibn Aissa** (d. 1553), the founder of a sect of Islamic mystics which was later much encouraged by Moulay Ismael (no admittance to non-Muslims). The cult, known as Aissaoua, was one of the most violent in Morocco: its devotees worked themselves into a frenzied trance, ate snakes and cut themselves with knives. Today the *moussem* still takes place on the eve of Mouloud, but with all the unpleasant extremes expunged.

You should not leave old Meknes without visiting the **Dar Jamai Museum**, which is housed in a 19C palace built by one of the Jamai brothers, both of whom held high office under Sultan Moulay el Hassan and were then ruined and incarcerated at the hands of the succeeding sultan. (The Palais Jamai in Fes was built by the other brother.) The Dar Jamai is situated at the medina end of Place el Hedim, with its entrance exactly opposite Bab el Mansour. Here you can relax and enjoy the perfect peace of the inner garden, which always seems to be filled with birdsong. Although less rich than the Dar Batha in Fes, the museum offers some interesting wrought-iron work, some beautifully simple Andalusian-style tiles, Meknes pottery (including a soup bowl said to have belonged to Moulay Ismael), Berber jewellery, traditional kaftans and lots of embroidery. Best of all are the Berber carpets, mainly from the Middle Atlas. The building itself is a joy, with fine cedarwood ceilings, and some upstairs rooms are furnished in 19C style, including a fascinating *salon* with a large central throne for the man of the house and a chair in each corner for his four wives. **Open** 08.30–12.00 and 15.00–18.00; closed Tues; entry 10dh.

Built—like new Fes and new Rabat—by the French during the Protectorate, the **Ville Nouvelle** is separated from the old city by a deep ravine, at the bottom of which runs the river **Boufekrane**. It is a thriving town of prosperous-looking white buildings, and it lives on the produce and profits of the surrounding fertile agricultural land.

Horse-lovers will wish to visit the **Royal Stud** (Haras Royal) in the south of the new town (well-signposted from Avenue Mohammed V). Here there are some 600 superb animals, of which 160 are pure Arab and the rest Berber (mainly kept for *fantasias*) and half-breeds. One may walk in the gardens and peer into stables at leisure. This is the most important thoroughbred Arab stud in Morocco.

Excursions from Meknes

Meknes is the ideal centre from which to visit the Roman provincial capital of Volubilis and the holy Arab city of Moulay Idriss, which lie about 28km to the north. There is a new hotel—the *Volubilis Inn*—on the P13 outside Volubilis. There is also a campite—*Camping Zerhoun*—on the Meknes road 11km before Volubilis. Moulay Idriss has no hotels.

Take the Tangier road out of Meknes and after c 15km turn right on to a minor road which curves and climbs steadily up to the **Zerhoun Plateau**. The road is lined with olive trees and agaves, and in spring there are wild flowers and the pink feathery blossom of the tamarisk tree. The view over patchwork plains and misty mountains is unique.

Volubilis

Soon, to your left, you will see the distinctive forms of the Roman city of Volubilis. Few people are not moved when they first catch sight of the lonely remains of this far-flung Roman outpost glinting in the sun in a setting of serene beauty. From a distance the site is dwarfed by the vast plain on which it stands and is overshadowed by the nearby Zerhoun mountains.

You should allow at least an hour for your walk through the ruins, more if you want to examine them closely and take photographs (although many of the statues and small pieces have been removed to museums, particularly the Museum of Antiquities, Rabat). For such an important monument there is a remarkable lack of formality and very little in the way of written material to help you round. There is no shortage of guides, however, who permanently hang around the ticket office at the only entrance from the road, through a gap in the walls. Next to the ticket office is a small museum. **Open** daily from sunrise to sunset; entry 20dh.

History of Volubilis

Archaeological evidence suggests that there was a settlement here from the Neolithic period. By the time the Romans arrived, in the 1C BC, there was undoubtedly already a town of some importance, built by **Berbers** who had become relatively prosperous in this fertile and well-watered region under the civilising influence of the Carthaginians. In 25 BC the Emperor Augustus granted the Berber kingdom of Mauritania to **Juba II** and added to it the whole of Numidia (now Algeria).

Juba is thought to have been a descendant of Hannibal, a very fine bronze head of whom was found at Volubilis in 1944 and is presumed to have belonged to Juba. Juba was educated in Rome, and in 19 BC married Cleopatra Silene, the daughter of Mark Antony and Cleopatra. He was scholarly and ruled his kingdom wisely. He is said to have written some 50 learned books, and also to have discovered that the milky juice from a kind of spurge growing freely throughout the Atlas mountains was a cure for conjunctivitis. He named the plant Euphorbia after his physician, Euphorbus. Opinions differ as to whether he actually lived in Tingis or Volubilis: both were by now important cities in the western half of Mauritania.

Juba died in AD 19. He was succeeded by his son **Ptolemy**, who was murdered by the Emperor Caligula in AD 40, leaving no heir. Four years later the kingdom came under direct rule from Rome and was divided for easier administration into two provinces: Mauritania Caesariensis (eastern) and Tingitana (western), but not before there had been serious rebellions by Berber tribes determined to avenge the murdered Ptolemy. Under their leader Aedemon, who was a freedman and minister of Ptolemy, the Berbers threw themselves into a fierce and bloody **revolt** against the encroaching power of imperial Rome. This was finally quashed in AD 47 by Marcus Valerius Severus, a Roman official in Volubilis, with the help of citizens of the town. Having successfully quelled the rebellion he returned immediately to Rome, where the Emperor Claudius conferred Roman citizenship and immunity from tribute for ten years on the city of Volubilis for its loyalty. It was probably for this reason that the seat of **provincial government** was placed firmly in Volubilis and not in Tingis, despite the fact that the province was named after the latter.

From this time on the town of Volubilis grew and prospered. The region became one of the granaries of Rome and also a major producer of olive oil and of copper, which was mined in the hills. At this time there are thought to have been some 15,000 inhabitants. The town was also a base from

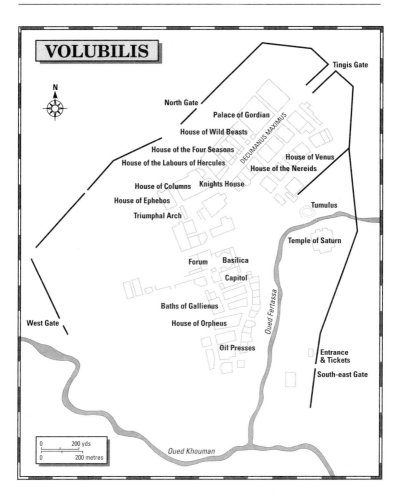

VOLUBILIS

N

Tingis Gate

North Gate

Palace of Gordian

House of Wild Beasts

DECUMANUS MAXIMUS

House of the Four Seasons

House of the Labours of Hercules

House of Venus

House of the Nereids

House of Columns   Knights House

House of Ephebos

Triumphal Arch

Tumulus

Temple of Saturn

Forum   Basilica

Capitol

Baths of Gallienus

Oued Fertassa

West Gate

House of Orpheus

Oil Presses

Entrance & Tickets

South-east Gate

| 0 | 200 yds |
| 0 | 200 metres |

Oued Khouman

which to control the uneasy and often rebellious Berber tribes in the nearby hills. Four **military outposts** were built to protect the town, and one of these, Tocolosida, was situated where the village of Ain el Kerma stands today, just off the Sidi Kacem–Rabat road. By AD 168 the great encircling ramparts of Volubilis, sections of which still remain, were complete. They are thought originally to have extended over 2km and to have had six gates. Most of the great buildings which remain as ruins today—the Capitol, Basilica, and Triumphal Arch of Caracalla—were constructed at the beginning of the 3C and some historians believe that they replaced earlier buildings that had previously been destroyed, probably in some particularly violent Berber uprising.

By the end of the 3C the Romans were beginning to withdraw, probably in the light of mounting Berber pressure and of more urgent problems else-where, and the seat of administration moved north to Tingis. Volubilis remained a centre of **Roman culture**, however, preserved by its Romanised and increasingly Christian population. Unlike neighbouring Spain, Mauritania Tingitana was never totally overrun by tribes from the north, and Volubilis kept its Latinised traditions more or less intact until the arrival of the Arabs and their all-embracing and uncompromising **Islam** at the end of the 7C.

The new culture took over absolutely. By the time Moulay Idriss I arrived in 786 the Romanised Berbers had already converted to Islam and Volubilis had been renamed **Oulili** (after a local flower). It was at this point that the town was abandoned. We know that Moulay Idriss I preferred to live in the neighbouring hills. His son, Moulay Idriss II (804–828), also disdained to live in Oulili and founded Fes as his capital. Neither, fortunately, took it upon himself to destroy the Roman city, which remained standing, although decaying and empty, throughout the centuries until it was severely damaged by the Lisbon **earthquake** of 1755. This was very nearly its end, but towards the close of the 19C a party of foreign diplomats travelling from Fes to Tangier via the shrine of Moulay Idriss stumbled on some of its remains. Serious excavations were begun by the French at the beginning of the Protectorate in 1915, and now the Moroccan government continues the work. There is much still to do but enough has already been revealed of this important Roman town to suggest how life was lived by the Roman colonisers and latinised Berbers of that time.

You will be taken first along an original paved road past a series of oil presses. The first major point of interest is the **House of Orpheus** on your left, so called because one of its mosaics is dedicated to Orpheus, the musician of Greek legend. (For want of a better system many of the houses and smaller buildings have been named after the mosaics or statues found therein.) This seems to have been an important house. The domestic quarters include a kitchen and three rooms for family bathing: the *caldarium*, *frigidarium* and *tepidarium*. Bathers would enter the hot room first for a bath, then plunge into a cold-water bath in the second room, finally emerging to enjoy a leisurely massage and oiling of the skin in the open court or peristyle. The *tepidarium*, as the name suggests, was a room of medium temperature and was probably used only in the winter. There would have been a hypocaust underneath the floor where hot air from a furnace circulated between the supporting pillars before passing up the walls through hollow tiles and bricks to heat the water and the air in the rooms above. One of the rooms has a mosaic depicting dolphins, which were considered by the Romans to bring good luck. The reception areas consist of further rooms arranged around a larger court where there is a charming mosaic of Amphitrite in a chariot drawn by a sea-horse and surrounded by other exciting sea crea-tures. One of these rooms contains the Orpheus mosaic, which shows the musi-cian with a fascinating collection of animals, such as elephants and lions, which roamed the countryside in those days. Indeed, we know that the hills around Volubilis were an important source of lions for the Roman games, a source exploited to the point of the animals' total extinction.

Next, on the left, are the old **public baths** restored by the Emperor Gallienus in the 3C AD. Bathing was taken very seriously by the Romans and public baths fulfilled an important social role, enabling people to relax together, eat and drink, talk business and exchange gossip. There is very little left here of a decorative nature to suggest any of this and the Volubilis baths were probably not very big.

You now approach the great administrative centre of Volubilis, comprising the capitol, basilica and forum, whose ruins today make a proud and impressive sight. The **capitol**, dated by inscription AD 217, is thought to have been constructed over an earlier building of similar nature. It comprises a rectangular court surrounded by Corinthian columns, with a temple at one end approached by a flight of steps. At the foot of the steps is a sacrificial altar. The temple was dedicated to Jupiter, Juno and Minerva. The tall, slender columns are particularly fine and some have been well restored.

Volubilis, the capitol

Adjoining the capitol is the **basilica**, or lawcourts, which would have had an apse at both ends of a large rectangular area probably divided into five aisles. An important and central part of Roman life, this building would have been used not only for dispensing justice but also as a centre for commercial exchange. The blind arcades here have been restored recently.

The **forum**, nearby, is a large open space which served as a place for public meetings and political speeches—the focal point of city life. Surrounding it would have been the main administrative buildings and temples. It was probably built during the reign of the Emperor Septimius Severus (193–211), and it is his family which is commemorated on stone plinths to the right of the path; also included is the bust of Marcus Valerius Severus who put down the Berber revolt led by Aedemon (see above). Other statues which no doubt lined the Forum have been removed to the museum in Rabat.

Next you pass the remains of the house where the famous **bronze dog** was found (now also in Rabat). This is one of the finest pieces to come out of Volubilis and should be seen if at all possible. Not far away is a house which has amusing mosaics of fishermen and acrobats, including one riding backwards on a horse.

Next comes the **triumphal arch** which was the only edifice to survive the earthquake intact. It provided the clue which provoked the initial excavations. It was erected in honour of the Emperor Caracalla in AD 217, the year of his death, and seems to have had a purely ceremonial function as it does not really lead anywhere—to the west of it is an empty space. Only the east face and the two sides have been lavishly decorated with statues, columns of imported marble, and medallions, including four charming ones representing the seasons. The top section of the arch is now missing and one can only imagine how it would have looked surmounted by the bronze figure of Caracalla himself driving a six-horse chariot.

On the far side of the arch is the **House of Ephebos** (named after a bronze head of Ephebos now in Rabat), and next to it is the easily identifiable **House of Columns**. Both would have belonged to patrician families. They are large and have traces of splendid mosaics in the public and private rooms, which are grouped, as was the fashion, around three separate courtyards. One particularly charming mosaic shows the three gods, Bacchus, Venus and Cupid; others portray sea-nymphs (a favourite theme) or have geometric designs of interlocking circles or squares.

Next comes the **Knight's House**, in a ruinous state apart from one lovely mosaic of Bacchus discovering the sleeping Ariadne. Next to it (up a little side street) is the **House of the Labours of Hercules**, which contains what is probably the most famous mosaic of all, in excellent condition, with the hero's well-known exploits easily recognisable in ten out of twelve scenes. The mosaic is in what was probably the banqueting hall, whch has stone benches on three sides where guests would have reclined and feasted. These four noble houses occupied a prime site on Decumanus Maxuimus, the main street of Volubilis, where there would have been market stalls and shops behind the shade-giving colonnades which lined both sides as far as the Tingis Gate in the northeast town wall. Notice the marks of chariot wheels still visible on some of the paving stones.

The houses further up the street are somewhat smaller but also contain fine mosaics—the most remarkable being that of the **Four Seasons**, each season depicted in its own medallion. Another mosaic shows nymphs bathing. Only the **House of the Wild Beasts** disappoints, for its mosaic has been removed. Next to it, and nearest to the Tingis Gate, is the **Palace of Gordian**, so called because of an inscription which dates its construction to the reign of Gordian III (238–44). It impresses by its size and its large bath house, and is thought to have been the residence of the provincial governor, which seems reasonable in view of its close proximity to the Tingis Gate.

Most of the houses on the south side of Decumanus Maximus are in total ruin and indistinguishable one from another; however, the **House of the Nereids**, opposite the House of the Four Seasons, merits a closer look by virtue of its mosaics. The streets alongside it join Decumanus Maximus to a lesser street that runs parallel to the south. Here, standing out amongst the mass of ruins, is the **House of Venus**, notable for having been the source of the bronze heads of Cato and Juba II which are now in Rabat. This was undoubtedly an important house owned by someone with superior artistic taste. Its many courtyards and rooms are decorated with **mosaics** of woodland nymphs and mythological scenes. Facing the entrance, across the central court, is a group of rather worn mosaics, including one that depicts ducks pulling chariots in a hippodrome. The real treasures are beyond, in what must have been the public rooms, where the mosaics are better preserved. The two most outstanding mosaics—thought to be slightly later than the others (possibly early 3C)—are of Diana bathing with her nymphs and surprised by Actaeon, and of Hylas captured by nymphs.

From here it is possible to rejoin the well-trodden visitors' path and follow the ravine of the river **Fertassa** back to the southeast gate. You will pass by a tumulus and, on the far side of the river, a large rectangular ruin known as the **Temple of Saturn** which is thought to pre-date the advent of the Romans and to have had its name changed by them. The walk back to the gate offers those with a little imagination a good opportunity to appreciate the extent of the encircling ramparts.

Hotels

Volubilis Inn, on P13. ☎ (05) 544 469 fax (05) 636 393. ****A (54 rooms). Fine views over the Roman site. Good Moroccan and international restaurants, swimming pool.

Campsite

Camping Zerhoun, on the main Meknes road 11km out of Volubilis. Snack bar, showers. 4km from the bus station.

Moulay Idriss

If Volubilis is Morocco's chief monument to Roman civilisation, Moulay Idriss, the shrine of Sultan Moulay Idriss I (788–91), founder of the first Arab dynasty in Morocco, commemorates the beginnings of Islam in the country. The view of Moulay Idriss from Volubilis is a striking and provocative one, exuding mystery and a rare other-worldliness, and there is everything to be said for visiting the two sites in this order. You return to the main road from Volubilis and then climb 3km to the foot of the great massif which supports the little holy city, whose houses seem to grow out of the rock.

Moulay Idriss is a city apart. Conscious that the possession of the tomb of the founder of Moroccan Islam is sufficient reason for its existence, it really awakens from its torpor only once a year in August and September, when thousands of pilgrims from all over the country come to the **moussem** to honour their first king, called El Akhbar ('The Old') to distinguish him from his son, who is buried in Fes. Indeed, Moroccans who cannot afford to go all the way to Mecca are allowed instead to make five pilgrimages to Moulay Idriss (which ranks fifth amongst holy cities in the Muslim world) though this does not entitle them to adopt the courtesy title of *el Hadj*. The *moussem* at Moulay Idriss is one of the most important in Morocco, and is sometimes attended by members of the Royal Family. Primarily it is a religious festival but it is also a lively affair with *fantasias*, markets, singing and dancing. The surrounding countryside is dotted with tents, and the feasting and rejoicing continue for many days and nights. The spectacle is one of the most colourful that the visitor to Morocco can see. However, it is essential to remember that it is, above all, a holy festival and should therefore be treated with great respect. There are no hotels in Moulay Idriss and there never will be, since non-Muslims are not permitted to stay overnight in the town. (There are no Jewish or Christian inhabitants.) Tourists are welcome during the day but must never be encouraged to such a degree that the intrinsic apartness of the 'city of the Shrine' is lost.

At any time other than August and September, Moulay Idriss is a peaceful corner. A certain amount of controlled expansion is now taking place, however, and you cannot but notice the over-large white building alongside the road as you approach, which turns out to be a new covered market. Cafés are springing up around the squares, craft stalls are proliferating and the number of 'student'-guides is certainly increasing.

The **Great Mosque and Shrine of Moulay Idriss** stand in the hollow between the two hills which make up the town. They were rebuilt by Moulay Ismael in the 17C and are firmly barred to non-Muslims by a wooden barrier. Alongside stands a modern palace belonging to the present king. The hills are known as Khiber and Tasga; the latter is still spoken of as *'la ville sainte'* and some sections of it are still completely closed to visitors; Khiber, which is the higher of the two, can be freely and extensively explored and its narrow, winding streets are a joy.

It is now possible to drive up to the deservedly famous viewpoint on Khiber known as the **Terrace of Sidi Abdallah el Hajjam**, though purists will still prefer to climb the steep path and steps (which start to the left of the main square), if only to enjoy the enchanting views back through alleyways as they ascend; look out too for the ancient **Moulay Idriss Medersa**, which incorporates stones taken from Volubilis. Its cylindrical minaret is covered in the text of a chapter of the Koran, worked in green-and-white mosaic, and was restored in 1939.

From the terrace you can look down on the hill of Tasga, which is a perfect dome—a symphony of white and various gradations of white, through grey to light brown, with the occasional green-tiled roof of a mosque. The general hum of activity rises towards you: cocks crowing; donkeys braying; children crying; but all muted like the colours. There is also a good aerial view of the Great Mosque and of the complex series of courtyards and outbuildings that surround it: behind the white arcades is accommodation for pilgrims; the white dome covers the tomb of Rachid, Moulay Idriss' lifelong companion and friend, and, after his death, regent until the infant Idriss ibn Idriss became king.

Also strongly recommended is a drive around the well-signposted **Zerhoun Circuit** (about 10km in all) which takes you to the foot of the **Jbel Zerhoun mountains** and offers some magnificent views over the Meknes plain. The plain is one of the most richly cultivated areas in the country, with particular emphasis on vines. You can then either take the road north from Volubilis, passing a new hotel (see above) and continuing 10km through olive groves to join the main Sidi Kacem–Fes road just before the Zegotta Pass; or you can take the equally beautiful road from Moulay Idriss east for about the same distance and join the same road a little closer to Fes, at Nzala-des-Beni-Amar. From here it is 35km to the junction with the main P1 road coming from Meknes, and a further 10km to Fes.

Fes

Fes is the oldest of Morocco's four 'Imperial Cities' and it dominated the country's religious, cultural and political life for a thousand years—until the French arrived in 1912 and removed the seat of government to Rabat. In fact it consists of three cities: Fes el Bali (the medina) founded in the early 9C; Fes el

Jdid, founded alongside it in the 13C; and the Ville Nouvelle built by the French at the far end of Fes el Jdid at the beginning of the 20C.

The medieval city of Fes el Bali remains complete and is unspoiled. It is fervently Islamic, deeply traditional, and closed to the motor car. Its physical collapse over the centuries has been halted by UNESCO, which has made it the object of a Cultural Heritage plan and has restored many of its glorious buildings. Fes remains the proud centre of Islamic Morocco, able to retain its dignity and traditions the better for having handed over the burden of government administration to the new capital, Rabat.

History of Fes

The Idrissides. The traditional story of the foundation of Fes, as it appears in the chronicle *Raoud el Kartas* by Ibn Abi Zar el-Fasi, the 13C historian from Fes, states that in 808 **Idriss II** decided that Volubilis, the old Roman capital, was too small and sent his vizier to search for a new site. The vizier discovered a fertile plain watered by many springs which were the source of a river. He followed the river down into a long flat valley enclosed by ranges of hills and chose this place as the site for the new city. Idriss was well pleased and gave orders for construction to begin. The story states that first he built a walled settlement on the right bank of the river with a mosque— Mosque of the Sheikhs (*El Sheikh*)—and a year later he built an exactly similar walled settlement on the left bank and another mosque—Mosque of the Cherifs (*El Chorfa*).

This story is sometimes questioned by modern historians who doubt whether Idriss II would have built a second separate town exactly like the first and so close to it in time and space. Levi-Provençal quotes the Arab historian Abou Bekr er Razi, who wrote that it was Idriss I who considered Volubilis too small and that it was he who built the first town of Fes in 799. Moreover, this story goes, when he began digging the foundations he uncovered a golden pickaxe (*fas*) and so the place was named *Madinat Fes* ('Town of the Pickaxe'). Nineteen years later, when Idriss II succeeded his father, he decided that this little settlement (which was essentially Berber in character) was not grand enough and he began to build a more dignified capital on the other side of the river which was to have a predominantly Arab feel. The second explanation seems more likely to be true.

The **etymology** of the word *Fes* is also a subject for speculation. The French historian Henri Gaillard, writing in 1905, listed four legends, the first of which is mentioned above. The second concerns a group of Persians, known as *Fars*, who were present at the moment when the boundary was being marked out and were buried under a sudden rock fall. The place was therefore named to commemorate them. Another relates that when Idriss was asked what the name of his new capital should be, he replied it should be called after the first man who passed by that morning: someone duly appeared and answered that his name was Fares, but as he lisped it sounded like Fes. The fourth claims that Idriss was visited by a very old monk who was overjoyed to learn about the plans for a new city because he had read in a holy book that one day a man called Idriss who was descended from the Prophet would build a city called *Sef* (sic) in this very spot where, he said, there had earlier been a great city.

Moulay Idriss II was a good leader who spent the 24 years of his reign (804–828) strengthening and enlarging his father's kingdom and consolidating the capital. He was assisted by the timely arrival in 818 of some 8000 Arab families who had been expelled from Andalusia by the Christians. Idriss welcomed them and installed them in the city on the right bank, which from that moment became known (and still is) as **Fes el Andalous**. These people brought from Spain the skills in mosaic, wood-carving and stucco-work which later made Fes famous. Seven years later 2000 Arab families came to Fes from Kairwan in Tunisia, also seeking a peaceful place to live. They, too, were welcomed and were offered a place on the left bank of the river, which thereafter became known as **Fes el Karaouyine**. In *Raoud el Kartas* it was said that the inhabitants of el Andalous were 'strong, brave and good at cultivating the soil'; those of el Karaouyine were 'better educated and more given to luxurious living; the men were handsome but the women were less pretty than those of *el Andalous*'.

In 828 Idriss II died and his tomb became the principal shrine of the city that he had created. He left many sons who subsequently divided the kingdom between them, usually a recipe for disaster but in this case, at least at first, Fes remained the most advanced and prosperous town in Morocco. In 859, during the reign of Idriss II's grandson, Yahia, the two great **mosques** of Karaouyine and Andalous were founded (on the sites of the original El Sheikh and El Chorfa mosques, which had become much too small). In keeping with Islamic law the two mosques soon became centres of culture as well as prayer. Since Islamic learning centred around the Koran, which was read aloud in mosques, what more natural than that they should become not only places of prayer but also of religious and scientific knowledge. Under the Idrissides, houses, shops, public baths (thanks to the glorious abundance of water) and flour mills were built on both banks of the river. Merchants from far and wide poured in to buy and sell in the prosperous markets, and *fondouks* (lodging houses) were built to accommodate them.

The Berbers. This peaceful period of self-assured progress was shattered in the second half of the 10C by the Zenata Berber tribe of Meknassas who came from the south and made sudden and repeated attacks on the totally unprepared Fassis. A period of unprecedented violence followed, during which the two halves of the city found themselves fighting one another. To make matters worse the attackers were soon joined by another tribe of Zenatas, and the two leaders, who were brothers, installed themselves one on each side of the river, which exacerbated the feud. Their arrival coincided with (or perhaps caused) a period of intense **famine**. Such was the desperate hunger of the occupying Berbers that whenever they saw smoke rising from a Fassi's home they forced entry and grabbed whatever food was being prepared. The people soon grew wary and began to dig caves in which to hide their food.

The Almoravides. This situation continued until the arrival of the Almoravides in the 11C. The leader of this group of fanatically religious Sanhaja Berbers was **Youssef ibn Tachfine**. He had already founded Marrakesh as his capital in 1062, but he knew that Fes, the traditional capital of Morocco, must be forced into submission before he would be able to declare himself sultan of the whole country. The people of Fes, already exhausted by hunger and in-fighting, could offer little serious resistance. Nevertheless, there were many battles and the remaining Zenatas either fled or were massacred.

The unpleasant preliminaries over and his right to power established, Youssef ibn Tachfine proceeded to embellish and enlarge Fes to such an extent that the quality of life for Fassis surpassed anything else in Morocco at that time. He made use of resident Andalusian talent—and probably imported more—to erect all kinds of public buildings, including mosques, baths, fountains, markets, and *fondouks*, to accommodate the increasing flow of merchants to the city. The river was ingeniously harnessed so that by 1069 every house had running water available to it. One outstanding act forms a milestone in the history of Fes: Youssef ibn Tachfine joined the two halves of the city together by demolishing the wall which had divided them and building a bridge across the river. He was the first to see that in order to achieve real progress, the two quarrelling factions must unite. In fact the two welded together only very slowly, and some would say never completely.

The Almohades. Peace reigned for over 70 years until the next dynasty of religious fanatics, the Almohades, arrived c 1154. The people of Fes barricaded themselves inside the city. The Almohade leader Abd el Mumene built a dam across the river with wood and rubbish, so that on its release tons of water hurtled down, taking with it city walls, houses and people. Having captured Fes, Abd el Mumene had much of the delicate Almoravide carving in the mosques plastered over, declaring that it was too ornate. He also demolished the Almoravides' town walls, saying 'only justice and the sword shall be our ramparts'. His successors were to regret this impetuous act and started building **new walls and babs**. One of the best preserved today is Bab el Mahrouk ('Gate of the Burned One'), so called because a rebel leader was suspended from its arch and burned. It was built so high that a soldier could enter on horseback without having to lower his standard. The city is still enclosed by what is left of the massive Almohade walls. Fes el Bali (Old Fes) is no bigger today than it was in Almohade times and herein lies the secret of its unique harmony and authenticity.

Although the Almohades also chose Marrakesh as their capital, Fes became even more prosperous under their positive and educated guidance and was soon the centre of a vast Islamic empire comprising much of Spain and almost the whole of North Africa. Cultural and spiritual life flourished and the Karaouyine became a regular meeting place for learned men, scientists and doctors from all over the empire. The *Raoud el Kartas* recounts that at this moment of supreme greatness, at the beginning of the 13C, there were 785 mosques, 80 fountains, 93 public baths, 9082 shops, 372 flour mills, 135 bread ovens, 467 *fondouks*, 89,236 houses, and 125,000 permanent inhabitants, with hundreds more people passing through, all of which must have made Fes easily the biggest town in the Moorish empire at that time. Such was the intensity of **cultural activity** in the city that most of the smaller mosques became places of learning with their own libraries and professorial chairs—all under the aegis of the Karaouyine. In the Arab world it became the dearest wish of anybody with power and influence to send his son to be educated in Fes.

The Merinides. The city continued to prosper under subsequent dynasties, with only the occasional outbreak of inter-tribal violence. During the late 13C the Merinide sultan Youssef returned from successful conquests in Spain to find the city closed to him. On regaining entry he executed six of the rebellious Fassis and fixed their heads to the ramparts. His son, Yacoub II (1286–1307), forgave this infidelity and made Fes his capital.

The Merinides had arrived in vast numbers and the old city could expand no further. A new town was built outside the Almohade walls, close but not too close to the old town and dominating it from higher ground. Called *Fes el Jdid* (New Fes), it was essentially a garrison town and one is still struck by the military character of its ramparts. The army was permanently stationed here, mainly for the purpose of continuing the campaign against Spain, but also to be on hand should there be any further revolt by the people of Fes el Bali. A royal palace and mosque were built and many fine houses for high-ranking Merinides. The new city did not compete with its neighbour for spiritual or educational superiority but it did provide administration and protection. It also provided somewhere for the increasing Jewish population to live. Hitherto, Jews had been scattered throughout the old city in isolated groups, officially tolerated by the Muslims but not welcomed, often mistreated and frequently made scapegoats. The Merinides built a Jewish quarter, which was protected by high walls pierced by only one gateway. Today the remains of the **mellah** are recognisable by the unusually high walls, and houses with tiny windows.

Yacoub II was one of the first Berber sultans to show any signs of philanthropy. He actually sought to improve conditions for the people, especially the blind, the sick, and above all the poor students who could not afford lodgings within the city. The Merinides are best remembered in Fes for their **medersas**—buildings comprising two storeys of small rooms, some of them bedrooms and others classrooms, around a central courtyard. Here the students found board and lodging for little or no money. Some *medersas* even had their own mosques, or at least an oratory where students could retire to say their prayers. Although the little rooms were simple inside, the carved decoration and mosaics around the courtyards were crafted with a degree of expertise formerly reserved only for mosques. *Medersas* were not just students' lodgings, they were monuments to Islam. All were grouped around one or other of the two big mosques—the Karaouyine and the Andalous—and only one was built in Fes Jdid, which is proof that the Merinides were content for the older town to remain the spiritual centre.

The Merinides built very few mosques in Fes el Bali because it already had so many. They did, however, manage to squeeze in more houses, more fountains and more palaces, all more exquisite than anything put up by the sober Almohades. These palaces, created by master craftsmen from Spain, were fairylands of marble, carved cedarwood, stucco, and fine mosaics. Today one must visit the Alhambra in Granada to see a typical example of the flamboyant palatial style of the Merinides. No such palaces survive today in Fes, though many of the *medersas* are still well-preserved and remain a faithful reflection of the Merinides' penchant for elegance and grace.

The Saadians. With the death of the last Merinide sultans in 1465 there followed a series of weak rulers from the related El Wattas tribe. Chaos ensued throughout the country as Christian invaders arrived unchecked from the north and rebellious Berber tribes rose up to try and take control of the interior. Religious leaders prayed for a strong ruler and in 1541 the Saadians arrived from the Draa valley under Mohammed. He drove the El Wattas out of Fes but found the people hostile and scornful of his uncouth ways. He humiliated them by banishing their leaders to the desert and then made Taroudannt in the south his capital. The defeated Fassis lived a quiet and fearful existence until 1576, when **Abd el Malik**, a grandson of Mohammed esh-Sheik, swept into the city and, with the help of Turkish troops from neighbouring Algiers, made Fes the Saadian capital. Once enthroned he quickly paid off the troops and sent them back lest they should decide to stay, although for some weeks prayers were said in the name of the Turkish caliph.

An English ambassador visited Fes for the first time in 1577, sent by Queen Elizabeth I to 'the king of Maruecos and Fesse'. Abd el Malik tried hard to negotiate a political alliance with England against the Spaniards but failed. A **trade agreement** did follow, however, by which English cloth was exchanged for sugar, dates and almonds. Once secure in Fes the Saadians settled down to continue the process of embellishment which their predecessors had left unfinished. This was done in the same Hispano-Moresque style and their only innovation was the use of Italian marble, which they imported in large quantities together with the skilled artisans to work it. They paid for the marble, weight for weight, in locally grown sugar. By this time (the late 16C) the Saadians had shed their rough manners and were even adopting some of the refinements of the Fassi way of life: dressing in silks, eating at intervals during the day instead of all at once like desert nomads, and holding discussions with scholars. In 1578 Abd el Malik was succeeded by Ahmed, nicknamed *Edh Dhahabi* ('The Golden One'), who was only interested in plundering gold and slaves from Timbuktu. He put the people of Fes to work minting gold coins, but he preferred to live in Marrakesh, where he spent most of the new-found wealth. At his death in 1603 his three sons battled for the throne, and a period of **civil war** followed during which Fes was sacked repeatedly. Fes el Bali and Fes el Jdid were ranged against each other, family fought family, and even the call to prayer from the minarets was suspended.

The Alouites. In despair the people of Fes invited another race of Shareefs (descendants of the Prophet) to take control. These were the Alouites, who came from the Tafilalet region having arrived from Arabia three centuries earlier, and who still reign today. The first sultan, Moulay Rachid, was welcomed to Fes in 1666, where he restored order, lent money to the ruined merchants and brought back strict observance of Islam. But he was a cruel tyrant and his successor, Moulay Ismael (1672–1727), even more so. Ismael chose Meknes as his capital. He mistrusted the Fassis and appointed a number of governors to rule Fes in his absence. They were so fearful for their own heads that they punished the slightest misdemeanour with death. Many eminent Fassis left the town and the population dwindled for the first time in its history. When Moulay Ismael died, aged 81, he was succeeded by a series of quarrelling and incapable sons and grandsons. Real power now lay in the hands of the infamous 'Sudanese' or Black Guard which the old Sultan had built up for his own protection, mainly from descendants of slaves. They owed loyalty to no one and could make or break sultans at will. This they did and Fes was severely affected, with one seige by the Guards lasting 27 months.

Not till 1757 did an Alouite sultan emerge who was able to bring the over-extended Black Guard under control. This was Mohammed III, and he gradually restored Fes to something approaching its former glory. But the two years of his son Yazid's (1790–92) reign were by contrast most destructive. He was nicknamed by his contemporaries 'the Bloodthirsty', and his ruling principle was that a sultan should keep a continuous stream of blood flowing from the palace gates to the city walls, so that the people would live in fear and obedience. This he managed to do until he was removed by his jealous brothers. He was followed by a string of uninspiring monarchs who did nothing to improve the sterile condition into which Fes and the whole country was sinking. The reign of **Moulay el Hassan** (1873–94) was comparatively peaceful. At first the people of Fes el Bali shut their gates to the new sultan, and he, not daring to use firearms for fear of damaging the holy shrine of Moulay Idriss, had to wait outside until one of his men had penetrated the walls and persuaded the Fassis to lay down their arms and open the gates. Subsequently he joined Fes el Bali and Fes el Jdid together by constructing the Dar Batha Palace between them, with an entrance at each end; and by constructing an avenue joining Bab el Mahrouk with the Royal Palace in Fes el Jdid. He died in 1894, worn out by his struggle to quell the country's increasingly ungovernable tribes. His sons, Abd el Aziz and Moulay Hafid, were no more successful and in 1912 Fes was occupied by the French and a treaty was signed relieving Hafid (1908–12) of his power to govern and declaring the greater part of the country a French Protectorate.

Post-Independence. Fes played a crucial role in the struggle for independence and the Declaration of Independence was actually prepared in the Karaouyine Mosque. Since that time, and the retention of Rabat as capital by Mohammed V on his regaining the throne, Fes has lost much of its political power, even though individual Fassis hold many important posts in government.

Like Casablanca, Fes has a large and overcrowded urban population (more than 200,000 people live in the medina, and several families now occupy houses which were designed to accommodate just one), and in 1990 the young people of Fes were provoked into rioting for better employment opportunities and a more democratic political system. The latest Constitution, of September 1996, was designed to provide this.

Despite the recent unrest, Fes has remained the proud centre of Islamic Morocco, able to retain its dignity and traditions—at least on the surface—thanks to UNESCO's Cultural Heritage Plan, which ensures the city's survival as one of the most complete and fascinating medieval cities in the world.

■ Practical information

Tourist information. ONMT. Pl. Mohammed V, ☎ (05) 622 041 and Pl. de la Resistance, ☎: (05) 623 460.

Banks. Blvd Mohammed V/Ave de France.

Post office. Corner of Blvd Mohammed V and Ave Hassan II.

Trains. Railway station at Rue Imarate Arabia. ☎ (05) 625 001. Trains to Casablanca, Tangier and Oujda.

Air transport. Royal Air Maroc, 52 Ave Hassan II. ☎ (05) 620 456. Saiss airport is 11km south on Route d'Imouzzer. ☎ (05) 624 712. Internal flights to all major cities. Airport bus from Pl. Mohammed V.

Buses. Ave Mohammed V. ☎ (05) 622 041; also Pl. Baghdadi (by Bab Boujeloud). Services to Rabat, Casablanca, Marrakesh, Meknes, Chaouen, Oujda, Tangier, Azrou and Sefrou. Buses for Taza and Oujda leave from Bab Ftouh.

Taxis. The best way to get around in Fes—as in any large Moroccan city—is by *petit taxi*. This is particularly relevant to your walk through the medina, when you are likely to enter by one *bab* and leave by another.

Grands and *petits taxis* can both be found at stands at Pl. Baghdadi (next to Bab Boujeloud), Bab Ftouh (southeast gate), and Pl. Mohammed V (Ville Nouvelle). *Petits taxis* can also be found at Dar Batha (south of Bab Boujeloud), Bab er Rsif (close to the Karaouyine Mosque), Bab Guissa (by the *Palais Jamai* hotel), Ave Hassan II, by the main post office (*ville nouvelle*), and Pl. des Alouites (Fes el Jdid).

Hotels

Hôtel Palais Jamai, Bab Guissa. ☎ (05) 634 331 fax (05) 635 096. ***** (100 rooms and 20 suites). See text below. Situated in Andalusian-style gardens within the ramparts of the medina, this place is legendary. It has two restaurants (one Moroccan and one international), swimming pool, sauna, tennis courts and a night club. A twin room in the new section with a view over the medina costs 1650dh, or 1100dh without the view. Suites in the old part can cost up to ten times as much.

Hôtel Les Merinides, Bordj Nord. ☎ (05) 646 040 fax (05) 645 225. ***** (90 rooms). The hotel's interior has been completely restored since the fire that destroyed it in 1990. While definitely lacking the atmosphere of the *Palais Jamai* it is somewhat less expensive and does have an equally fine view of the medina from its terrace.

Hôtel Jnan Palace, Ave Ahmed Chaouki. ☎ (05) 652 230 fax (05) 651 917. ***** (249 rooms). Only built in 1992, in a 7ha park in the heart of the new town. Vast and good for package tours.

Hôtel Batha, Pl. Batha. ☎ (05) 636 441. **** (61 rooms). A new hotel very conveniently located opposite the Dar Batha Museum, close to Bab Boujeloud and the medina.

Hôtel Moussafir, Ave des Almohades. ☎ (05) 651 902 fax (05) 651 909. ***A (98 rooms). Close to the railway station. It also has a pool and restaurant.

Hôtel de la Paix, 44 Ave Hassan II. ☎ (05) 625 072. ***B (42 rooms). Quite comfortable for its category, and centrally placed. No pool.

Hôtel Kairouan, 84 Rue du Soudan. ☎ (05) 623 590. *A (20 rooms). Recommended as excellent (within its category) and cheap.

Restaurants

The following are all in the medina and should be booked in advance.

Les Remparts, Bab Guissa. ☎ (05) 637 415. This new restaurant is very close to

The Merinide tombs

the *Palais Jamai* and serves excellent Moroccan meals in a traditional palatial setting. Recommended.

Al Fassia in the *Hôtel Palais Jamai*. ☎ (05) 634 331. Faultless Moroccan cuisine and worth the price.

La Djenina, also in the *Hôtel Palais Jamai*. ☎: (05) 634 331. The hotel's international restaurant. Also outstanding. Menus at 280dh.

Palais de Fes, 16 Rue Boutouil. ☎ (05) 634 707. Very close to the Karaouyine Mosque. Open for lunch only. Caters for package tours in season.

Dar Saada, 21 Attarine. ☎ (05) 633 343. In the Attarine Souk in a splendid old palace. Recommended especially for its *pastilla*.

Dar Tajine, 15 Ross Rhi. ☎ (05) 634 167. Another traditional restaurant.

Palais M'Nebhi, 15 Souiket Ben Safi. ☎ (05) 633 893. Off the Talaa Seghira in a fine 19C palace.

The remaining restaurants are all in the Ville Nouvelle.

La Cheminée, 6 Rue de l'Indonesie. ☎ (05) 624 902. Near the railway station. Good French food.

Roi de la Biere, 59 Blvd Mohammed V. ☎ (05) 625 326. International/French cuisine.

Les Voyageurs, 41 Blvd Mohammed V. ☎ (05) 625 537. Adequate, but not exciting.

El Ambra, 47 Route d'Imouzzer. ☎ (05) 641 687. Out of town but worth the effort for good Moroccan cooking.

Campsites
Diamant Vert, Ain Chket forest, 5km west of the city. ☎ (05) 640 810.

A panoramic drive

An initial drive (15km) around the **Route de Fes** is strongly recommended. It follows the rim of the basin in which the medina is tightly wedged and so provides very good views—the best times are early in the morning or at sundown. The route is well signposted and you can join it at almost any point. If you are approaching from the *ville nouvelle*, leave by Avenue Hassan II and Avenue Moulay Youssef; turn left where the ramparts begin (along Boulevard des Alouites) and follow them round, turning right along Boulevard des Saadiens, and right again where the road is joined by another coming from Meknes. Continue along the ramparts and you will pass the early 14C Merinide gate—**Bab Segma**—with its single remaining octagonal tower, reminiscent of the Merinide gate of Chellah in Rabat; on the left is the **Cherrarda Kasbah**, which was built in the late 17C by the first Alouite sultan, Moulay Rachid, as a vantage point over the city (it now contains an annexe to the university and a hospital); and also **Bordj Nord**, a 16C fort built by Christian slaves and now containing a museum of weapons. Just beyond is the 5-star *Grand Hôtel des Merinides*, which has a panoramic terrace overlooking the medina.

Very little is known about the nearby **Merinide Tombs** (late 15C), except that they constitute one of two Merinide necropoli, the other, earlier, one being at Chellah in Rabat. All that remains are a few crumbling ruins with a place to stop your car (or the taxi) to take advantage of what is probably the best view of the medina. Far below you will see a conglomeration of buildings in shades of brown, grey and white, interspersed by the colourful minarets and green-tiled roofs of the mosques. This is also a wonderful place from which to appreciate the call of the **muezzins** from the minaret tops at prayer time. The first call comes from the Karaouyine Mosque, followed a second or two later by all the other mosques and producing an extraordinary ripple of sound which dies away as the last muezzin finishes his cry. At dawn or at night, the minarets light up one after the other and then fade when the call is over. The effect is magical.

The road zigzags down to reach **Bab Guissa** and then on to **Bab Jamai** (through which is the famous *Hôtel Palais Jamai*, built just inside the walls) and continues to wind round, leaving the roads from Ouezzane and Taza on the left, to the south side of the city. It passes **Bab Ftouh** (giving access to the **Quartier Andalous**) and eventually arrives at **Bordj Sud** (equivalent to the look-out fortress you saw on the north side). From here there is another fine view of the city. Continue past the ramparts, **Bab Jdid** and **Bab el Hadid**, to return to the *ville nouvelle*.

Fes el Bali

The **medina** comprises 187 *quartiers* and in each of these there are, by law, a mosque, a Koranic school, a bakery (a bread oven to which families bring their own dough to be baked on the spot), a water fountain and a hammam. There are six *medersas*, 14 city gates and over 300 mosques in all here.

No cars are allowed in the medina (the streets are too narrow). Mules and donkeys are the only form of transport and the cry of *Balak!* ('Attention!') is frequently heard: it means 'please stand aside as I need to get past you with my mule/donkey.' It is just as well to act quickly or you can find yourself pinned against the wall by a pannier full of table legs, or iron pots. Everyone seems to be busy making, selling or carrying something. The skills of the craftsmen are those of Andalusia, brought back to Morocco by victorious sultans in the 13C and 14C, and by Muslim Andalusians in the 15C and 16C when they were expelled by the Christians. Their way of life has changed very little over the centuries. They have their proud traditions and unique skills, their strong sense of family loyalty and deep Islamic faith. It is perhaps an irony that the ebullient craft economy is now sustained by the tourist trade, either through personal purchase or export. It is to be hoped that the delicate balance will remain and

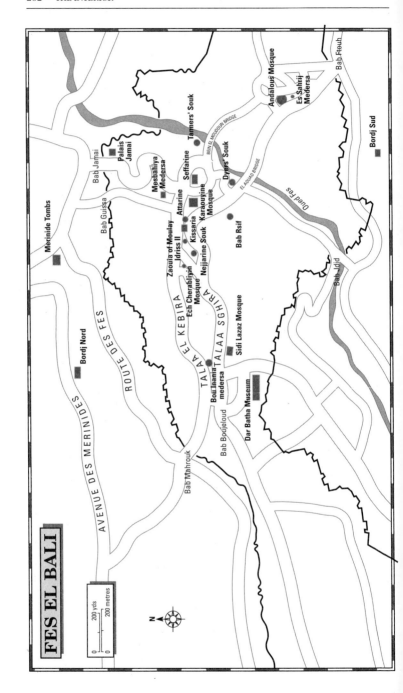

FES EL BALI

Andalous Mosque
Es Sahrij Medersa
Bab Ftouh
Bordj Sud
Tanners' Souk
BEN EL MOUDOUN BRIDGE
Palais Jamai
Mesbahiya Medersa
Seffarine
Dyers' Souk
EL ADOUD BRIDGE
Oued Fès
Bab Jamai
Attarine
Karaouyine Mosque
Merinide Tombs
Bab Guissa
Zaouia of Moulay Idriss II
Kissaria
Neijarine Souk
Bab Rsif
Ech Cherabliyin Mosque
TALA A EL KEBIRA
TALAA SGHIRA
Bab Jdid
ROUTE DES FES
Bordj Nord
Sidi Lazaz Mosque
Bou Inania medersa
Dar Batha Museum
AVENUE DES MERINIDES
Bab Boujeloud
Bab Mahrouk

200 yds
0
200 metres
0

N

that this enchanting city will be able to retain its quintessential character despite all the flattering attention from outside.

Fes el Bali is not just shops and workshops. Over 200,000 people also live here and many of the unpromising windowless walls that line the side streets hide beautiful and rich interiors. Houses are built on a square around a central patio, often with gardens and fountains, and all the windows look inwards.

You will probably need to take a guide the first time you walk through the medina, not only to avoid getting lost but also to fend off other well-wishers who will flock to help you once they see you hesitate. It is also a good way of ensuring you include all the significant monuments. Most of the Fassi guides are proud of their city and can produce fascinating snippets of information if encouraged. It is important, however, to do some homework and make clear what you want to see. Otherwise you run the risk of being whisked at speed through the maze of narrow alleyways from one carpet or kaftan cooperative to another, for the obvious reason that any purchase you make will activate a rake-off for your guide. An uninformed tourist is considered fair game. Generally, however, hassle is a lot less intense nowadays than it was in the 1980s and early '90s. If you stick to the main arteries through the medina and look as if you know where you are going, you may be able to walk from one end to the other without a guide at all. You should allow at least a day, or preferably two separate half days for your walk; an in-depth visit obviously takes longer. All the streets have been paved over the last few years and this is a vast improvement over the dirty, muddy alleyways it was previously necessary to navigate.

A logical place to start is the **Bab Boujeloud** (at the Fes el Jdid end); there is a parking area outside it and taxis come and go all the time. This is one of the newest city gates (1913), built in the traditional style and covered in ceramic tiles, blue outside and green inside. The view through it gives a foretaste of what is to come: the green minaret on the left is that of the 14C Bou Inania Medersa, and the grey minaret on the right is that of the 11C Sidi Lazaz Mosque.

Go through the *bab* and plunge into the noise and excitement of the **Talaa al Kebira** (Rue du Grand Tala), which bends round to the left of the two minarets, through an archway with the sign *Kissariat Serajine*. It is the more interesting of two main streets and will take you right into the centre of the medina. The **Talaa Sghira** (Rue du Petit Tala) runs parallel to, and below, it: the two join up at Souk el Attarine.

The smell is of oranges, mint and spices, laced with the occasional tantalizing aroma of charcoal-grilled kebabs. The pollution caused elsewhere by revving moped engines is thankfully absent, though some might not think mule dung much of an improvement. Most of the way you are protected from the sun by a rough covering of rushes over the street. You will pass first the butchers (offering somewhat flyblown produce) and the fruit and vegetable section. Notice the cords hanging from the roofs of the stalls by which the vendors swing themselves in and out over the piles of produce; there is often no other way.

You will soon come to an impressive entrance (on your right), which is the way into the **Bou Inania Medersa**. This was built as a lodging-house for students of the Karaouyine by the Merinide sultan Abou Inan in 1355. Generally considered to be the finest of all Moroccan *medersas*, this beautifully restored example

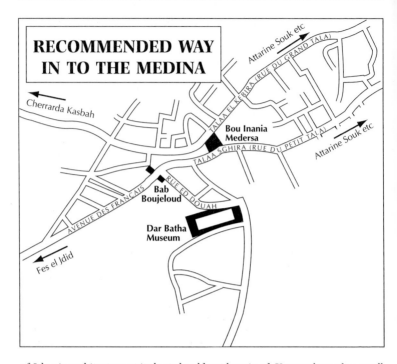

RECOMMENDED WAY
IN TO THE MEDINA

Cherrarda Kasbah

Attarine Souk etc

TALAA EL KEBIRA (RUE DU GRAND TALA)

Bou Inania
Medersa

TALAA SGHIRA (RUE DU PETIT TALA)

Attarine Souk etc

AVENUE DES FRANCAIS

Bab
Boujeloud

RUE ED DOUAH

Dar Batha
Museum

Fes el Jdid

of Islamic architecture at its best should not be missed. You go through a small entrance-hall, with its own splendid stalactitic (*muqarnas*) dome, into the glory of the building, which is the **court**. The walls are quite breathtaking; it seems that not a centimetre has been left undecorated, and yet because the colours are so muted and the proportions so near perfect the overall effect is not confusing. The whole is framed from above by a layer of finely carved cedarwood, while below is a terrace of delicate stucco. Stucco-work like fine threads of lace outlines the simple openings of the tiny, cell-like, students' rooms. These were still in use by students until 1956, but are now seriously decayed. (It is worth climbing one of the flights of stairs, which ascend from the entrance hall to the terrace, for an exceptional view of the court and nearby buildings.) Below the stucco on three sides of the court is a horizontal band of black Kufic script painted on wood. The columns beneath it are covered with minutely worked *zelliges*, which form the only point of colour, other than browns and creams, in the whole complex structure. Between the columns are elegant wooden grilles, and behind these are the rooms which would have served as lecture halls.

In the centre of the court is the small ablutions fountain, fed by waters from the river Fes, a spot of perfect peace in its natural surround of plain flagstones, an acceptable contrast to the contrived perfection around it. At the far end of the court, opposite the finely proportioned door through which you entered, is the **oratory**, with its delicately sculpted mihrab, where the imam stands facing Mecca to lead the prayers. This part of the *medersa* is still in use and, depending on the good nature of your guide, it may or may not be possible to peer in. The green-tiled minaret is one of the most elegant in Fes. **Open** 08.00–17.00; closed Fri morning; entry 10dh.

Leaving the *medersa* you will notice a curious phenomenon high on the wall opposite: a row of 13 wooden blocks projecting below 13 windows—seven of the original brass bowls remain on the blocks. This was once a **water-clock**, created c 1317 by a local craftsman. It was discovered in about 1355 by Sultan Abou Inan, who erected it opposite the *medersa*, which was being completed at that time. The clock was undoubtedly intended to draw the attention of passers-by to the *medersa* and also to ring out the hours of prayer. There is much specu-lation as to how it worked, the most likely explanation being that there were two water-tanks hidden inside the house behind the wall; water flowed at a controlled rate between them, and the falling level in one or the rising level in the other activated a series of levers which caused a weight to fall through a window into one of the brass bowls. The clock is currently screened off from the street for restoration. Next door to it, and also part of the Bou Inania complex, are the original 'Turkish-style' latrines; even they are built around a central court and have a carved plaster ceiling. These too were closed at time of writing.

As you continue down the Talaa al Kebira, keep a look out for *fondouks* on both sides. These are now often used by craftsmen as workplaces or warehouses and no one will mind if you wander in. One *fondouk*—on the left—is a small tannery. The smell of animal skins, heaped up and waiting to be scraped and cured, is foul, and the complete process is better seen at the big tannery by the river Fes. In pleasanter vein, as you penetrate deeper into the medina remember to keep looking up at the countless minarets which are one of its special charms. Notice particularly that of the 14C **Ech Cherabliyin Mosque** ('Slipper-makers' Mosque') on the right. Its decoration is said to have been modelled on that of the Almohade Koutoubia in Marrakesh, and is still in its original form. By this point the street has changed its name to Rue ech Cherabliyin and passes through stalls selling *babouches*, leather pouffes and book covers tooled with gold. Then come the brass souks, where there is a man who says his father designed the seven gates of the Royal Palace in Fes el Jdid and who will gladly chisel for you an intri-cate pattern on a sheet of brass which will turn into a tray before your eyes.

Continue in this general direction and you will eventually reach (although not necessarily in this order) the *zaouia* and mausoleum of Moulay Idriss II, Place Nejjarine, the Attarine souk and *medersa*, the Karaouyine Mosque, and the Place Seffarine with its *medersa*, before arriving at the river which divides the city into its two halves—Fes el Karaouyine and Fes el Andalous.

The **Zaouia of Moulay Idriss II** was built by the Idrissides in the 9C but later fell into disuse and decay during the rule of the Almoravide and Almohade dynasties. It was rebuilt in the 13C by the Merinides who rekindled the cult of the Idrissides and of Moulay Idriss in particular. It was the succeeding dynasty of Wattasides who rediscovered Moulay Idriss's tomb, and from that moment this became the most revered sanctuary in Morocco, the object of pilgrimages and a source of comfort to rich and poor alike. Until quite recently the *zaouia* also held the documents of allegiance from all the tribes to each new sultan. It is still a place to gather in time of trouble and, even to this day, it retains the right of *horm* (holy asylum) and the streets leading to it are barred by wooden beams which mark the boundary of the *horm* area. These effectively kept out all non-Muslims until the arrival of the French in 1912. Significantly, Sultan Moulay el Hassan, who found himself shut out of the city in 1873, forbore the use of gunpowder for fear of damaging this sacred place (see above).

The four doors are often open, so it is possible, discreetly, to peer in and look at the magnificently carved Merinide wooden ceiling, and at the tomb in white marble, with people sitting cross-legged in front lightly touching it and praying. Old men sit and chant verses from the Koran. It is unwise to try to photograph it. Notice, as you approach, the copper plaque on the outside with a hole into the wall where people can place their hands for a moment of comfort and blessing (*baraka*). All around the *zaouia* there is an area of specialised souks: nearest the building are the candle-makers; next are the jewellery-makers and goldsmiths.

Next door to the *zaouia* is a **kissaria** (covered market), built to replace one that burned down in 1954. Traditionally a *kissaria* is a place where imported goods are sold. This one seems to be filled with fabrics—it is a treasure house of silks, brocades and woollen materials (much of which appear to have been made locally) and the guides refer to it as 'the fabric souk'.

Nearby are the carpenters' workshops of the **Souk Nejjarine**, which give off a heady aroma of cedarwood. Here men sit on the ground and hold table legs between their toes whilst they use both hands to plane the wood, or carve intricate patterns on table tops. There is a huge demand in Morocco for this highly specialised work. You are now in the **Place Nejjarine**, with its 17C **fountain**, beautifully decorated with mosaic tiles and carved and painted wood, and its early 18C **fondouk**, which has a magnificent entrance under an imposing porch roof (presently being restored).

The **Attarine Souk**, on the northeast corner of Place Nejjarine, is the centre for herbs and spices and is said to be the busiest souk in Fes. The more everyday spices like coriander and turmeric are piled in great heaps on open display, whilst the rarer varieties are kept in small jars in murky shop interiors; the rarest and most expensive of all is musk. Recommended are the ready-made mixtures of five or seven spices which will transform an everyday chicken casserole into a feast. Notice the strange twists of dried grasses on sale to Berber women, who use them for cleaning their teeth. Also in this souk, with its door on the main street, is the *Restaurant Dar Saada*, housed in a 19C palace and also functioning as a carpet shop. Close by is the **Henna Souk** presenting every kind of beauty aid including henna paste and leaves, kohl and phials of exotic perfume. And if all else fails, there are lizard skins and terrapin shells for magic potions and aphrodisiacs.

At the end of the souk is the bronze door which leads into the **Attarine Medersa**. Built in 1325, it has the same ground-plan as the Bou Inania Medersa but it is considerably smaller. It also has the same sequence of wall decoration: *zelliges*, stucco, and carved wood. In the courtyard, tile-covered piers support an arcade with particularly finely carved capitals. The floor is also tiled—unlike that of Bou Inania—and the whole effect is one of an infinite variety of geometrical patterns comprised of squares and circles and ten-pointed stars, each design a point of visual repose in its exquisite symmetry. The oratory is by comparison very simple. It is no longer in use and so may legitimately be entered. The entire building has recently been well restored and its first-floor terrace affords an excellent view into the courtyard of the Karaouyine. Look across the green-tiled roofs and you see three minarets: the left-hand one is that of the Zaouia of Moulay

Idriss; on the right are two belonging to the Karaouyine, the slimmer of the two being the oldest Islamic building in Fes, dating from 956. **Open** 09.00–12.00 and 14.00–18.00; closed Fri morning; entry 10dh.

Until the completion of the Mosque of Hassan II in Casablanca, the **Karaouyine Mosque** was the biggest in North Africa, with space inside for some 20,000 people who enter through 14 separate doors. It was founded in 859 by Fatima el Fihri, a young girl originally from Kairwan, who sponsored the building of the first mosque as a tribute to God in memory of her father, a wealthy merchant. It is said that she consulted local wise men as to the siting and planning of the mosque in relation to Mecca and that she had the original building made out of materials extracted from the chosen site so as to avoid the introduction of any impure substance. The building started as a simple rectangle measuring 32m by 36m. It was raised to the status of cathedral mosque in 933, and in 956 given a new minaret, simple to the point of austerity, which still survives. Both the Almoravides and the Merinides enlarged the mosque, and by the end of the 13C it had reached its present dimensions.

In keeping with Islamic law it very soon became a centre of culture as well as prayer—a **university** as well as a mosque. Learned men lectured students who crowded round them in circles squatting on the floor—the most interesting teacher collecting the biggest circle. The lectures could take place only between the times allocated for prayer. Teaching centred on the Koran, but at an early stage subjects such as law, geography, astrology and arithmetic were introduced. It is believed that Arabic numerals and the zero may have been developed here. Many famous scholars, including the historian Ibn Khaldoun, studied here. Much of the learning was by rote (as it still is in the Koranic schools) and it is doubtful whether many students actually learned how to apply the knowledge they had so painfully absorbed. They might have attended classes for ten years or more before gradually starting to teach their own pupils, either in the mosque or in the neighbouring *medersas*. Today the students have moved out to more comfortable premises in the modern town, both to live and to work, and the Karaouyine has reverted to its original sole function as mosque.

It is ironic that such a vast place, so central to the life of Fes throughout the ages, is actually quite difficult to find. It is so hemmed in by lesser buildings, alleyways and stalls, all tightly packed against its very ordinary walls, that the unguided visitor can quite easily pass by without noticing it. It does not tower above the city in the style of a Christian cathedral. The only hope for a non-Muslim to see anything at all is to be fortunate enough to find one of the doors open.

The Almohade interior of 16 aisles is simple: the arcades of identical horse-shoe-shaped arches and undecorated columns give a great sense of space. Far more ornate is the open courtyard built by the Saadians in the 16C. It has a black-and-white tiled floor, and at each end a pavilion with carved stucco arches over slender columns and a green-tiled roof. On one side of the courtyard is the main archway through which the king himself passes: an elaborate textbook of Muslim architecture covered with fine stucco-work, mosaics and, at the top, the stalactitic plaster carving for which the Saadians were renowned (compare the workmanship with that of the Saadian tombs in Marrakesh). The courtyard strongly resembles the Courtyard of Lions in the Alhambra at Granada.

Walking round the outside of the Karaouyine, in a clockwise direction from the Attarine, you pass the rather dilapidated but once elegant **Mesbahiya Medersa** (1346). It has a floor of Italian marble and a very splendid marble basin which was brought over from Andalusia by the Saadians. It also has finely carved wooden decoration above the door. The rest of the woodwork has been taken to the Dar Batha Museum (see below). Next you pass the **Tetouani fondouk**, once a hostelry for merchants from Tetouan and now a carpet shop.

The **Karaouyine Library** is housed in a simple building separate from the mosque. Believed to date back to the foundation of the mosque in the 9C, in the 14C it received a unique collection of copies of the Koran and other Islamic works returned from Andalusia as part of a peace treaty by the King of Castile. It contains 30,000 books, including a superb 9C Koran and an original copy of Ibn Khaldoun's *History*, and is considered to be one of the most prized collections in the Muslim world. In the late 1950s, King Mohammed V added a spacious reading room for students of the university. (It is closed to the public.)

In front of the library is the pretty Place Seffarine ('Metalworkers' Square'). All around there is furious activity and noise, for men are hammering huge cauldrons into shape. There are treasures in every conceivable metal here—copper urns, silver trays and family-sized pots for making couscous. Here too is the **Seffarine Medersa**. Built in 1280 by the Merinide sultan Youssef, it is the oldest of the Fes *medersas*. The entrance (through a heavy studded door) is hidden down a narrow lane which leads out of the left-hand corner of the square. In need of some restoration, its 30 students' rooms are tucked away behind a fine, arched balcony above the court. It was built in the style of a traditional Fassi house.

By now you are approaching the river Fes, the waters of which are used by the dyers and tanners. The **Dyers' Souk** (*Souk des Teinturiers*) is directly below the Seffarine Medersa and, until recently, was instantly recognisable by the brightly coloured skeins of silk and wool draped across the street to dry. Underneath were the dyers themselves, crouching over cauldrons of hot, steaming liquids which gave off an acrid, choking vapour. On our last visit, there was none of this and the street was occupied by metalworkers. 'Not enough work for the dyers,' our guide explained.

The **Tanners' Souk** (*Souk des Tanneurs*) is close by (just above the Bein el Moudoun bridge). Either the constant stream of tourists or the sickly smell should lead you there. It is an extraordinary and unique sight. Row upon row of round, dried-earth vats are filled with different coloured liquids, some for treating the skins and some for dyeing them. Scantily clad and nimble-footed tanners hop from vat to vat, nursing the skins through the various processes.

The skins (sheep, camel, kid and cow) are first scraped free of hair and fat in lime baths, then soaked for two or three days in water mixed with sulphuric acid and salt to soften them; they are then immersed in vats of oils mixed with tanning agents and subsequently laid out to dry. After this they are lubricated with oils to make them supple, and then scraped and smoothed out ready for polishing. The final process is that of dyeing: only vegetable dyes are used—indigo, poppy flower, mint and saffron, among others—after which the skins are laid out to dry once more, usually on neighbouring rooftops, before reaching the hands of the craftsmen who turn them into the familiar leather goods on sale all over Morocco. This whole dramatic and colourful scene cannot have changed much since the 16C when Andalusian artisans first brought their skills to Fes.

The Tanneries

Only the tourists are new, cameras flashing and mint sprigs delicately held in front of noses. The workers seem to take no notice at all.

Cross the river to visit the **Andalusian Quarter** (Fes el Andalous). There are two bridges, **El Aouad** and **Bein el Moudoun**, both dating originally from the 11C and still in use. You can see that even now the Andalusian and Karaouyine quarters are only tenuously joined. The former is quieter, more spacious, even rural, but certainly not without points of interest.

To reach the **Andalous Mosque** (sister mosque to the Karaouyine), take either of the two bridges and continue steadily up the hill; Rue Sidi Youssef is the more direct route. Founded in 860 by Miriam—sister of the Fatima responsible for the Karaouyine—the mosque began as an oratory and achieved status as a mosque after the Almohades enlarged it in 1200, at which point it, too, began to fulfil an educational function like the Karaouyine. Most beautiful is the north portal (with a stepped street leading up to it), which dates from the Almohade period. It has been restored quite recently. The magnificent horseshoe arch is set off to perfection by the dark stucco-work around it, the verses from the Koran painted in black above, and the important carved cedarwood canopy above that. This is the highest gateway in Fes and from its top the *oulemas* (religious authorities) watch for the thin crescent of the Ramadan moon. To the left of the portal is a Merinide fountain for ablutions. (Although non-Muslims are subject to the usual frustration of not being able to look inside officially, there is a large crack in the south door.)

The Merinides built two *medersas* in the immediate vicinity to serve as annexes and sleeping quarters for students studying in the mosque library. These are the **Es Sebbayine** and **Es Sahrij Medersas**. The former, whose name means 'seven', was so-called because it was here that students were taught how to chant the Koran in seven different approved styles. (It is not open to the public.)

The latter is particularly worth seeing. It was built c 1320 and has extremely rich *zellige* decorations and fine wood carving in simple Almohade patterns of palmettes and pine cones. Es Sahrij is also remarkable for its large rectangular pool which creates an unusual optical effect: it appears to be deepest at whichever end you stand. This is a trick of the refracted light and the guides enjoy asking you what you can see and are highly amused when you peer in expecting to see a fish or perhaps some writing on the bottom. This *medersa* has recently been restored. **Open** 09.00–12.00 and 14.00–18.00; closed Fri; entry 10dh. To your left, as you continue up the hill, used to be the workshops and kilns of the potters. These have now moved out of town and the space is occupied by an unexciting mix of imported household goods.

The potters of Fes

The potteries can be found 3km east of Fes el Bali on the road to Taza. (A taxi from Bab Ftouh will get you there in a few minutes, and should be asked to wait as you are unlikely to find another for the return trip.) When you see the sign—Poterie Fakhkhari—and columns of smoke from traditional kilns, you know you have arrived. Jars, vases, plates, bowls, everything from the most homely shapes to the most delicate refinements of form and colour, can be found here, or be seen in production. Fes pottery, with its distinctive blue markings, is greatly valued throughout the country, and the showrooms here are a good place to buy it new, though you obviously need to hunt for antique pots in the medina itself. A little knowledge of the classic designs can be useful in your quest for the ultimate piece of Fes ware and should impress the merchant when you are bargaining.

Bab Ftouh is a little further up the hill and close by it is the gleaming white **Koubba of Sidi Harazem**, the 12C saint adopted by the students as their patron, and the subject of a colourful *moussem* every spring.

Cross back over the river and turn up the hill to the right towards Bab Jamai and the renowned **Palais Jamai Hotel**, which will provide welcome refreshment (at a price). It is the only luxury hotel within the medina walls. The oldest part of the hotel was a palace, built at the end of the 19C by Si Mohammed ibn Arib el Jamai, grand vizier to Sultan Moulay el Hassan. He was one of two brothers who became extremely wealthy and powerful during the reign of Moulay el Hassan, only to fall from grace under his successor Abd el Aziz. Their eventual fate is vividly described by Walter Harris in *Morocco That Was*. Si Mohammed in fact survived his brother but emerged from his dark dungeon broken both in mind and body, and financially ruined to boot.

The old palace has now been made into luxurious suites of two, three and four rooms, many with their own private Andalusian-style terraces, gardens and fountains. The rooms are decorated with all the lavish detail and colour of Moorish palaces, but with modern comforts added, and there is a faint smell of cedarwood overall. Such luxury must inevitably be paid for and most of us can only dream about it. Rather less exorbitant are the prices for rooms in the new section of the hotel (added in 1970) where, incidentally, the medina views are better for being unimpeded by palm trees. There is nothing to stop you wandering into the non-private sectors of the gardens of the old palace: the scent from the orange trees, the aromatic shrubs and medicinal herbs is intoxicating on a summer night.

For tired feet, it is a short taxi ride from the hotel back to Bab Boujeloud. Otherwise, return on foot by way of the Talaa Seghira, which starts just above Place Nejjarine and offers a slightly different sequence of craft shops and also a view of the sculpted roof of the Bou Inania Medersa. It will eventually rejoin the Talaa al Kebira and take you back to Bab Boujeloud.

Co-operatives and restaurants

At some point you will probably allow yourself to be persuaded into a co-operative. Co-operatives are often housed in former palaces and usually display a very wide range of merchandise, about which the 'front man' will be glad to impart a limitless flow of information. Do not take too seriously the claim that 'here prices are fixed'; it is surprising how fast they become unfixed once you walk towards the door. The goods in these highly organised establishments generally start at higher prices than the smaller independent merchants and you may wish to search more widely.

Some of the larger palaces have been turned into restaurants where traditional Moroccan food is served in a suitably authentic setting. This is probably the best way of tasting such delicacies as *pastilla*, which are usually only made in large quantities. (Fes claims to be the birthplace of *pastilla*.) Many of these places are also open in the evenings, when there might also be a floor show, but you may need to book in advance from your hotel. The price often includes transport to and from your hotel and a guide to get you there from the nearest *bab*.

It is not certain whether Fes el Bali or Fes el Jdid should lay claim to the **Dar Batha Museum**, for the palace it occupies was built by Sultan Moulay el Hassan in 1873 for the purpose of joining the two cities together and has a gate at each end. It is certainly worth a visit for an overview of Fes culture through the centuries. It is a five-minute walk from Bab Boujeloud: facing the *bab* and looking in towards the medina, walk down the street going off to the right—Ed Douah—turn right again and the museum entrance is on the right.

The palace was built in the form of a square around a central patio with a fountain and cypresses (a lovely place to catch your breath after a walk in the medina). The museum within consists of some eight rooms stuffed with the cultural trappings of former dynasties: there are fine Berber carpets, embroidered gowns, 13C and 14C tiles, plasterwork, pottery, and a collection of *mushrabiyyas* (carved wooden screens used in mosques to divide women from men and made in such a way that the women can see through but not be seen). All of this is visited in the company of a guide, usually a very old man, who, although informative (he will attempt three or four languages), will usually be incapable of answering questions. It is sad that the collection of arms—spears and daggers finely ornamented in silver and gold and encrusted

FES EL JDID & MODERN FES

N

0   200 yds
0   200 metres

Tetouan and Ceuta

ROUTE DE FES

CHERRARDA KASBAH

AVENUE DES FRANÇAIS

Makina

BAB SEGMA

BAB DEKAKKEN

Vieux & Petit Mechouar

GRANDE RUE DES MERINIDES

Great Mosque

Jardins de Boujeloud

FES EL JDID

Mosque of Moulay Abdallah
Jardins Lalla Mina
Royal Palace

MELLAH

BAB SEMMARINE

Ketama, Taza and Oujda

PLACE DES ALOUITES

ROUTE DE FES

Meknes and Rabat

BOULEVARD DES SAADIENS

BLVD. DES ALOUITES

AVE MOULAY YOUSSEF

Railway Station

AVE DES SPORTS

AVENUE DES ALMOHADES

PLACE DE LA RESISTANCE

i

PLACE MOHAMMED V

Post Office

ABDALLAH CHEFCHAOUENI

MODERN FES

AVENUE HASSAN II

BLVD MOHAMMED V

Meknes and Rabat

Handicraft Centre

with precious stones, as well as antique rifles and pistols—has been moved elsewhere (we were unable to discover whether this is a permanent or temporary situation).

The palace is a worthy exhibit in its own right. It has splendid painted ceilings, some superbly carved wooden doors and one particularly evocative little courtyard displaying fine metal grilles. **Open** 08.30–12.00 and 14.30–18.00; closed Tue; entry 10dh.

Fes el Jdid

Fes el Jdid, or 'New Fes' (so-called to distinguish it from Fes el Bali), was built by the Merinides in the 13C. Unlike former dynasties they were not motivated by religious fervour but rather by the desire for power and property, and a love of ostentatious wealth. Fes el Jdid was built to house the Merinide sultans in splendour and also as a centre of administration. It therefore has a very different character from the older city. Inside the long stretches of wall are palaces and military and administrative buildings, but very little private housing (except in the *mellah*). There is a great deal of space, and the enormous squares and courtyards lack animation.

Fes el Jdid has not really found a role for itself. Some of its royal splendours are on show to the public—but only from the outside—and it is essentially a **museum** town as all the administration has been transferred to the modern city. From Bab Boujeloud, walk down the Avenue des Français. This is a good 10min walk and you may want to rest a while in the **Jardins de Boujeloud**—on your left, having crossed the Avenue de Unesco—which are open to the public. They are cool, restful and full of fountains and there is a small café by an ancient waterwheel at the far end.

At the end of Avenue des Français, turn right and you come into a small walled square known as the **Petit Mechouar**. Go through one of the three arches to reach the **Vieux Mechouar** which dates from the 18C and was used at that time for royal parades. It is dominated by the monumental **Makina**, once an arms factory but now a carpet factory. On the right is **Bab Segma** which leads to the **Cherrarda Kasbah** built by the first Alouite sultan, Moulay Rachid, as a fortress from which to guard against possible insurrection by the citizens of Fes el Bali. It is now an annexe of the Karaouyine university.

Return to the Petit Mechouar and go through the smaller of the two gateways on the right, which leads to the relatively tranquil—and once forbidden—District of Moulay Abdallah, where you will find the 13C **Great Mosque**. A little further on is the 18C **Mosque of Moulay Abdallah**, recognisable by its slender minaret with vertical bands of green tiles; it has become a mausoleum for Alouite sultans including Moulay Youssef, the grandfather of the present king.

Return once more to the Petit Mechouar and turn right through the monumental **Bab Dekkaken**, which was the main entrance to the city until 1971. You are now in the **Grande Rue des Merinides** (formerly Rue du Mellah), which is lined with metalworkers' and jewellers' shops and leads eventually into the old *mellah*, through another monumental gate, the **Bab Semmarine**.

The **mellah**, thought to be the largest in Morocco, was constructed by the Merinides to rehouse Jews who were living in the precinct of the Karaouyine in order to make space for *medersas*. No doubt the Merinides also realised that if all the Fassi Jews were kept in one place, and close to the central administration

(*Makhzen*), their commercial activities could be overseen and taxed to provide a useful source of income. Jews were offered protection within the *mellah* in exchange for their absolute loyalty to the sultan and they were discouraged from ever leaving the precinct by being forbidden to wear shoes outside it, right up to the French Protectorate (1912). The use of the word *mellah* (meaning salt) in this context originated in Fes and is thought to refer to the task allotted by the early Fassis to the Jews in their community—salting the heads of vanquished enemies before they were set up on the *babs* as trophies. Nowadays there are very few Jewish families left, most of the population of 17,000 having emigrated at the end of the Protectorate in 1956 or during the late 1960s after the Arab–Israeli war. The *mellah* has become a somewhat melancholy place though the high-walled houses with their tiny windows, wrought-iron grilles and wooden balconies have a certain charm. Within the *mellah* is a Hebrew cemetery with clean white gravestones, restored recently under the UNESCO Cultural Heritage Plan.

The Grande Rue des Merinides will take you right through the *mellah* into the **Place des Alouites**, a very exotic site. It is a huge court with many palaces, pavilions and audience halls, built over 700 years by the various dynasties (for no sultan would have wished to live in anything built by his predecessors). It includes the present **Royal Palace (Dar el Makhzen)**, built in 1880 and recently restored. This has seven doorways, three doors on each side of a central portal. The doors are superbly worked in brass and surrounded by green and blue ceramic mosaics. An essential and colourful, but slightly anachronistic, part of this whole 'Arabian Nights' scene is the Royal Guard, dressed in traditional costume. It is unfortunate that one cannot enter any of these palaces.

The **Ville Nouvelle** was built by the French at the beginning of the Protectorate and is an entirely separate city c 1.5km from Fes el Jdid. To reach it from Fes el Jdid, simply continue along the Grande Rue des Merinides, which changes its name to Avenue Moulay Youssef and takes you to the main Avenue Hassan II. The new town is crossed by some fine boulevards, and has many good shops, hotels and restaurants, a railway station and a **handicraft centre** (*centre d'artisanat*) on Avenue Allal ibn Abdallah (a continuation of Avenue Hassan II), which is open every day. This is a good place to visit before launching into the medina and, as with so many such centres, it is the surrounding workshops which prove to be most rewarding. The craftsmen are often happy to chatter about what they are doing, and why, and their prices are not usually fixed (unlike those at the handicraft centre).

Excursions from Fes

Moulay Yacoub lies 20km northwest of Fes. Take the P1 Meknes road and after about 5km branch off to the right along the S308, which allows good views down on to the Sais Plain. Moulay Yacoub is thought to have been the Roman settlement of Aquae Dacicae. The waters are rich in sulphur and are particularly beneficial to sufferers from rheumatism, skin conditions, and ear, nose and throat complaints. There are swimming pools, and massage and 'special' treatments are available by appointment (which your hotel or the tourist office in either Fes or Meknes should be willing to book for you). There is a large hotel-restaurant (see below).

On your way back to Fes, you will notice a rough road going off to the right signposted **Ras el Ma**. It leads a few kilometres to the high point on which, history tells us, Moulay Idriss II stood and decided to build his city. *Ras el Ma* is Arabic for 'head of the water' and it is here that the Fes bubbles out of the ground to become, further downstream, the powerful river that provides the main water supply for the city.

Hotels
Hôtel Soterme, ☎ (06) 694 074. **** (120 rooms). Overlooks the spa. Very large but a good enough restaurant.

Sidi Harazem lies 15km southeast of Fes. Take the Taza road out of the city (starting near Bab Ftouh) and after 11km there is a right-hand turn to Sidi Harazem. In ancient times this was just an oasis of palm trees watered by natural hot springs, with a saint's tomb in the middle. Since the time of the first Alouite sultan, Moulay Rachid, however, the shrine has been the object of an annual *moussem* every April. Increasingly nowadays, the **spa** is visited all the year round for its thermal waters, of proven benefit both externally and internally. It is possible to take a medicinal bath and there is a pleasant hotel-restaurant on the spot (see below). The bottled water from here—without any mineral taste—is widely available all over Morocco.

Hotels
Hôtel Sidi Harazem, ☎ (05) 690 057. ****B (64 rooms). Overlooks the thermal swimming pool and has nice gardens and a good restaurant.

The Middle Atlas and the Jbel Ayachi region

About an hour's drive from either Fes or Meknes brings you up into the Middle Atlas, a region of folded mountains and high, windswept plateaux; of vast forests of cork oak and cedar, and lakes and streams full of trout or coarse fish; an area of warm, dry summers and very cold, snowy winters. This is Berber country and sheep and goat-rearing is the main occupation of these tough but friendly people. Rugged-faced, tall, thin men, and sometimes quite small boys, muffled up in thick brown djellabahs even in summer, can be seen tending flocks high up in the rocky valleys. Many of them are semi-nomadic: they do have homes but they also think nothing of following their flocks in search of fresh pasture and spending months in black, weatherproof tents.

This is a most rewarding region to tour. There is a good network of mountain roads (sometimes blocked by snow in winter) giving access to an unbelievable variety of scenery within quite short distances. There are a few modest but well-run hotel-restaurants, many of them started by the French during the Protectorate.

Imouzzer Du Kandar to Demnate

Lying just 36km south of Fes at an altitude of 1345m, the attractive little town of **Imouzzer du Kandar** is much visited by the people of Fes during summer, when the air is fresh and cool compared with the heat of the plain; in winter it can be very cold indeed, with temperatures down to minus 18° C. Imouzzer is a very open town with two landscaped artificial lakes in the centre and one or two good buildings such as the **Mahakma** (courthouse). At the southern end of the town are prehistoric troglodyte caves, until quite recently inhabited by members of the Berber Ait Seghouchen tribe.

There is not much to keep you in the town itself (apart, perhaps, from the Monday souk held in the ruined kasbah), but the countryside around it is lovely and there are some breathtaking views. **Jbel Abad** (1768m high) lies a short distance to the east and there are many natural lakes in the area—indeed one is struck by the abundance of water everywhere—for this is the great watershed of the country. To the south and east are stony deserts and dry river beds but here and immediately to the north is verdant land.

A few kilometres south of Imouzzer is a left-hand turning to Dayet Aoua, starting-point for the delightful **Circuit des Lacs**. Aoua is the largest of the lakes (150ha); it has a road going right round it and a hotel-restaurant (see below) with facilities for swimming, rowing boats for hire, and daily permits for fishermen. The lake is stocked with pike, perch, black bass, carp, and roach, but tends to be over-fished. Serious fishermen will go to the smaller lakes further away from the hotel, such as **Dayet Ifrah** or **Dayet Hachlaf**, which complete the circuit and lead you to Ifrane. The lakeland tour adds about 25km to the direct route from Imouzzer to Ifrane by the P24, but in the spring is good for picnics and walks through flower-filled meadows.

Hotel-restaurants

Hôtel des Truites, Ave Mohammed V, Imouzzer du Kandar. ☎ (05) 563 002. Lovely views.

Le Chalet du Lac, Dayet Aoua. ☎ dial 0 and go through Ifrane PTT

Ifrane

Ifrane offers the visitor a remote tranquillity and fresh, dry mountain air. It is sited in an old volcanic crater at 1650m and is bounded on all sides by forests of cedar and of cork oak. The cedar woods are wonderful to walk and picnic in. They offer welcome shade in summer, and in the winter they are covered with snow.

Ifrane is a fairy-tale town unlike any other in Morocco—a conglomeration of white-walled villas with steep red roofs and gables. It was built in 1929 by the French at the time of their greatest expansion as a kind of permanent holiday village and means of escape from the humidity of the coast and the heat of the interior. No expense has been spared recently to upgrade it. Ifrane now has wide, tree-lined avenues (probably the best-kept roads in Morocco), a skilfully land-scaped artificial lake surrounded by parkland and ornamental gardens, a stadium, tennis courts, even a new university, as well as European-style shops, hotels and cafés. Overlooking the town is a large mansion with a green-tiled roof; this is one of the king's palaces and Ifrane is one of his favourite places for relaxation. In the middle of town there stands, somewhat incongruously, a magnificent stone lion said to have been carved by an Italian prisoner of war. It is guarded all day long by a policeman, supposedly to stop anyone posing for photographs alongside it.

The **Al Akhawayn University** was inaugurated in January 1995. It occupies some 50ha of woodland above the town and offers undergraduate and graduate degree courses. Grounded in African, Arab and Islamic culture, its organisational structure, curriculum, method and language of instruction are modelled on the American system of higher education.

Ifrane, and indeed other Middle Atlas towns, has a particular attraction for **storks**. Every respectable villa has its stork's nest, which is returned to every spring. The clacking of the birds beaks in mutual appreciation is one of the most characteristic sounds of Ifrane.

Below the town (running northwestwards) is the river **Tizguit**, a delicate stream with tiny waterfalls bordered on either side by meadows and copses, weeping willows, oaks and many other trees. This is a paradise of wild flowers in the spring, and it is pleasant to leave for a while the exotic bougainvillaeas and hibiscus below to see violets and primroses growing here. In the autumn there are mushrooms, including the highly prized morelle. This enchanting spot is known as **Les Cascades de la Vierge** and the minor road signposted to Zaouet Sidi Abdeslem (itself a picturesque village) passes right through it.

From Ifrane you should certainly do the 20-minute drive up to the **Mischliffen**. (Take the Boulemane road and turn right after 9km.) You drive through dark, mysterious forests up over the **Tizi n'Tretten** (1934m) and then turn left to plunge down into the volcanic, cedar-topped crater which is the Mischliffen. In summer this view is magnificent. In winter the place is one of the busiest skiing stations in the Middle Atlas. There are only two ski-lifts and one big bowl to ski in and around but this satisfies people from Meknes and Fes in search of easy family skiing. There is more skiing a little further along the road at **Jbel Hebri**, with a wide piste, a ski-lift and an auberge at the top. Skiing is perhaps slightly steeper here but the facilities are fairly poor. These stations do have the advantage of being easily accessible by road and equipment (fairly basic) can be hired from the *Café Chamonix* in Ifrane. Hot food and drinks are available at the **Ski Club Ifrane**.

Hotel-restaurants

Hôtel Perce Neige, Rue des Asphodelles. ☎ (05) 566 404. **A (23 rooms). In the centre and particularly recommended. It has recently been refurbished and improved. It belongs to an oil company (Samir), but is also open to the general public. The restaurant is impressive.

Grand Hôtel, Ave de la Marche Verte. ☎ (05) 566 203. **A (38 rooms). Also centrally placed and pleasant.

Hôtel Mischliffen, ☎ (05) 566 607. ***** (90 rooms). Large and insensitively placed overlooking the town. Expensive and lacks atmosphere.

Restaurants

La Rose In town centre. Offers a simple and copious meal.

Campsites

On the Meknes road. ☎ (05) 566 156.

The main road between Ifrane and Azrou has one of the loveliest **panoramas** in Morocco, across range after range of mountains in varying shades of blue, blurring eventually into infinite nothingness. The view is best from the point where the road plunges down from the oak forests below Ifrane to the plateau of Azrou. Clever little Berber boys, knowing that all motorists will stop here, have organised a thriving amethyst industry. The gemstone can be found in the surrounding rocks and some of what they offer for sale may be genuine, but most is not. They will not mind if you lick your fingers and rub to see if the purple paint comes off. They will also probably try to sell you wild peonies, and wild asparagus, mushrooms and strawberries (which are very good).

14km along the road from Ifrane is a turning to the **Cèdre Gouraud**, which leads to a gigantic cedar 10m in circumference and named after a French Resident-General. Its neighbours are almost as majestic and this whole section of forest is worth stopping for.

Azrou is as Moroccan in appearance as Ifrane is French. It lies in a wide, flat valley, dwarfed by its backcloth of mountain slopes, upon which perches the original Berber village, home of the Beni Mguild tribe, and consisting of rows of beaten-earth houses with flat, white roofs. The modern town below has a particularly colourful Tuesday market attended by Berbers from neighbouring villages intent on selling their carpets (not necessarily to tourists, and therefore reasonably priced) as well as fruit and vegetables. Also worth visiting is the **Centre d'Artisanat**. It exhibits a wide range of carved cedarwood objects, metalwork, Berber rugs and the sequinned cushion covers which are typical of the region. It is exactly opposite the huge rock (*azrou*) which stands in the middle of the road and gives Azrou its name. **Open** 08.30–12.00 and 14.30–18.00.

Hotel-restaurants
Hôtel Panorama, Rue El Hansali. ☎ (05) 562 010. ***B (36 rooms). Central with a modest restaurant.
Auberge Amros. ☎ (05) 563663. ****A (83 rooms). 3km out of town on the Meknes road. Recommended. Good restaurant.

A forest road ~ Azrou to Khenifra
The main P24 road to Khenifra via **Mrirt** is unexciting. Much more rewarding is the mountain road (S303—a left-hand turn off the P24 about 8km after Azrou) which takes you, via **Ain Leuh** (another typical Berber village with flat-roofed houses) into the remote and mysterious heart of the mountains, winding through oak and cedar forests. Through clearings in the trees you catch sight of misty mountain landscapes. The road has recently been paved but parts of it can still become impassable after heavy rain. Cross tracks will tempt you deeper into the forest and will deteriorate the further you penetrate, and boggy patches and boulders can catch you out if your vehicle is low slung. It is also extremely easy to get lost. That said, this is wild and beautiful country and you may be lucky enough to glimpse a family of Barbary apes playing alongside the track or coming to the streams to drink. The ancestors of the apes which today amuse the tourists on the Rock of Gibraltar are thought to have come originally from here.

About 30km south of Ain Leuh you come to the headwaters of Morocco's longest river, the **Oum er Rbia**, which eventually finds its way out to the Atlantic by way of Azemmour. You will know you have arrived when you reach a small carpark off the road with plenty of little boys in attendance ready to walk you up to the main source (about 10min).

If you have time to spare thereafter, it is worth taking the short left-hand track signposted to Aguelmane Azigza, south of the headwaters. This is a large, indigo lake well-stocked with coarse fish. The shores are alive with butterflies and grasshoppers and there are wild flowers in glorious abundance in season. A memorable place for a picnic.

Khenifra lies on the banks of the Oum er Rbia and is the home of the Zaiane Berbers, once a very important tribe and renowned for their outstanding horsemanship. The small medina is busy, with good souks. There is a fine kasbah alongside the humpbacked bridge. From Khenifra a road (2516) has recently been constructed to the spa town of Oulmes, and this is probably the quickest way of reaching Rabat, should you wish to do so after your Middle Atlas tour. About 17km out of Khenifra another road (3409) turns off left to **El Kbab**, a small village specialising in a variety of handicrafts.

The P24 from Khenifra to Kasba Tadla more or less follows the Oum er Rbia river and crosses the rich agricultural **Tadla plain**. About 22km before Kasba Tadla a road goes off left to **El Ksiba** (9km) whose pleasant hotel-restaurant (see below) is located in a woodland setting much favoured by the local monkeys, who swing excitedly from branch to branch screaming at the visitors. There is also a campsite. About 34km along this road, at **Tiz-n-Isly**, you can take the wild and beautiful track south for a slow but spectacular drive up to the high plateau of Imilchil (see below) and Dayet Tislet. This track is often blocked by snow in winter but at any other time of year should not cause problems. At Imilchil another track runs east along the crest of the Jbel Ayachi range all the way to Midelt (see below).

Kasba Tadla was one of Moulay Ismael's outposts. He built the kasbah (17C) here in order to control the wild Tadla Berbers and discourage them from coming any nearer to his citadel at Meknes. The **kasbah** consists of two walled sections each with its own mosque. There is a lively Monday market in the square which contains a mosque with a white minaret. Moulay Ismael was also responsible for building the noble 10-arched **bridge** across the river. It is worth crossing for a good view of the town from the top of the hill on the other side.

Hotel-restaurants
Hostelerie Henri IV, El Ksiba. ☎ (03) 415 002. Nice location in the woods.

Beni Mellal lies 30km further south. It has another of Moulay Ismael's fortresses but is really memorable only for its delightful setting amidst olive groves against a backcloth of gentle hills. Recommended for lunch is the hotel-restaurant *Ouzoud*, situated on the outskirts of the town, its peaceful gardens stretching out towards the hills. There is a change in atmosphere here: *Le grand sud* and Marrakesh lie ahead, and Beni Mellal is as much a 'gateway to the south' as is Midelt at the east end of the Jbel Ayachi range.

Take the P24 out of Beni Mellal and after 6km turn left towards the lake and dam, signposted Bine el Ouidane (the name means 'between the rivers'). The lake is good for fishing and a licence can be obtained from the hotel, *Auberge du Lac*. The dam is very impressive; it is said to retain 1500 million cubic metres of water, which is used to irrigate a huge surrounding area. From the lake continue 28km along the S508 to the village of **Azilal**. This is a spectacular road, worth every inch of the steep climb. At Azilal the road turns west.

Continue c 22km to a right-hand turning signposted to the **Cascades d'Ouzoud**. This is a famous beauty spot—a row of waterfalls which tumble over the vertical side of a deep canyon, spanned by an almost permanent rainbow rising out of the mist. Rare climbing plants and strange eroded rock forms give the setting a unique beauty. There are marked trails which zigzag down to the pools in the chasm below the falls and along the valley. There is a modest café with rooms at the top of the falls, somewhat garishly painted in bright pinks and blues, but offering a courtyard where you can sit in the shade of an orange tree and sip your cool drink before scrambling down the somewhat precipitous path. There are several small campsites nearby and generally the place is delightfully uncommercialised.

Hotel-restaurants
Hôtel-Restaurant Ouzoud, Route de Marrakesh, Beni-Mellal. ☎ (03) 483 752. ****B (60 rooms). Good food and lovely garden with views.
Auberge du Lac, Bine el Ouidane. ☎ (through operator) 5. *A (42 rooms). Charmingly sited on the lake's shore. Good food.

If you are heading towards Marrakesh anyway, continue westwards along the S508 and you will come to **Demnate**, an interesting small hillside town, arguably more High than Middle Atlas. It is surrounded by ancient ramparts and has a very colourful souk on Sundays, when the streets are filled with stalls brimming over with the lush produce of this fertile area. Whilst there it is worth taking the track (6km) up to **Imi-n-Ifni**, a natural bridge formed by the eroding effect of the river. There is an air of mystery here. The place is haunted by crows and has its own annual *moussem*, usually around the Islamic festival of *Aid el Kbir*.

From Demnate it is 59km back to the main road (P24) and then another 55km to Marrakesh.

Meknes to Imilchil
Leave Meknes by the P21 which follows the Boufekrane river and after 31km reaches the fast-developing town of **El Hajeb**, perched on the edge of the plateau. There is nothing worth stopping for here except the view back over the Meknes plain with its crops of cereals, oranges and vines. At El Hajeb the road divides, the left-hand fork going up to Ifrane and the right-hand one going to Azrou via the Berber village of **Ito**, from where there is an extraordinary view to the right over a strange lunar wasteland of small hillocks which form the basin of the river **Tigrigra**.

The road from Azrou to Midelt follows the valley of the river **Gigou**, which winds through lush green meadows. After passing through the unremarkable town of **Timahdite** the road rises to the **Col du Zad** (altitude 2178m). On either side in the distance are the misty pink shapes of some of the highest peaks in the Middle Atlas. Just before reaching the pass, you will notice a turning on your left signposted **Aguelmane Sidi Ali**. A kilometre down this turning is a very large, deep lake which is rich in pike, perch and other coarse varieties, but which has been closed for fishing since December 1990. This is a region full of streams and as such is a favourite summer pasture for Berber herds.

Once over the Col du Zad the landscape changes. Behind you are the cedar forests and in front stretches a bare, arid, sandy plateau. There is another range of mountains in the distance, rising far more abruptly than the Middle Atlas, a thin cordillera, black and forbidding in summer, snow-covered in winter. This is the **Jbel Ayachi** range and at the foot of it is **Midelt**, which is, as its name implies, right in the middle of Morocco, and embodies the characteristics of many regions. It is cold and windswept in winter and very hot, dusty and dry in summer. It does have an adequate, if rather depressing, hotel-restaurant, where the dining room extends into a caidal tent (see below).

Midelt is, however, distinguished by its position as the starting-point for one of the most spectacular drives in Morocco—along the spine of the Jbel Ayachi past the amazing **Cirque de Jaffar**. This is a noble circle of peaks (about 26km from Midelt), and the skilfully engineered track takes you up to a pass 3700m high, from which you gaze down into this vast amphitheatre. The track is very steep in places and should not be attempted after heavy rain or in snowy conditions.

The track continues along the ridge for many kilometres, with views over range upon range of peaks. Driving conditions do not get any easier, however, and progress is slow because you are constantly having to stop to remove quite sizeable boulders from the track. Many people are content to see the Cirque de Jaffar and then return to Midelt. Brave spirits drive all the way through (96km) to Imilchil at the other end of the Jbel Ayachi range. But do not do so without making sure that the track is open; even then you should be prepared for the possible disappointment of having to turn back. The drive can easily take all day.

Hotel-restaurants

Hôtel Ayachi, Rue d'Agadir, Midelt. ☎ (05) 582 161. ***A (28 rooms). Adequate. See above.

Imilchil

Imilchil, high and solitary in the mountains, is certainly worth visiting, particularly in September when it has a large *moussem* and the **fête des fiançailles**— a kind of marriage fair held by the Ait Haddidou Berber tribe.

The setting for all this colourful tradition and festivity is magnificent: Imilchil lies on a vast tableland, broken by the uneven line of distant purple mountains. It is fit only for sheep and goat raising, is very hot in summer and cold and snow-covered in winter. There are several lakes and rivers in the vicinity which offer some of the best **trout fishing** in Morocco, but they are often difficult of access. Imilchil itself consists of little more than a few red-earth kasbahs surrounded by a small area of well-watered green fields, which contrast strikingly with the dry-as-dust landscape beyond.

The marriage fair

On this occasion the bare plateau is covered with tents of all shapes and sizes. The merchants are there to buy and sell, the singers and dancers have come to entertain. The young girls of the tribe are dressed from head to foot in striped woollen djellabahs with pointed hoods, around which are draped necklaces and silver ornaments. Their faces are not covered. Their high cheekbones are reddened with henna and their eyes are smudged with khol. The young men wear white djellabahs and carry their best silver daggers. Contracts of marriage are discussed between families, complicated dowries are arranged and festive dances begin. The **dancing** grows more and more compulsive as the festival progresses. Men and women, huddled together, shoulder to shoulder, move up and down as one human mass to the irresistible rhythms of the drums and the wailing voices of the poets and singers.

Amongst all these celebrations wander bemused tourists, not so numerous yet as to spoil the authenticity of the occasion. Accommodation consists of tents and food of mass-produced couscous and brochettes, although there are now a couple of very basic hotel-restaurants. The occasion is unforgettable, and, to many people, worth a small degree of discomfort.

Bahlil to Boulemane

Bahlil lies about 24km southeast of Fes on the P20. It is a picturesque Berber village clinging so hard to the rocks that they and the houses appear to be one and the same. A charming legend attaches to this very ancient village: when **Moulay Idriss**, the founder of Fes, rode there one day, hoping to convert the inhabitants to Islam, his horse suddenly became exhausted and nearly collapsed. The young king fell to his knees and prayed for water, whereupon a spring gushed forth from the ground where his horse stood. Doubting Berber onlookers, now convinced that the Muslims' god was a very powerful one, converted forthwith to the faith. The spring was named *Ait Reta* and is said to flow still from a spot between the bridge and the great mosque.

Another 4km will bring you to **Sefrou**, a town of great antiquity, famous for its **cherry festival** in June. The history of Sefrou is said to go back to the end of the 7C (before the arrival of the Arabs), when the agricultural Sefrioui tribe built themselves fortified *ksours* as protection against the many fierce nomads who roamed the countryside. Traces of these beaten-earth fortresses still remain along the Aggai river. Later, Moulay Idriss used Sefrou as a base while Fes was being built. Later still, the town achieved notoriety as a stopping-place for gold-laden caravans on the way from the desert to Fes, and it became a significant trading centre. Many Jews came to live there, as is evidenced today by the colourful *mellah* with its very narrow streets and taller-than-average houses. There is also a lively medina which is full today, as then, of local crafts, including jewellery, pottery and metalwork. Waterfalls and 18C ramparts complete the picture of this interesting little town in its setting of cherry orchards at the eastern edge of the Middle Atlas.

Hotel-restaurants

Hôtel Sidi Lahcen Lyoussi, ☎ (05) 660 497. **A (22 rooms). Good restaurant and an atmospheric, chalet-style hotel.

The road continues southwards towards Boulemane and ultimately joins the P21 between the Col du Zad and Midelt (see above). It climbs steadily across a wild and featureless mountain landscape consisting mainly of cork oak forests. Boulemane itself is unremarkable.

The South

Marrakesh

The first thing to strike you on entering Marrakesh is that everything is pink: the ancient castellated ramparts around the medina, the buildings within, and the modern buildings in the new quarter (known as Gueliz) are all in varying shades of the same colour, derived from the local red earth. Marrakesh lies north of the Atlas Mountains and is therefore very accessible from the northern half of the country. It is also a natural starting-point for a journey to the south, either by one of two spectacular roads across the mountains (over the Tizi-n-Test and on to Taroudannt, or over the Tizi-n-Tichka to Ouarzazate and the valleys of the kasbahs beyond) or by a faster route west of the mountains through Chichaoua and Agadir.

Marrakesh is the jewel of Morocco's tourist industry, combining as it does a perfect climate, a wealth of ancient monuments, and a unique setting of palm trees against the High Atlas peaks. Alas, the jewel is in some danger of becoming tarnished by the sheer number of well-heeled tourists who arrive by coach and unwittingly destroy the magic of the place by their very presence. The ONMT claims there are more than 10,000 tourist beds in and around Marrakesh. And it shows. The discerning visitor will take in the principal monuments and the souks early in the morning or late in the afternoon, leaving the fabulous Place Djmaa el Fna until the evening. Marrakesh is well served by all categories of hotels and restaurants, two golf courses and a casino.

The city's climate is considered by many to be one of the best in the world, except in the high summer months when it can become very hot (up to 38° C), though never humid. For the rest of the year the temperature ranges from warm to pleasantly hot. There is very little rain and the air is light and particularly good for anyone suffering from chest, ear, nose or throat complaints. The sun is only occasionally obscured when a sandstorm arrives suddenly and violently from the desert.

History of Marrakesh

Marrakesh, founded in 1062, was twice the capital of Morocco: first under its creators the Almoravides, followed by the Almohades; secondly under the Saadians in the 16C.

The Almoravides originated within the nomadic Sanhaja Berber tribes of the desert and at the end of the 10C were engaged in conquering and converting to Islam the black countries south of the Sahara. Their campaigns were inspired by an overpowering lust for the gold that was flowing into Morocco from the region of the river Niger; they were determined to find its source, though they never did. In 1050, however, one of the Almoravide princes went to Mecca on a holy pilgrimage and returned convinced of the need to reform not only himself but also his fellow men and particularly his greedy kinsmen. Many joined him and soon a large band of pious Berbers began to roam the south of Morocco, forcing everyone in their path to submit and repent of their lustful ways, in particular the drinking of wine and the taking of more than four wives. Their version of orthodox Islam spread quickly all over the south.

Out of this fierce puritanism emerged one of Morocco's truly great leaders, **Youssef ibn Tachfine**. Arab historians record that he was the personification of all the virtues claimed by his people, being renowned for his wisdom, sense of justice, courage, and, above all, his simplicity. He was, apparently, a modest man who clothed himself in rough woollen garments, ate only camel meat and drank only camel's milk. He was slight in build and had brown skin, with little hair on his face. His eyes were black and his voice was soft. Even when he became the ruler of a vast empire, he retained a deep-felt consideration for the humblest of his subjects.

In 1062, after leading his men over the Atlas mountains, Youssef decided that the plain to the north, which was warm and protected by the mountains from the cruel Saharan winds, was a good place to pitch camp. He built a mosque and a kasbah and Marrakesh was founded. A serious problem was shortage of **water**, so the enterprising leader had wells dug and underground conduits built linking one with another. The few skimpy palm trees eventually became the lush palmery we see today, and the efficient system of channels is still in use to water the many ornamental gardens. The camp gradually became more permanent (a totally new concept for formerly nomadic Berbers), with buildings made of the distinctive red earth which still gives the city its characteristic pink glow. Youssef ibn Tachfine set about the task of pacifying the whole country. This was not difficult: once Fes had fallen all other resistance collapsed.

In 1085 Youssef was called away to Andalusia, where Christian armies had managed to win back the old Visigothic capital of Toledo. The Christians were defeated and he returned to Marrakesh victorious and hugely enriched in both reputation and material wealth. He went back to Spain in 1090 and this time firmly annexed the provinces of Granada and Malaga to the Almoravide empire. During this time his son **Ali** consolidated and continued the building of the city and, some years later, erected the first enclosing ramparts, few of which still remain. Inside the walls, mosques, palaces and gateways were being created with the help of craftsmen from Andalusia. This was the beginning of the blending of two cultures, the rough vigour of the desert Berbers with the advanced refinement of Islamic Spain. Gradually Marrakesh became a centre for men of learning, for artists and makers of fine textiles and leatherwork.

In 1106 Youssef ibn Tachfine died, aged over 100 years. Predictably perhaps, Ali (1107–44), who had received much of his education in Andalusia and had never experienced tough desert life, was less vigorous and purposeful than his father; and his successors were even less so. The influence of the easy-going and luxury-loving Andalusian court was beginning to take hold of Almoravide society. The drinking of alcohol was tolerated and women began to walk unveiled in the streets. Serious moral decline set in and the time was ripe for another tribe of zealous reforming Berbers to take over.

The Almohades arrived from their stronghold at Tin Mal in the High Atlas and made their first, unsuccessful attack, on Marrakesh in 1130. They were inspired by **Ibn Tumart** (died 1133), a remarkable man whom many thought to be the *Mahdi* (Messiah). He had an unshakeable belief in the unity of God and a profound understanding of the Koran, which he had taught for the first time in the Berber language. He was already very old but he had prepared a young, intelligent and deeply religious Berber to take over the leadership from him. This was **Abd el Mumene** (1133–63), the son of a potter. He launched a successful attack on Marrakesh in 1147. The remaining Almoravides were put to death and their monuments destroyed. The rest of the country put up little resistance and the Almohades went on to conquer Algeria and more of southern Spain. It was Abd el Mumene's grandson, known as **Yacoub el Mansour** ('Yacoub the Conqueror', reigned 1184–90), who was responsible for much of the great architecture in Marrakesh. For a time he transferred his capital to Seville so as to be on hand if Christian armies should threaten again, and this marked a period of peace and prosperity in Marrakesh. The gardens of Menara and Agdal, with their emphasis on ornamental fountains, date from this period. But the most significant legacy is the Koutoubia Mosque, started by his forefathers but completed by Yacoub in 1190 on the spot where, 100 years earlier, the Almoravides had built their mosque. During his reign the court became a fashionable centre of learning for much of the Western world.

However, Yacoub's son **Mohammed** (1199–1213) was a mere 17 years old when he succeeded his father and morally incapable of carrying on the example of dynamic and single-minded rule set by his ancestors. He had to face a major revival of Christian vigour in southern Spain almost as soon as he began to reign, and in 1212 his army was defeated at **Las Navas de Tolosa** in Andalusia, a terrible battle which proved to be a turning point in the Christian reconquest of Spain. From that moment on the fortunes of the Almohades, both at home and abroad, declined and Mohammed's successor **Youssef el Mostansir** (1213–23) proved even less capable of stopping the decline.

The **Merinides** arrived in 1262. They showed little interest in Marrakesh, which lost its capital status to Fes and fell into decay until the arrival of the Saadians 300 years later.

The Saadians had originally come from Arabia in the 12C and had settled down peacefully in southern Morocco, around Zagora. However, with the decline of the Merinides and with all the assurance that their undisputed descent from the Prophet Muhammad gave them, they surged north in the early 16C, quickly dispatched the incompetent Merinide rulers and then turned their attention from Fes (which they found too sophisticated) back to crumbling Marrakesh. Fabulously wealthy after many successful forays across the Sahara in search of gold, they spared no expense or effort in making it a glorious city once more. Just two **Saadian monuments** survive, however, and one of those, the Badi Palace is in ruins. It was destroyed by the infamous Moulay Ismael of the succeeding Alouite dynasty. The other is the Saadian Tombs, a palace built to house the graves of the Saadian princes, so superb in craftsmanship that even the vengeful Alouite sultans could not bring themselves to pull it down, though they did build a wall round it to hide it from view.

Never again was Marrakesh to find itself the centre of so much lavish attention, for it gradually lost its status, first to Meknes, then to Fes and ultimately to Rabat. Two notable buildings were created in the 19C, however, during the reign of the Alouite sultan Moulay El Hassan. They were the Bahia Palace and the Palace of Dar Si Said, now a museum.

It was Moulay el Hassan who appointed Thami el Glaoui **Pasha of Marrakech**, in recognition of hospitality and safe conduct provided to the sultan and his 3000-strong army by the El Glaoui brothers at Telouet in 1893. When the French arrived in 1912 they flattered El Glaoui whilst, at the same time, using his immense power and influence to control the otherwise constantly warring Atlas tribes. El Glaoui played a crucial role in the exile and eventual return of Mohammed V (see *History of Morocco*).

As well as a shrewd statesman, El Glaoui was an energetic and lavish entertainer of world figures, including Winston Churchill, both at Telouet and in his Marrakesh palace, Dar el Glaoui on Rue Bab Doukkala. This is now occupied by the Ministry of Culture and offers little of tourist interest, since it was badly looted in 1956, the year of Independence and of El Glaoui's death. The curious can sometimes gain access to the outer sections by finding the *gardien*, but Telouet offers a much better insight into the lifestyle of this extraordinary man.

The French built modern Marrakesh—known as **Gueliz**—alongside the west walls of the old town, soon after they arrived in 1912. By this time the medina was in a sad state of neglect, the Alouite dynasty having switched its allegiance to other Imperial cities. The French, with their enlightened policy of preservation of Islamic monuments and culture, rebuilt and expanded the medina alongside Gueliz and today the old and new cities together form a prosperous and homogenous whole, not unlike Rabat, but very different from either Meknes or Fes, where there are definite divisions between the old and the new.

▦ Practical information

Tourist offices. **ONMT**. 176 Ave Mohammed V, ☎ (04) 432 097 and Pl. Abdelmoumen Ben Ali, ☎ (04) 431 088.

Bank. Pl. Djmaa el Fna/Ave Mohammed V.

Post office. Pl. du 16 novembre (on Ave Mohammed V in the new town).

Air transport. Royal Air Maroc, 197 Ave Mohammed V. ☎ (04) 436 205 or (04) 446 444. Airport 5km southwest of the city, signposted off Ave de la Menara. Flights to Paris and London via Casablanca; also to Agadir, Ouarzazate and Tangier.

Trains. Railway station at Ave Hassan II. ☎ (04) 447 768 or (04) 447 703. Trains to Casablanca, Meknes, Fes, Oujda, Tangier and Rabat.

Buses. For services to all long-distance destinations, the bus station is just outside Bab Doukkala, ☎ (04) 433 933. The station for local buses (to Ourika, Asni etc.) is outside Bab er Rob.

Taxis. *Grands taxis* go from Bab er Rob, Djmaa el Fna and Bab er Raha, south of Bab Doukkala. *Petits taxis* are all over town, especially around Pl. Djmaa el Fna, and very good for sightseeing purposes.

Horse-drawn calèches. These can be caught all over town, especially outside the main hotels and in the Djmaa el Fna. Sitting in one of these, making slow, aristocratic progress through the streets, is one of the most restful and delightful ways of getting to know your way around, and particularly to be recommended at sunset when the whole town and palmery is bathed in a hot, rosy hue. Prices can be high and should definitely be negotiated in advance.

Hotels

Hôtel La Mamounia, Ave Bab Jdid. ☎ (04) 448 981 fax (04) 444 660. ***** L (232 rooms). See description above. There are six restaurants, a casino and a nightclub. The hotel is outside the ONMT's classification scheme and prices are extremely high; less so, however, if one books it as part of a package with a tour operator, such as Cadogan Travel.

Palmeraie Golf Palace, Route de la Palmeraie. ☎ (04) 301 010 fax (04) 302 020. ***** L (314 rooms). This new and outrageously expensive hotel, set in the palm grove, must be a paradise for golfers, for there is an 18-hole course within the 77ha grounds. Every luxury has been thought of, there is a state-of-the-art fitness centre and eight restaurants. Like the *Mamounia*, it does appear on the itineraries of some tour operators.

Hôtel Es Saadi, Ave Quadissia. ☎ (04) 448 811 fax (04) 447 644. ***** (152 rooms). Outside the walls of the medina, 10min walk from the souks. An elegant hotel with a beautiful garden.

Hôtel Les Almoravides, Arset Djnane Lkhdar. ☎ (04) 445 142 fax (04) 443 133. ****A (105 rooms). Located just off Ave Mohammed V, midway between the new town and the medina, close to the *ensemble artisanal*. Has delightful gardens and a pool.

Hôtel Le Marrakech, Pl. de la Liberté. ☎ (04) 434 351 fax (04) 434 980. ****A (365 rooms). Conveniently located, with pool. Tends to cater for large groups.

Hôtel Toubkal, Rue Haroun-Errachid. ☎ (04) 448 872. ****A (124 rooms). Just outside the walls. Modern, with pool and gardens. Recommended.

Hôtel Imilchil, Ave Echouhada. ☎ (04) 447 653 fax (04) 430 171. ***A (94 rooms). Outside the walls but not far from the souks. Good value. Has a small pool.

Hôtel Koutoubia, 51 Blvd Mansour Eddahbi. ☎ (04) 430 921. **A (60 rooms). In the new town, just off Ave Mohammed V. Lovely garden. Has a garage.

Hôtel de Foucauld, Ave El Mouahidine. ☎ (04) 445 499. **B (33 rooms). Just off the Djmaa El Fna. Modestly comfortable and with a Moroccan restaurant in the basement. Recommended.

Grand Hôtel Tazi, corner Rue Bab Agnaou and Ave el Mouahdine. ☎ (04) 442 452 fax (04) 442 787. **B (61 rooms). Inside the town walls and very convenient to the main monuments. This old-fashioned hotel has seen better days but is well run and good value. There is a roof-top terrace but no pool.

Hôtel CTM, Pl. Djmaa el Fna. * Very basic, but usually clean and overlooks all the action from a conveniently placed roof terrace.

Restaurants

The town is rich in restaurants to suit every mood and purse. If you want something really atmospheric and have a long evening to spare, try the Moroccan restaurants, most housed in former palaces in the medina. There will probably be a small 'Andalusian' band, maybe some dancers and even a snake charmer. It is all created for the tourists. On the whole, the more expensive the restaurant, the more discreet the entertainment, with the *Restaurant Morocain* at the *Mamounia* topping the list with menus at 700dh a head.

Recommended are the following:

Dar el Baroud, 275 Ave Mohammed V (very close to the medina walls). ☎ (04) 426 009. Good food and a modest floor show. 280dh a head.

Restaurant Ed Douira, 14 Derb Jdid Hay Salam. ☎ (04) 442 802. Right by the Bahia Palace, and therefore much frequented by groups. 380dh a head.

La Maison Arabe, 5 Derb Ferrane, close to Bab Doukkala. ☎ (04) 423 604. Exceptionally good food, but pricey at around 500dh a head.

El Baraka, 1 Pl. Djmaa el Fna. ☎ (04) 442 341. Good food. Medium priced.

Palais Gharnatta, 5 et 6 Derb el Arsa, Riad Zitoun Djdid. ☎ (04) 445 216. The 'Arabian Nights' floor show brings in the tour groups. Good food.

The Kasbah Restaurant, Derb Lamnabha. ☎ (04) 435 355. Recommended. Excellent Moroccan food and a roof terrace overlooking the medina. Expensive.

Even more exotic are one or two enterprising places out in the Palmeraie, where you sit in huge tents and, at the end of a copious meal, have the chance to see a real *fantasia* performed. There will usually be troops of Berber musicians and dancers. The whole is definitely touristy but can be great fun. Recommended is *L'Oasis de Marrakech*, Route de Casablanca. ☎ (04) 430 368. 400–500dh a head.

All the above should be booked well in advance. The price will sometimes include transport to and from your hotel, and it is worth asking about this.

At the other end of the scale—and definitely for the locals—are the delicious-smelling food stalls in the Djmaa el Fna itself, where you choose your food, watch it grilling over charcoal, and sit at a long table to eat. This is very cheap, but the quality of the meat or fish can be a lottery. Steaming bowls of the traditional soup, *harira*, are usually delicious.

There are a number of modest French restaurants in the new town, notably *La Jacaranda*, 32 Blvd Mohammed Zerktouni and *Le Petit Poucet*, corner Ave Mohammed V and Rue Mohammed el Bequal. Both are moderately priced and quiet.

Holiday villages

Club Mediterranée, Pl. Djmaa El Fna.☎ (04) 444 016. A luxury holiday village hidden away in a corner of the Djmaa El Fna, standing in its own palm grove. You do not know it is there until you arrive inside the gates.

Golf

The Marrakesh Royal Golf Club, Ancienne Route de Ouarzazate. ☎ (04) 444 341 fax 430 084. 18 holes, 6200m, par 72.

The Palmeraie Golf Club, Les Jardins de la Palmeraie, Route de la Palmeraie. ☎ (04) 301 010 fax (04) 302 020. 18 holes, 6214m, par 72.

A tour of the city

Dominating the centre of town with its 70m-high minaret is the **Koutoubia Mosque**. It was begun by the first Almohade sultan, Abd el Mumene, in 1158, and completed by his grandson, Yacoub el Mansour, in 1190. It is one of the largest mosques in Africa and accommodates over 20,000 people. Its name derives from the word *kutubiyin* (booksellers) and relates to the bookstalls estab-lished all around the mosque in its early years, when it undoubtedly combined the functions of library, university and Koranic school with that of a mosque (as did the Karaouyine in Fes).

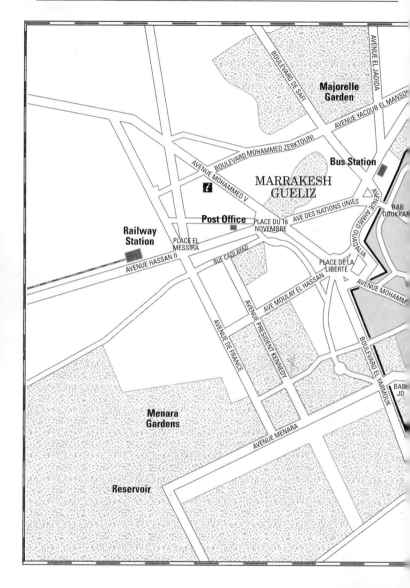

Today's mosque stands on the site of the original mosque erected by the founder of Marrakesh, Youssef ibn Tachfine and subsequently destroyed. It is the second to have been built by the Almohades, their first attempt having been pulled down almost immediately because the orientation towards Mecca had been incorrectly calculated. (Traces of this earlier building can be detected along one of the outside walls.) The exterior is simple to the point of ordinariness.

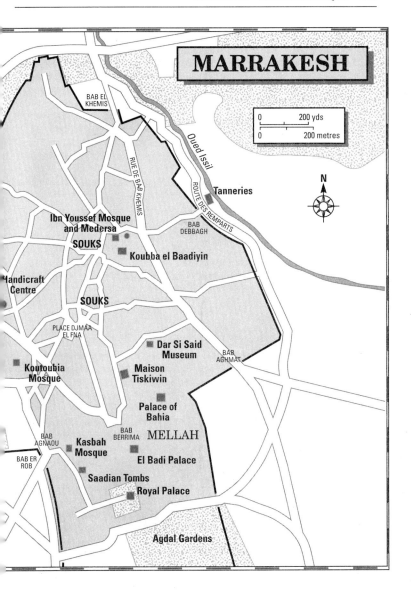

MARRAKESH

BAB EL KHEMIS

RUE DE BAB KHEMIS

Oued Issil

ROUTE DES REMPARTS

Tanneries

0   200 yds
0   200 metres

N

Ibn Youssef Mosque and Medersa

BAB DEBBAGH

SOUKS

Koubba el Baadiyin

Handicraft Centre

SOUKS

PLACE DJMAA EL FNA

Dar Si Said Museum

BAB AGHMAT

Koutoubia Mosque

Maison Tiskiwin

Palace of Bahia

BAB AGNAOU

BAB BERRIMA

MELLAH

Kasbah Mosque

BAB ER ROB

El Badi Palace

Saadian Tombs

Royal Palace

Agdal Gardens

Inside, its purity of line, its 17 aisles with identical **horseshoe arches** and the total lack of any decoration on its white walls achieve a simple elegance typical of buildings founded by the Almohades, who disliked excessive ornamentation. But it is the minaret for which the Koutoubia is most famous.

The **minaret** is similar to but a little earlier than the Giralda in Seville and the unfinished Hassan Tower in Rabat, for which Sultan Yacoub was also respon-

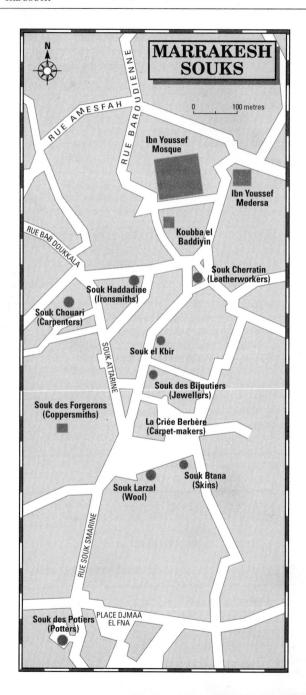

N

MARRAKESH SOUKS

RUE AMESFAH

RUE BAROUDIENNE

0   100 metres

Ibn Youssef
Mosque

Ibn Youssef
Medersa

RUE BAB DOUKKALA

Koubba el
Baddiyin

Souk Cherratin
(Leatherworkers)

Souk Haddadine
(Ironsmiths)

Souk Chouari
(Carpenters)

SOUK ATTARINE

Souk el Kbir

Souk des Bijoutiers
(Jewellers)

Souk des Forgerons
(Coppersmiths)

La Criée Berbère
(Carpet-makers)

Souk Btana
(Skins)

Souk Larzal
(Wool)

RUE SOUK SMARINE

PLACE DJMAA
EL FNA

Souk des Potiers
(Potters)

sible. It is perfectly proportioned in relation to the main body of the mosque. The square lantern supports a rounded dome crowned with four golden balls (the topmost one is invisible from the ground), said to have been presented by the wife of the sultan as a penance for not observing three hours of Ramadan. The decoration, in the form of stone tracery, is simply designed to set off the windows, and is different on each of the four sides. This purity of form is not disturbed by any superimposed ornamentation except for a narrow band of blue tiles at the top, which serves to reflect the sky. Inside, as in the case of the Hassan Tower in Rabat, there are several chambers and a ramp leading up to the top floor, from which the muezzin calls the faithful to prayer five times a day.

Very close to the Koutoubia is the most exciting and exotic part of Marrakesh: the square called **Djmaa el Fna**. The name, literally translated as 'the Mosque [or Assembly] of the Dead', is taken to refer to the custom of displaying the heads of vanquished rebels or criminals, since the square is known to have been a place of **public execution** even up to the last century. Since then, and particularly in the pre-Independence days, it has been a centre for public meetings and even riots. There have been one or two unsuccessful attempts to close it down and part of it has been covered over and turned into a corn market, but the Djmaa el Fna is still the heart of Marrakesh.

Today it provides constant, ever-changing **entertainment**, which reaches its climax at sundown and continues late into the night. This is not for tourists but for local tribesmen who come to buy and sell, or just to see each other, talk and generally enjoy themselves. There are story-tellers (for most of the Berber audience cannot read), spell-binders and witch doctors: you can have a love potion made or a mixture concocted which will kill your worst enemy, if you can find a language in which to ask for it; if you have a pain to be cured you can overcome the language problem by pointing to the place where it hurts on a sinister tattered chart of the human body, although it might be unwise to rely on the prescription; there are dentists displaying rows of teeth that they have pulled out during the day, and even some sets of false ones to put in their place; there are religious mystics who often work themselves into a trance, followed by many of their audience; there are letter-writers, usually sitting under umbrellas with the tools of their trade scattered around them; there are sellers of brightly coloured dyes, piles of old bones and little bottles of sickly perfume; and there are the ubiquitous water-sellers and snake-charmers, who after putting a cobra through its paces will take it out of the basket and wave it under the noses of the bemused spectators. **Music** is provided by the Gnaoua, black musicians of a religious brotherhood descended from slaves, who play either the *guembri* (a kind of lute) or the *garagab* (metal castanets), or beat huge drums with long curved sticks whilst their companions jump up and down. The sound of the snake-charmers' flutes adds to the mystical cacophony.

Acrobats, usually children who manage to bounce on their heads like rubber balls, finishing the right way up with their hands outstretched for coins (a concession to tourism), pass between the circles. Many of them drag monkeys along on leads, and the animals will perform for you whether you want them to or not. Towards evening the hot-dog stalls and charcoal grills get under way and tables and chairs are set up. It is hard to resist small herring-like fish, *kefta* (meat-balls), unidentifiable pieces of meat and corn-on-the cob, all sizzling and smelling quite delicious. This smell, mixed with the inevitable scent of mint tea, the hotchpotch sound of the musicians, the hum of the story-tellers' voices and the occasional screeches of the holy men are what most characterise the Djmaa el Fna. If you keep your head down and avoid looking conspicuous, it is perfectly possible to wander about unmolested. If you do feel it is all getting too much, there are several conveniently placed cafés around the square, from the terraces of which you can often have a splendid view of the whole entertainment, without noise or hustle. But the temptation to become part of the pageant usually returns quite quickly, and you slip down and join the throng once more.

The main entrance to the **souks** is in one corner of the Djmaa el Fna, opposite the hotel-restaurant *Café de France*, via Rue Souk Smarine (the textile workers' souk). (See the plan of the souks on page 232) The souks cover a vast area and, if you want to see as much as possible in a limited time, it is advisable to take a guide, at least on your first visit. (Guides can be arranged either through your hotel or through the tourist office, though it is also possible to pick one up on the spot, with the usual proviso of agreeing terms in advance.) Two things struck me the last time I visited Marrakesh: one was the awful pollution caused by mopeds rushing through narrow alleyways at full throttle, which almost negates the timeless charms of the souks; the other was the almost complete absence of pestering by hustlers and drug pushers. It is said that the government carried out a major clean-up operation recently, to the point of transporting frequent offenders some way out of town, and this at least is a most welcome development.

The souks are a riot of colour, noise and activity, a wealthy storehouse of all the treasures of this vast and varied country. They are grouped into corporations. Thus you will find all the silver merchants in one corner, all the gold merchants in another, and rows of stalls selling exclusively leatherwork (**Souk Cherratin**) or copper goods (**Souk des Forgerons**) or jewellery (**Souk des Bijoutiers**). The real fascination is to watch the craftsmen at work, gilding on leather, or inlaying with enamel the sheaths of ornate silver daggers, hammering out copper, embroidering silks or smoothing out the surface of a cedarwood table. You can easily spend a day or two exploring the full extent of the tangle of little streets and absorbing the extraordinary excitement of this industrious and colourful world, with its spicy smells and weird music. Most of the alleyways are covered by a trellis of latticed reeds so they are relatively cool even in high summer. The best time to visit the souks is fairly early in the morning or late in the afternoon (after 17.00). The siesta is taken very seriously and very little happens in mid-afternoon. However, business does continue until quite late in the evening.

The **Ibn Youssef Medersa** is to be found in the northern part of the souks, just beyond the leather section (Souk Cherratin). It is the largest *medersa* in Morocco and is reputed to have housed over 800 students at one time. They would have attended lectures in the adjacent mosque of the same name and probably at other nearby mosques. Built by the Merinides in the 14C it was completely rebuilt by the Saadians in 1562 in their exuberant Andalusian style. It is possible that it was constructed on the foundations of an earlier religious monument built by the Almoravides. It has recently been restored.

The tour first passes through a small entrance hall and a long outer corridor to reach the great rectangular court with its upper storey of students' rooms (approached by a stairway from the entrance hall). The court contains a large **pool**, rather than the small ablutions fountains of the Fes *medersas*, which is set in a floor of white marble. The pool is said to date back to the 11C and is perhaps the original reason for the *medersa* being located here. The walls are the most remarkable feature, decorated with characteristic Saadian flamboyance. The decoration is comparable with the Courtyard of Lions in the Alhambra of Granada, and it seems likely that Andalusian craftsmen of the same school were responsible for all the most lavish Saadian monuments in Morocco (compare the Saadian Tombs, described below, and the two pavilions added to the central court of the Karaouyine in Fes).

Around the base of the walls is a layer of softly-coloured mosaic tiles, then delicate stucco arches, with panels of criss-cross patterns carved in stone above, and, at the top of the walls, cedarwood lintels carved with Kufic script and a pine-cone design. The horseshoe-shaped **mihrab** in the oratory is a particularly fine specimen, with arabesques incorporating quotations from the Koran, and around it a stucco frieze of swirling designs and more pine-cone motifs. A sculpted marble wash basin, which used to stand in the small entrance hall, has been removed to the Dar Si Said Museum. The figurative nature of its decoration—small heraldic birds—betrays its non-Saadian origin, and it is thought to have been brought from Cordoba in the 10C. **Open** 08.00–12.00 and 14.30–17.45; closed Fri mornings; entry 10dh.

The **Ibn Youssef Mosque** stands across the road from the *medersa*, on the foundations of a 12C mosque commemorating one of the city's seven patron saints, Sidi Youssef Ibn Ali. This was rebuilt in the 16C and again in the 19C so very little is left of the original building. The main point of interest to the non-Muslim visitor is the 42m-high minaret which towers over other buildings.

If you stand with your back to the south wall of the mosque and look straight ahead towards the souks, you will see the **Koubba el Baadiyin**. (The entrance is down some steps opposite the mosque.) Built by the Almoravides when they founded the city in the 11C, it is thought to have covered a ritual ablutions basin serving worshippers at the original mosque. This is the only Almoravide building remaining intact in Marrakesh, and was discovered as recently as 1952, half-buried in rubble from recent demolition and with less interesting structures hard up against it. It is a small and simple square building of brick and stone, with a rough dome, but it is worth a closer look, for it manifests the beginnings of what were to become very familiar Almohade and Merinide designs. It has pointed horseshoe and lobed arches, and stepped merlons surround the dome. The interior is decorated with floral and pine-cone motifs. There seem to be no official opening hours but, as soon as you show interest, a *gardien* will come forward and offer to take you in for 10dh.

Turn right from the medersa and walk down Rue Bab Debbagh and, after about 10min, you will come to the **Bab Debbagh** itself. Outside the ramparts, on the left of the gate as you face outwards, are the **tanneries**, ranged alongside the river Issil which fulfils their constant need for water. The tanneries have existed here since the 12C, far away from the medina centre because of the unpleasant smell produced in the tanning process. Traditional methods are still used here, as they are in Fes (see the description on page 208). The busy time for the tanners is the morning and nobody minds if you wander in and take photographs. The leather workers, who turn the skins into the familiar bookcovers, desktop ware and belts, can be found inside the gate, within the medina walls.

Leave the south side of the Djmaa el Fna by the Rue Bab Agnaou and after a few minutes' walk you will reach a small square; on the left is the **Bab Agnaou** itself. It is the only surviving Almohade monumental gate without restorations in Marrakesh. It is very large and simply decorated, with stone carving in the manner of that on the Koutoubia minaret, unlike the gates of later dynasties which tend to be laden with tiles and decorative columns (as in Meknes). Go through it and, facing you, is the **Kasbah Mosque**, also called El Mansouria after the Almohade sultan Yacoub el Mansour who built it at the end of the 12C. Its minaret is exactly contemporary with that of the Koutoubia and it too has a band of coloured tiles around the top. It was restored in 1965. To reach the Saadian Tombs, take the narrow path which passes to the right of the mosque.

The **Saadian Tombs** represent one of the most perfect examples of Saadian art anywhere in Morocco and (mosques and *medersas* excepted) are considered by many to be the finest monument in Marrakesh. This royal mausoleum was built in the late 16C by Ahmed Edh Dhahabi (1578–1603), the greatest of the Saadian rulers, and paid for with the gold that he had brought back from Timbuktu. The palace, which houses the tombs of 66 Saadian kings, comprises two buildings, each with three rooms, set in a garden.

On your left as you enter the garden is an oratory with a superb mihrab and a lantern supported by four elegant columns. Leading from the oratory and visible from the garden through the next opening is the **Room of the Twelve Columns**, which Ahmed Edh Dhahabi created for his own tomb and those of his sons. Their graves lie beneath the ceramic mosaic floor marked by finely carved marble slabs, the large central tomb being that of the sultan himself. Here are stalactitic (*muqarnas*) cupolas and very delicate stucco-work; carved and gilded cedarwood ceilings; and walls decorated with soft-coloured mosaic tiles. Light comes from a hidden internal glass dome and creates a special atmosphere. A third room contains the tombs of wives and children.

The second building, a little older and almost sober in its decoration by comparison, contains the tomb of Lalla Messaouda, the mother of Ahmed, and that of Mohammed esh-Sheik, the first Saadian sultan, together with those of more princes.

The gardens are always full of birdsong and have palms and datura standing amidst rosemary, jasmine and roses. In the centre is a square containing simple tombstones belonging to the servants of Saadian royal households. Even the Alouite sultan Moulay Ismael, whose policy was to destroy all relics of the preceding dynasty, left the Saadian tombs intact. He did, however, have the area encircled by a wall which no one had succeeded in penetrating until the French discovered it in 1917; it is they who were responsible for the path which today leads from the Kasbah Mosque. **Open** 09.00–12.00 and 14.30–18.00; closed Fri mornings; entry 10dh.

Ahmed Edh Dhahabi also built the **El Badi Palace**, which means 'the incomparable'. To reach it, return through the Bab Agnaou and turn immediately right towards Place des Ferblantiers: El Badi is on the south side of the square through Bab Berrima. The contemporary historian El Oufrani (1511–1670) relates that 50 tons of marble was imported from Italy and paid for, on a pound-for-pound basis, with sugar; he also states that skilled craftsmen came from many different countries to build the palace, and were amply rewarded for their work (unlike the creators of Moulay Ismael's royal palaces, mostly cruelly exploited Christian slaves). The walls of this incredibly sumptuous palace were 2m thick and the inner courtyard measured 135m by 110m, and enclosed gardens watered by 100 pools and fountains (placed above ground level so that irrigation was easier) and with several elegant pavilions faced with marble columns.

All this can now only be imagined because the palace lies in ruins: it was systematically destroyed by the jealous Moulay Ismael, but not before all the treasures had been stripped from the walls and dispersed among his own extravagant palaces in Meknes. Traces of one or two of the pavilions still remain, the most complete being that of *El Khemsin* ('The Fifty'), on the west side, which was once a vast reception hall named after its 50 marble columns. Another half-ruined pavilion houses a small museum which contains, among other things, an early Almoravide pulpit. It still has its original painted ceiling. Vestiges of other royal palaces lie around the perimeter of the courtyard, and on the south side is the enclosure housing today's **Royal Palace (Dar el Makhzen)**, built on Saadian and Almohade foundations and recently superbly restored. It is used by the royal household and is therefore not open to visitors.

Today the ruins of El Badi are brought to life by a two-week **Folk Festival** (*Festival National des Arts Populaires*) held every September in what used to be the courtyard. On this occasion the pools are filled and the fountains play. Groups of dancers and musicians are brought in from all over the country and the atmosphere—in such a setting—can be magical. Performances usually start around 21.00 and go on until midnight. The exact date varies from year to year but details are usually available from local tourist offices.

Next to the Badi Palace is the **mellah**, reached by returning to the Place des Ferblantiers and passing through an archway on the right of Bab Berrima. The *mellah* was created by the early Saadian sultan Abd Allah (1574–76), ostensibly to protect the sizeable Jewish population from Muslim threats and insults, but also to have them easily accessible for taxation purposes: the Jews in Saadian times represented a considerable source of revenue for the Makhzen. The *mellah* was once a thriving city within a city. It covered an area of some 18ha and included synagogues (a few of which still remain), shops, gardens and houses. Today it differs from the rest of the city only in the unusual height of its houses and the lack of space between them. There are very few Jews left now and the various souks have been taken over by Muslim craftsmen. Having lost its identity it now seems rather sad and neglected in comparison with the colourful souks that lie immediately around Djmaa el Fna.

The splendid **Bahia Palace** lies immediately north of the *mellah*. It was once the residence of Bou Ahmed, a black slave who, by means of ruthless cunning and corruption, rose to positions of immense power and wealth, first as chamberlain to Sultan Moulay el Hassan, and subsequently as vizier and regent to the young Sultan Abd el Aziz. It is said that Bou Ahmed employed up to 1000 craftsmen for a period of six years to construct the palace to his satisfaction (*bahia* means 'brilliance'). In his book, *Morocco That Was*, Walter Harris, *The Times* correspondent between 1887 and 1933, recalls how he once dined at the Bahia Palace with Bou Ahmed and describes 'the hot jasmine-scented air of the courts, for it was late in spring, and the great dinner served in one of the saloons, while a native band discoursed anything but soft music just outside; and Bou Ahmed himself—short, dark and of unprepossessing appearance—none the less an excellent host'. When Bou Ahmed died in 1900, the palace was sacked by his slaves and concubines and his family was driven destitute out of town.

The Bahia Palace is still empty but merits a visit as an interesting example of somewhat ostentatious, Andalusian-style, 19C domestic architecture. You will see some of the harem apartments, and a fine council chamber with painted cedarwood ceiling and tiled walls, grouped around a large central courtyard with gracious colonnades, fountains and a green-and-white mosaic floor, which creates an effect of infinite coolness. The palace is approached through an avenue of orange trees, geraniums, datura, jasmine, and a few lofty palms. This is typical of old Marrakesh: one minute the hectic bustle of donkeys and men in crowded squares; the next the enchantment of a scented tree-lined path of absolute peace. **Open** 09.00–12.00 and 14.30–17.30; entry 10dh.

Si Said was Bou Ahmed's brother and he, too, managed to achieve rank and riches sufficient to build a fine, late 19C palace for his residence. This is now the **Dar Si Said Museum**, probably one of the best in Morocco, with its wide variety of treasures and everyday objects from the region. The palace itself is so finely crafted that it would deserve special attention even without the artefacts it contains. Particularly striking are the ceilings, each more beautiful than the last.

The palace is Andalusian in style, built around a patio crowded with fountains and plants. You enter the building along a passageway lined with ancient wooden doors complete with heavy and intricate locking devices. First there is a room containing a variety of children's wooden toys, including what must surely be the forerunner of the Big Wheel, with carriages, each large enough for one child, hanging on four spokes, making a kind of vertical roundabout. The jewellery room is dominated by great Roman-style fibulas as worn by Berber women, together with earrings and elaborate head-dresses. Then there is a room full of weapons, including the long, heavy *fantasia* rifles which are traditionally held aloft in one hand and shot in the air as the rider gallops along at top speed.

Another room contains nothing but copper and brass household utensils; here are the kettles with their ornamental stands still used in the hand-washing ceremony before and after a traditional Moroccan meal. Coffee pots, hexagonal sugar boxes typical of Marrakesh, incense-burners to drive out evil spirits, and very ornate bowls with conical lids for containing bread. There is also a room filled with kaftans from all over Morocco.

Upstairs is the main reception room, obviously intended for family occasions and today arranged as for a wedding. It holds two major pieces of furniture, both made of cedarwood: one is a many-sided, two-tiered table used for displaying wedding presents; the other is a traditional marriage chair, intricately painted and with the usual very high seat. The reason for its elevation is two-fold: it was always necessary for the bride to be clearly visible to all the guests; and, perhaps more importantly, it was necessary to discourage her from running away should the first sight of her intended husband be too awful to contemplate (traditionally she would not have met him before the ceremony).

The last rooms contain carpets, mainly Berbers from the Middle and High Atlas mountains. The colours are predominantly dark red and gold. **Open** 09.00–12.00 and 14.30–18.00; closed Tues; entry 10dh.

A more modest but beautifully presented museum, housed in a turn-of-the-century mansion, the **Maison Tiskiwin**, is located between the Bahia Palace and the Dar Si Said, at No. 8 Rue de la Bahia. It represents a quiet and tasteful antidote to the opulence of the two palaces. There is a good collection of carpets, jewellery, clothes and other objects from northern and central Morocco, put together by the Dutch anthropologist, Bert Flint, resident in Morocco for some 40 years. (His collection from southern Morocco can be seen in Agadir, at the Folk Art Museum.) The central courtyard of Maison Tiskiwin is beautiful in its own right and the various rooms around it have fine ceilings. There is a detailed guide sheet—in French—to take around with you. **Open** 10.30–12.30 and 15.00–18.30; entry 10dh.

Marrakesh is justly famous for its **gardens**, where the visitor is free to wander and where time has little meaning. They are, however, some distance from the centre of town and it is a good idea to take *petits taxis*. Most refreshing is the **Menara Garden**, created by the Almohades in the southwest corner of the town. (Take the Avenue de la Menara from the Koutoubia Mosque.) It is a vast olive grove containing a large reservoir which is overlooked by a sober 19C pavilion (*menzah*), for which there is an admission charge of 5dh. Today, busloads of tourists stop at the steps leading up to the reservoir, gaze a moment into the brackish water, take a quick photo of the pavilion or the ever-present water-sellers, and then drive back into the town. The gardens themselves remain untouched by all this commotion and await the more leisurely visitor. The drive back along the Avenue de la Menara affords an unforgettable view of the Koutoubia.

The **Agdal Garden** lies to the south of the Royal Palace and was created by the 12C Almohade sultans to provide shade from the desert sun. Some of the irrigation channels they had dug are still used to water the garden's fruit trees. Take the road southwards below Bab Agnaou and then turn left along Rue Bab Ahmar to reach the entrance to the garden. (It is a good 3km from Djmaa el Fna.) The garden extends some 3km and contains olive, apricot, fig, orange, plum and pear trees, as well as an assortment of pools and walkways. It was redesigned in the 19C by Sultan Abd er Rahman whose son, Mohammed, was later drowned in the largest of the pools called, somewhat ironically, *Es Sahraj el Hana* ('The Pool of Health'). From the roof of the pavilion that stands alongside the water there are distant views of the High Atlas.

Quite different from the other gardens, and probably one of the loveliest spots in Marrakesh, is the **Majorelle Garden**. The entrance is in a small street off Avenue Yacoub el Mansour in the north of the new town (north of Bab Doukkala). The garden was created during the Protectorate by the French painter Jacques Majorelle (1886–1962), and is now owned and maintained by the couturier Yves Saint Laurent. It is a place of great tranquillity and contrast of colour and shape: of sun and deep shade, of intense blue pergolas covered in purple bougainvillaea and crimson geranium; of huge curvaceous pots scattered amongst spikey palm fronds, agaves and bamboos. Wherever you stand, or sit, there is a vista. And all this to the sound of bulbuls and turtle doves. It is truly the perfect antidote to the noise and pollution of the souks. There is also a museum, which costs a further 15dh and is housed in Majorelle's former studio. It contains some of the artist's paintings, as well as fine examples of carpets and pottery collected by Saint Laurent. **Open** 08.00–12.00 and 14.00–17.00 in winter; 08.00–12.00 and 15.00–19.00 in summer: entry 15dh.

The new town, **Marrakesh Gueliz** (so-named after a type of sandstone quarried to the northwest of the city), is traversed by wide boulevards, lined on both sides by orange and lemon trees or by jacarandas; the scent of the former and the colour of the latter when in flower are unforgettable. The main artery is Avenue Mohammed V, which starts in the district of modern shops, hotels and restaurants, and sweeps through the walls of the medina right up to the Koutoubia itself. About halfway down this street is a government-run **handicraft centre** (*ensemble artisanal*), which gives a good idea of the range of local craftwork available in the souks, and of prices. As usual, however, it is the workshops surrounding the centre which are most interesting: there, craftsmen are hard at work, young men and women are being taught their various skills, and prices are negotiable. **Open** 09.30–17.30. ☎ (04) 423 835.

The palmery, which lies to the north of the city, covers over 1214ha, contains some 180,000 palm trees, and is one of the great wonders of southern Morocco. The 14km **Route de Palmeraie** starts by the Oued Tensift bridge on the Casablanca road, and there are usually plenty of *grand taxis* and calèches around waiting for your custom, should you not be motorised already. The legend surrounding the palmery's origins has it that the Almoravide founder of Marrakesh, Youssef ibn Tachfine, pitched camp here and that, after a meal, his men scattered their date stones far and wide, some of which fell into holes already made by their lances, from which the palms grew.

A tour of the ramparts along the **Route des Remparts**, which could be added on to a drive through the palmery, takes you for about 8km around the medina walls, originally 12C Almoravide but later extended, and in places replaced, to allow for expansion of the medina. The walls incorporate ten monumental gates, mostly reconstructed since Almoravide times, the most notable of which are as follows (starting from Bab Doukkala, by the bus station, and driving clockwise round the town): **Bab el Khemis**, guarding the northeast entrance to the medina and overlooking a square where a souk is always held every Thursday; **Bab Debbagh**, protecting the eastern entry, close to Oued Issil and the tanneries (see above); **Bab er Rob** ('Gate of the Raisin Juice'), a reconstructed Alomohade gate south of the medina, so-named because it was the only entry route permitted for consignments of this drink; **Bab Agnaou**, described above; and **Bab el Jdid**, which bestrides Avenue de la Menara and is next door to the luxurious *Hôtel La Mamounia* (see below). From here, return to Bab Doukkala via Boulevard el Yarmouk.

Only five minutes' walk from the Djmaa el Fna, the **Hôtel La Mamounia** is the place to be if money is no object. It is a luxurious palace—built in 1923 and completely renovated in 1986—set in 13ha of beautiful walled gardens. The

Ramparts and the High Atlas

atmosphere is dignified and the style of architecture inside is Moorish with a touch of Art Deco from Jacques Majorelle, responsible for the Jardin Majorelle (see above). The original building contains the famous 'Winston Churchill suite'; this was said to be his favourite hotel in all the world and he would spend many weeks at a time relaxing and painting here. Most of the bedrooms are at the back and face the Atlas. Below you is the swimming pool in its setting of leaning palms, orange and lemon trees, datura and cypress; beyond are the snow-capped mountains.

The High Atlas

The highest and most majestic of Morocco's many mountain ranges and a natural physical barrier between the developed north and the pre-Saharan south, the High Atlas extend some 700km from Agadir in a northeasterly direction, and offer some of the most grandiose and varied scenery anywhere in the land. This is Berber country, scene of many historic struggles and stronghold of notorious and ruthless tribal chiefs right up to the early part of the 20C. Now peace reigns once more and the people have come down from their protected mountain villages to a gentler life in the valleys below. Trekking is now the major activity in the region, and local people are glad to act as guides to walkers and to those wanting to see the area's prehistoric rock-carvings. There is a good network of tracks, and there are many accessible summits (including a dozen exceeding 4000m and more than 400 reaching 3000m).

Grands taxis depart regularly, summer and winter, from Marrakesh (Bab er Rob) to Oukaimeden. Alternatively, **buses** leave from the same point and go as far as Ourika, where it is usually possible to take a taxi onwards to Oukaimeden. The first option is certainly quicker and not much more expensive, if the *grand taxi* is full (about 20dh a head). Car hire from Marrakesh is the alternative. The three major routes into the mountains from Marrakesh are described below.

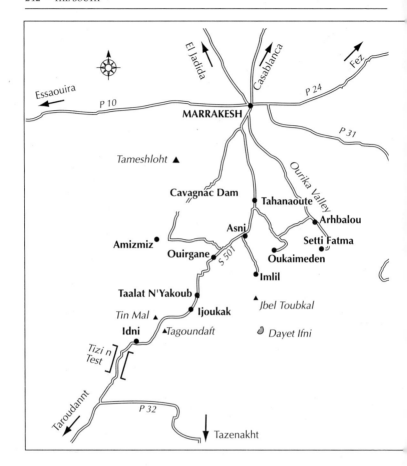

The Ourika Valley and Oukaimeden

Take the main road to Taroudannt out of Marrakesh. The S513 road to Ourika branches left just before you leave the southern outskirts of the city. After a flat stretch of about half an hour it begins to climb in gentle spirals alongside a rushing torrent of icy water which is the river **Ourika**. Villages cling to the almost vertical sides of the valley. They are difficult to spot from a distance because they are made of the same red earth as the valley itself. Wildly romantic to photograph, they must be less romantic to live in; some of them are indeed deserted and in the process of being slowly eroded away by the wind and rain. No longer under threat of attack by hostile tribes, the inhabitants have moved down into the fertile valley, where they cultivate every space. It is particularly lovely in spring when the tiny valley-bottom fields first emerge from the winter snow, their horizontal lines softened later by clouds of almond blossom.

The road continues as far as the hamlet of **Setti Fatma** (63km from Marrakesh,

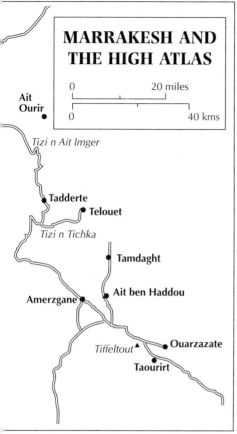

MARRAKESH AND THE HIGH ATLAS

0 — 20 miles
0 — 40 kms

Ait Ourir

Tizi n Ait Imger

Tadderte
Telouet

Tizi n Tichka

Tamdaght

Ait ben Haddou

Amerzgane

Tiffeltout ▲

Ouarzazate

Taourirt

1500m) and then gives up as the gorge closes in. This is a good place to start walking and if you call in at the village café you will probably be directed to the 'Walk of the Seven Waterfalls', which starts as a rough path from the grassy sward behind the café and fairly quickly becomes more of a scramble up the rocks. For the less energetic there are more moderate paths. For serious walkers there is a trek eastwards to the **Plateau Yagour**, a rich hunting-ground for rock-carvings. Take a guide.

Setti Fatma is known for its annual four-day *moussem* in August (the exact dates vary), which takes the form of a huge and colourful fair in addition to religious cere-monies around the Koubba of Setti Fatma, forbidden to non-Muslims. Berbers come from far and wide and the festivi-ties, particularly the dancing, can be fun to watch, or even join in.

There are several hotel-restaurants in the Ourika valley, which you will have passed on the way to Setti Fatma (see below).

Hotels

Ourika Hotel, ☎: (04) 433 993 ****B (27 rooms). Swimming pool.
Auberge Ramuntcho, ☎ (04) 446 312 **B (14 rooms). You can eat copiously on the terrace whilst gazing down into the ravine or up at the soaring peaks.

The road to **Oukaimeden**, which branches off the Ourika road at Arhbalou (24km back towards Marrakesh from Setti Fatma), is only slightly hair-raising and rises gradually to 2650m by means of rather gentle hairpin bends. It is paved all the way. The little settlement of Oukaimeden should certainly be visited, for here the mountains rise even more abruptly and splendidly to their great heights and one really feels on top of the world. There are three small hotels—the *Imlil*, *Chouka*, and *Chez Juju*—which are ski-lodges with cosy accommodation and good food, and there is at least one refuge belonging to the Club Alpin Français.

In summer the village overlooks an **alpine prairie** crowded with livestock and Berber tents. Each tribe has its own area which it jealously guards. The summer pastures open on 10 August each year.

In winter Oukaimeden offers the best **skiing** in Morocco. The season runs from December to May, but the best snow usually arrives in January. There are three ski-lifts and a day pass costs 60dh. Equipment may be hired from the shop next to *Chez Juju*. This is not beginners' skiing however; the snow tends to be icy and most of the runs are steep. Nor can one be sure of the snow: it may not come at all or it may come in such superabundance that the only access road is cut off. For non-winter visitors, **trekking** and **climbing** are obvious attractions and guides are available to take you up **Jbel Oukaimeden** or to indicate one of the many tracks going southwest towards Imlil (the principal starting-point for the ascent of **Jbel Toubkal**). You may also be fortunate enough to spot some **prehistoric rock-carvings**. Oukaimeden is one of three principal sites in the High Atlas for such carvings. If you want to see them, it is worth calling in at the Club Alpin chalet in the village, where there is a map.

Hotels
Hôtel Imlil, ☎ (04) 459 132 ***B (32 rooms).
Auberge chez Juju, ☎ (04) 319 005 **B (17 rooms).
Le Chouka, ☎ (through operator) 6. 8 rooms and 30 dormitory beds. Open only in winter.
Club Alpin Français Refuge. Can sleep 100 in dormitories. Has a restaurant and hires out ski equipment.

The Tizi-N-Test road to Taroudannt
This picturesque and unforgettable road soars to a precipitous height of 2100m at the Tizi-n-Test, plunges somewhat frighteningly down for some 30km and then levels out as it approaches the plain of the Souss river and Taroudannt. For savage beauty of a kind rarely seen, this is a drive worth saving your energy for. As it nears the pass, the road becomes little more than a roughly patched single track with passing places, hugging the mountainside, twisting and turning around the head of each gully. The scenery is ever changing: sunburnt villages perched on high escarpments, terraced fields cut into steep slopes, masses of wild flowers in spring, goats climbing trees, rushing torrents and, above all else, the mysterious, permanent and untouched snowfields.

It is 222km from Marrakesh to Taroudannt and you should allow at least five hours for the journey. The road was constructed by the French at the beginning of the century as a first step in the pacification of the all-powerful 'Lords of the Atlas' (in this particular area, the Goundafi clan, the ruins of whose kasbahs crown the heights at strategic points along the way). Sadly it is no longer well maintained since most travellers to Taroudannt and Agadir prefer the much quicker route via Chichaoua.

Coming from Marrakesh, the road is flat as far as the small town of **Tahanaoute**, which overlooks the Gorges of Moulay Brahim and from where a track leads to the ski resort of Oukaimeden (see above). It then climbs a further 13km to **Asni**, which appears almost completely surrounded by mountains and has a lively Saturday market. Asni can be a delightful spot to spend the night—a fitting halfway house between the hot and exotic attractions of Marrakesh and the cold and rugged Berber country to come. A track starts here for Imlil

(17km), the starting-point for the trek to the top of Jbel Toubkal. There is a some-what pretentiously named hotel in Asni, the *Grand Hôtel du Toubkal* (see below), and there is also a youth hostel.

13km further on is **Ouirgane**, also highly recommended as a stopping-place. It has a distinguished hotel, *La Roseraie*, an idyllic place surrounded by rose gardens, lime and lemon groves and carpets of wild flowers (for facilities, see below). From the village there are plenty of tracks to tempt you into the mountains. Ouirgane has a market on Thursdays.

Hotels

Grand Hôtel du Toubkal, Asni. ☎ (through operator) 3 Asni. ***A (26 rooms). Small, but very adequate.

La Roseraie, Ouirgane. ☎ (04) 432 094 fax (04) 439 130. ****A (30 rooms). Offers facilities for hunting, fishing and particularly riding, and has its own string of horses which can be hired by the day or used for longer treks.

Next comes the village of **Ijoukak**, which spans the Agoundis river and also has a small hotel. A kilometre further on is the village of **Taalat N'Yacoub** with a ruined Goundafi kasbah.

A poorly signposted track, 3km beyond the kasbah on the right, leads to the roof-less but otherwise restored **Tin Mal Mosque**. In autumn 1996 the road bridge over the fast-moving river was broken and the only footbridge was a couple of tree trunks with a few branches laid over the top. We took a deep breath, made it over the river and walked for 10min up the hill to what is one of Morocco's most hallowed monuments.

History of the Tin Mal Mosque

Built in 1153, this is the stronghold from which the Almohade chief, Ibn Tumart (hailed as the *Mahdi*) and his disciple, Abd el Mumene, first went out to preach the need for reform and then to attack the decadent Almoravides in Marrakesh and Fes. It was also to Tin Mal that the last of the Almohade leaders retreated when the Merinides drove them out of Marrakesh in 1262. The Merinides ruthlessly sacked the town in 1276 but, significantly, left the mosque itself standing, as if even they respected the teachings of Ibn Tumart, who was buried there.

Noble in its stark setting, Tin Mal affords a unique opportunity for the non-Muslim to see what a mosque is like inside. It still retains its framework of trans-verse arches and some splendidly tenacious **stalactite vaulting** (*muqarnas*), particularly under the arches either side of the **mihrab**, which is original in design, though displaying typically Almohade patterns of powerful geometric forms around arabesques and rosettes. It closely resembles that of the Koutoubia in Marrakesh (which it slightly pre-dates) and it is almost certain that the two were designed by the same craftsman. There are some very lovely **capitals** in the area of the mihrab as well as columnettes, attached to the piers where the arches begin; these are typical of the Almohade period, deriving originally from Cordoba. Notice too the old **doors** which have been casually stacked in one corner, having been replaced now by modern, more secure, doors. Tin Mal is

Interior of the Tin Mal Mosque

unique in that the **minaret** is placed above, and partly behind, the mihrab—minarets are usually positioned at one end of the north wall and no one knows why the architect of Tin Mal decided otherwise. A 'guide' sits on the steps of the mosque, watching as you toil up the path, and asks 15dh per person for the benefit of his company, which is of doubtful value, but one is not in a positon to argue.

A little further on the road passes close to another kasbah, perched on a hilltop, called **Tagoundaft**. This, too, was built by the Goundafa tribe who ruled in feudal style over this whole area until the early 20C, when they were extinguished by the even more powerful Glaoui clan. Being privately owned, it is in mint condition but is therefore not open to visitors.

The magnificent Tizi-n-Test, 12.5km beyond **Idni**, offers breathtaking views, especially south over the Souss valley. Below the pass on the other side (37km) the road meets the P32, which goes east towards Tazenakht and is part of the great west–east route across the south of Morocco, linking the major towns of Agadir, Ouarzazate and Errachidia. A further 67km along this road is the small town of **Taliouine** with a splendid Glaoui kasbah which seems to flow down the hillside. This has good stalactite carving on the towers, and almond trees all around. Next door to it is the 4-star *Ibn Toumert* hotel, while the more modest *Auberge Souktan* overlooks the kasbah from the opposite side of the valley. It makes a pleasant excursion and there is a rough road going southwest to Irherm and to Tafraoute. From the junction with the P32 it is 52km easy driving to Taroudannt.

Hotels

Hôtel Ibn Toumert, Taliouine. ☎ (04) 882 225 fax (04) 882 319. ****B (100 rooms).
Auberge Souktan, Taliouine. Unclassifed (4 rooms).

Taroudannt

Wedged into the valley of the river **Souss**, between the High Atlas to the north and the Anti-Atlas to the south, Taroudannt is an attractive red-earth town completely enclosed in ancient, crenellated walls some 6m high. Within this forbidding exterior are olive groves, palm trees and fertile, well-watered fields.

History of Taroudannt

This is a town which instantly speaks of past splendours: it has early origins but it was the **Saadians**, arriving from the Draa valley to the east in the 16C, who made Taroudannt their capital. They stayed for 20 years, embellishing and building palaces and ramparts. The town became a prosperous commercial centre, exporting sugar, cotton and indigo to the region of Timbuktu in exchange for the gold which became a Saadian obsession. Greatly enriched, the Saadians then moved to Marrakesh and Taroudannt's importance dwindled fast till it became what it is today: an unremarkable town but one whose magnificent walls lend it great elegance. Because it is down on the plain and inland it is very hot in summer, and warm and windy in winter.

Taroudannt's souks are animated and the craftwork—carpets, and objects of brass, leather and wrought iron—is attractive if not exactly unique. More collectable is the heavy Berber jewellery. There are also figurines and objects carved out of the soft local stone, which appear more African than Islamic. The best places to find a wide range of these objects are the **Souk Arab Artisanal**, next door to Place Assarag (entrance opposite the *Hôtel Taroudannt*), and the **Marché Berbère**, 10min walk from here to the south of Place Talmoklate, its entrance next door to *Hôtel Mentaga*.

Just inside the main walls and to your right as you approach from the Marrakesh direction, is the old **Kasbah Quarter** where the Saadians had their palaces, most of which were destroyed by the Alouite sultan, Moulay Ismael, in the 17C when he put down a rebellion, massacred the entire population and replaced it with Berbers from the Rif. He built a fortress here, of which sections remain. Here too is the *Palais Salam*—once a 19C pasha's palace, it is now probably one of the most enjoyable hotels in Morocco, as much for its friendly service (complimentary fresh orange juice appears the moment you arrive) as for the splendour of its air-conditioned, split-level rooms opening on to idyllic gardens, where the wind rustling through palm fronds sounds just like rain. There is also the *Gazelle d'Or*, an inordinately expensive hotel 2km out of town. It is completely self-contained behind its solid red ramparts and offers every conceivable luxury and amusement, including swimming, tennis, riding and falconry in a 10ha park.

It is 80km from Taroudannt to Agadir through the **Adminin Forest** and across the prosperous farmlands of the Souss valley.

Hotels

Hôtel Gazelle d'Or, ☎ (08) 852 139 fax (08) 852 654. ***** (23 rooms). Luxury hotel set in its own park (see above).

Hôtel Palais Salam, ☎ (08) 852 130 fax (08) 852 654. ****A (143 rooms). Good facilities and service, and a garden setting (see above).

Hôtel Saadiens, ☎: (08) 852 589 fax (08) 852 118. ****A (56 rooms).

Hôtel Taroudant, ☎ (08) 852 416. *A (31 rooms).

Naturally Morocco Ltd. rent out two, self-contained apartments, one for 2–9 persons and one for 4–12 persons (the latter for the use of vegetarians only). The house is located in a quiet neighbourhood 5min walk from the town centre. ☎ and fax (01267) 233 279.

A few kilometres out of Marrakesh on the Taroudannt road, a right-hand turn (S507) is signposted to Amizmiz, which lies 53km to the southwest. On the way you pass several kasbahs including that of **Tamesloht**, and the **Cavagnac dam** with its great lake behind it.

Amizmiz is a small and charming Berber settlement. Its houses are clustered around a kasbah and a *zaouia*. It has a small inn and there is a colourful market on Tuesdays, usually attended by a large number of people from neighbouring villages.

After Amizmiz the road becomes a rough track, but none the less scenic as it winds its way through oak and juniper trees before petering out in the middle of nowhere.The quickest way back to Marrakesh is by the way you have come, but a rewarding circular trip (140km in total) can be made by taking a turn east at Amizmiz along a wildly beautiful track across the gorges of the **Nfiss** river, rejoining the main Taroudannt road just to the south of Asni.

The Tizi-n-Tichka road to Ouarzazate

The Tizi-n-Tichka, at an altitude of 2260m, is a higher but slightly less spectacular pass than the Tizi-n-Test on the Marrakesh–Agadir road. Nevertheless, this is a driving and visual experience not to be missed, and in this case the road is well-maintained and the inclines are properly graded.

The first town, still on the plain, is **Ait Ourir** which has nothing special to recommend it except its Tuesday market, and the fact that about 12km further on a road (RP31d) leads to prehistoric rock-carvings on the Plateau Yagour. 20km further across this fertile plain, planted with olive groves and fruit trees, the road begins to climb and to cross, first of all, the **Tizi-n-Ait-Imger** in the foothills, and at 1470m a kind of practice run.

From this point on, standing at every hairpin bend and often perilously close to the edge, are sellers of amethysts and other semi-precious **minerals** such as cobalt and topaz. The stones are usually still uncut and sometimes remain within the original rock casing. Small boys with boxes of these treasures run up the hill by some hidden short-cut in order to overtake you and be waiting at the next bend but one. There are also co-operatives with several permanent stalls and a more professional take-it-or-leave-it approach. The range of merchandise is enormous and often includes fossils and local pottery as well as stones. You will need—and be respected for—your best bargaining skills.

The road soars higher, between slopes spotted with oleanders and scrubby oaks, and the last village before the pass is **Tadderte**—a picturesque Berber settlement surrounded by walnut trees and with a modest inn (see below). After 16km you come to the pass itself, and once over it the atmosphere changes quite markedly. You are now facing the desert and the **Draa valley**; to your left are the valleys of the rivers Dades, Todra and Ziz, slicing through the mountains until they reach the hot sand. This is the land of oases, kasbahs and *ksour*—what the ONMT is pleased to call 'The kasbah trail' or 'Land of a thousand kasbahs'.

Hotels
Auberge les Noyers, Tadderte. ☎ (through operator) 3 Tadderte

Ksour and kasbahs

Ksour and kasbahs are a phenomenon of southern Morocco. A **ksar** (pl. *ksour*) is a fortified village: the bigger *ksour* can house hundreds of families and have mosques, squares, shops and communal bread ovens behind their defensive walls. A **kasbah** is the fortified house of a single family, or the palace of a chief with rooms for his harem and his retainers. Very often *ksour* and kasbahs are linked together: *ksour* will contain kasbahs (as in the case of Ait Benhaddou, see below) or will adjoin them (as at Taourirt in Ouarzazate, for example), and it is hard to distinguish where one begins and the other ends.

The concept is essentially a Berber one and the main purpose has always been that of **defence**. Throughout history—up to and during the Protectorate—Berber tribes in the south were in a near constant state of war with each other and, from 1912 on, with the French. Nowadays, with peace restored, it is quite common to see hilltop *ksour* and kasbahs abandoned in favour of more accessible dwellings on the plains, or at least on the lower slopes, the fertile river basins being reserved for crops.

The walls of both kinds of structure are made of **pisé** (mud and straw mixed together) on a foundation of mud and stones, often river shingle. This leaves them particularly vulnerable to erosion by the weather, rain in particular; it also means they are cheap to build and very often it is easier to start afresh with a new construction rather than try to repair an old one. Hence the fairly frequent sight of a kasbah built alongside the ruins of an older one (as at Telouet), which in time just melts away, lending a picturesque and romantic flavour to southern landscapes as it does so. *Ksour* are the same; inside what appears to be a ruined outer wall there may be new, or at least perfectly habitable, dwellings.

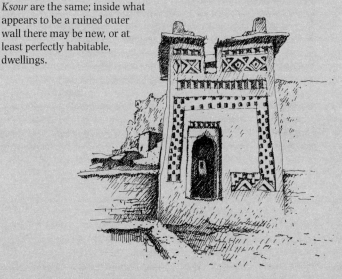

Kasbah in the south

Most kasbahs have a **tower** at each corner—either crenellated or topped with stepped merlons—used largely for surveying the surrounding countryside but also as a store for weapons and grain in time of seige. There is a primitive, almost childlike quality about the **decoration** of the older buildings. Wavy lines, chevrons and all kinds of geometrical shapes have been carved out of the *pisé* in what seems like glorious abandon. **Windows** are often unevenly spaced across walls and of varying sizes; sometimes outlined in white, sometimes not, they are usually covered by delicate metal grilles, which are made by local artisans. The overall result of all this is enchanting to the onlooker.

Interiors are wholly practical. The ground floor is reserved for **livestock**; above will be a domestic floor for cooking and family eating and there is usually a hole in the centre down which kitchen waste can be thrown for instant consumption by the sheep, goats and chickens below. Richer dwellings will have a floor above for sleeping and reception of guests. Every building has a **terrace** open to the skies, be it ever so small, for sleeping in summer, for hanging out clothes and sometimes for livestock. Very often the rooms below are built around a central well so light and fresh air can enter from above. Ceilings tend to be made of palm branches laid over wooden beams. Floors are simply earth, usually swept meticulously clean. Doors often last longer than walls because they are made of wood and are of immensely solid construction, with original bolts still intact although some are as much as three centuries old. If defence is the first consideration, then **coolness** in summer (when temperatures can rise to 50° C) is the second. These structures are immensely cool inside and often, it must be said, extremely dark.

The best *ksour* and kasbahs are in the Draa valley, between Agdz and Zagora, and all along the Dades and Ziz valleys, but most particularly in the oasis of Skoura (42km east of Ouarzazate). They tend to be in, or on the edge of, oases which are skilfully irrigated and minutely cultivated. In principle, every family living in a *ksar* or kasbah owns a patch of land where they will grow cereals, lucerne (for livestock), and vegetables as well as dates and olives.

A good guide will show you round a *ksar* or kasbah first and then take you for a walk through the **oasis**, the latter experience being the perfect antidote to the slight claustrophobia one can feel during the former. The fact that he will know everyone will make you feel more comfortable as you walk past men and women hard at work in order to survive.

Telouet

Shortly after the pass there is a turning left to Telouet, the spectacular kasbah of the **Glaoui** family. The drive itself—over 21km of narrow but tarmacked road—is a joy, taking you into the remote heart of the mountains past terraced slopes and scattered villages hanging over brilliant green valleys, frothing with almond blossom in early spring. The Glaouis dominated a large part of the south in the days before and during the Protectorate, and this palatial kasbah was the very centre of their power, guarding as it did the only caravan route across the Atlas between Marrakesh and the Sahara.

El Glaoui

The story of the most famous member of the family, Thami el Glaoui (1879–1956), also known as the Pasha of Marrakesh or, quite simply, El Glaoui, is a fascinating one. In the aftermath of World War II, which had brought Morocco out of its isolation, the desire for self-determination and independence from France was growing apace. The Independence Party, Istiqlal, regrouped and the sultan, Mohammed V, gave tacit support to the cause by omitting all reference to the French in his speeches, later declaring himself openly supportive of independence.

Meanwhile, Thami el Glaoui, the most powerful man in the south, was showing himself to be a staunch supporter of the French, probably because he and others like him feared that any independent Moroccan government would very soon put an end to their almost limitless power and extravagant lifestyle. Aided and abetted by the French he did all in his power to stem the tide of nationalism, publicly denouncing the sultan for having sold himself to Istiqlal and calling him 'Sultan of Istiqlal but not of Morocco', whereupon Mohammed V bade him leave the palace and never return.

The French continued to support El Glaoui, building up his reputation as 'the uncrowned king of the real Morocco'. In August 1953 he issued a request to the French Government, signed by hundreds of the traditionally rich and powerful, calling for the immediate removal of the sultan whom, he claimed, the people of Morocco no longer recognised. The next day the sultan and his family were duly exiled to Madagascar. An uncomfortable two years followed during which Morocco was ruled by an elderly puppet sultan, and support grew for the banished ruler, matched by increasing mistrust and dislike of the French. This period of growing disquiet and confusion finally ended in 1955 when El Glaoui once more took the lead; sensing defeat, he made a complete volte-face and requested the return of the 'true sultan' on the grounds that his previous dismissal had been illegal. Tired of the whole affair the French Government acquiesced and brought Mohammed V back from Madagascar. He went first to Paris where El Glaoui, ever the opportunist, met him and fell to his knees begging forgiveness, which Mohammed V granted with the words: 'we must forget the past and look forward now to the future.'

The **Kasbah of Telouet**, former palace of El Glaoui, is now a sad shadow of its former splendour. Built in the late 19C and first part of the 20C, the earliest sections have been seriously eroded by the weather, leaving a sorry mix of half towers and grotesquely shaped walls (imagine a sandcastle before it finally gives way to the sea). The 20C section is, however, in relatively good shape and is visitable. There is a resident *gardien* who will show you round, locking and unlocking huge doors as he goes, but who is quite unable to do more than recite a few dates and basic facts. He is there every day and payment is '*comme vous voulez*'(never a satisfactory situation, but 10dh per person should more than suffice). The only way to have an informed guide is to book one in advance through the local tourist office (Telouet is 105km from Ouarzazate). The next best thing is to read up on the whole Glaoui saga in *Lords of the Atlas* by Gavin Maxwell.

A door inside the Glaoui Kasbah

You will be shown the main courtyard with its minstrels' gallery (a nice European touch), the tribunal—with an 18C door—where justice was dispensed, and the splendid **reception hall** which was only built in 1942. It is decorated in the familiar sequence of cedarwood, stucco and *zellige*: the fine columns are encased in *zellige* and have delicate stucco capitals of palm leaves and geometric patterns. No expense was spared and 300 artisans were brought in from Fes to produce this extravagant Andalusian-style decor for a man who considered himself equal to royalty. (El Glaoui even went so far as to have the roof covered in green tiles, which are usually seen only on mosques and royal palaces.) Around the reception hall are similarly resplendent dining rooms and the harem bedrooms, one of which is trimmed with a luxurious frieze of brightly coloured silk belts embroidered with the emblems of families who served the Glaoui clan. At the end of the reception hall is a delicate **window grille** from which El Glaoui could look right down his fertile valley before, presumably, demanding payment from passing Saharan caravans. One is struck by the resounding emptiness of these vast rooms, which must in their day have been filled with superb carpets and the very best of French and Moroccan furniture. Nothing remains now, for the whole building was looted after El Glaoui's death in 1956. A climb up steep, dark stairs to the terrace offers an interesting overview of the whole complex structure in its varying stages of decay: one or two walls still manage to retain vestiges of ornamentation and even, in one or two cases, a crazily skewed fireplace.

A wander around the outside of the kasbah is an evocative, if depressing, experience. In front of it are the scant remains of an older palace, built in the 19C by an earlier Glaoui and now reduced almost to its foundations. Many remnants of the mud walls are now used as livestock enclosures by local villagers; dogs and children play in heaps of rubble and the vast crenellated 20C walls that tower above give a sense of unreality to the whole scene.

The adjacent village of Telouet goes about its daily business as if the kasbah were not there at all. Few tourists, it seems, come this way now, and the *Auberge de Telouet* has probably seen better days.

The road to Ouarzazate winds gradually down past the terraced Berber village of

Irherm-n-Ougdal, with its typical dark-red, square kasbah with a tower at each corner. The road follows the river **Imini** and at Amerzgane (60km from Tizi-n-Tichka) puts out a right-hand branch (P32) which eventually joins up (via Tazenakht) with the Tizi-n-Test road over the High Atlas, 220km to the west.

A turning 12km beyond Amerzgane leads east to the village of **Ait Benhaddou**. Just 10km along a paved road, Ait Benhaddou is a spectacular fortified *ksar* with houses piled up around several decorated kasbahs, all seeming to defy the laws of gravity as they perch on the steep mountain slope. These fortified villages must have been almost totally inviolable but extremely awkward to live in. Ait Benhaddou looks like a film set, and indeed it

Carved plaster detail inside the Glaoui Kasbah

was used by Orson Welles when making *Sodom and Gomorrah* and by David Lean for *Lawrence of Arabia*. Since then the lower section of the village has been rebuilt under the auspices of UNESCO which recognises it, quite rightly, as one of the most beautiful villages in southern Morocco. Its historic importance lies in the fact that, like Telouet, it stood on the only caravan route through the Atlas. The track connecting it with Telouet still exists and is drivable (47km), though only in a four-wheel-drive vehicle as there are several fords to cross, including one deep one just north of Ait Benhaddou, where the bridge was washed away by floods and has not, as yet, been replaced.

A walk through the village is highly recommended. First you must brave the stepping stones across the river where strategically placed small boys wait to help you and then guide you through the maze of narrow passages, first to the principal kasbah halfway up, which is still inhabited and said to be at least four centuries old (the owner asks 5dh each to take you up to his terrace for a splendid view), and then to the ancient and now ruined *agadir* (grain store) which stands at the top of the hill. It is an energetic walk but worth every step. Back on the main road, it is just 24km to Ouarzazate.

Marrakesh to Agadir via Chichaoua

This fast road across the lower reaches of the western High Atlas was only completed in 1973. It is straightforward, easy driving and scenically a little dull (266km in all). First, follow the main Marrakesh–Essaouira road as far as **Chichaoua**, an ordinary town distinguished only by its carpet industry. The carpets have pink or red backgrounds and are produced in quantity by several co-operatives which will welcome the interested visitor. After Chichaoua the road turns south and climbs gently to the small town of **Imi-n-Tanout** and then crosses the Tizi-n-Maachou which, at 1300m, must be one of the lowest and easiest passes in the High Atlas range. The road continues to pick its way through the foothills and finally descends towards the fertile Souss plain with Agadir and the ocean beyond.

Prehistoric rock-carvings in the High Atlas

Rock-carvings in Morocco tend to be clearly visible, cut into vertical outward-facing rock faces, rather than hidden away in caves, as in Europe. They are therefore fairly easy to spot, particularly if you enlist the help of a guide who will show you where to look for images of animals—cattle, elephants, hyenas—people and weapons. There are three principal sites.

1. Oukaimeden. There are four zones: (i) in the village itself, by the dam and south of the road; (ii) between the lake and the junction of l'assif-n-Ait Irene with l'assif Tiferguine; (iii) beyond l'assif Tiferguine, up the little pass of Igountar; (iv) on the slopes of Jbel Ifir, northeast of the village, to the left of l'assif-n-Ait Irene, and north of the road.

2. Plateau Yagour. There are two routes to the site. The first starts from the Ourika valley: leave the car at the *Auberge Ramuntcho*, cross the river and the bridge and take a path towards Anammer (45min). Alternatively, from the P31 going towards Ouarzazate, take a right-hand turning (RP31d) 12km after Ait Ourir. The road follows the Oued Zat as far as Arba Tighedouine (16km). Leave the car there and follow a *piste* in the direction of Azgour.

3. Jbel Rat. From Demnate, take CT6715 to Imi-n-Ifni (6km), then the CT6712. After 7km you will find traces of dinosaurs on red rocks left of the *piste*. If coming from Azilal, take the RS508 towards Ait M'hamid, 1km before which you take the CT1808. Go over the Tizi-n-Oughbar and then follow the valley of Oued Lakhdar as far as Sebt Bouwlli (60km of *piste*—3 hours drive in a four-wheel-drive vehicle).

There is also a 'secondary site' close to the village of **Tainant**, accessible from the Tizi-n-Tichka road, south of the pass. The village itself is no more than an easy 20min scramble away from some good examples.

Anyone seriously interested in the carvings should get hold of an excellent booklet, *Gravures Rupestres du Haut Atlas: la Grande Traversée des Atlas Marocains*, which gives detailed descriptions and itineraries for all the sites. It is available (in French only) from the tourist office, or direct from the Ministry of Tourism, 1 Rue d'Oujda, Rabat. ☎ (07) 722 643 fax (07) 722 156.

Ouarzazate, the Draa Valley, and Zagora

Ouarzazate

The town of Ouarzazate lies at an altitude of 1160m at an important junction between the main routes from the Draa and Dades valleys and Marrakesh. Standing as it does on the edge of the desert and accessible by three major roads,

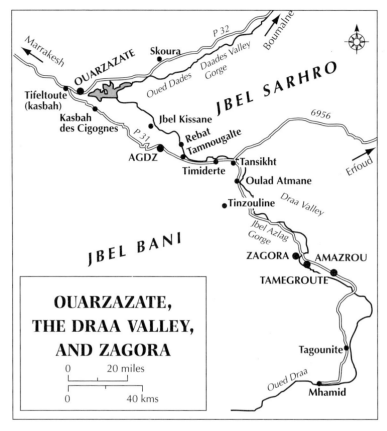

Marrakesh
OUARZAZATE
Skoura
P 32
Daades Valley
Oued Dades Gorge
Boumalne
JBEL SARHRO
Tifeltoute
(kasbah)
Kasbah
des Cigognes
P 31
Jbel Kissane
6956
Rebat
Tamnougalte
AGDZ
Timiderte
Tansikht
Oulad Atmane
Erfoud
Tinzouline
Draa Valley
Jbel Azlag
Gorge
JBEL BANI
ZAGORA
AMAZROU
TAMEGROUTE

**OUARZAZATE,
THE DRAA VALLEY,
AND ZAGORA**

0   20 miles

0   40 kms

Tagounite

Oued Draa

Mhamid

Ouarzazate has become an important stopping-point for international package tours. Some 15 years ago it was decreed a major tourist centre and it now has an impressive range of luxury hotels with fine swimming pools, all grouped together in a *zone hotelière* some way north of its one main street, Avenue Mohammed V. It also has its own airport, conveniently located 1km north of the hotels.

The town began as a strategically placed French outpost from which to pacify neighbouring Berber tribes. It therefore lacks a medina and there is a marked shortage of atmospheric restaurants and local colour. It does, however, have breathtaking mountain scenery close at hand and makes a fine starting-point for the 'Kasbah Trail' along the Draa, Dades, Todra and Ziz valleys.

■ Practical information

Tourist office. ONMT. Ave Mohammed V. ☎ (04) 882 485.
Banks. Ave Mohammed V.
Post office. Ave Mohammed V (opposite ONMT).

Air transport. Royal Air Maroc, 1 Ave Mohammed V. ☎ (04) 885 102. The airport is 1km north of town, along Rue de l'Aviation. ☎ (04) 882 348. It is served by *petits taxis*. Flights to Casablanca, Agadir, Marrakesh, and Paris.

Buses. The station is on Ave Mohammed V, near the ONMT. Services to Marrakesh, Taroudannt and eastwards along the Dades.

Grands taxis. Pl. Mouhadine.

Car hire. Hertz, 33 Ave Mohammed V. ☎ (04): 882 084.

Hotels

Hôtel Azghor, Blvd Moulay Rachid. ☎ (04) 882 612 fax (04) 882 319. ****A (106 rooms). The old 'Grand Hotel du Sud', set in lovely grounds with a good pool and views.

Hôtel Belere, Blvd Moulay Rachid. ☎ (04) 882 803 fax (04) 883 145. ****A (264 rooms). A modern palace built around a vast pool. Good international restaurant with Moroccan buffet every Friday night. Moroccan restaurant opens mid-March until September.

Hôtel Tichka Salam, Ave Mohammed V. ☎ (04) 882 393 fax (04) 882 766. ****A (105 rooms). Not far from the Taourirt kasbah.

Hôtel La Gazelle, Ave Mohammed V. ☎ (04) 882 1561. **B (30 rooms). On a much more modest scale. Pleasant and with a good restaurant.

Restaurants

Tifeltoute. ☎ (04) 882 813.
For details, see below. A whole experience. Booking essential.

Hôtel La Gazelle (see above). Good food and good value.

Restaurant Es-Salaam, Ave Prince Heritier Sidi Mohammed. Cheap and delicious.

Chez Dimitri, Ave Mohammed V. Also cheap. Greek and Italian specialities.

Holiday villages

Club Mediterranée, Blvd Moulay Rachid. ☎ (04) 882 650 fax (04) 882 814.
Excellent if you want a sporty holiday with high quality food and wine included. Not cheap.

Campsites

Camping Municipal,Quartier Sidi Daoud. ☎ (04) 884 636. Just beyond Taourirt kasbah, alongside town swimming pool.

Ouarzazate is proud of its two Glaoui kasbahs. The first is **Tifeltout**, 5km out on the Marrakesh road, up a side turning on the left. Its harmonious proportions and soft outlines make it one of the most frequently photographed and filmed kasbahs in Morocco. It is now a restaurant renowned not only for its excellent Moroccan cuisine but also for folklore displays and Berber dancing, which take place in the huge courtyard most evenings between mid-March and mid-September. There are also eight rooms and space is available on the flat roof, either for sleeping or simply for escaping from the somewhat repetitive sound of the Berber troupes. As with the paradors in Spain, little has been altered on the outside and a high standard of comfort has been installed without defacing the essential Moorish dignity and splendour of the building.

In the centre of town, at the end of Avenue Mohammed V, is the fine kasbah of

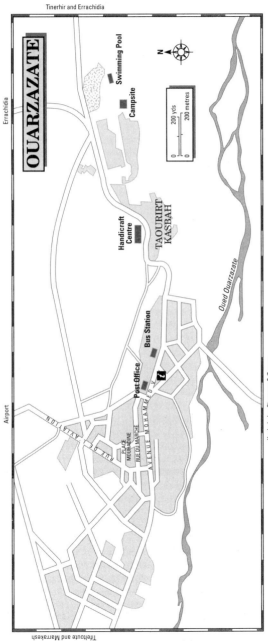

OUARZAZATE

Tinerhir and Errachidia

Errachidia

Airport

Swimming Pool

Campsite

200 yds

200 metres

Handicraft Centre

TAOURIRT KASBAH

Oued Ouarzazate

Bus Station

Post Office

i

RUE DE L'AVIATION

PLACE MOUHADINE

RUE DU MARCHE

AVENUE MOHAMMED V

Kasbah des Cigognes & Zagora

Tifeltoute and Marrakesh

Taourirt. Much of it is in need of repair but a short tour of the rooms which are accessible is worthwhile. A guide, without whom the maze of corridors will not make much sense, can be picked up at the entrance and his price negotiated in advance. (The writer hired a guide for two hours, which included a walk around the adjoining *ksar* and a drive out to the Kasbah des Cigognes—see below.)

Constructed in 1754 of the usual *pisé* (mud and straw) with a foundation of stones and mud, it is not surprising that much of the kasbah is in a ruinous state after years of failure to make good after rains. You walk first across a courtyard where ceremonies and dancing would have taken place. It is graced by a German cannon which was apparently given to the Glaoui family by the sultan, Moulay el Hassan, to encourage them to control the southern tribes. In its heyday the kasbah would have housed hundreds of people: members of the Glaoui clan (though not El Glaoui himself, whose main residence was Telouet, described above), their harems and their servants. You are then shown the ground floor which was essentially for livestock and domestic affairs, kitchens, and stores. More interesting is the floor above, where the main reception rooms have fine, painted, cedarwood ceilings, the family's private mosque and the women's apartments, the biggest being reserved for the 'favourite wife' (in other words, she who presents the current lord of the kasbah with his first son). All the women's rooms have *mushrabiyyas*, many still in place, through which they could peer at the outside world without being seen. One is struck forcibly by the prison-like quality of this building and the incredibly limited lives that the women of the harem must have led well into the 1930s. From the terrace above there is a good view of the village behind and of the reservoir created in 1972 by the impressive **El Mansour Eddahbi dam**, which is accessible along a track from the Zagora road. **Open** 09.00–12.00 and 13.00–18.00; entry 10dh.

The village, or **ksar**, which adjoins the kasbah was once divided into two sections, Jewish and Berber, but the Jews have long since gone and the synagogue is occupied by a Berber carpet-weaver called Mohammed Negib, who is keen to chat if only because he feels very cut off from the main tourist route. A wander through the streets of the *ksar* can be a very sociable affair, especially if you are accompanied by one of the local guides who will know everyone. Few tourists bother to come here after visiting the kasbah and the place is pleasantly laid back and undemanding.

Opposite the kasbah, on the other side of the road, is the government-run **handicraft centre** (*ensemble artisanal*), which is open every day and displays the usual local crafts, particularly Berber carpets and painted mirrors, at fixed prices. All around it, and competing hard for your attention, are the workshops producing similar goods (which officials would claim were of inferior quality) at very flexible prices.

To reach the **Kasbah Des Cigognes**, take the road signposted to Agdz and turn left about 2km after crossing the river on to a *piste* which leads you through the village of Telmasla. This kasbah on the banks of the Draa river is little more than a romantic ruin in a wonderful setting. However, parts of it are being restored, not all that authentically, by film companies who use it for their biblical epics. (And does it really matter if a Roman forum appears in the middle of a Saharan kasbah?) The local 'caretaker' knows more about the film stars than he does about the history of the kasbah. No matter. It is really the **storks** which make it memorable, nesting precariously on every ruined turret. According to our guide, they come here in particular because of the plentiful supply of fish in the river. *Ouarzazate* is Berber for 'without noise' (*ouar*—without, *zazate*—noise); you really have to come this far out of town to believe it. The setting is truly peaceful and very lovely.

The Ouarzazate ~ Zagora road

The road from Ouarzazate to Agdz (73km) is arid and, in parts, quite dramatic as it cuts through the strange surrealistic shapes of the **Jbel Sarhro**. Looming up on the left is the extraordinary **Jbel Kissane**. Approached from this direction, it looks like a single mountain until you pass it and realise that it fronts a massive range. The outline reminded the writer of a gateau topped with meringue; a passing Berber announced that the locals thought of it as a Moroccan teapot surrounded by glasses: *chacun à son goût*.

Agdz is a most attractive market town, with a huge main square busy with cafés and stalls which are hung with colourful Berber carpets and scattered with local pottery and jewellery. This is an excellent place to seek out and bargain for **carpets**: the selection ranges from quite small prayer rugs, to others made of silk that need to be hung on the wall, to large, room-sized carpets in vibrant colours. They do not necessarily have the lasting quality of the more solid Berber rugs from the north, and their price should favourably reflect this fact. Wandering through all the cheerful hubbub of the town are the desert people, tall thin men of aquiline feature and noble gait, looking somewhat aloof. Agdz has its souk on Thursdays. It also has one or two unclassified and basic hotels, notably the *Hôtel Kissane*, which has a good restaurant.

The **Draa Valley** between Agdz and Zagora must be one of the most intensely populated ribbons of land in the pre-Saharan region. The **Draa** is one of Morocco's longest rivers, rising in the High Atlas, cutting through the Jbel Sarhro range and then turning west along the southern flanks of the Anti Atlas, sometimes disappearing into the desert sand to reappear further on. It eventually pushes its way out to the Atlantic at Foum-el-oued-Draa ('Mouth-of-the-river-Draa') about 80km southwest of Goulimine.

From the road there is nothing but arid, sandy wasteland above, while on the valley floor not an inch of space is left unused. There are cereals of all kinds, and almond, lemon, orange, date and olive trees. Just above the fertile ground live the people in their villages, their simple houses coloured red or ochre, with heavy wooden doors and tiny windows so that the sun does not enter. These people are industrious. The women who are not working in the fields spin and weave, the old men tan hides or make *babouches*, the young men tend their crops. The women dress in typical southern Berber style, swathed in metres of fine black material embroidered with silver, and their faces are unveiled. They wear heavy, often beautiful, jewellery regardless of how menial their everyday tasks; this is an integral part of the family capital, to be sold off in times of drought and poor crops, or to be increased and displayed in greater profusion in periods of prosperity.

A left-hand turning 4km south of Agdz leads to a *piste* up to **Rebat** (c 3km) which gives a splendid view of the whole Draa valley and its wonderful palmery, starting here and stretching all the way to Tamegroute, south of Zagora. From now on you will pass *ksar* after *ksar*, and kasbah after kasbah, some ruined, some restored, some right on the road, others some way back, probably up a rough *piste*. Many of these fortified villages are not signposted on the road and you must stop to ask the name (if this is important), whereupon you will be besieged by small boys wanting to show you round and/or sell you dubious dates.

One of the best of the named *ksour* is **Tamnougalte**, 5km beyound Agdz and accessible by a *piste* turning left off the road; the village is guarded by a fine kasbah which is empty and seems almost too neat to be true. This is because it has been used by a film company that has obviously repaired it. 2km further on are two more, unnamed kasbahs, one on either side of the road. Next is **Timiderte** with a ruined village on the left and the new one on the right. At **Tansikht** the gorge opens out into a wide valley.

Oulad Atmane—a big village with a lovely, compact kasbah on a hill to your right—comes next. 30km north of Zagora is **Tinzouline**, a modern, developed *ksar* with a ruined kasbah above it. Rock-carvings (*gravures rupestres*) are signposted here, allegedly 7km along a *piste* to the right, but the writer was unable to find them.

Notice, as you go, the domes of the *koubbas* in this region, which are pear-shaped, almost pointed—quite unlike the rounded forms seen further north. Notice, too, the way in which superbly carved towers can sometimes rise out of plain, undecorated, even ruined, walls. The road now passes through the **Jbel Azlag Gorge** and then emerges on to the great palm-filled oasis which is Zagora.

Zagora and Amazrou

Zagora was once an important stopping-place for camel caravans on the journey between Timbuktu and Sijilmassa (south of Erfoud). Indeed there is a sign in Zagora which states that it is just 52 days by camel to Timbuktu. The Saadians set off from this region in the early 16C, going on to conquer the whole of Morocco and also to penetrate deeper than ever before into the region south of the Sahara in search of gold and slaves. Other dynasties had been here before and it was the Almoravides who built the **fortress** on top of **Jbel Zagora**, the hill on the opposite bank of the Draa, ideally placed for guarding the caravan route. Behind the hill are traces of earlier occupation in the form of heaps of stones, probably marking the burial places of prehistoric chieftains. There is a track which crosses the river and goes up to the fortress which is now, once again, used for military purposes. Casual visitors are therefore discouraged from approaching it closely. The views are nevertheless spectacular from well below the top.

Zagora does not pretend to be anything other than an **oasis**—a stopping-place for weary travellers—a take-off point for the journey into the unknown. It has markets on Wednesdays and Sundays which are almost exclusively given over to dates, for centuries the staple food of desert dwellers. The best time to visit would be at Mouloud—the Prophet's birthday—when there is the big *moussem* of Moulay Abdelkadir Jilali, which is well worth seeing.

Hotels
Hôtel Reda, Route de M'Hamid. ☎ (04) 847 249 fax (04) 847 012. ****A (155 rooms). A new hotel, mainly catering for tour groups.

Hôtel Tinsouline, Ave Mohammed V. ☎ (04) 847 252. ****B (88 rooms). In typical kasbah style, with a pool and all reasonable comfort.
Hôtel de la Palmerie, Ave Mohammed V. ☎ (04) 847 008. *A (16 rooms). Probably better as a restaurant than a hotel. It organises treks.

Campsites
Camping Sindibad, Ave Hassan II.

There is really very little to see and do in central Zagora and you are strongly recommended to continue 2km southwards to the delightful palm-filled oasis of **Amazrou** across the Draa river. Here are not only the most enjoyable hotel-restaurants, but also the **Kasbah des Juifs**—Zagora's one 'tourist sight'. It is a huge, rambling and part-ruined kasbah formerly inhabited by Jewish silver-smiths making jewellery. It is 3km from Amazrou, along a *piste*: you will need someone to show you the way and also to lead you to one of the three remaining jewellery workshops, whose occupants are now Muslims.

The jewellers of Amazrou
The silversmiths—who today make mostly **fibulas**—are usually very willing to show you the traditional Jewish methods they still practise. They make a soft clay paste, hammer into it an existing silver fibula, and then bake it to produce a mould. Silver is then heated in a furnace and (with the addition of 10% tin) is poured through a hole in the mould. Once hardened, the silver object is taken from the mould and chased, engraved and polished.
Fibulas are worn by Berber women, one below the right shoulder if they are not married, and two—one on each side—if they are either married or divorced. They are also popular with tourists and these silversmiths sell in bulk to middle-men who retail them in the souks of Marrakesh and other cities at twice the price. The good thing about this—if you happen to be in Amazrou—is that you are under no pressure whatsoever to buy (unless you want to), though it is usual to make a small donation to the silversmith himself.

After visiting the smiths, take time to wander around the kasbah, where hundreds of Berber families still live, some underground and all, it seems, in a state of semi-darkness and refreshing coolness in the hot weather. There is a great sense of community here.

Hotels
Hôtel Kasbah Asmaa, ☎ (04): 847 241 fax (04) 847 527. ***B (20 rooms). Tucked away in the palmery, this hotel is a delight with very friendly staff. It really is an old kasbah and the rooms are decorated in traditional Moorish style. There is a small pool set in peaceful gardens and you dine in style, *à la Marocaine*, in Berber tents. The hotel organises camel treks into the desert, tents and all food provided, from one to seven days.
Hôtel La Fibule du Draa, ☎ (04) 847 318 fax (04) 847 271. ** (26 rooms). Similar in setting and style to the above. It also organises camel treks.

Campsites

Camping de la Montagne. Located in the Amazrou oasis below the Jbel Zagora mountain.

Tamegroute and the Naciryin library

A short excursion from Zagora 22km to the village of **Tamegroute** is recom-mended. (Continue southwards along the main road signposted to Mhamid.) Tamegroute was once the seat of the **Naciryin**—a religious brotherhood that came originally from Iraq and was renowned for keeping the peace amongst Draa Berber tribes. In the 17C they settled in the *ksar* of Tamegroute, which already had an 11C *zaouia* and was a revered seat of learning. There remain today a *medersa* (still in use as a college for theological students), a *zaouia* with a mosque which houses some 50 tombs of members of the brotherhood, including that of the founder, Abou Abdallah Mohammed ibn Naceur, and a library containing some 4000 priceless books. The mosque is closed to non-Muslims. All around, in the courtyard of the *zaouia*, are pilgrims who have come to pray, to touch the tomb and to be cured of their mental illnesses. Many of them have come far and are given food and drink by the members of the broth-erhood which (it was alleged by the guide) is still active.

The **library** itself is a rare and fascinating treasure and, unlike the Karaouyine in Fes, is open every day to visitors. Here are ancient manuscripts and books (the earliest is a Koran dated 1063), with beautifully executed illumi-nations in gold, indigo, saffron and henna on gazelle skin. As well as religious works, there are books on astronomy, medicine, history and Arabic grammar. Of particular interest are a biography of the Prophet Muhammad dated 1103, a 14C plan of Alexandria, a 15C history of Fes, and a very complete medical dictionary, listing maladies in black and the appropriate medicines in red. Some of the books are left permanently open in their locked cabinets, presumably in the interests of tourism, and are just beginning to show signs of fading from the sun. All are catalogued and there are suitably erudite guides who can explain some of the mysteries. **Open** 09.00–12.00 and 14.00–18.30; entry 10dh.

The *zaouia* and library are on the left as you enter the village, behind the *Hôtel Riad Dar Naciri*, which is still signposted although it is no longer a hotel.

Also of interest is the **'Kasbah Souterrain'** built in the 17C by the Saadians to house hundreds of black slaves brought in from the Timbuktu region. People still live there today, mainly Berbers, and it is used specifically for storing sugar because 'it is dark and therefore there is no problem of flies'.

Tamegroute is also known for its distinctive green pottery. The **potteries** can be visited and are signposted on the left of the road, just after the hotel. They are run by a German cooperative which exports much of the produce. Apparently it recently tried to introduce modern gas furnaces but local people preferred their traditional methods, using locally gathered thorn bushes and grass for fuel; this, too, is controversial since the grass is needed to stabilize the sand dunes. The pottery itself is a rather uninteresting green colour (from locally mined manganese and copper) and comes in the form of roof tiles (for mosques and royal buildings) as well as pots.

11km south of Tamegroute is the *Hôtel Repos du Sable* and 200m beyond it is a *piste* which takes you into the tiny village of **Tinfou**. Tinfou is having a serious problem with encroaching sand, which blows in from the Sahara through the gap in the mountains created by the Draa river. Major efforts are being made to grow grasses and knit them together to make a stabilising network, but it looks rather as if the battle is being lost.

Hotels
Hôtel Repos du Sable, BP6 Tamegroute, Zagora.

South of Tamegroute the landscape is quite changed. The road leaves the river and you drive over a bare plateau of black rock. The sun shines relentlessly on the distant, sinister silhouettes of the **Jbel Bani** range and the view seems unreal. **Tagounite** (48km from Tamegroute) has little to offer the visitor other than a *piste* going west to Foum Zguid (strictly for four-wheel-drive vehicles only). **Mhamid**, 30km beyond, is in the dunes south of Jbel Bani. It was once a strategic point on the trans-Saharan trade route but now it is a rather forlorn administrative centre, fast disappearing altogether under the sand. For some time after an attack by the Saharan nationalists, Polisario, in 1980 Mhamid was out of bounds to visitors. Now it is open again but has little to show other than its dunes and its old, pre-1980 *ksar* on the far bank of the Draa. The road ends here. Even the waters of the great Draa disappear into the sand soon after.

The Dades Valley, Tinerhir and the Todra Gorge

The P32 out of Ouarzazate follows the course of the **Dades** river, taking you north of the El Mansour Eddahbi reservoir. Not without justification is this road called **La Route des Kasbahs**, for as you approach Skoura (41km) they become ever more plentiful and ornate, with intricate carving on the towers and delicate wrought-iron grilles over the windows. The first sign of joys to come is the oasis and village of **Oued el Hajaj**, where there is a kasbah complete with storks' nests.

The first visitable kasbah is that of **Ben Moro**, on the left just 2km before Skoura. It stands at the beginning of the Skoura oasis, which extends for 4500ha. There is no sign on the road to indicate the kasbah, but if you stop the car, or even slow down, its owner, whose name is Mohammed, will spring out of the adjacent modern house he has inhabited since 1970 and offer to take you round. This is worthwhile as an introduction to kasbah life. Ben Moro Kasbah was built by a Muslim escaping from Spain in the 17C. The ground floor was occupied by livestock and grain stores, and the first floor by ten families, each with its own two rooms and oven; the second floor was for sleeping, and the terrace above was a point from which to survey the surrounding land 'and watch for nomads who might steal the dates' and presumably, a few decades back, for hostile Berber tribes or even the French. One cannot but comment that if Mohammed is so keen to attract passing tourists, he really should do something about lighting the steep, uneven stairway up to the terrace, and perhaps even repair some of the holes.

Two more fine kasbahs lie behind Ben Moro, accessible either by a *piste* which

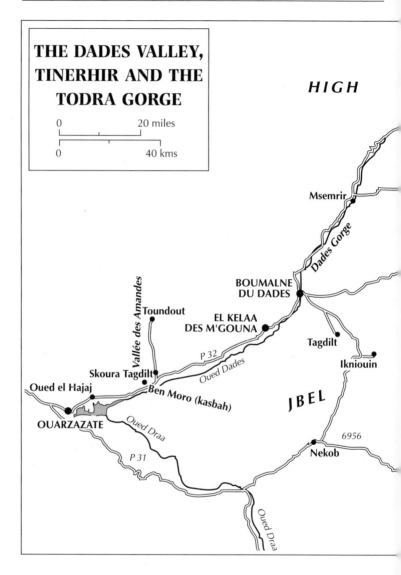

THE DADES VALLEY, TINERHIR AND THE TODRA GORGE

0   20 miles

0   40 kms

HIGH

Msemrir

Dades Gorge

**BOUMALNE
DU DADES**

Vallée des Amandes

Toundout

**EL KELAA
DES M'GOUNA**

Tagdilt

Ikniouin

P 32

Oued Dades

Skoura Tagdilt

J B E L

Oued el Hajaj

Ben Moro (kasbah)

OUARZAZATE

Oued Draa

6956

Nekob

P 31

Oued Draa

runs off left just before Skoura or, preferably, on foot through the palmery. It is a deeply satisfying and calming experience to walk amongst the date palms, and olive, apricot, fig and almond trees, marvelling at the intricate pattern of irrigation channels which keep everything so astonishingly green, and listening to birdsong and, perhaps, the low murmur of women's voices as they work amongst their crops.

The first kasbah to appear is **Amerhidil**, built by a Middle Atlas tribe of that

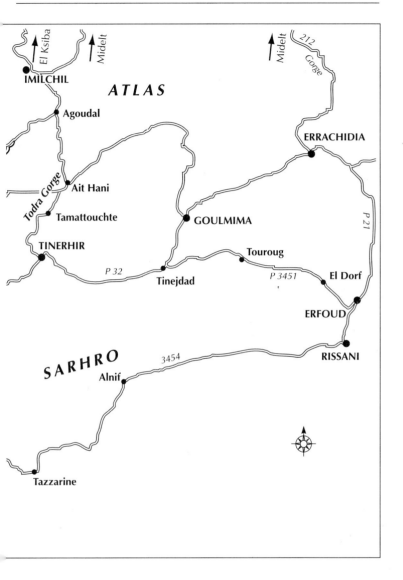

name and later taken over by the Glaoui family. It now belongs to a direct descendant of that family and the interior cannot be visited. A further 10min walk southwest along a track leading from Amerhidil is the impressive kasbah of **Dar Ait Sidi el Mati**. It has the same layout as Ben Moro but is definitely better maintained and more visitor-friendly, as well as being more remote. From this point you can either take a short track eastwards, past the ruined **Kasbah El Kabbaba**, to rejoin the main road, or return through the palmery.

Skoura itself is little more than a small market town. If you have an hour to spare, take a minor (tarmacked) road heading north from the centre and sign-posted to **Toundout** (21km). The point of this short excursion is really the road itself, which winds through almond trees and kasbahs towards the tiny village of Toundout, nestling in a palmery against the glorious backdrop of the High Atlas mountains. It is known locally as **'La Vallee des Amandes'**. After Toundout the road becomes *piste* and goes higher into the mountains—wonderful to explore if you have unlimited time and four-wheel-drive vehicle. Otherwise, turn back to rejoin the Dades Valley. After Skoura the palm trees cease temporarily, to be replaced by a sweeping mountain landscape.

El Kelaa des M'Gouna, 50km further on, is famous for its rose water (*eau des roses*), which every other shop in town appears to sell. It is bought in large quantities by Moroccan women who rub it into their faces and hands, and most of it comes from here. The rose bushes look so insignificant out of season that it is easy to miss them, growing as they do between cultivated plots in the palm groves. But in May, when they are covered in tiny pink blooms, they are a joy to behold—and to smell. A festival is held in late May or early June each year when the petals are harvested. The one classified hotel in this small town is the *Hôtel Les Roses du Dades*. Once very grand, it still retains considerable charm and style, with friendly service to match. The views from the back rooms, over the Dades valley—wide here and meticulously cultivated—are memorable.

Hotels
Hôtel Les Roses du Dades, on a hill alongside the old kasbah. ☎ (04) 883 807. ****B (102 rooms). See above. Has a pool and fine views.

There are one or two good kasbahs on the 24km stretch between El Kelaa and Boumalne, especially one on the right at El Hart. **Boumalne du Dades** is only of interest as the starting-point for excursions up the Dades Gorge, and southwards into the Jbel Sarhro by way of La Vallée des Oiseaux and Tagdilt. Its one classified hotel, the *Madayeq* (****B) is—at time of writing—closed until further notice.

Hotels
Hôtel Soleil Bleu, Boumalne. ☎ (04) 344 163. Unclassified.

The **Dades Gorge** is not a drive for the nervous. The road soars up the sides of the gorge, turns round and round on itself, plunges down and serpentines up again. But it is perfectly feasible in an ordinary car, the views back down the gorge are superb, and the kasbahs clinging to craggy outcrops look especially impressive.

After the village of **Msemrir**, the gorge widens. A *piste* running east from Msemrir crosses a range of mountains to **Ait Hani** at the northern end of the Todra Gorge (42km). This is quite one of the most spectacular drives in Morocco but has areas so steep and hairpin bends so tight that your nerves, not to mention your car, are strained to the utmost. This is rugged mountain scenery on a leviathan scale and quite untamed. There are no people. The rock is highly mineral and it is tempting to collect specimens of rock crystal, quartz and amethyst. If, on arrival at Ait Hani, you want more of this excitement, continue north to Imilchil (66km). But it will take all day and there are easier ways of approaching Imilchil.

The recently tarmacked road to **La Vallée des Oiseaux** leaves the P32 1km after the town of Boumalne. It is signposted to Ikniouin. After 8km there is a junction and you should take the right-hand track (now rocky *piste*) for a further 8km to Tagdilt. The valley is said to be a birdwatcher's paradise, with falcons, buzzards, and even the occasional bustard. Far from being a verdant place alive with twittering birds as the name suggests, however, the valley is a vast empty basin of stony desert (hammada), ringed by the volcanic peaks of the Jbel Sarhro in every hot colour under the sun. It is very lonely and very beautiful. As for birds ... we saw several birds of prey, a wheatear and some larks.

You can penetrate deeper into the Jbel Sarhro by returning to the junction and taking the left-hand fork to Ikniouin, thence driving southwards for 56km over the Tizi-n-Tazazert (2283m) to **Nekob** which is on the main west–east road between the Draa Valley and Rissani. This drive is very steep in places and takes you up to what seems like the roof of Morocco. The views over apparently endless ranges are beyond description.

Tinerhir

From Boumalne there is an easy drive of 53km along the P32 to Tinerhir, at the southern entrance to the Todra Gorge. Tinerhir is one of the great tourist-frequented centres of the pre-Saharan region, and understandably so, for it is in a bowl high in the mountains, ringed round with huge sculpted peaks which create a magical silhouette against the setting sun. The colours are dramatic: the green of the palm grove—tightly wedged in amongst the vertical rock walls—making a vivid contrast with the dry dusty red. Most of the group tours stay at the *Hôtel Sargho* which stands high above the town and provides the best views (see below).

The town itself is, however, well worth exploring. Walk into the **medina** from the market place behind the *Hôtel Todra*. (There is a market every Monday.) You will find yourself in the main street, known locally as *La rue des Femmes* because the shops sell kaftans and all things female. There are also **spice merchants**; look for the *Pharmacie Berbère* on the left, which has a superb array, including a *ras el hanout* containing 45 different spices, and very reasonably priced, high-quality saffron. Here too there is magic, in the form of bird skeletons, wolf skins and all manner of strange, unidentifiable objects which can cure just about any complaint, it seems.

Also in the medina are carpenters, and metalworkers fashioning grilles for windows. Here too are the **rug-weavers**—women from the Ait Atta tribe who work with their daughters weaving traditional carpets from camelhair or lambs-wool, sometimes incorporating silk from silkworms kept in mountain villages. These women are few in number and you certainly need a guide to take you to them, and to interpret if you are seriously interested in bargaining for a rug, as most speak only Berber. Traditionally they would work in their villages, but now there is increasing demand for their products and more and more can afford small houses in the medina where they set up their looms, thus avoiding the exhausting walk through the mountains laden with heavy rugs. These women do their own dyeing, still using vegetable dyes such as henna (red), indigo (blue), saffron (yellow) and kohl (black). The rugs are often covered in symbols to bring good luck or ward off the evil eye (see *Traditional crafts*), the colours are usually vibrant and the workmanship is of high quality, though with a definitely home-made look, which includes the fringe at one end only (machine-made rugs have fringes at both ends).

A walk through the old **mellah**, adjoining the medina, brings you out into the palmery. The Jews have long since left the *mellah* and some 20 Berber families now live behind its massive wooden door. It all seems very dark and gloomy but is no doubt very desirable in the heat of summer. The contrast as you walk out into the sunny **palmery** is striking. It extends for some 40km into the Todra Gorge and is minutely irrigated and cultivated in small family plots growing vegetables in summer and cereals and lucerne for livestock in winter. Palm trees remain only on the periphery but cutting them down is nowadays strictly controlled. Livestock are pastured on less valuable land higher up the mountains and women heavy-laden with animal feed on their backs are one of the characteristic sights of this region. It is women who tend the crops, arriving in the early evening after their household chores are done. Men, it seems, 'do the heavier work'.

Tinerhir has another palmery which extends southeastwards. To reach it take the turning to Waklim (4km) which is on the right just before the ceremonial entrance to Tinerhir. There are **potteries** in this region, specifically at El Harat and (further south) at Agoultine. Both involve driving over rough *piste* and are difficult to find without a guide.

Hotels

Hôtel Sargho, ☎ (04) 834 181. ****B (62 rooms). Geared towards tour groups. Poor service but superb views.

Hôtel Kenzi Bougafer, Blvd Mohammed V. ☎ (04) 833 280 fax (04) 833 282. ****B (98 rooms). Very new with Moroccan and international restaurants, pool, and conference room to seat 150. On the edge of town and 15km away from the Todra Gorge.

Hôtel Todra, 37 Ave Hassan II. ☎ (04) 834 249. *B. Has a modest restaurant and is very central for exploring the medina.

The **Todra Gorge** is one of Morocco's most spectacular sights, a vast fault in the plateau which separates the High Atlas from the Jbel Sarhro. The road from Tinerhir runs along the bottom, never taking off and soaring up the sides as it does in the Dades, but sticking to the river, and frequently disappearing into it. There is a drive of about 10km through the first palmery, described above, before one reaches the dramatic entrance to the gorge. At this point it really is best to park the car and proceed on foot, preferably wearing walking- or wellington boots. The river is quite fast-flowing and stepping-stones have been strategically placed just far enough apart for most people to need a helping hand over the jumps; predictably, well-organised groups of boys are waiting for this eventuality with hands outstretched for dirhams. As one café-owner explained wryly, they only have to place the stones a bit closer together to make it easy for everyone to cross ... but then they would not earn their dirhams. Irritating little boys apart, this is a wonderful place: the sky becomes a slit of light at the top of the canyon and the rock walls, dark and forbidding, are brought to life here and there by waterfalls looking like lengths of glinting silver ribbon.

There are plenty of cafés on the way up, and even some hotels in the very mouth of the gorge, including the huge *Yasmina* surrounded by tourist buses and postcard stands, and the more modest and recommended *Hôtel Restaurant El Mansour*, where you pay 50dh for one of their four double rooms, and the same for a plentiful three-course meal. There are also campsites, but these tend to be further back in the palmery. From the *El Mansour* it is about 1km to **Tamattouchte**, after which the road begins to improve and you can consider whether to go on to Ait Hani and cross over to the Dades Gorge (see above), or return to Tinerhir.

Hotels

Hôtel Yasmina, ☎ (04) 833 013. See above. Has a good restaurant.
Hôtel Restaurant El Mansour See above. Basic accommodation with hot showers around a courtyard. Food is excellent value.

The small town of **Tinejdad** lies 55km east of Tinerhir and has just one interesting feature—an art gallery, *Galerie d'Art, chez Zaid* (well signposted off the main road). Established in 1995 it is really more like a museum, with an eclectic mix of exhibits including fossils, locally made jewellery, pots, Korans, a collection of model bicycles made of wood, and paintings by contemporary Moroccan artists. There are also lengths of fine material, and shawls and other items embroidered—somewhat gaudily—in wool (this is a local speciality). There are gardens to sit in, alongside a magnificent white bougainvillaea, a row of working telephone boxes (a rare sight in the Moroccan south), and a modest restaurant. The inspirational force behind all this is a colourful character called Zaid, who has been collecting for many years, and who proudly takes you round. He is himself a painter and his works are for sale, as are most of the exhibits. There is no entry charge. ☎ (05) 786 798.

At Tinejdad there is a choice of routes: either northeastwards through Goulmima to Er Rachidia (24km, following the P32) or eastwards along a minor, but adequate, road to Erfoud (87km).

Goulmima has a very fine 15C **ksar** which still houses some 400 families. Walk through the grand entrance (sadly one of its two decorated towers has fallen down) and you are in a cool, tranquil, well-ordered world with a mosque, shops, main

Entrance to the Ksar

square and houses built on a grid pattern and usually comprising two floors and a roof terrace. Many have centuries-old wooden doors and—surprisingly—beehives set into the walls, the bees entering through tiny grilles to make their honey. 'Rich' people apparently move out of the *ksar* and build their own detached houses elsewhere, only to regret it when the summer heat arrives. The inhabitants of the *ksar* are proud that they now have electricity and a health worker who visits their children once a month. Each family owns a plot of land in the surrounding palmery as well as an enclosed space within the ruined walls for their livestock.

All in all, Goulmima is a pleasant, laid-back little town where tourists rarely stop. The people are friendly and our guide—Youssef Tebri—was one of the best we had experienced anywhere. There is just one small hotel.

Hotels

Maison d'Hôtes Les Palmiers, 6 bis, Hay Ouatmane, Secteur 2. ☎ and fax (05) 784 004. Located in the palmery. A good restaurant with a few rooms and camping facilities. Owned by Mme Odile, who is French.

The road from Tinejdad to Erfoud passes some attractive villages, **Touroug** in particular, and several splendid kasbahs. It follows the river **Rheris**, which has created a lush strip of continuous palmery, populated and exhaustively culti-vated by the Ait Attas, who once dominated the region and demanded tribute from other, less warlike Berber tribes. Ruined kasbahs and an extensive grave-yard marked with pointed stones (to discourage jackals from digging up the bodies) betoken furious battles in the past. Notice also the mounds of sand and stones—in lines on one or both sides of the road—which once served as access points to irrigation channels known as *khettara*. These are no longer active, but similar mounds within cultivated palmeries in the region certainly are, and each family will be responsible for servicing a number of them.

El Dorf (58km) is a sizeable village with a huge *ksar* occupying one side of a long street that is said to house 6000 people. El Dorf has a fine triumphal arch and a cool colonnaded centre. From here it is palms and kasbahs all the way to Erfoud, with a particularly fine kasbah on the left, just 5km out of town.

The Ziz Valley, Erfoud, Rissani and Merzouga

The river **Ziz** cuts the most easterly route through the High Atlas to the Sahara. From Midelt the southbound P21 climbs up into the mountains crossing the range via the **Tizi-n-Talrhemt** ('Pass of the She-camel', 1970m) which marks quite brutally the change between temperate and desert vegetation. The road descends, crossing a bare plateau before reaching the valley of the Ziz at Ait Koujmane (7km south of Rich). **Rich** was important to the French as a base from which to control the warlike Ait Haddidou Berbers, but is now little more than a small market town approached from the main road by an unnecessarily pretentious avenue. From Rich there is a long but comparatively simple route across the plateau to Imilchil (110km).

The Ziz has carved a dramatic corridor through the mountains only to become lost in the desert sands south of Erfoud. The scenery is spectacular as the road

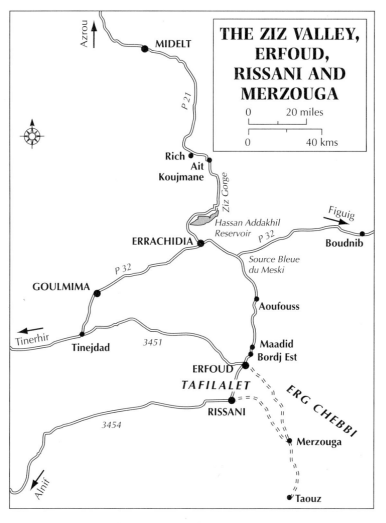

THE ZIZ VALLEY, ERFOUD, RISSANI AND MERZOUGA

enters the **Ziz Gorge**, passing first under the **Tunnel du Légionnaire** (built by French legionnaires during the Protectorate years and still always guarded). The river forms a narrow green strip, punctuated here and there by *ksour* and palms, and enclosed by stark, precipitous rock walls. It may almost completely disappear in the dry season but it can become a violent torrent after rain. It is now disciplined by a complex system of dams and reservoirs of which the **Hassan Addakhil dam** just north of Errachidia, completed in 1971, is a good example. Ziz water now irrigates the Tafilalet plain and the area to the south, instead of flooding and destroying Berber villages, as it did in the late 1960s. The damage to crops and homes at that time was incalculable and a decision was made to invest in a number of dams to keep the river within bounds and profit from its energy. This done, the region is now an agricultural success story and Errachidia is its focal point. **Errachidia** was created by the French as the administrative and commercial capital of the province of **Tafilalet**. Its geographical location gives it an obvious strategic importance: it stands at the crossroads between the great west–east route that crosses Morocco south of the High Atlas, and the main north–south route connecting Fes with the Tafilalet region and Erfoud by way of the Ziz corridor. For this reason, the town bristles with military and there are barracks to right and left of its magnificent triumphal arch. These exuberant arches are a feature of major southern towns and tend to set high expectations of what is to come—hopes that are all too often unjustified.

Because it was created by the French, Errachidia (formerly called Ksar es Souk) has no medina or historic buildings. It is built on a typical grid pattern, has a **handicraft centre** (*complexe artisanal*) on the main street, Boulevard Moulay Ali Cherif, and a covered market off the same street.

■ Practical information

Tourist office. **ONMT**. Blvd Moulay Ali Cherif
Buses. Bus station on the main square, Pl. Hassan II, leading off Blvd Moulay Ali Cherif.
Grands taxis. From the bus station.

Hotels
Hôtel Rissani, Route d'Erfoud. ☎ (05) 572 186 fax (05) 572 585. ****B (60 rooms). Not central, on the far bank of the river, but has a good restaurant.
Hôtel Oasis, 4 Rue Abou Abdellah. ☎ (05) 572 519. **A (46 rooms). Near the covered market, good restaurant and good value. If you must spend a night in Errachidia, this is the place to be.
Hôtel Meski, Blvd Moulay Ali Cherif. ☎ (05) 572 065. **B (25 rooms). An old hotel, with pool, out of town on the Midelt road.

Restaurants
Any of the above hotels, plus:
Restaurant Imilchil, Blvd Moulay Ali Cherif. Good value. Nice terrace.

The journey between Errachidia and Erfoud 77km away, by way of **Meski**, is delightful. The village of Meski is famous for its spring, which is 2km off the main road. Clearly signposted **La Source Bleue du Meski**, it gushes out from a cleft in the rock into a tank erected by French legionnaires for the purpose of swimming. It is now looking very sanitised within concrete walls and swimming is not permitted: it costs 5dh just to go and have a look. Overlooking the spring is a pleasant enough café-restaurant and there are various touristy shops below. There is also an attractive campsite amongst the palms by the water from the spring, with the river Ziz running alongside (beyond the wall).

Small boys—whose average age is around 9 years—who are not allowed into the campsite area, leap out of the bushes before you get to the spring and invite you for a guided tour of the adjacent palmery. They are very persistent and highly organised and take you on a delightful 10-minute walk past channels of crystalline water, oleanders and a distant *ksar*. From Meski a road runs eastwards 245km to Bouarfa.

After Meski you begin to catch glimpses of palm trees and fields of crops through gaps in the rock wall. In the middle of the valley the Ziz waters, in friendlier mood now, glint in the sun. From now on the *ksour* become more numerous and the valley throbs with life. Built throughout in beaten earth, or *pisé*, they are the most characteristic feature of the Ziz valley, surrounded by high walls, often minutely decorated with traditional Berber designs and pierced by richly carved archways. Inside are friendly people living a free and tranquil life in the privacy and cool shade afforded by the walls. These are Berber tribesmen, descended from desert nomads, who have come north in search of fertile plains and rivers. Similar people, living in similar conditions and working every inch of the land, are to be found in the Draa and Dades valleys (see above).

The road comes right down onto the bed of the Ziz and you drive amongst the palms, oleander and almond trees; children will rush out to wave and to try to sell you baskets of apricots or dates, or bunches of flowers. Seen from above, the Ziz valley must look like a green ribbon winding over an infinite stretch of sand and sunburnt rock. It is one endless oasis of date palms.

Aoufouss, midway between Meski and Erfoud, has three impressive *ksour* at its northern edge, each with its own mosque. **Maadid**, just before Erfoud, has another three, claiming to be 300 years old. Inside they are very dark and cool with narrow passages leading between houses, which appear lighter inside because they are built around central, open patios.

Erfoud

Erfoud is an attractive town, red and sandy and exuding desert atmosphere, though like Errachidia it was built in straight lines by the French in the 1930s as a base for controlling the Tafilalet region.

▓ Practical information

Buses. Station at Ave Mohammed V in the centre of town.
Grands taxis. From the bus station.

Hotels
Hôtel Salam, Route de Rissani. ☎ (05) 572 186 fax(05) 572 585. **** (156 rooms). At the west end of town. Traditional decor and glorious flower-decked swimming pool.
Hôtel Sijilmassa, ☎ (05) 576 003. ****B (75 rooms). Commands one of the loveliest desert views in Morocco.
Hôtel Tafilalet, Ave Moulay Ismael. ☎ (05) 576 535 fax (05) 576 036. ****B (20 rooms). Old style hotel. Very central. Also owns the *Auberge de Merzouga* next to Erg Chebbi, which offers tented accommodation (30dh a night) as well as camel expeditions into the desert. Bookings through the *Tafilalet*.

Restaurants
The above hotels, plus *Café des Dunes*, Ave Mohammed V.

Campsites
Camping Erfoud, by the Ziz river. Bookings through the ONMT in Errachidia.
Camping Source Bleu du Meski.

The town has a market place which is worth exploring for local produce and particularly for **dates**. Old men preside over crates of them and your aim should be to buy from a newly opened crate which has not yet developed a cloud of flies. Flies or not, the dates are wonderfully cheap, come in many different varieties and are undoubtedly a better buy than those sold in baskets by small boys on the roadside, which are of doubtful age and quite often turn out to be maggoty. Erfoud has its main date harvest in September each year and there is a major date festival in October, when the town really comes to life.

Erfoud is right on the edge of the sandy Sahara and is therefore a centre from which to make many trips. Tracks branch out in all directions towards the dunes, joining one oasis with the next and disappearing into the desert horizon. A good overall view used to be had by driving up to **Bordj Est**, a hillock on the edge of town, approached by a *piste* going left off the route to Merzouga (just across the Ziz). However, the *piste* has deteriorated so much, with ruts and rocks around every hairpin bend, that few small cars can make it, even to the military post stationed half way up, further than which one may not go anyway. The soldiers, who seemingly have little to do, watch from on high as you stop for the twentieth time to remove a rock.

Rissani
Rissani lies 22km to the south of Erfoud. The drive is through a continuous oasis of brilliant green squares of flourishing crops, irrigation canals and palms.

Sijilmassa
Just before entering the town, notice the crumbling sections of wall on the left. This is all that remains of Sijilmassa, an Arab city dating back to the early 8C. Well-placed on the earliest **caravan route** from the Sahara to Fes, it became notorious for greed, vice and slave trafficking and was several times sacked by both Almoravides and Almohades in their early, most pious years. Barely discernible a few metres up the rough track are the remains of a palace, whilst in the foreground are a *marabout* and a cemetery. This site was in danger of disappearing altogether beneath the encroaching sands, but excavations by the Moroccan Institute of Archaeology are now under way. Information on the site can be had from a small museum in Rissani.

Rissani's triumphal arch is grand and richly decorated and suggests greater prosperity than is to be found now. The town comprises a cluster of *ksour*, small houses grouped within impregnable walls with decorated towers and ornate entrances. Inside are all manner of souks and narrow passageways to be explored, and a charming arcaded market.

This region is proud to have been the cradle of the reigning Alouite dynasty, for it is from here that they emerged in the mid-17C, first conquering the southern oases and then taking Marrakesh and Fes from the Saadians. Many traces of their origins lie here, on the southeast side of Rissani, and are accessible either by walking through the town or by taking the well-signposted, 21km *Circuit Touristique* around the outside.

First there is the **Mausoleum of Moulay Ali Cherif**, founder of the Alouite dynasty. It was rebuilt in 1955 after the Ziz river overflowed its banks and carried much of the original building away. It is now open to non-Muslims. In front is a huge square where lively markets are held, usually on Sundays. There is a donkey park, but no car park. Men from different desert tribes, wearing flowing robes and turbans, bring their wares here to sell: strangely shaped pots, leather chests studded with brass, old jewellery, rugs and blankets. It is a fascinating scene. Behind the mausoleum—and worth the short walk or bumpy drive—is the beautiful carved entrance to a royal *ksar* known as **Ksar d'Akbar** which once served to house disgraced members of the Alouite family and the widows and concubines of its leading members.

Oulad Abd el Halim is another royal *ksar*; its remains include two fine gateways whose design and ornate carving remind one of the great *babs* of Meknes. It is thought to have been lived in by the early governors of the Tafilalet, many of whom were members of the royal family. Today what is left of it houses one or two carefully chosen families who subsist amongst the ruined walls, courtyards and overgrown gardens. Remarkably, some of the painted ceilings survive in apparently excellent condition because, the guides say, they were painted with egg tempera.

Merzouga and Erg Chebbi dunes

The journey from Erfoud to **Merzouga** (53km) to see the group of massive dunes collectively known as **Erg Chebbi** is a must. (*Erg* is the Arabic word for 'sand dune'.) People have often been disappointed by the Moroccan desert because so much of it is stony but here—in the Tafilalet—it surpasses all expectations, which explains why film companies love it and the locals are experts on all the movie stars.

The road from Erfoud—turning to *piste* after 16km—is perfectly feasible by small car (though four-wheel-drive enables you to go faster) but you should always take a guide unless you are very experienced in sand driving. Quite apart from the danger of getting stuck, or lost in a sand storm, the *piste* divides and divides again a number of times. Approaching Merzouga is fine because such is the size of the dunes that they become visible very early on, but returning is more tricky as there is nothing to point the car at. There is also the slight risk of straying into Algeria 80km to the east, though the military would almost certainly prevent this. Guides are available in the main hotels in Erfoud; Mokhtar at the *Tafilalet* is highly recommended. (There are 40km of *piste* between Rissani and Merzouga but this route is more difficult to follow and travelling in convoy is usually advised.)

Once you have crossed the Ziz and passed the turning to Bordj Est, you will see stalls selling both fossils and objects made of local marble, at half the price you pay in the hotels. Also for sale in the more remote areas are tiny guinea pig-like creatures, known as *poissons de sables* by the locals, who eat them. Paying children along the way simply to let the pathetic creatures go can become rather expensive. Other wildlife—which you probably will not see unless you camp under the stars—includes desert foxes, lizards and a number of snakes. Gazelles are no longer seen because of the drought, and flamingoes no longer congregate around the lake known as Dayet Srji, 2km west of Merzouga and approached by a *piste* leaving the village by the PTT building. Even in the 'wet season' from December to March it has been dry for the last few years.

There are various *auberges* along the way, the first being *Auberge Kasbah Derkaoua*, 6km from the beginning of the *piste*. It is run by a Frenchman and has ten rooms, but it is still some way from the dunes. Accommodation becomes more plentiful once you reach the first village—**Hạs el Beida**—which is 3km before **Merzouga**. Neither village is beautiful in itself, having adapted too fast to increasing attention from tourists, film-makers and the Paris–Dakar rally which passes this way. (There is even a *Depot Nomade Artisanal* selling carpets.) Forget the villages and look at the dunes, burning orange in the evening sun and truly magnificent: the biggest is 200m high. They are said to be growing in size and moving very slowly northwards. Well-informed visitors get up at 03.00 in the summer to see the sun rise, or arrive at 18.00 in the evening. Moroccans also come (we were told) to bury themselves in the sand at temperatures of 60–80°C to cure their rheumatism.

At the foot of the biggest dune is the *Auberge de Merzouga* (an annexe of the *Tafalilet* in Erfoud) which has a few rooms, but whose main attractions are its caidal tents; a night under canvas with hot showers laid on costs just 30dh; camel trips are available to take the intrepid even further. There is a doubtful track continuing south a further 24km from Merzouga to rejoin the Ziz river at the much smaller oasis of **Taouz**. Beyond lies the Algerian border and the wilderness of the Sahara.

The East ~ Figuig

There is little of interest in the neglected, eastern flank of Morocco other than Figuig, right by the Algerian border. It is accessible either from Errachidia via Meski (399km) and the windswept mining town of Bouarfa, or from Oujda (376km). Both routes are featureless and empty; the former passes through various mining villages, and the latter is relieved by fairly frequent old forts (*bordjs*), many now in ruins and little more than picturesque silhouettes on the desert skyline, recalling vividly the story of *Beau Geste*. The roads are good, however, there are no mountain ranges to cross and the going is fast. Both journeys give some idea of the huge extent of the country, and those addicted to isolation and vast open spaces will enjoy themselves. Tourists are almost non-existent. Needless to say, there are no filling stations along the way, though there is one as you enter Figuig from the north.

Figuig has great character and charm. It is one of the largest of the southern oases and is said to have over 200,000 palm trees. It consists of seven separate *ksour*, each with its own individual palmery enclosed within crumbling turreted ramparts, and signposted from the main road. It is not hard to believe that until the beginning of this century the seven were constantly in a state of simmering and sometimes quite bloody dispute, usually over the scarce water supplies. This explains the number of towers erected to watch over precious irrigation channels (they now make good vantage points from which to survey the whole fascinating oasis scene).

■ Practical information

Buses. Services leave daily for Errachidia and Oujda from the northwest corner of the 'El Oudarhir' ksar.

Hotels
There are no classified hotels.
Hôtel Diamant Vert, Zenaga *ksar*. ☎ (06) 699 030. Recommended; it has a very few basic rooms and a pool, but no food.

Restaurants
Café Oasis, Zenaga *ksar*. Good quality, simple Moroccan cooking—usually no choice of menu.

Campsites
The *Diamant Vert* allows camping in its garden.

Figuig's strategic position on the border with Algeria has frequently involved it in wars with that country, not least during the reign of the expansionist sultan, Moulay Ismael, who in the early 18C first lost the settlement and then won it back again. It was also until recently a departure point for pilgrims leaving by camel for Mecca. At time of writing, Figuig is once again full of soldiers and the mood is tense.

Figuig is, however, different from anywhere else in some indefinable way, its palms providing welcome coolness wherever you go (and this is just as well, as it has the reputation of being the hottest place in Morocco). Of the seven *ksour*, some are worthier of a visit than others: the largest is **Zenaga** with a modern administrative centre and a welcome café. **El Maiz** is probably the most picturesque with its maze of narrow shady streets and terraced houses. **El Hammam**, as the name implies, boasts a hot spring where people can perform their ablutions before entering the mosque.

The Anti Atlas, Tiznit and Tafraoute

The **Anti Atlas** range runs parallel to the High Atlas and to the south of it. Between the two ranges at the western end is the very fertile plain of the rivers Souss and Massa and from here the land rises gradually eastwards towards the great volcanic mass of the **Jbel Sirwa**. Some of the peaks rise to over 2500m. All of this mountain area is good for trekking, with a network of tracks and frequent villages with willing guides.

The road from Agadir to Tiznit (88km) crosses the coastal plain described above. The Oued Massa is found about two thirds of the way down and has been dammed upriver by the **Youssef-ibn-Tachfine dam**, to make an enormous reservoir which provides irrigation for fruit and early vegetables. A major attraction here is the **Souss Massa National Park**, created in 1991 and now covering some 32,500 acres around the estuary of the river, where reed beds and sand banks provide a perfect environment for hordes of over-wintering and

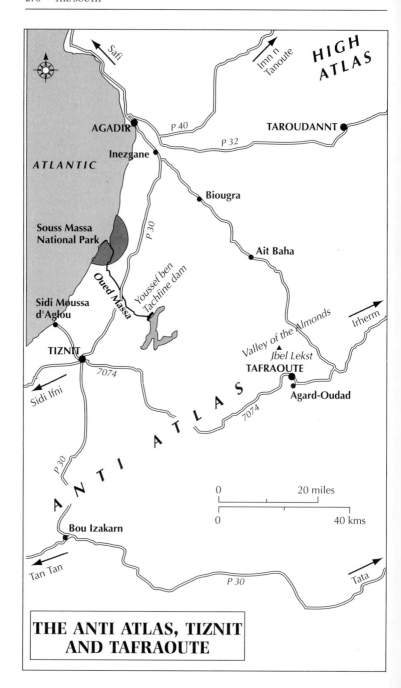

Safi

Imn n
Tanoute

HIGH
ATLAS

AGADIR

P 40

TAROUDANNT

P 32

ATLANTIC

Inezgane

Biougra

Souss Massa
National Park

P 30

Ait Baha

Youssef ben
Tachfine dam

Oued Massa

Sidi Moussa
d'Aglou

Valley of the Almonds

Irherm

Jbel Lekst

TIZNIT

TAFRAOUTE

7074

A N T I   A T L A S

Agard-Oudad

Sidi Ifni

7074

P 30

0   20 miles

0   40 kms

Bou Izakarn

Tan Tan

P 30

Tata

THE ANTI ATLAS, TIZNIT
AND TAFRAOUTE

migrating birds including flamingoes, herons, storks and ospreys. Some of the rapidly dwindling world population of bald ibis is also said to nest here.

The village of **Massa**, a little way inland from the coast and acessible from either Tiferhal or Ait Bella on the main road, is thought to be the spot where, in 670, the first Arab invader, Oqba ibn Nafi rode his horse into the sea, triumphantly proclaiming that only the ocean prevented him from from carrying Islam's conquest even further.

Tiznit

Tiznit lies at the western end of the Anti Atlas. It is a typical pre-Saharan walled town of considerable charm, with houses that are flat-roofed and red or ochre-coloured. It is set in a cluster of palm trees which form a romantic backcloth to the crenellated walls and stocky square towers which are so characteristic of pre-Saharan architecture.

History of Tiznit

Surprisingly, perhaps, this is not an old town at all but was built by Sultan Moulay el Hassan in 1881, albeit enclosing within its 6km of walls several existing *ksour*. The town's function was military. It was built as a base from which to pacify the Chleuh Berbers and later the French were to use it for the same purpose. They kept a large garrison there and used what is today the main square, the Mechouar, as their parade ground. Today, the Mechouar is the focal point for banks, the post office, and a *centre artisanal*, as well as being the main stopping-place for buses.

◼ Practical information

Buses leave from the Mechouar to Tafraoute, Goulimine, Agadir and Casablanca.
Grands taxis go from the far end of Ave du 20 Août, which leads off the Mechouar.

Hotels

There are three classified hotels in Tiznit, all bunched together by the main roundabout south of town.

Hôtel de Tiznit, Rue Bir Inzaran. ☎ (08) 862 411. ***B (40 rooms). Despite its unpromising-looking site next to a petrol station, this hotel is peaceful inside and the rooms are grouped around a charming courtyard with bougainvillaea cascading over the walls, and oleander and rosemary surrounding the small swimming pool. Recommended.

Hôtel de Paris, Ave Hassan II. ☎ (08) 862 865. **A (20 rooms). A new hotel with quite a good restaurant.

Hôtel Mauritania, Rue de Goulimine. ☎ (08) 862 072. *A (16 rooms). Very modest but clean.

Restaurants

There are several restaurants grouped around the Mechouar, with nothing much to choose between them. Probably the best place to eat is at one of the above hotels.

Campsites

Camping Tiznit, located on the road which runs between the main southern roundabout and the town walls, near Bab Oulad Jarrar.

Tiznit is often referred to as Morocco's **'silver capital'** and its people have long been known for their delicate work in silver—filigree bracelets and necklaces, belts, daggers encrusted with semi-precious stones and much else. The craft goes on in small workshops, somewhat grandly called *fabriques*, which are dotted around the town. You will certainly be pressed to go and see at least one and will notice that the most delicate filigree work is done by young boys, often working in poor light: 'small fingers and good eyes' the explanation goes, but one feels the eyes will not stay 'good' for long in those conditions. A complete range of this work is for sale in the jewellery market (**Souk des Bijoutiers**)—a square of shops with little to choose between them, to be found behind the **Mechouar**, just inside the **Gate of the Three Doors** (*Les Trois Portes*).

But the real glory of Tiznit is its antique jewellery, and no one should miss the **Ancien Souk** in Rue Si Belid with its rose-coloured walls and its collection of stalls where the old men display their wares. (Any small boy will take you there.) Tiznit is a trading post between north and south: much of the new silverware is taken by nomads down to the Saharan region (perhaps as far as Mauritania or Mali) where it is exchanged for antiques—filigree jewel boxes lined with camel-skin, caskets in silver with coral or turquoise, ink wells made of camel-bone and silver (for writing Koranic texts), heavy necklaces made from silver coins and tiny pieces of coral mounted on fine chains. Much of this is then sold to merchants from the big cities like Fes or Marrakesh, who sell it on to the tourists in the souks. The lesson here is obvious. Tiznit (or Goulimine further south) is the place to buy from the widest range and at the lowest prices. But be warned: such treasures often look less impressive (or perhaps too exotic) in a Western setting.

Apart from the permanent Ancien Souk, there are other places to buy. Some of the Berber middle-men rest a while before heading either south to buy or north to sell, and will be delighted to display their wares, which they keep in their houses in vast wooden chests. Since their progeny tend to roam the streets as (often very knowledgeable) guides, it is difficult to avoid the experience, which will follow a very precise protocol: you are invited in to take tea—first in the outer room and then in the inner sanctum; the treasure chest is pulled from the wall and the items are lifted out with great pride (the guide acting as interpreter); once everything has been laid before you, 'not for buying, just for looking', a wooden bowl is offered in which to place the objects which particularly please you. (If you really do not want to buy anything at all, it is better to stop at this point, admire the goods and gracefully withdraw.) That done, you are asked to write down on a piece of paper, conveniently to hand, the prices you would be prepared to pay for any of them. The paper will pass backwards and forwards between you in solemn silence as each side changes the figures up or down. Finally a compromise is reached, the articles change hands, the money is counted, the silence is broken and more tea is served. There is an elegant and timeless inevitability about the whole process which is quite delightful.

Tiznit does not offer much in the way of interesting buildings but the **Grand Mosque**, in the centre of town, has an unusual minaret with small wooden stakes sticking out of it, said to facilitate the dead in their climb up to Paradise. Next door to the mosque is a sacred spring. Legend claims that a town was founded here some 1500 years ago in memory of a reformed prostitute who was martyred; it is said that at the moment of her death a miraculous spring gushed forth from the spot where she fell. The lady in question is the town's patron saint and the spring, still revered as a holy place, is called **Source Bleue de Lalla Tiznit**, though sadly it is now no more than a dirty, stagnant pool.

From Tiznit a road goes west 17km to the attractive beach of **Sidi Moussa d'Aglou**, with its troglodyte fishermen's huts dug into the rock face. There is very little else to see apart from the vast stretches of untouched sand and the magnificent Atlantic rollers.

Another road leaves Tiznit heading westwards before running down the coast to Sidi Ifni (43km). The coastal stretch is lovely and—about 2km after the head-land village of **Mirhleft**—there is a particularly good sandy beach overlooked by a *marabout*'s shrine set inside ancient walls.

Sidi Ifni was built in 1934 by the Spaniards, who were finally taking up a right granted to them by the Treaty of Tetouan in 1860 to have a small enclave within reach of the Canary Islands.They did not leave until 1969. Today Sidi Ifni is a rather depressing, has-been sort of place. The large central Plaza Mayor, now renamed **Place Hassan II**, retains its central Andalusian garden, with a typical pebble mosaic pavement. Ranged around it are the sad and locked-up Consulate-General and a collection of decaying pink-and-white official buildings. Here too the Moroccans have built a new town hall, boldly candy-striped in pink and white as if to revive the jolly, Art Deco, mood. There is also a memorial commem-orating the date of the Spanish surrender on 30 June 1969, and a Moroccan fort up on the hill to guard against any future invaders.

Hotels

Hôtel Ait Baamran, Rue de la Plage. ☎ (08) 875 267. *A (20 rooms). Has a good fish restaurant.

Hôtel Belle Vue, 9 Pl. Hassan II. ☎ (08) 875 072. *A (16 rooms). Up to 1969 this must have been the place to be. The building still retains vestiges of grandeur but little in the way of comfort.

Restaurants

Restaurant Tamimt, Ave Hassan II. Good simple food, mainly Moroccan.
Restaurant Atlantic, 1 Ave Houria. Satisfying German cooking.

Campsites

Camping Sidi Ifni, Ave Sidi Mohammed.

From Sidi Ifni there is a picturesque and winding coastal road to Goulimine (57km).

Tafraoute

Tafraoute lies 111km east of Tiznit in the heart of the Anti Atlas. This is a beautiful, if fairly wearing, drive of some three hours through rugged and gargantuan landscapes. The tarmac strip in the middle of the road is just wide enough for one car and the battle to stay on it rather than move on to the rocky hard shoulder is usually won by large and tight-packed Mercedes *grands taxis*, which claim it as their right. That said, this scenic and dramatic drive should on no account be missed: houses of red earth, sometimes painted an ochre colour, are built high up on the rocks, one above the other, backed by great vertical rock masses in chaotic shapes. (There is a good example of gravity-defying boulders around the village of **Adai**, just 3km before reaching Tafraoute.) The area is sparsely cultivated and only the almond trees seem to flourish. Indeed, Tafraoute is much visited in early spring when the almond trees are in blossom. The **almond festival** is in mid-February but the exact date changes from year to year.

Tafraoute

The town of **Tafraoute** lies at 1300m in a kind of amphitheatre—a complete circle of rose-coloured granite rocks perched on top of one another and studded with date palms and almond trees. The best view of the town is from the terrace of the *Hôtel Les Amandiers* which is built high above it in traditional kasbah style. Tafraoute itself is soon explored and merits less time than Tiznit, though it has a range of shops and modest restaurants and a fair amount of local **craftwork**, notably at *Coin des Nomades*, *Artisanat du Coin* and the *Maison Touareg*, all in the town centre. There is a lively souk every Wednesday.

■ Practical information

Buses leave from the main street, a 5min walk eastwards from *Hôtel Tafraoute*.
Grands taxis also leave from there, as well as Pl. Massira, in the centre of town.
Mountain bikes can be hired from a shop on Pl. Massira (opposite the post office).

Hotels

Hôtel Les Amandiers, ☎: (08) 800 080. ****B. Caters for tour groups and the service is sometimes slapdash. But the wonderful views make up for it, and there really is not much choice in Tafraoute.

Hôtel Tafroute, Pl. Moulay Rachid. ☎ (08) 800 121. * A cheaper option—in town and next to a filling station.

Restaurants

L'Etoile du Sud. Good Moroccan food served in a rather touristy tent. But it can be fun.

Campsites

Les Trois Palmiers, off the Agard-Oudad road.

The best thing about Tafraoute is the surrounding countryside, which offers a wealth of villages to explore and mountain tracks to walk or drive. This is prehistoric rock-carving country and local guides are available at the *Hôtel Les Amandiers* to show you where to go. The hotel also has a good large-scale map of the area to enable you to plan your walks.

Particularly recommended is the Ameln Valley or the **Valley of the Almonds**, which forms a shallow cresent north of Tafraoute. The 20 or so Ameln villages stand on the south-facing slopes of the Jbel Lekst (2359m), their red houses clinging precariously to the mountainside, with irrigated fields on narrow terraces beneath them and their tiny gardens dotted with palm trees. One of the most picturesque and accessible of the villages is **Oumesnat**, which lies 8km northeast of Tafraoute. From here there is a delightful walk westwards along the valley, picking your way over the many streams and irrigation channels which flow down the mountain. The road eventually joins up with the Tiznit–Tafraoute road (7074) at **Souk Ad Tahala** (c 15km in all).

Valley homes

Some of the houses in the area seem remarkably richly decorated and well-maintained. This is because many of them are the family homes of local men who have moved north, perhaps even to Europe, and worked long and hard for many years as shopkeepers, usually grocers (*épiciers*), in the big towns. They are part of the tribe of Chleuh Berbers who are well-known for their business acumen and energy. As time goes on they convert their earnings into land and houses back home. Children stay in the valley with their mothers and grandmothers, who tend the almond trees, while fathers continue making money elsewhere, affording themselves the occasional holiday on their 'country estates' and eventually retiring there. This unusual lifestyle probably dates from the early 1880s when there was serious crop failure and men had to find work elsewhere in order to feed their families. Now they have the best of both worlds. The houses tend to be square and flat-roofed and are built around a central courtyard: there is usually a squat tower at one corner. The windows are usually outlined in white, doors are often bright blue.

Another recommended excursion is to the village of **Agard-Oudad**, 3km south of Tafraoute on the 7075 road. It is sited hard up against a dramatic spur of rock known locally as *le chapeau de Napoléon*. One kilometre further on are the 'painted rocks' or **Les Pierres Bleus**—a somewhat bizarre cluster of blue and pink rocks which were painted in 1984 by a Belgian artist, Jean Veran, and which undeniably fit quite comfortably into this grandiose and already brightly coloured setting.

If not driving back to Tiznit, from Tafraoute you can either go northeastwards to Irherm (62km)—but note that the road surface deteriorates to *piste* after about 24km—and thence north to Taroudannt (a further 89km); or you can stay on the main road all the way to Agadir (127km), a route which offers spectacular mountain scenery and an endless succession of hilltop villages as far as the small market town of Ait Baha; thereafter it crosses the Souss plain.

The Pre Sahara: the oasis route

Bou Izkarn to Tata

The route from Bou Izakarn to Tata (245km and paved all the way) runs from west to east through the stony pre-Saharan desert. It is generously scattered with oases teeming with activity thanks to frequent streams coming down from the mountains north of it, which are harnessed for sophisticated irrigation systems enabling the cultivation of a wide range of cereals, fruit and vegetables. Added attractions are the prehistoric rock-carvings, particularly around Foum el Hassan, the vast herds of camels and the friendly Berber people. The desert

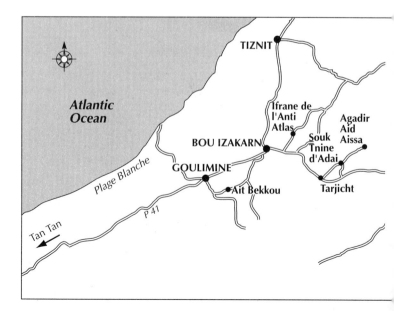

terrain at this point is disappointingly grey and rocky and anyone hankering after 'real' sandy desert should go to Laayoune or to the Tafilalet region further east (see above).

There is very little in the way of filling stations, accommodation or refreshment along the way, except at Tata. Moreover (at time of writing) there are fairly frequent military road blocks, where your passport will be requested and possibly taken away for checking. This can be both time-consuming and irritating.

Take the P30 eastwards out of **Bou Izakarn**, which itself has little to offer, other than one classified hotel, the *Anti Atlas*, Route de Goulimine, ☎ (08) 874 134 (**B, 10 rooms). The first point of interest is **Ifrane de l'Anti Atlas** lying some 8km north of the main road along the 7076, which turns northwards 14km east of Bou Izakarn. It is a large and colourful oasis, divided by walls into three administrative zones, each with its own kasbah. It once had a huge Jewish community that dated back to pre-Islamic days and the ruins of the *mellah* are still very much in evidence, as indeed is the Jewish cemetery up the hill, with Hebrew-inscribed tombstones, many of them now broken. This is a sad but very evocative place, said to be one of the last to convert to Islam. From here, incidentally, a track continues 50km northwards to join up with the main Tiznit–Tafraoute road at the **Kerdous Pass**.

Back on the P30, continue east to the oasis of **Tarjicht** where a minor road goes off left to **Agadir Aid Aissa**, by way of Souk Tnine d'Adai (21km in all). The main attraction here is the impressive and very ancient *agadir*—a traditional fortified storehouse for food (mainly dates) and weapons which would have served the whole community, and was undoubtedly necessary in the days before the Protectorate when Berber tribes preyed on each other's villages. This is one

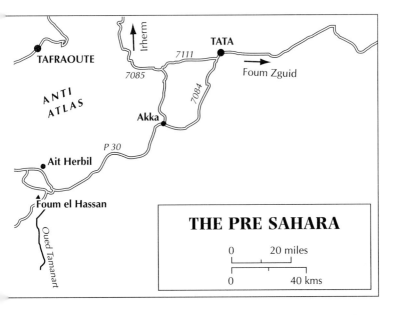

of the biggest and best preserved *agadirs* in the south, made more imposing by its position on a hill (which you can walk up if you want to peer inside).

On your return, the left-hand fork at Souk Tnine d'Adai will take you further along the P30 in the direction of **Foum el Hassan**, an oasis which lies by the river Tamanart. This region is rich in **prehistoric rock-carvings** and there will be no shortage of small boys in the village (or in Ait Herbil just before it) to lead you to them. There are images of gazelles, bison, birds, and even elephants, which would have roamed the Sahara around 2000 BC when these carvings are thought to have been made. It is a rare treat to be able to see such unique treasures in so informal and uncrowded a setting. There is no need to crawl through dark and slippery caves; these rocks are widely scattered beneath the desert sun, albeit requiring a steepish scramble (10–15min) from the road.

Akka lies 58km further east. Located on one of the ancient Saharan caravan routes, it is the largest of ten villages in a very fine palm grove stretching northwards. The whole oasis is noted for a particularly sweet and delicious variety of date, known as *bousekri*, and people also grow barley and maize, figs, grapes and vegetables, thanks to an intricate network of irrigation channels. This is a lush, cool place in which to pause awhile, take a walk, and eat some dates; but beware of tempting pools which may well harbour bilharzia. There is a lively souk every Thursday.

Tata

Continue 62km to Tata, a large and relatively sophisticated oasis town watered by three streams from the Anti Atlas, which have made possible a surprisingly green central square—**Place Marche Verte**—from which buses run to Tiznit and Agadir, or to Taroudannt via Irherm. (This is also the place to negotiate the cost of a *grand taxi*, if you want to continue eastwards and do not feel your vehicle is up to rough *pistes*.) Tata has a bank, a filling station and even a **handicraft centre** (*centre d'artisanat*), all located around the Place Marche Verte, and there are various restaurants and two classified hotels.

Hotels

Le Relais des Sables, Ave des F.A.R. ☎ (08) 802 301. ***. A new hotel with good restaurant, gardens and a swimming pool.
Hôtel La Renaissance, Ave des F.A.R. ☎ (08) 802 042. **B. Restaurant but no pool.

Campsites

There is a campsite on Ave Mohammed V, beside the municipal swimming pool.

At Tata there are several route options: the road eastwards to **Foum Zguid** (142km) is now tarmacked but poorly maintained. Foum Zguid is an oasis with welcome shade but little in the way of refreshment. From there it is possible to drive north to **Tazenakht**, on mountain track which is tough going but has plenty of villages along the way, or continue eastwards a further 120km to Zagora and the Draa valley (see above). The Foum Zguid–Zagora stretch is *piste*, there are far fewer oases, and it is extremely easy to get lost. It is not recommended without a 4WD vehicle.

Alternatively you can drive from Tata to **Irherm** and on to Taroudannt. This is a spectacular mountain road which is paved all the way. Take the 7111 westwards out of Tata and rejoin the 7085 coming from Akka. Continue northwards along the palm-lined Akka Valley, over the **Tizi-Touzlimt** to Irherm (120km), and thence to Taroudannt 88km further on. Irherm is a small market town selling mainly copper pots. Copper used to be mined here and Irherm was an important staging-post for Saharan caravans. The last alternative is to go back to Bou Izakarn and thence onwards to Goulimine (41km).

Goulimine, Tan Tan and Tarfaya

Goulimine is frankly a disappointment. This once dignified and eminently Saharan town, which was an important stopping-point on the caravan route from Timbuktu, has now expanded into a noisy commercial centre depending largely for its prosperity on the groups of tourists who are brought here regularly by coach to see a way of life which no longer exists. The charming colonnaded section (now called **Place Hassan II**) is still there, right in the middle, but completely engulfed.

■ Practical information

Buses run from the old Sidi Ifni road, at the northern end of town.
Grands taxis go from the southern end of Blvd Mohammed V.

Hotels
Hôtel Salam, Route de Tantan. ☎ (08) 872 057. **B (19 rooms). Still retains its Saharan character and has a flat roof to escape to on a hot, airless summer night. The restaurant is good, too.
Hôtel Tighmert, Ait Bekkou. ☎ (08) 873 053. ****. An imposing-looking, kasbah-style hotel amongst the palm trees. Large and often nearly empty, but that must be because it is so new and little known. The restaurant is good.

Restaurants
Apart from the *Hôtel Salam*, there really is not much to recommend in Goulimine itself. However, the *Tighmert* at Ait Bekkou and *Fort Bou-Jerif* are both outstanding in their way.

Campsites
Camping Goulimine, on the edge of town.
Fort Bou-Jerif, BP 504, Goulimine.

The once famous Saturday camel market (1.5km out of town on the Tan Tan road) is now almost exclusively given over to goats. The few camels there are have probably been brought in for butchery only, and trading in fine camels goes on in the less accessible oases to the south. 'Now it is the camels who photograph the tourists,' our guide said, somewhat cynically. Two facts that help to explain the demise of the camel market are the tendency of the region's Berbers to give up their nomadic lifestyle and settle down to raise livestock and grow crops in the plentiful oases, and to see trucks as an easier option for transport.

At least the local Berbers retain their very fine romantic image—swathed in sand-repellent indigo blue cotton robes whose dye is so little fixed that the colour comes off on their skins, which are permanently tinged with blue—hence their popular name of 'blue men'. They wear the ends of their blue, black or white turbans wound round their mouths as a protection against the sand-carrying wind which never ceases to blow, and this undoubtedly adds a touch of mystery to their noble demeanour.

The traditional *guedra* is also a thing of the past. This erotic dance performed (sometimes for hours on end) by a woman on her knees and moving only the top part of her body, to the accompaniment of clapping and drumming, is now only ever put on for visiting tourist groups. The memorable hot, sticky *guedras* in cafés and tents are gone for ever, it seems, at least from Goulimine.

For a night or two in an unspoilt oasis, take a minor road southeastwards to Asrir and then a further 6km on *piste* to **Ait Bekkou**, where a new, traditional style, hotel has just opened—the *Tighmert* (see above). Whether you stay there or not, the drive is worth doing, past scores of grazing camels (all the ones you did not see in Goulimine) and a good sprinkling of typical black Berber tents, made of woven camel hair. These tents are surprisingly cool and spacious inside, last for some 20 years and are usually lined with brightly-coloured rugs.

Ait Bekkou oasis is a pleasure to walk around, especially at sundown, and there is a surprising amount of activity going on amongst the palm trees. Thanks to a constant supply of water, the people are able to grow barley, maize, grenadines and quinces, as well as the ubiquitous prickly pear, known locally as 'Berber figs'.

An excursion to **La Plage Blanche**—a long stretch of white beach extending over 50km southwest of Goulimine—is also worthwhile. There is paved road for 13km (to Tiseguenane) and then 18km of good *piste*, which will bring you to the northern edge of the beach and an old French Legion fort—Fort Bou-Jerif—where an enterprising French couple run a restaurant with rooms and a camp-site.

Tan Tan

Tan Tan lies 125km southwest of Goulimine, an easy drive over a rather bleak stretch of desert. (Note there is a filling station with a cafe 50km south of Goulimine.)

■ Practical information

Buses. Daily services to Agadir and Laayoune from Pl. de la Marche Verte.
Grands taxis also congregate at Pl. de la Marche Verte and can be negotiated as far as Agadir or Laayoune.
Air transport. Royal Air Maroc, Ave de la Ligue Arabe. ☎ (08) 877 259. The airport is 9km from town. ☎ (08) 877 143. Flights to Agadir, Casablanca and Laayoune.

Hotels
Hôtel Amgala, Ave de la Jeunesse. ☎ (08) 877 308. *A (29 rooms).
Hôtel L'Etoile du Sahara, 17 Rue El Fida. ☎ (08) 877 085. (34 rooms).

Restaurants

Nothing to speak of in town other than a few cafés around the Place de la Marche Verte. There is a good fish restaurant (*L'Etoile de l'Ocean*) at Tan Tan Plage and more are promised.

Two stone camels bestride the road as you enter the town, to form a sort of *arc de triomphe*. Tan Tan achieved instant fame on 5 November 1975 as a starting-point for the Green March, described below. Today it has returned to being a modest outpost, which really comes to life only once a year, in June, when it hosts the **moussem of Sidi Mohammed Laghdari**. This event attracts a huge gathering of Saharans and 'blue men' with their camels, some of whom will have come from as far south as Mauritania. Camel racing, rather than *fantasia*, is the order of the day, and it is all far more colourful and exciting than anything Goulimine has to offer.

Not surprisingly, the centre of Tan Tan has been renamed **Place de la Marche Verte** and it is here that the main administrative buildings, hotels, banks, *grands taxis* etc. are concentrated.

The main P41 road continues 25km westwards to **Tan Tan Plage**, and the port which is responsible for much of the country's sardine industry. The beach could be lovely but, at time of writing, has a rather neglected and grubby feel to it. There are apparently big plans for tourist development in the future.

The road from Tan Tan to Tarfaya is tarmacked for all of its 236km. For most of the way, it hugs the shoreline and only deviates from it to encompass the salt lake of **Sebkhat Tazra**. Somewhat surprisingly, the road is set up on a cliff for much of the way, and fishermen can sometimes be seen swinging their baskets over the brink to collect the catch their colleagues have snatched from the sea. It is they who most probably inhabit the tents scattered about the cliff edge. There are a few other features to break the journey: the river **Chebeika** about 40km south of Tan Tan Plage, for example, forms its own lagoon, surrounded by dunes and attractive to flamingoes, where it reaches the sea; the village of **Sidi Akhfennir**, at about the halfway point, has rudimentary cafés and a filling station (which could quite easily be empty); there are more inlets and lagoons along the way, particularly the **Lagoon Khenifis** 80km north of Tarfaya, which is rich in fish, migratory birds and other wildlife and has been registered as a natural park—moreover, fishing boats are available for hire from the lagoon. As you approach Tarfaya the cliffs disappear and the road rejoins the coastline, scattered with shipwrecks from times past.

Tarfaya

Tarfaya was occupied by the British in 1876, when a Scot called Mackenzie used it as a trading post. He built a fort and lighthouse, known locally as **La Casamar** ('House of the Sea'), of which but a single-storey bastion remains offshore. At that time the town was called Port Victoria. Mackenzie left in 1884 when, it is said, he fell out with the sultan, Moulay el Hassan.

The Spaniards established themselves here in 1920, during their Protectorate, and renamed the place Villa Bens. They built a few houses, a church, and a fort which overlooks the town. It was all returned to Morocco in 1958 when the town became, once more, Tarfaya.

Tarfaya was also an important staging-post and resting-place for pilots of the French **Service Aéropostale** delivering mail to and from West African countries in the 1920s. There is a memorial to the aviator and novelist, Antoine de Saint Exupéry who wrote his novel, *Courrier Sud,* in Tarfaya. A nearly lifesize model of his Bréguet biplane stands on a plinth on the sandy shore, seemingly poised to take off over the Atlantic once more. The service is commemorated every October by the Toulouse–Dakar Rally when pilots land their small planes at Tarfaya for a night of feasting in caidal tents on the beach before continuing on to Senegal the next day. Opposite the memorial is the **pasha's house** and the **old souk**; the latter is worth walking through, but the former is closed.

Until quite recently, Tarfaya was an important sardine port, but this has now declined because of a serious problem of sand encroachment. Our guide boasted that Tarfaya sardines were the best in Morocco, much better than those from Safi which, he alleged, is seriously polluted. We tasted them, freshly grilled on the roadside and absolutely delicious.

There are no classified hotels or restaurants in Tarfaya, just one or two very basic cafés, and the sardine grills.

The Western Sahara, Laayoune and beyond

The **Western Sahara** is gradually opening up for tourism. Indeed, the Moroccan government is positively encouraging visitors to go to Laayoune, the capital of the region, which is receiving major investment in hotels, roads, an airport (with direct flights to the Canary Islands), and a desalination plant on the coast to provide drinking water for the growing population, and has a very efficient and friendly tourist office. There are five classified hotels, of which two are in the luxury class, and many of the major banks have set up branches. There are also regular long distance and 'local' bus services and plenty of *grands taxis.*

The Western Sahara is the most rewarding and beautiful region to visit. You really have not seen, or experienced, desert until you come here. It is a very complete experience and quite unlike any other. There is the desert landscape itself, with glistening white and hazy pink salt pans, many of which are stilll worked (Sebkat Tazra just north of Tarfaya, for example, produces 20 million metric tonnes of salt a year), and the occasional white buildings along the road-side are almost certain to be salt cooperatives. Then there is the sudden and incongruous blue of a lagoon or river glimpsed between the dunes, and the wonderful array of robust and free-roaming dromedaries.

The road between Tarfaya and Laayoune (115km) is highly recommended. There are salt pans and lagoons along the way, herds of dromedaries and, above all, the sort of sandy desert that dreams are made of (the Erg Lakhbayta). Why are so many signposts along the road bent or otherwise damaged? The 'vandals' turned out to be the dromedaries themselves, scratching their necks ecstatically on the hard posts. Indeed, at one obviously irresistible signpost, two were queuing up, one behind the other, awaiting their turn. It has to be said that

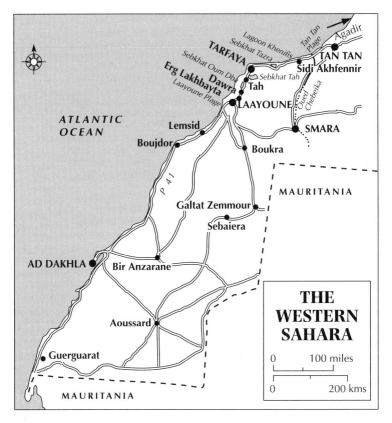

many lagoons and salt-workings are some way off the road and it is wise to have with you a local guide who will know just where to stop the car and lead you (sometimes as much as half an hour's drive or walk over *piste*).

35km south of Tarfaya is a historic spot called **Tah**. This is where the Western Sahara officially starts, for Tah marks the spot where the old Spanish province of Seguiet el Hamra fell in 1975. On either side of the road there is a memorial stone: one reads '1886 Visit of Hassan I' and the other commemorates a visit by the present king, Hassan II, on 3 March 1985.

Sebkhat Tah is an extremely deep salt lake which is below sea-level. It is best seen by walking or driving a little way along a *piste* which runs eastwards immediately after Tah. There have been ideas of turning the lake into a tourist attraction but, apparently, no money with which to do it.

A few kilometres south of Tah, on the seaward side of the main road, is **Sebkhat Oum Dba**, approached along a track for some 3km. Here, in the midst of so much scrubby, sandy nothingness, in a shallow gorge, is a river—the **Oum Dba**—which runs for 20km and then completely disappears into the sand. In the dry season it disappears altogether. It is an almost miraculous sight and probably quite unfindable without a guide. Overwintering flamingoes and other birds sometimes come here; jagged chunks of rock resistant to wind erosion stand out of the sand; and salt crystals give the scene an unearthly translucence.

Dawra, the next point of interest, is a village dating from Protectorate times. It has 120 palm trees and 5000 people, who can live there because of numerous wells and a river which enable them to grow cereals and vegetables. It lies a little way east of the main road and is worth the short diversion.

The Green March and its consequences

On 5 November 1975, 350,000 unarmed Moroccans led by King Hassan II walked across the old frontier and reclaimed the former Spanish provinces of Seguiet el Hamra and Rio de Oro (now called the Western Sahara). From the Moroccan point of view there was some historical justification for reasserting Morocco's **sovereignty** over the area, going back as far as the Saadian conquests in the 16C, and a visit in the late 19C by Moulay el Hassan. A very readable book by King Hassan II himself, *Le Défi*, spells it all out.

At the time of my last visit, in October 1996, the Western Sahara was still officially regarded by European, US and Canadian governments as 'occupied territory'. The United Nations had, at that time, stopped trying to identify voters for its referendum (see *History of Morocco*) as there was still disagreement about criteria and—the UN claimed—people were being 'shipped in' to swell the number of voters. The Identification Commission had, it was alleged, gone home, though I discovered Laayoune hotels still full of UN personnel, amongst whom I was the only tourist. There have been various positive developments in 1997, including revitalised attempts by the UN to mediate between the governments and organisations involved (Morocco, Algeria, Mauritania and the Polisario), and the creation of autonomous Moroccan regions, of which the Western Sahara is one.

A second negative factor arising from all this is the number of police or **military checks** on the roads and ringing the towns of Tarfaya, Laayoune and Smara in particular. You really feel as if you are entering foreign territory and need to have your passport, and a cheerful smile, at the ready. All should go smoothly unless you say you are a journalist, or even a writer. Filling stations are very few and far between and no-one should travel without adequate reserves of both fuel and water.

Laayoune

During the Spanish Protectorate, Laayoune was little more than a large oasis in a sea of sand dunes on the southern bank of the **Seguiet el Hamra** river. The new provincial capital has been built on the plateau above the river and now has a population of 140,000. The Moroccans have put in massive investment and people have been encouraged to settle here with tax exemptions and cheap housing, food and fuel. The population is a mix of 65% Saharan nomads, many of whom were driven by drought to seek a more secure and settled way of life, and 35% people from the north seeking work and tempted by the financial incentives.

■ Practical information

Tourist office. ONMT. Ave de l'Islam. ☎ (08) 891 694 fax (08) 891 695.
Banks. On or around Ave Mohammed V.
Post office. Ave Hassan II.
Air transport. Royal Air Maroc, Pl. Dchira. ☎ (08) 894 071. Hassan I Airport
is 2km from town centre. Tel: (08) 893 346. Flights to Casablanca daily except
Tuesday; Tan Tan, Agadir and Tangier, every Friday; Dakhla, Monday and
Saturday; Las Palmas, Wednesday and Friday.
Buses. CTM station at 20 Ave de la Mecque. ☎ (08) 894 229. Services to Agadir
and Tan Tan.
ONCF station at Pl. Oum Saad. ☎ (08) 894 224. Services as above, also to
Smara and Tarfaya.
Grand taxis. Pl. Lamkhakh (end of Ave Hassan II).
Car hire. Soubai, Pl. Dchira, ☎ (08) 893 661 and Laayoune, Pl. Dchira, ☎ (08)
894 744.

Hotels
Hôtel Parador, Rue Okba Ibn Nafi. ☎ (08) 894 500. ***** (33 rooms).
Hôtel Al Massira, 12 Rue de la Mecque. ☎ (08) 894 225. ****A (75 rooms).
Hôtel El Alia, 1 Rue Kadi El Ghalaoui. ☎ (08) 894 144. *** (34 rooms).
Hôtel Lakouara, Ave Hassan II. ☎ (08) 893 378. **A (40 rooms).
Hôtel Marhaba, Ave Hassan II. ☎ (08) 893 249. *A (36 rooms).
The first two of these hotels are brand new and have pools and every possible
luxury.

Restaurants
There are none. Best to eat at the *Parador* or the *Massira*.

Of positive interest to visitors is a **festival**, only recently
programmed into the official annual calendar, which is to
be held around the last week of February each year
(check the ONMT for exact dates). This will
include camel racing—featuring 400–600
camels—*fantasias*, folklore and
gastronomy, and should be a spectacular and highly colourful event.
There are many very prestigious and costly buildings in the
new town, the centre of which
is the **Mechouar**, an imposing
square whose vast emptiness is
broken only by four towers
topped with golden crowns and
a series of concrete canopies
designed to keep the sun off the
anticipated milling crowds.
(The traditional Spanish
custom of the *paseo* should be

The Mechouar

encouraged here.) The square is floodlit at night. Overlooking the Mechouar is the French-designed **Palais de Congres**—a surreal mix of glass and concrete which can accommodate up to 1200 people for conferences and seminars. Just off the square, on Avenue de la Mecque, is the new **Grand Mosque** which, like all Moroccan mosques, has an unremarkable exterior: it is closed to non-Muslims. Not far from here is the incredible **football stadium** built in 1985 to accommodate 35,000 spectators. The pride of the stadium—and of its military caretaker—is the real grass, which must be watered every day and mown every fortnight. The place cries out for international events. It is immaculate, lacking only players and spectators.

Also on Avenue de la Mecque is the **Ensemble Artisanal**, where cooperatives of woodcarvers, jewellers and metalworkers have been housed in a row of white-domed huts to ply their trade and display their wares. Some of the work is very fine indeed. The huts are copied from the originals in the old Spanish quarter: the domes have holes at the top which provide ventilation and make working conditions just about bearable in summer.

Less interesting, depending on your point of view, is the **Colline des Oiseaux**, a rather depressing bird sanctuary with one or two baboons and monkeys added. Once the oleanders between the enclosures and pools have grown a bit more, the place will undoubtedly look more welcoming. Much more lively, by definition, is the Saturday **livestock souk**, in which goats and camels are bought and sold at an astonishing rate by blue-robed Saharans to whom bargaining is a traditional way of life. This unchanging scene is the more poignant as one remembers the remarkable extravagance of the Mechouar nearby.

Below the new town, the old Spanish quarter stands picturesquely against a backdrop of seemingly endless dunes. There is a lot of domestic building going on here and modern houses are appearing alongside the domed buildings. There is a sad old cathedral which is usually closed.

There are big plans for **Laayoune Plage**, 20km south along the main P41 road. One day it will have a corniche road with restaurants and hotels along the seafront. I saw the beginnings of 'le Champignon complexe touristique' with two- and four-person bungalows grouped around a swimming pool and restaurant. At time of writing there is still much to do. There are a few assorted private villas along the long, pebbly and apparently clean beach; the campsite is no longer open and the supermarket is closed. There are, as yet, no tourists, but the possibilities are immense. In the distance you can see the conveyor belt which brings phosphates from the mining town of Boukra to the port of Laayoune (a distance of 30km). A track runs alongside it, but tourists are not welcome in this heavily militarised area.

Smara

Smara lies 245km south of Tan Tan or 240km east of Laayoune. Both routes are fairly featureless but the former is probably the better road, being relatively new.

History of Smara

Smara was built in 1890 by order of the sultan, Moulay el Hassan (Hassan I), by a local leader and learned man, Sheikh Ma el Ainine. Hassan I was the first Alouite sultan to attempt to pacify the Saharan tribes and the purpose of Smara, like Tiznit which he also built, was to house a permanent garrison and show that law and order were here to stay. Inside the walls, which were pierced by five monumental gates, there was a kasbah, a mosque, a library containing many of the sheikh's own religious works, grain stores and living quarters.

The town soon became a focal point of control over trans-Saharan caravans and over the tribes in general. It was also a significant rallying point against the French, who first attacked it in 1913. In 1936 it was bombarded by joint French and Spanish forces which reduced it to its present ruinuous state. All that survives of the original town are some of the arcades and pillars of the mosque and some sections of wall, rapidly disappearing under the sand. Smara started as a garrison town and today, over a century later, it still fulfils that function. In view of the relative proximity of Algeria it is not surprising that most of the inhabitants are either military or from the UN.

There are no classified hotels in Smara but there are several unclassified ones, including the *Hôtel al Maghreb Al Arabi*. There is also a campsite on the edge of the Sakia Al Hamra canyon 20km north of Smara on the Smara–Tan Tan road, called *Bah Naama*. It is much used by passing caravans and also by rally drivers.

Ad Dakhla

The best way to cover the 540km south from Laaoyoune is to fly. The flight takes just over one hour and there are three per week. The alternative is to drive down on the perfectly good road, time-consuming though it may be. The only reason for going to **Ad Dakhla** must be for the deep-sea fishing, which is said to be marvellous. Tuna, swordfish, marlin, grouper and barracuda are all to be had, and conditions in this as yet virtually undiscovered place must be near perfect. Serious fishermen will turn to *Sochetur* at 72 Boulevard Zerktouni, Casablanca, ☎ (02) 277 513, which organizes inclusive fishing trips to Ad Dakhla. Alternatively, consult the ONMT in Ad Dakhla itself, ☎ (08) 898 228.

Hotels

Hôtel la Sargha. ****
Hôtel Doums, Ave Al Walla. ☎ (08) 898 045. ***A (28 rooms)
Hôtel Al Wahda. *
Hôtel Sahara, ☎ (08) 897 773. *
Hôtel Miramar. *

Campsites

There is a site at the entrance to the town, by the sea.

TRAVELLING TO MOROCCO WILL ENJOY

MOROCCO

Feast for the Senses

For further information on Morocco please contact :

THE MOROCCAN NATIONAL TOURIST OFFICE

205 Regent Street - London - WIR 7DE
Tél : 0171 437 00 73
Fax: 0171 734 81 72

HOLIDAY MAKERS

GOLF AND ABUNDANCE OF SUNSHINE.

BEACHES, MOUNTAINS, DESERT,

A WIDE VARIETY OF ACTIVITIES TO CHOOSE FROM NAMELY, CULTURE,

Index

Peoples' names are given in *italic* and the most important places are given in **bold**.